BETWEEN FLOPS

Preston Sturges, c. 1948

A BIOGRAPHY OF PRESTON STURGES

BETWEEN
FLOPS

JAMES CURTIS

LIMELIGHT EDITIONS

NEW YORK

Also by James Curtis

James Whale

First Limelight Edition, September 1984

Copyright © 1982 by James Curtis

Published in the United States by Proscenium, Publishers Inc., New
York, and simultaneously in Canada by Fitzhenry & Whiteside Limited,
Toronto. Published by arrangement with Harcourt, Brace, Jovanovich,
Inc.

ISBN 0–87910–026–5

Manufactured in the United States of America

Library of Congress Cataloging in Publication Data

Curtis, James, 1953–
Between flops.

Reprint. Originally published: New York : Harcourt,
Brace, Jovanovich, c1982.
Filmography: p.
Includes index.
1. Sturges, Preston. 2. Moving-picture producers
and directors—United States—Biography. 3. Screen
writers—United States—Biography. I. Title.
[PN1998.A3S884 1984]   812'.52 [B]   84–7129

For Priscilla

ACKNOWLEDGMENTS

In justifying the preparation of his autobiography in 1959, Preston Sturges suggested a ". . . good reason for writing your *auto*biography is that it may prevent some jerk from writing your *bio*graphy . . . and this is all to the good, if only because what you write *yourself* about persons and facts you knew at first hand will contain only such voluntary departures from the truth as you consider necessary to prevent a few husbands from shooting their wives for instance, or vice versa, as opposed to the mountains of false statements, misspelled names, wrong dates, and incorrect loci the well-meaning biographer usually comes up with after tracking you down through the morgues of deceased newspapers, the old letters of some of your friends, and the very unreliable memories of people who knew you slightly."

Readily conceding these drawbacks, I embarked upon this project with the at least slightly comforting knowledge that Sturges had left a wealth of letters, screenplays (both produced and unproduced), and other memorabilia, carefully preserved and placed at my disposal through the kind auspices of his widow, Sandy. I have quoted these sources with her permission as well as drawn heavily from the aforementioned autobiography, a rambling and only slightly edited dictation which chronicles the first thirty years of Sturges' life.

I am grateful to Brook Whiting, James Mink, and the staff of the Department of Special Collections, University Research Library, UCLA (where the Sturges papers reside), for their valuable assistance. I am also grateful to Bob Gitt of the UCLA Film Archives for his tireless help in seeing most all of Sturges' films.

My special thanks to the many friends and co-workers of Preston Sturges who contributed recollections and other data: Lucinda Ballard, Larry Blake, Eddie Bracken, Bill and Lucille Demarest, the late Robert Florey, Edwin Gillette, the late Richard Hale, Katharine Hepburn, Ted Kent, the late Carl Laemmle, Jr., Dominick and Peggy Maggie, Rouben Mamoulian, Joel McCrea, Maxine Merlino, Colleen Moore, the late Emory Parnell, Frances

Ramsden, Robin Sanders-Clark, Lionel Stander, Barbara Stanwyck, Herb Sterne, the late Eddie Sutherland, the late Fran Templeton, the late George "Dink" Templeton, Rudy Vallée, Orson Welles, Billy Wilder, and the late William Wyler.

Particularly generous with their time and encouragement were Priscilla Woolfan, Sandy Sturges, Charles H. Abramson, and Louise Sturges, all of whom reviewed early drafts of this book and contributed much to its accuracy.

For varied courtesies, encouragements, and assists, I am also indebted to: Jon Costello, Marvin Coyle, Mike Hawks, Charles Higham, Bob Hope, Ronnie James, Larry Kleno, Miles Kreuger, Bob Scherl, David Shepard, Anthony Slide, Tom Sturges, Kay Taylor, James Ursini, Marc Wanamaker, Larry Ward, The Academy of Motion Picture Arts & Sciences, and The New York Public Library at Lincoln Center.

Karen Swenson and Nancy Dragoun typed the manuscript with patience and superior spelling.

My agent, David Stewart Hull, provided the encouragement that got this project going. I was also fortunate in having the counsel of Marcia Magill, a superb and attentive editor.

Lastly, I must thank David Lewis, who taught me much about writing during the course of this effort and whose devotion made the difference in its completion.

James Curtis

Los Angeles
1981

PROLOGUE

The date was August 7, 1959, a seasonably humid evening in New York City. In the stately Frank E. Campbell Funeral Chapel at 81st and Madison Avenue, a young widow stood alone before the casket of her husband.

Preston Sturges' face reflected not so much make-up as a set, stone-like tenseness that was both disquieting and unnatural. His hair, perfectly combed as it had never been in life, was stiff with hair spray. The lips were drawn tight, as not in repose, and she thought that he must have died in pain that the mortician was unable to conceal.

The demise of Preston Sturges is sad and, yet, intriguing. For ten years he had been among the brightest talents in Hollywood, but he had spent the decade of the 1950s in virtual obscurity. He was by no means inactive, but that next great hit—the one that would restore him to prominence, move his reputation from the past tense—never came. He viewed his entire life as a succession of failures, with only occasional intermissions of greatness. But he never counted himself out and knew he needed nothing more than the time to wait out his slump and seize the opportunity when it again presented itself.

Alexander King once called him the "Toscanini of the prat-fall," *Reader's Digest* a "genius with a slapstick." In the Hollywood of the early 1940s he was thought to have no peer—with the exception perhaps of Frank Capra—as a maker of rousing satires. He wrote eight produced stage plays and twenty-five produced screenplays—twelve of which he also directed.

Several of Sturges' films made fortunes in the forties; one year the IRS identified him as the third highest-paid executive in the country. He owned a popular Hollywood restaurant, a motion picture production company (with partner Howard Hughes), and an engineering firm bearing his name in Wilmington, California. He won the Academy Award once and received a total of three nominations. Having earned over $3 million in his lifetime, he died with practically nothing.

Sturges had been dictating the night of his death, and had phoned down to room service for a plate of coleslaw and a glass of beer. He had simultaneously been at work on a new play and a book of memoirs to be called *The Events Leading Up to My Death*. The meal provoked severe heartburn, and as he lay on the bed popping antacid tablets and belching quietly, he delivered his standard line for such occasions: "I hope to God I don't croak tonight." But the pain grew worse and a worried secretary phoned the front desk for a doctor. Sturges' face contorted as he gasped for air and then—suddenly—his heart stopped and efforts to revive him proved futile. The doctor theorized the gas had applied intolerable pressure on his heart, but an autopsy was waived and no one seemed terribly interested in exactly what had precipitated the attack.

Mrs. Sturges received the news when UPI called to confirm his death and flew from California with her stepson the next day. A family friend accompanied her to the undertaker's to deliver a fresh suit of clothes. Underwear and socks had been requested, but, oddly, no shoes.

"Between flops, it is true, I have come up with an occasional hit," Preston Sturges had once written, "but compared to a good boxer's record, my percentage has been lamentable." Still, remarkably, he wrote and directed two films a year between 1940 and 1943—eight films honored today for their deftness and originality. But he quarreled with his studio, seeking an independence that eventually did him in. Like the mythological Icarus, Sturges soared higher and higher until his single pair of wings could carry him no farther.

"In twenty-two years," he observed, "I managed to alienate every one of the seven major studios and soon found myself out of work." Admitting to impudence seemed unworthy of him.

"He was truly a Renaissance figure," said his friend and colleague Billy Wilder. "There were very few that came down the pike with his vision. If he had a little luck—and the financing—it was there on the screen. A new voice that spoke with wit. Incisively. Daringly. Compared with the ninety percent of drivel that went on the screen, there was thought. There was a man of intellect, of size. A man who wrote literature."

Sturges' funeral wouldn't have pleased him, although the trip to the cemetery—with the procession of cars moving slowly along the streets of Manhattan and then accelerating on the turnpike to keep pace with the hearse—might well, with little exaggeration, have been a scene from one of his movies. Rain fell lightly and the Unitarian minister eulogized a man he had never met as one "who practiced his own religion and whose influences in our lives were many and varied."

He then intoned the Beatitudes:

Blessed are the poor in spirit: for theirs is the kingdom of heaven.
Blessed are they that mourn: for they shall be comforted.
Blessed are the meek: for they shall inherit the earth . . .

Mrs. Sturges expected her husband to rise from his bier and call a halt to the proceedings at any moment.

It was August 8, 1959—almost twenty years to the day since Preston Sturges had struck the deal to direct one of his own screenplays, a deal that would eventually win him the Academy Award and fulfill the promise he had long felt within him.

BETWEEN
FLOPS

1.

In 1939, a driver traveling east along Melrose came upon the Paramount studios almost by accident. In Hollywood proper—to the bewilderment of tourists—there were remarkably few major studios: M-G-M lay southwest in Culver City; Universal and Warners' due north in the Valley; and 20th Century-Fox settled snugly into a section of West L.A. known, without coincidence, as Fox Hills. Remaining were the United Artists studios on Formosa; the Chaplin facility on La Brea; Columbia off Sunset in that dusty Boot Hill of independents known collectively as "Gower Gulch"; and then, a few blocks south past Santa Monica on Gower, RKO and Paramount. The two were butted together like dwellings in a land-poor housing tract, but it was the RKO globe with its neon radio tower that was right at the corner of Gower and Melrose and the first to be seen. As one drove past, it took a quick glance down Bronson to see the famous guard gate and archway at Marathon and the words PARAMOUNT PICTURES.

In those days few people actually drove onto the cramped lot as the streets were narrow (though uncluttered) and there was truly no place for cars. There was no employee parking lot; most people had to park at a garage across the street and enter through the administration building to the left of the gate.

Except for the archway and gate the studio was merely a long wall with windows. The overall impression was summarized by an inmate of the period as "shit stucco." The lobby of the administration building was spare; only a security guard and a buzzer by which people were admitted. No portraits lined the walls except in the casting office, which, possibly to control unauthorized traffic, was entered through the front gate.

Casting was on the first floor, to the right of the guard with the buzzer, and the executive offices were to the left. Looking out onto the lot from the north side of the building was the office of Y. Frank Freeman, an inoffensive Southerner who held the nebulous title of Vice-President in Charge of Operations. Freeman had spent most of his life in exhibition, and for several years was in charge of

Paramount's theatre operations in New York. Then one day he appeared at Hollywood's buzzing door, presumably to help keep an eye on things for the New York office.

Freeman was a short, graying man in his late forties who had no discernible function on the lot other than to walk and feed the boxer dog kept in a cage outside his window. He rarely meddled in production, except when the honor of the South was at stake. He lobbied such controversies with the fervor of a Civil War veteran, but otherwise maintained a low profile. The studio line was always: "*Why* Frank Freeman?"

Across from Freeman's office—overlooking Marathon—sat the office of William LeBaron. LeBaron was in charge of production under Freeman, a position he had held since 1936—shortly after the company was reorganized under the Bankruptcy Act. Prior to that, Paramount was known as the studio of Mae West, Gary Cooper, W. C. Fields, Maurice Chevalier, Marlene Dietrich, and the four Marx Brothers. The directors included Rouben Mamoulian, Cecil B. DeMille, Josef von Sternberg, Henry Hathaway, and Ernst Lubitsch. In 1939, however, only DeMille remained and the year's program leaned heavily upon radio personalities like Jack Benny, Bob Hope, and Bing Crosby; Hopalong Cassidy Westerns; and the Bulldog Drummond mysteries. DeMille made one picture a year and, from Florida, Max Fleischer supplied Popeye cartoons.

LeBaron was a large, easygoing man with a writer's background who had been producing films since the late teens. Before joining Paramount he had been in charge of production at RKO where he made, among other films, *Cimarron* and *Rio Rita*. At Paramount, he had worked primarily with Fields, West, and Crosby—the studio's top moneymakers apart from DeMille— which is probably the reason he was put in charge.

Because LeBaron had a strong background in comedy and was a playwright himself, he was quite taken with the writer Preston Sturges. Sturges was a tall, heavyset man of imposing vocabulary, resonant voice, and piercing eyes. With his broad, jowly face and curly black hair only a brief moustache kept him from resembling a plaster cherub of the type commonly molded into the ceilings of old movie palaces.

Sturges was a warm, gregarious character whom LeBaron instantly liked. Like the production chief, Sturges had spent several years as a playwright in New York, but unlike him Sturges had enjoyed a blockbuster hit with his play *Strictly Dishonorable*. Sturges, in fact, had ridden out a crest of popularity on Broadway before using Hollywood as a sort of employer of last resort. There again he made a splash with his extraordinary screenplay *The Power and the Glory* before gradually settling into the comfortable position of one of the industry's top writers. Sturges joined Paramount about the same time LeBaron rose to power; the two enjoyed an entirely satisfactory relationship.

Sturges was difficult, yet undeniably brilliant. Such men rarely made good staff writers because they were inalterably convinced that collaboration weakened their efforts and diluted their points of view. The pride of authorship was mother's milk to them and they fought constantly with producers accustomed to using multiple writers. They objected loudly to directors and actors changing their lines, believing that their way was the only way to make the films they wrote and their words the key contribution: all the administrators, technicians, sound stages, and theatres in the world were useless without the thoughts and the words of the writer.

LeBaron sympathized with such viewpoints, but motion pictures represented business, not art, to him and the medium was—by its very definition—a collaborative enterprise. Still, it was men like Sturges who gave the industry many of its finest hours. Some were worthy of the controls they demanded; others weren't. Discipline was a virtue often foreign to the creative mind; sound business judgment was even rarer. When "A" pictures routinely cost a company several hundred thousand to a million dollars or more, that judgment, LeBaron insisted, had to come from somewhere.

Sturges was known as an erratic fellow who worked nights and loathed deadlines. Nonetheless, he had been trying to break into directing since *The Power and the Glory* had demonstrated to him the creative influence a film's director could have. The director was royalty, ennobled in the days prior to talking film when he was truly the creator and storyteller. The aristocracy lingered; Sturges considered each one, whether rightly or wrongly, a prince of the blood. "When a good picture is made," he would say, "everybody's a prince but the writer."

Some directors were men of great taste and were reasonable about collaboration; others were merely dramatic traffic cops. When it was thought *The Power and the Glory* might hit big, there was interest from more than one studio in Sturges' directing his next original, a political comedy-drama called *The Vagrant*. But *The Power and the Glory* flopped in almost every market but New York and interest quickly dried up. Art was one thing, but you couldn't bank reviews and in 1933 all the majors—excepting Metro—were reporting losses.

So Sturges withdrew *The Vagrant* and began to build a reputation based principally upon the films he wrote as a hired hand— *The Good Fairy, Diamond Jim, Easy Living,* and *If I Were King.* The last was a beautiful adaptation of the McCarthy play about

François Villon for which Sturges not only did his own translations, but added some original Villonesque poetry of his own.
Sturges spoke fluent French, and there were many who believed he
was born and raised in France. He was certainly quick to invoke
his European education whenever the talk turned to his qualifica-
tions to direct.

Sturges turned forty in August of 1938 and seemed to be
mellowing as he married his third wife and talked of starting a
family. He completed an unabashedly sentimental romance called
Beyond These Tears and then renewed the pitch LeBaron was used
to hearing upon the completion of every Sturges script: why not let
him direct the next one?

The next one, at first, was to be an adaptation of a book called
Triumph over Pain, about William T. G. Morton, the disputed
discoverer of anesthesia. LeBaron had no taste for the subject, but
Sturges doggedly pushed forward, making casual comments about
free-lancing like Ben Hecht and selling his scripts to the highest
bidder. But then there was also *The Vagrant*, which LeBaron had
read and liked.

Sturges had redated *The Vagrant* and retitled it *Down Went
McGinty*. A political yarn, it was definitely not commercial, but it
was a good piece of work. The problem was that Sturges was more
valuable to the company as a writer than as a director. Directors
were a dime a dozen; really good writers were always scarce.
LeBaron preferred to see Sturges write another picture and leave
the actual filming to a man like Mitchell Leisen—who was only as
good as his material. Nonetheless, LeBaron understood Sturges'
genuine frustration with his lack of control over things like *Easy
Living*, which Leisen had filmed with no sense of pacing Sturges
could discern. So Sturges was getting increasingly restless and
difficult. He took every reasonable opportunity to slam Leisen's
alleged talents and it was apparent the two men would be unable
to work together much longer. Sturges spoke openly about moving
to another studio. LeBaron knew any company that would be
willing to entrust a "B" feature to Sturges could have him easily.
He didn't want to lose him. What's more, LeBaron knew that
Sturges longed to remain with Paramount, where he was settled
and comfortable, but would be driven to wherever his ambition
might take him.

Privately, Sturges was growing weary of the pitch and proposed to LeBaron an irresistible offer: *Down Went McGinty* for only
$1.00—on condition that Sturges be allowed to direct it. That, in
itself, would put the company many thousands ahead. If LeBaron
couldn't trust him with a film even at a discount, then there was no
future at Paramount and no choice but to get out. Once more,
Sturges retold his story—of his successes on the stage, his experi-

ence as a photographer, designer, and painter; and of his education in the arts under the influence of his mother and the dancer Isadora Duncan.

LeBaron's defenses began to crumble. If Paramount could hang on to Sturges long enough to let him find out what a lousy, demanding job directing was, maybe he'd go back to writing and be happy. But whatever Sturges seemingly lacked in good sense he compensated for with an infectious enthusiasm for his work. Sturges knew beyond all doubt he could make a hit of *McGinty* if given a chance, and LeBaron knew he had nothing to lose.

"Go ahead and get it out of your system," LeBaron finally told him. "But just remember one thing: it's a terrible job. You have to get up at seven o'clock in the morning and listen to a lot of damned actors muff their lines all day. You are already a very successful writer with many credits to your name. If you make yourself ridiculous as a director, you will be less valuable as a writer. You are doing a very dangerous thing. Remember that old proverb . . ."

"I know," answered Sturges. " 'Shoemaker, stick to your last.' But I've got to do it even if it ruins me. I've wanted to for so long. There's only one job in pictures and that's making them. And the director is the man who makes them. Everything else is secondary and I am not by nature a second-fiddle player."

LeBaron nodded. A dollar, he told Sturges, somehow didn't sound legal enough for the purchase of *Down Went McGinty*. "Let's make it ten." Sturges happily agreed and the papers were drawn up.

"Be it on your own head," warned LeBaron as Sturges turned to leave. He paused.

"As a matter of fact," said Sturges, "I'm going to make you a wonderful picture."

"As a matter of fact," LeBaron smiled, "I know it. I've never known anyone with that much enthusiasm and confidence who failed."

A check was promptly issued for the sum of $10. Sturges had a photostat made and pasted it in his scrapbook. That night, he dined with friends and delightedly recounted the day's events. But his companions questioned the significance of what he had done. Normally, the screenplays he wrote cost Paramount $30,000 and up. Why would Preston sell one for $10? Surely the job of directing wasn't so important to him that he would, in effect, pay for the privilege of doing it.

"Why, Preston?" a friend finally asked. "Why for only ten dollars?"

Sturges eyed her squarely. "Because," he replied, "I want to be a prince of the blood and nothing less!"

2.

The irony of Preston Sturges' life up to age forty was that for three quarters of it he had only the vaguest idea of what to do with himself. Before he had reached the age of two, his mother had decided to raise him—in her own loving, crazy-quilt manner—to be an "artist" and, consequently, formulated no master plan for his education. The goal was nebulous and emotional and against it stood Preston's unwavering devotion and admiration for the Chicago stockbroker who was his father. The ambition inside young Preston was largely dormant and took decades to surface. Perhaps it was the time it took to find the true course of his life—that one special thing he was meant to do above all others—that contributed to the intensity of his later work. There was a lot of wasted time, he would later note, and a deeply ingrained inertia he would always have to fight.

Contrary to popular presumption, Sturges wasn't an unrepatriated Frenchman, nor was he even born a Sturges. He was actually born in Chicago and his biological father was one Edmund P. Biden, after whom the boy was named. Mr. Biden was evidently not a man of great personal charm or stoic endeavor. He was, in fact, at the time of his first son's birth, connected with a Chicago collection agency. He was five feet seven, reportedly expert on the trapeze. He parted his hair in the middle and drank excessively. He called Preston's mother, the former Mary Dempsey, "Mamie," a name she hated, and played the banjo, an instrument Mary abhorred even more than her nickname.

Mary Dempsey was an attractive woman, five feet five but large-boned, with piles of curly blue-black hair and a magnetic personality. What it was about Mr. Biden that appealed to her is uncertain, for she was a person of lofty standards, loath to tolerate an unpleasant relationship. Indeed, she was married five times in her life and courted by males from virtually every social stratum.

For Mary exaggeration was a natural part of the thought process. She was blessed with a vivid imagination through which she strained every recollective utterance of nearly sixty years of life. "Anything she said three times she believed fervently," her son observed. "Often twice was enough." Stories of her improbable adventures were common in family circles and usually perpetuated by Mary herself. At age sixteen she was supposedly a brilliant young medical student at the Herring Homeopathic Hospital in Chicago, where she was known to one and all as "Dr. Dimples." However, she later told Preston she had given birth to him at age fifteen and thereafter was unable to explain successfully what she had done with him during her medical studies. It is a matter of record, though, that she was indeed one of the founders, around 1905, of the Chicago Home for Convalescent Women and Children. In the early days of World War I, she was also the principal founder of the Hospital Mititan, established on the floor of the famous casino at Deauville, in Normandy, supplies for which she single-handedly appropriated with the aid of nothing more than a borrowed Red Cross truck and the goodwill of the local pharmacies and luxury hotels.

Of the many fanciful notions Mary's mind gave birth to, the most public was the one concerning her maiden name and illustrious Italian origin. No such plebeian a name as "Dempsey" could possibly have been hers, Mary felt. With minimal genealogical research, she saw d'Este gradually molded into Desmond, and from Desmond to Dempsey. The name, she reasoned, was bestowed upon her in error by the Irish associates of an ancestor, a distinguished Italian prince on the lam in Ireland in the wake of a romantic duel. "Dempsey," Mary declared, was a perversion of the Italian "d'Este," which made her an Italian princess.

These points, once settled in her mind, prompted Mary to readopt her true Italian name, and she became Mary d'Este Dempsey, and then, simply, Mary d'Este.

The name served her comfortably until the year 1911 when, in Paris, she founded her renowned perfumery at 4 Rue de la Paix. It was called, quite naturally, the Maison d'Este and promptly incurred the wrath of the French descendants of the famous Italian family who threatened legal action if the name and the vulgar electric sign she had hung were not instantly removed. A natural fighter, Mary became the picture of righteous indignation and there was much growling and baring of teeth before a grouping of the finest legal minds in Europe was able to negotiate a compromise: the sign could stay, but the name would change... slightly. Thus Mary became Mary Desti, and her shop the Maison Desti.

When Mary's son was born, according to her, absolutely no one, least of all herself, knew anything at all about the pregnancy up to the very last moment. At first, Mr. Biden—who was reportedly fond of operations—thought the baby was a tumor and was

9

preparing to dispatch his wife to a local hospital for its removal. This plot was hatched in the evening of August 28, 1898. Fortunately, on the following morning, about five o'clock, the baby was born and Mr. Biden, having regained his composure, promptly christened it Edmund Preston.

"I saw Mr. Biden only once in my life," Preston later remembered. "This was in 1914 when Mother had sent me to America from Paris so that I wouldn't enlist . . .

"Mr. Biden, who had a new wife and a new baby, heard I was in New York and invited me to dinner. I went, but sometime during the evening he said something rude about my mother, so I left and never saw him again during his lifetime, although he was very anxious to see me after I became rich and well known and things were going badly for him. But I never forgave him . . . especially an insane and sadistically imaginative letter he wrote later expressing his great joy at my mother's death."

Concluded Preston, "Mr. Biden never did sound like much of a husband to me, but it must be remembered that he was one of Mother's very first ones and that, like the celebrated Mrs. Simpson, she did better later."

Little is known of the events immediately following the birth of Edmund Preston Biden, other than that the marriage ended and Mary and her infant son fled to Europe.

Mary later wrote a book covering this trip called *The Untold Story*—about her meeting, friendship with, and tragic parting from Isadora Duncan. In Chapter II, Mary wrote, "In January, 1901, after a disastrous runaway marriage and later divorce, I tucked my little year and a half old babe under my arm and started for Paris to study for the stage. This I did under the advice of Dr. Ziegfeld, Flo Ziegfeld's father, who had the Conservatoire of Music in Chicago. At this moment I had rather an extraordinary voice and, as I was scarcely more than a child myself, great things were hoped for from my Paris trip."

The "year and a half old babe" was, of course, Preston, except that in January 1901 he was approximately *two* and a half years old. And it obviously pleased Mary to be "scarcely more than a child," although she had been on earth since 1871. "I am probably lucky that she never introduced me as her brother," said Preston, ". . . which happened to some of my friends also with pretty mothers." Mary clung to youth as long as she dared, then settled down and, in her final years, started to cook and sew and generally attend to all the womanly things she had despised during most of her adult life. Had she lived longer, Preston speculated, she might have learned to knit.

Mary encountered Isadora Duncan in Paris through the office of an American real estate agent. She was dazzled.

"Had I been ushered into Paradise and given over to my guardian angel," Mary wrote, "I could not have been more uplifted." Isadora's beauty and grace overwhelmed her completely. ". . . a little retroussé nose . . . gave just the slightest human touch," she continued, "otherwise I should have thrown myself on my knees before her, believing I was worshipping a celestial being."

Such hyperbole was typical of their lifelong friendship: Isadora, the younger, as goddess; Mary, the older, as adoring follower. Both were subject to distraction along the way, but, ultimately, before husbands—*before children*—before anything, came each other. Shortly after their first meeting, it was Mary who moved into Isadora's Paris studio while old Mrs. Duncan, Isadora's mother, took little Preston (Mary could not bring herself to utter the hateful name of Edmund) to Geverney to live. Twenty-six years later, in Nice, it was Mary who hand-painted the red Chinese shawl that broke Isadora's neck when the fringe became tangled in a wheel of the Bugatti car in which she was riding.

Preston could later remember nothing of Geverney, and Mary, after spending almost a year with Isadora in Paris, returned to America at the behest of her mother. There, she acknowledged, she married "an old sweetheart—the kindest, truest friend a woman ever had . . ." a Chicago stockbroker by the name of Solomon Sturges. Sturges was a grandchild of the founder of Solomon Sturges and Sons (1860), one of the first reliable banks in the Midwest, from which the Continental Illinois National Bank and Trust Company of Chicago was directly descended. The two were married in Memphis, Tennessee, in January of 1902, at which time Solomon adopted Mary's child and became the only true father the boy would know.

Mary's second trip to Europe, in 1904, took her first to Berlin, and then on to Bayreuth, in Bavaria. Swathed in the Grecian robes in which Isadora preferred her, she spent six months working under the sponsorship of Frau Wagner and the Wagner summer festival. Preston, approaching six, was left at a local inn in the company of a governess and Isadora's niece Temple. Mary and Isadora shared a sort of peasant's villa not far away.

Preston fell hopelessly in love with little Temple Duncan, only a few months older than he. "She kept me broke for years," he recalled, "buying her highly perfumed soap and doll-sized Singer sewing machines." The two children were essentially the only playmates available for one another and they lived together twenty-four hours a day. After their stay in Bayreuth, the party moved on to Berlin and Hanover and then by boat to the island of Helgoland. Preston could remember a man with a beard and a red woolen shirt standing up to his wishbone in the ocean off Helgoland, holding him by the slack of his bathing suit and teaching him to swim. "I remember that my head was always going under water and that I screamed bloody murder," he said.

For a time, Preston was parked in a place in Berlin called a "Gymnasium," where he sat dumbly, unable to understand a word, "amongst a bunch of little short-cropped German jerks," until a kindly professor took pity on him and showed him how to draw a fish by attaching an unending quantity of u's to each other, and how to draw a tree employing the same technique with a series of y's. These exercises constituted the commencement of his formal education.

While in Germany, Preston was also compelled to attend the State Opera in Dresden as part of his artistic indoctrination, Isadora evidently believing that if a child enjoyed continuous (and compulsory) exposure to painting, sculpture, theatre, and music, he would naturally develop into an artist of some kind. Preston's walls were plastered with prints of the Renaissance masters, and concertgoing was deemed far more beneficial to the boy than random play with children his own age. Preston reluctantly napped in the afternoons instead of playing in the municipal gardens, and this, he said, "poisoned my existence."

It wasn't long before the boy developed an intense dislike for most things cultural. Exposed to some of the greatest minds of the age, the experiences were next to meaningless to him. Only as an adult could Preston finally appreciate his meeting the likes of Caruso, Ernst Haeckel, the king of Spain, Ganna Walska, Clemenceau, Mae Mossies, Monet, and the Prince de Polignac. Feverishly, he was once rushed into the presence of aged tragedian Jean Mounet-Sully lest the actor expire before bathing Preston in his aura of genius. Still the boy came to dread a night in the theatre, and loathe the words of Shakespeare and Molière.

Isadora would not allow her friend Mary to return to America without first seeing Italy. "We arrived at Florence one night at midnight," recalled Mary, "when the whole town was bathed in gorgeous moonlight. Isadora instructed the man to take our baggage to the Hotel de l'Europe, after which she, Preston, and I danced gaily through the deserted streets, over Dante's bridge, singing at the top of our voices, 'I am the Romeo. I am the Romeo. I am the Romeo that won Juliet. I am the Juliet. I am the Juliet. I am the Juliet who loved Romeo.'"

This trip ended in Venice, where the patient Mr. Sturges came to collect his family and take them home to Chicago. He arrived to find his wife and son attired in Grecian dresses, shawls, and sandals, and declaring (via Mary) that they would never wear anything else again. "What will you do in Chicago with the cold lake winds?" Solomon inquired. It would not matter, replied Mary, for she had adopted these clothes for life. Without further comment, Mr. Sturges put Isadora on a train for Berlin and then left for Paris with Mary and Preston.

"We arrived in Paris in a terrific rain storm," wrote Mary, "and as the water splashed through our sandals, I must admit my son and I looked very bedraggled and anything but artistic at our very fashionable hotel.

"My dear kind husband told me I had 'carte blanche' in Paris to buy what I liked if I would only be good enough to confine my Grecian clothes and sandals to the house."

Mary agreed, although evidently with crossed fingers, as there was one disastrous day not long after when Mary sent Preston to a Chicago grade school in similar dress. It was Preston's first experience with an American school, and he received a violent lesson in standards of attire from fellow students.

"We sailed for home," Mary concluded, "and I did not see Isadora again for several years, but when I did, it was when I finally came to Paris to remain permanently and when she and I were inseparable; every event of her life was entwined with mine."

3.

Preston was fond of telling the story of a night around 1907 at the family house in Glencoe, Illinois, when his mother and father had a terrible row. Mary had just brought him back from Europe, and the fight had to do with the length of time she had been away. Chicago was a city young Preston had come to adore, a place to which his father was tied by virtue of his banking and brokerage business, but a place that Mary, having savored the delights of studying in Paris, had grown to despise. If Mrs. Potter Palmer, the acknowledged queen of society, started the season off with Duck Bigarade, Mary contended, you never got anything but Duck Bigarade wherever you went for the rest of the whole goddamn season and to hell with it.

Soon the couple burst into Preston's upstairs bedroom to offer him a choice. As Mr. Sturges weaved silently from the effects of several highballs, Mary said sweetly, "Mother is going to live in Paris, darling, and Father is going to stay here in Chicago. What do you want to do?"

Sleepily, Preston mulled over the proposal. "I adored this big man I had been reunited with," he later said, "this ex-football player, this ex-bicycle champion of Illinois (on the high bicycle, of course), this man who had brought me home another present every night of my life when I was little, and whose unfailing tenderness and gentleness toward me extended back into the diffused twilight before memory began. It was heaven to sit on his lap and the perfume of my father—a mixture of maleness and the best Havana cigars—was the breath of Araby to me."

The boy said, "I want to stay here with Father."

And Solomon said:

"I am *not* your father."

In stupefaction the boy looked at him for a moment, then to his mother to see if he was kidding, then back at his father. Then he started to cry. "I remember their telling me I cried for a week, undoubtedly in exaggeration, but I know the kind of crying it was because I've seen my own little boys that way when they are brokenhearted, and after a while, the intake of breath makes a gasping, hollow sound more distressing than the crying itself."

He cried long enough to sober his father, to awaken the servants, and the neighbors, who began phoning. Then Mary cried, and in desperation, Mr. Sturges rushed down the stairs to the glass case in which he kept the trophies, medals, cups, and awards he had won in school and college, and later at golf. There were honors for track and field, baseball, football, and bicycling, and he gathered them all up in his arms and ran back up to the bedroom, where he laid them, one by one, at Preston's feet. They were finely crafted, and golden, and fascinating to the eyes of an eight-year-old, but the one Preston liked best was a high bicycle made of gold with a sapphire in the hub of the big wheel and a diamond in the little wheel in back. The crying ceased, and, presently, his father became his father once again. The bicycle was forgotten and very soon it became lost, ". . . but I think that night," said Preston, "he thought I was going to die of grief."

Although the two loved each other deeply, they were to be separated for many years. Despite his express wish, Preston was eventually taken to Paris to live. The times he did spend with his father were cherished, and though he had not a drop of Sturges blood, Preston revered his father's memory and named his first son, Solomon Sturges IV, after him.

In 1909, Mary prepared Preston for incarceration in a French school in Paris. The school was presumably suggested by a handsome young French actor with whom she had taken up, a viscount who had evidently attended the institution himself. Before he knew it, Preston found himself in La Petite École—the small boys' half of the great Paris Lycée Janson de Sailly. He was a *pensionnaire* (boarding pupil) in this gloomy old academy, gray with blocks of dormitories and gravel-covered play yards, cold and impersonal.

Preston hated the place. "The whole thing was rather remindful of Sing Sing," he said. The buildings were bitterly cold. In one, a "poor little bearded Jewish man" called Professor Bloch tried to teach him to play the violin. Attired in mittens (with the fingers removed), spats, several sweaters, a derby hat, and a muffler, Professor Bloch shivered through five hour-long lessons a week. Preston's playing was clearly awful. The pained expression on his master's face was something he carried in his mind the rest of his life.

After two and one half uneventful years at the Lycée Janson, Preston never knew specifically what soured his mother on the place—perhaps Isadora had found the prison-like appearance distasteful during a brief visit. One day, without explanation, he was lifted bodily out of Janson and installed in the country in a fine Anglophile school in Normandy called the École des Roches. Instead of cold, gray buildings that could easily have served as tombs, Preston's new school bunked its pupils in relatively cozy houses, where the housemaster taught his young charges the value of daily renditions of "Rule, Britannia," sung in cracking pubescent voices augmented by the housemaster's own reedy tenor.

Mary's fourth marriage—to a Turkish fortune hunter called Vely Bey—was not an especially happy one. There was a cultural division, to be sure, but it was probably Vely's almost immediate dislike of Preston that sealed the union's fate. At first, the boy simply took him as another of his mother's many admirers. After a while, however, the ramifications of marriage began to sink in: Preston now had a new father. This didn't suit him at all, as his love and respect for his adoptive father, Solomon Sturges, naturally fostered resentment for anyone who might presume to take his place. Vely Bey was a strict disciplinarian; a man, by Turkish tradition, used to having fatherly commandments obeyed without question. Preston would have none of it and Mary stayed clear.

Preston had long been separated from the relatively stable environment of his father's home in Chicago and missed it. He had been dragged around Europe in an almost whimsical manner. No one set of experiences dominated any other; no lasting friendships were formed or encouraged. His mother was his anchor and he resented the people with whom he had to share her. Preston knew Isadora and Isadora's friends, and that was it. There were rarely children of his own age to play with; most of his time, when he was not boarded out, was spent in the company of adults.

Consequently, Preston's social perceptions were shaped greatly by the arts to which he was constantly and forcibly exposed, where emotions and moral values were contrasted at the will of the author and the grays of life were lightened or darkened accordingly. Gradually, he set himself apart from his mother's friends, actively disliking the way they conducted their lives. The more flamboyantly Mary lived, the more conservative and reactionary Preston seemed to become. He disapproved of her suitors and disliked his new "father." He could vividly recall awakening his mother (between husbands) each morning and sniffing the pillow to tell if a man had been with her the night before; he just never seemed to have her to himself.

It wasn't long before Vely Bey proved intolerable. Preston announced his wish to return to Chicago and live with Solomon; Mary was just as determined to keep him where he was. Then, without warning, Preston was plucked out of the École des Roches and placed in "a sort of cramming establishment run by a very nice guy with a beard called Professor Azambre." He was not allowed to leave the school or to go home on weekends. Vely Bey told the professor that Preston was a "wild child, badly in need of the severest kind of discipline." To his credit, the professor didn't buy this judgment, and disliked Vely Bey for offering it. The boy's mother went off with her Turkish mate and Preston was left in Paris in school . . . seemingly to rot.

Eventually, vacation came and Preston returned home to his mother's apartment on the Avenue Charles Floquet. He and his stepfather took particular pains to be nice to each other—Preston, so he would not be sent back to school; Vely, so he would not lose Mary to her son—and presently, Vely's father and mother came up from Constantinople to pay a visit.

As much as Preston disliked Vely Bey, he found himself enchanted with his new grandparents. His grandmother was enormously fat and jolly, drenched in yellow diamonds. His new grandfather, a distinguished and highly decorated physician, was Ilias Pasha. He had been the Sultan Abdul-Hamid's personal doctor, as well as one of the first practitioners of the operation for cataracts (he had been an assistant to the German who invented the operation). "He considered me his authentic grandson," Preston recalled, "gave me so much advice, and took me for walks."

Ilias Pasha, for all his charm, would have remained little more than a nice old man had it not been for a rash that appeared one day on Mary's face. After examining it carefully, Pasha concocted a purple lotion with a white deposit on it which he said was used by the ladies not only of Abdul-Hamid's harem but of all the principal Turkish harems. The rash disappeared, and suddenly the idea occurred to Mary to market the lotion under the imaginative name of "Le Secret du Harem."

Mary asked Pasha if he would tell her how to make it. He said he wasn't supposed to . . . as it was a very valuable secret formula . . . that not only improved the complexion . . . but also removed wrinkles. Mary's tongue began to dangle and, finally, after careful consideration, her father-in-law gave her the formula.

Thus was born the Maison d'Este, or, as it soon became, the Maison Desti. From Paris Singer, the sewing machine heir and father of one of Isadora's children, Mary obtained some money. Just how much is not known, but it was enough to accomplish quite a bit.

Mary found a small storefront on the Rue de la Paix and had it decorated by a prominent dressmaker and interior designer named Paul Poiret. One day, a local manicurist stopped by to visit and Mary invited her into the business. She then enlisted a hairdresser, two Chinese chiropodists, and, finally, an elderly chemist. Before she knew it, Mary had herself a beauty institute.

With this, she thought she had better introduce a line of perfumes, which she did with the help of an old French house called L. T. Piver and Company. Mary had some crystal bottles and alabaster jars made, and needed only some different rouges and face powders to market a complete line.

Maison Desti grew quickly. Satisfied that she had developed an enterprise to be proud of, Mary then set out to do what she could do better than anyone: promote.

With Preston in tow, she hurried to New York. Flush with enthusiasm, she registered at the Ritz and then started out one morning on a selling tour. With three Ritz bellboys carrying her sample cases, wearing her magnificent mink coat and real pearls, Mary marched into B. Altman & Company with an entrance befitting a foreign head of state. Immediately she found herself surrounded by every floorwalker, manager, and assistant manager on duty.

"Mr. Altman?" Mary inquired.

Unfortunately, they told her, Mr. Altman was deceased. Would anyone else do? "Oh yes," said Mary, and whoever it was bought $10,000 worth of Desti products: all that she had brought with her.

Preston, of course, enjoyed these visits enormously. He had his mother to himself for a change, and wasn't stashed away in some horrible private school. He used to hang out the window of the Ritz and watch the switch engines shunting the cars around in the New York Central Railroad yards. Upon her return to Paris, Mary introduced additional products, including kohl for the eyes, and two new rouges. One day, a gentleman called upon her and said, "I think that what you have done, Madame Desti, is one of the most remarkable adventures in our business that I have ever seen. Now it so happens that I do not manufacture any cosmetics, although I am the most successful perfumer in the world. I propose that you give up your several perfumes, although they are very nice, and allow me to manufacture your cosmetics. They should make a remarkable team with *my* perfumes, which are called Coty."

Mary, Preston would ruefully report later, turned Mr. Coty down, believing that he was trying to take advantage of her. Preston marveled at the act until the day he died, dreaming of the millions he would have been worth. It is entirely possible, however, that had he been so wealthy, he would never have written a word for the stage or the screen. During his marriage in the mid-twenties to a woman with a regular income, he did very little. The erratic years of Preston's youth left him incapable of prolonged periods of concentration or endeavor. Like his mother, his interests drifted, his ambitions slackened. He began to write only when left with nothing else to turn to. Mary's rejection of the Coty offer helped to seal Preston's fate: the millions he would have in his lifetime would be wholly self-earned . . . by his as yet unknown talents as a writer and humorist.

Preston was sent next to Switzerland, where the daily regimen at his school, La Villa, included running five kilometers after lunch in preparation for rowing or soccer, then rowing mile-and-a-quarter sprints in a four-oared yole or playing outside right for two halves at soccer, in which the players would run forty-five minutes in each half. "A sort of kill or cure regimen," Preston later commented.

"La Villa was a very high-toned school," Preston recalled, "stinking with barons and counts and marquis like the École des Roches. One perfectly charming and very well-mannered Spanish boy was the nephew of the Duke of Alba, and another of my great pals was Hans, Baron von Stohlterfoht, who played the piano. For some wonderful reason, my fiddle had not been sent along and I was now taking piano lessons."

Preston began to take a mild interest in composing; primarily his talent seemed to lie in the area of songwriting. During the time that he was at La Villa, he and his friend von Stohlterfoht wrote a ragtime piece in twenty minutes which was accepted for publication by a firm in Riga, Latvia. Said Preston, "It was really pathetic. Now the publishers in Riga, Latvia, didn't know any more about ragtime than von Stohlterfoht or I did, which was a fortunate happenstance, or they wouldn't have touched our effusion with a ten-foot pole. My own familiarity with the genre . . . consisted of having danced one turkey trot (in knickerbockers in the casino at Trouville) with Elsie Janis the previous summer (she wouldn't go for a second one), and von Stohlterfoht had never even heard anyone playing such stuff and relied upon me as the expert. He *could* play the piano, however, and write down notes, which was a lot more than I could do. I contented myself, therefore, with whistling a tune and drawing a three-color cover, allegedly in the American popular music style."

Sturges amused himself with "Winky," as their "musical crime" was called, but attempted no further composing. He seemed to dabble in such things out of boredom, entertaining no thoughts of writing for a living; indeed he entertained no thoughts of doing anything for a living. He was happy at La Villa; the future was nowhere in sight.

When two years at La Villa had passed, Mary evidently decreed Preston's formal education to be at an end. The money ran out and she sent Preston to Deauville one summer to supervise the running of the new Maison Desti seashore branch. There, Mary made a rather unusual arrangement with a Mr. Hobson, the owner of Ciro's, an elegant and expensive Paris restaurant with a newly established Deauville branch. Ciro's used only the large second floor of its building, allowing for shops below and apartments above. Mary rented one of the shops for the Maison Desti branch, and then had included in the rental the use of a large room and bath upstairs over the restaurant for Preston, with all his meals free. His familiarity with exotic and gourmet dishes stemmed from this experience, and he dreamed of one day owning his own exclusive restaurant—once he had made his mark in the cosmetics industry. Preston was approaching an age where he began to think in mildly avocational terms. He thought of his father in Chicago, to whom he wrote often. How pleased Solomon would be to see his son . . . wealthy . . . successful . . . independent of Mary and her husbands. A man of standing and respect, and a source of great pride to the man he so loved.

Amid the gamblers, millionaires, gigolos, and beautiful women, he spent a happy summer in Deauville, the nicest one for some time. Suddenly, on one of the last days of July 1914, an era came to an end. "Nobody knew this, of course," said Preston. "We all thought it was going to be just one of those nice quick little wars that last just long enough for everybody to get decorated and for a few characters to appear with a bandage around their heads, with a little red stain in the middle, supported by two pals, ready to sing the theme song. Somebody had assassinated some arch-duke or other at some place called Sarajevo, which was very regrettable, but why this should stop all the trains from Deauville to Paris was a little difficult to understand."

Preston was returned to Paris by Ciro's Mr. Hobson and Mary was greatly relieved to see him. Recalling her credentials as a medical doctor of sorts, Mary had already offered her services (and those of every other red-blooded American woman in Paris) to the American ambassador through the columns of the New York *Herald*. The American ambassador asked her, by telephone, to please keep her mouth shut and sit tight. This was going to be a very brief war, of no more than a few weeks' duration. It had nothing to do with America in general and American women in particular. Mary was furious about this and eventually got to establish her hospital in Deauville all the same.

The moment Preston appeared in Paris, Mary decided to send him at once to America, on the theory that all the pomp and ceremony might compel him to enlist. She took him to the Gare St. Lazare station and kissed him goodbye. He had a trunk with him which he was to fill in Deauville with Desti products; then he was to take the boat to Le Havre and a French Line steamer to New York.

Preston arrived in Manhattan with his trunk full of cut crystal and went directly to 347 Fifth Avenue, where a convivial lady named Daisy Andrews had established the headquarters of the Desti business in America. Miss Andrews was puzzled as to what to do with the young man, so she wisely sent Preston on to his father in Chicago.

In Chicago, Solomon decided to complete his son's education back in New York and enrolled Preston as a day student in the Irving Preparatory School, in preparation for Columbia.

Not long after, Mary arrived from France. At the store on Fifth Avenue, business was terrible. Mary couldn't import her products, with the result that she had an argument with Daisy Andrews, who quickly vanished. Mary then declared bankruptcy on the advice of a lawyer who told her this was the way to sort out what she owned and what she had contracted for. Mary was to regret this decision the rest of her life; it was December 1914, and she yanked Preston out of school to help keep the Desti doors open.

By the time America declared war on Germany, the Desti business was running smoothly once more. Mary had made a local deal for stock, and there was enough regular business to pay the $40 rent, the telephone bill, and Preston's helper's salary. Solomon was sending $15 a week, and Preston's store income was an additional $10. Preston entertained no romantic delusions of war. "I became absolutely certain that I was going to be killed," he said, "so all I tried to do was to arrange for as nice a death as possible. I didn't feel like dying in the mud of the trenches with cooties crawling all over me, so I wrestled with my courage for a couple of weeks, then, toward the end of April 1917, went down and volunteered as a flyer in the U.S. Signal Corps." He was not quite nineteen. After an elaborate physical examination, he was turned down for having a blind spot in one eye larger than permitted. Brokenhearted, he promptly signed up with the Royal Flying Corps in Canada. Mary told her son that if he wanted to go into the air service she would get him into the air service of his *own* country. She began some string pulling, and within days Preston was taking another physical for the American Air Service. This time there was no mention of an overlarge blind spot.

In July 1917 Preston was enrolled at the School of Military Aeronautics in Austin, Texas. It was a tough course, with examinations every Saturday. A student needed a 60 to get by and if he got less than that in any subject, he dropped back into the following class. If he missed a second time he was out of the Air Service and sent someplace else as an enlisted man. Preston's grades were in the 90s and he passed honorably. There were long hikes, trapshooting, machine gun practice, and endless classes in aeronautic mechanics.

After three months at Austin, the students were shipped to a flying field called Park Field, in Millington, Tennessee, about twenty miles outside of Memphis. Because of overcrowded conditions, their training didn't start immediately, but they were delighted finally to be where the planes were.

In time, Preston learned to fly from aeroacrobatic aces who conducted training flights by buzzing cotton field workers (called "Nigger-Jazz") and locomotive cabs (called "Express Train-Jazz"). It was a terrifying, stomach-churning indoctrination, but the people of Memphis were hospitable and the men were invited to country club dances on Saturday nights and Sunday dinners in private homes.

During his tenure, the camp newspaper, the *Park Field Airgnat*, asked Preston for "three hundred words of humor" for an upcoming issue. "Why," he said, "I don't know, as I neither looked very funny nor, so far as I know, had ever said anything very funny. I tried to write about my pajamas; my mother had sent me some olive drab pajamas of exactly the same color as our uniforms, and I had found that I could get a lot of extra sleep in each morning by standing reveille in them (in the dark they looked as if I were dressed), running around the barracks in them, and then diving directly back into bed in them. I tried to imagine some humorous circumstance in which some officer was waiting for me when we got back from the run, to take me over to the colonel's office, so that I would finally wind up over there in my pajamas, but nothing funny came to mind so I abandoned the idea and retold a stale anecdote about a lunatic asylum." The *Airgnat* didn't ask for any more humorous pieces, but having learned that he could draw, they asked Preston for a weekly comic strip, and he obliged with the "gruesome" adventures of a flying cadet and his instructor called "Toot and His Loot." He always referred to it as "gruesome" because it was supposed to be funny. He noted that all of his days became gruesome while he tried to think up his "weekly boffo." The strain of weekly production haunted him for the rest of his life, keeping him from accepting a humorous television series some forty years later.

On the eleventh of November, 1918, a terrible disaster overtook them all: the war suddenly ended. After five months with but one objective—to become first-class fliers and then first-class officers in the Army of the United States—Preston and his classmates were suddenly unneeded . . . and seemingly unwanted. "I wanted to take some shots at some Germans, engage some German ace in single combat, and what happened to the *poilus* in the trenches, or even our own doughboys, interested me damned little," he said.

The government mercifully decided to let the boys finish their flight training and at least get their reserve commissions and wings before they were sent home. Most of the fields, including

Park Field, were to be dismantled, but a few, such as Carlstrom Field at Arcadia, Florida, were to be kept going, and it was there that Preston was to finish his training. First, however, he was given a furlough, and he went home by way of Chicago to see his father.

Over dinner at the University Club, Solomon asked his son what he would like to do when he got out of the Army. Preston said that he didn't know; that he thought he had some talent for mechanics, having recently invented and drawn up a multiple-speed planetary gear arrangement for automobiles (although he had just discovered that Louis Chevrolet had patented the same idea in 1900). But that only proved that he was working in the right direction. Solomon asked why he didn't go out to Hollywood and engage in the motion picture business, which seemed to be developing into something quite solid and respectable.

"You mean as an *actor*?" asked Preston in horror.

"Of course not!" said Solomon, who disliked the few actors he had met. "I mean in the business end of the . . . business, or whatever you call it."

"I wouldn't know just how to start," Preston said.

"We'll talk it over some other time," Solomon promised.

Preston forgot about the movies and went on to New York, where he stayed for a few days with Mary, who had moved the Desti business from 23 East 9th Street to 4 West 57th Street and was running it with manicurists again, as she had in Paris. Preston fooled around in the lab in back, inventing a lip rouge that would stay on for twenty-four hours. He was close to finding the formula when his furlough was up and he had to leave for Carlstrom Field in Florida.

Life in the peacetime Army meant Preston was fed, housed, clothed, insured, all for nothing, and given, of course, free medical and dental care. There was nothing to do except fly and do stunts, for which he received a high base pay, plus flying pay. On weekends they went to Arcadia or Fort Myers and he began to understand how easily young men could be sucked into this trap and laze away their best years working for retirement pay and security: the enemy, he decided, of intelligence and initiative.

Finally, having learned everything about peacetime flying, Preston took his final examinations. These examinations were to be given him by the ex-editor of the ex-*Park Field Airgnat*, the gentleman with whom he had divided some of the *Airgnat* residuals. He passed brilliantly, with the highest rating that can be bestowed upon a beginning flier: Pursuit Pilot. Soon, his commission arrived from Washington and he had it framed and hung on his wall. It was 1919 and Preston Sturges was twenty years old. His adult life lay entirely ahead of him; he had absolutely no idea of what he would do with it.

4.

Sturges emerged from the Army an adult, no longer in his mother's charge, and free to chart any course he pleased. But exactly what, he had to wonder, had Mary Desti prepared him for? In retrospect, his education seemed a hopeless jumble of required courses and miserable instructors. Blanching at the thought of attending some college for four years, he read voraciously, certain his schooling was complete.

Preston decided he wanted absolutely nothing to do with the arts, wishing instead to become a successful businessman. It was really all he knew. As a consequence of his eccentric education, he could draw reasonably well, play the piano and violin poorly, and hated anything that smacked of "culture." He wrote verse but knew there was no living to be made at it, although the thought of becoming a songwriter interested him.

Sturges also seemed to have an aptitude for running the cosmetics business. He dealt with customers well, managed the books passably, and even fiddled with the chemicals once in a while. The problem with the Maison Desti, he was sure, was simply mismanagement and apathy on the part of his mother. Well intentioned and intelligent, she simply had no head for business. "My mother was living proof of the fact that judgment and intelligence do not necessarily, or even very often, walk hand in hand," he once said. "My mother had wonderfully bad judgment and a brilliant mind."

Taking a careful accounting of his talents and abilities, Preston decided that the family business was the best place for him. There were millions to be made with the Desti line—as with Coty and Rubinstein—just so long as a capable and forward-looking businessman was at the helm. His father would be proud of him.

In New York, where the shop was a modest storefront on West 57th Street, Preston found his mother delighted with his decision. Probably due, in part, to Isadora's disapproval of the business (she once proposed a party during which the store's entire inventory would be cast into the street), Mary easily grew bored with the shop and had all but abandoned it on at least two previous occasions. The Desti clientele were remarkably loyal, although—especially during the war—supplies were erratic and the quality inconsistent. It was, evidently, The Secret of the Harem that kept them coming in, and Mary found that business got better with a manicurist or two. The Maison Desti had its share of illustrious customers: Evelyn Nesbit ("The Girl in the Red Velvet Swing"); Madame Ganna Walska, the Polish opera singer; politicians Hamilton Fish of New York and Reed Smoot of Utah; vaudeville star Valeska Surratt; Peggy Guggenheim; Mae Marsh, the moving picture star; and the widow of the celebrated actor Richard Mansfield, whose son became a friend of Preston's and would help out in the store occasionally. Such people were used to the finest establishments New York and Paris could offer, and Mary was convinced that manicurists were mandatory furnishings for a successful salon. For all his enthusiasm, however, the perfume business struck Preston as being somewhat effeminate, and immediately after his mother turned the business over to him, he fired the head Desti manicurist, one Peggy Sage. Later, a horrified Preston contemplated the millions she made from her line of fingernail lacquers, all of which could have borne the Desti name.

Mary quickly washed her hands of her business affairs (she said for good), wished her son luck, and took off for France and Isadora. She would return at no particular date, she declared, and excepting an occasional telegram reading CABLE MONEY TODAY ABSOLUTELY URGENT. MOTHER, she left Preston entirely alone. This, of course, suited him. Blithely reducing the Desti staff to himself and an assistant, Preston moved the business to the Williamsburg district of Brooklyn and had painted on the window: PRESTON STURGES & COMPANY, IMPORTERS AND EXPORTERS. He tinkered with the chemicals some more, perfected the indelible lip rouge (which he called, after the red red rose, Red Red Rouge), and became more of a wholesaler than a retailer.

His moustache eventually filled in, which added to the continental demeanor he developed, and he began reading such trendy publications as *The Smart Set*, in which he first discovered the richly amusing prose of its co-editor, H. L. Mencken. Mencken's special brand of intellectual elitism was coupled with a tireless respect for the English language and his command of a seemingly infinite number of words within it. Preston read Mencken's massive study *The American Language*, which helped define his interest in words and word origins. It encouraged him to improve his vocabulary and pronunciations. The fact that most people knew only a small fraction of the language they spoke amused him. To Sturges, Mencken seemed always to have just *exactly* the right word to "vivify a thought." He learned much from Mencken's writings, and refined many of his personal attitudes with Mencken in mind. Mencken's harshly cynical eye fascinated him, as did his ready sense of quality and acutely critical mind. Preston saw Mencken as the spokesman for an entire generation of nimble young minds, and he hopefully counted himself among their number.

One day, Preston received an invitation from his friends Cecil and Laura Singer to spend the weekend with them at the Fairfield, Connecticut, estate of a Mr. and Mrs. Jonathan Godfrey. The Godfreys sounded like a couple of "old poops" to him, but the Singers said it would be fun and eventually he accepted.

Preston wasn't surprised to find Mr. Godfrey a very boring sixty-four. The shock came in meeting Mrs. Godfrey, a beautiful twenty-year-old with whom he found himself immediately enraptured. Her name was Estelle. She was five feet three, three years younger than Preston, with her hair parted in the middle and coiled flatly over her ears. The two talked impulsively—ignoring the other guests—and she told him about her family in Rhode Island and the fortune her great-grandfather had made as a privateer in the War of 1812. Estelle's mother—who married a wealthy man called Mudge—took drugs; it was when the girl turned eighteen that she accepted old Mr. Godfrey's proposal, primarily to get away from her.

They drank too much that weekend, laughed a great deal, and danced shockingly close. Monday morning, Preston returned to New York to prepare for a trip to see his mother in Paris. Estelle drove him to the station alone. As the train pulled out he whispered, "I love you . . ."

Preston spent several months in France and returned with no clearer idea of how to improve the Desti business. Sales remained constant enough to meet his expenses, pay an assistant, and, occasionally, justify a modest profit. But Preston wasn't yet a success—he was merely surviving. Six days a week, the company took all of his time. He was up at dawn, at work shortly after, and there until six. Consequently, he made few friends and generally spent his leisure hours in the local theatres. He saw most of the successful plays, the best of vaudeville, and the current movies, which fascinated him. He especially loved slapstick comedy and had a tremendous capacity for it. America was in a state of postwar playfulness, and the leisure industries prospered. There were more movies than ever before, and the Broadway stage was in the midst of its most prosperous era. Preston attended as often as possible, developing clear attitudes toward the things he liked and disliked. He began to analyze these dramas, asking himself what exactly it was that made one play so good, and another so bad. What excited an audience? What made it respond? Why weren't all of the plays he liked immediately successful? What was it that made them different? He toyed with the idea of writing a play himself, even a book of some kind. Preston Sturges & Company was clearly getting him nowhere, but, again, he had a steady, if meager, income and lacked the self-discipline to apply himself. He worked hard but grew lazy after hours; he was simply not desperate enough.

Preston heard again from Mrs. Godfrey; she invited him to have tea with her at the Ritz. They talked about business—Estelle had looked all over Brooklyn for his factory—and Preston suddenly began to worry about the impression he had made. He had been full of alcohol that weekend in Fairfield but somehow that didn't seem to matter. They made plans for another rendezvous later that week, then another, and another. Finally, she announced she had made up her mind: she was leaving Fairfield and her husband and would go to live with her Aunt Louise in Boston. Preston took the cue. "So the next time the young lady came to town, I took her down to the Battery and into the Aquarium, where, surrounded by schools of stupid-looking fish, I made one of those terribly honorable proposals that begin with 'When and *if* you should by any chance happen to be free someday, my dear . . .' The young lady cried gently while accepting me and I think I snuffled a couple of times myself. I wish I could say the fish cried also, but their expression did not vary in the slightest."

Estelle, from her father's estate, had an income, in trust, of $11,000 a year. This caused Preston to pause a moment, and think seriously about marrying a woman wealthier than he. "Much as I disliked the un-American idea of marrying a lady with a dowry," he said, "I must admit that little Mrs. Godfrey's little private income put everything in a faintly different light." They would not only live much more comfortably than possible on Preston's meager income, but there would be money to expand the business. Promptly, Estelle bought a small country place with a pool near Hackensack, New Jersey. Her next step was to buy a Stutz open car. Preston found a larger factory—also in Brooklyn—with room above for an apartment.

The business started prospering. Preston struck a deal with a perfumery distributing company that wished to become the exclusive distributor of the Desti products. For this, they promised to purchase no less than the enormous amount of $1,000 worth of merchandise a month. Preston grew dizzy with joy.

Estelle and Preston lived together above the factory for over a year, exchanging daily coy little notes of endearment and gossip. They probably could have continued this way indefinitely, but then, in 1924, Isadora Duncan and her new husband returned to Russia. Mary, stranded in Paris, her fifth marriage at an end, boarded a ship and, without warning, returned to New York. After a frantic auto trip through Germany, Mary, at fifty-two, was physically exhausted and emotionally drained. She had no one person or thing to cling to, excepting two: Preston and the Maison Desti. And so, upon docking in New York, she headed immediately for the factory at 33 Throop Avenue. To reclaim it. Again.

Preston was aghast when his mother walked through the door and announced her intention to take it back. In her mind, she had never actually *given* it to him, she had merely left it in his care. Preston objected with vigor: she had most definitely given the shop to him, and he had sunk over four years of his life into it. This meant nothing to Mary. After all, she *was* the Maison Desti. *She* founded it, it bore *her* name. A bewildered Preston wondered what he could do. Obviously, if she insisted upon taking the business back, there was nothing he could do. It seemed like a cold-blooded move on Mary's part, but it probably never crossed her mind that Preston might also have some claim to the business; some need to be involved with it. Angrily, he stomped from the premises in a quandary over what he could do with himself. Another job in a cosmetics firm? Not a chance. Some other line of work perhaps? What in the world was he qualified for? Back to school? Never! Automatically, he consulted Estelle. He was desperate; he truly loved her.

Preston had to get away from Manhattan. He had to start over completely. At twenty-six, he was a total failure with nothing to show for the first quarter century of his life. No money, no success, no real education. And, to top things off, he was being supported by his wife. Preston searched his mind for a great man who had survived on his wife's money. If he had wanted to be an artist, Estelle could be his sponsor . . . but he didn't want to be an artist. Just exactly what did he want to be? He really didn't know.

Preston and Estelle headed north, settling between Peekskill and Yorktown Heights, in Westchester County. There they purchased (or rather, Estelle did) an estate of one hundred and nine acres upon which to live—three houses with a nineteen-acre millpond. It was a beautiful area, a complete contrast to midtown Manhattan. Preston had never experienced such serenity. There were no worries about money or jobs. There was time for doing whatever they pleased. All young men, he acknowledged, should be so lucky.

It took him a few weeks to adjust himself. He walked the grounds and contemplated life. Small details impressed him that never would have caught his attention in the city. The couple bought a German shepherd; every morning, the dog would go out and leap into the stream. On warm afternoons, he would combat the heat by seating himself in the rush of cool water. Preston noted the dog's beautiful coat and reasoned the animal instinctively knew the best way to care for hair—not with soaps or shampoos, but simply with rushing water. Thus, Preston took to cleaning his own hair by standing under the shower head with two large hairbrushes. He never again used shampoo.

Such inspirations led Sturges to believe himself to be a man of extraordinary reason; someone obviously destined for great and uncommon things. Once he had even figured out a way to project ticker tapes with a postcard projector for his father. And he had developed simple perfumes and rouges for the Maison Desti.

After the war, Preston had approached Paris Singer about buying the government's surplus Martin bombers to start an airline between Palm Beach and New York. Singer had declined, indicating the time "was not yet ripe" (whatever that meant), but the plan definitely exhibited original thought and initiative. Through most of his life, Preston noticed that small but deceptively useful ideas would pop unsolicited into his mind. Was this the way men like Edison and Whitney functioned? Did some divine power plant these ideas in a specially designed brain when the time was deemed proper? Was he one of these chosen souls? Perhaps the events of the recent past had been part of a great plan for him. The situation seemed custom-made for a great inventor—quiet surroundings, a beautiful wife, and a steady income. There was nothing to distract him.

An ambitious Sturges set to work. Every idea, no matter how minute it seemed, was written down and developed. One might seize him at any moment, prompting a flurry of single-minded activity that could last for days—sketching, puzzling, writing, building, and then finally consolidating it all into a one-page pastiche of words and drawings, neatly inked and patiently witnessed by the town clerk.

Everything looked so professional in ink and on paper. Among the minor things he devised were grooved leaf springs for automobiles (to facilitate easy lubrication) and a way to carry plate glass windows in automobile side curtains. They were both workable ideas, but Preston had no conception of how one should go about marketing such brainstorms. In fact, living where he did, he had no way of telling if an idea had already been put to work. Just how would one approach Detroit with an idea as minor as a pocket in a side curtain into which could be slipped a piece of glass? And what would they pay for such a revelation?

Preston soon moved on to bigger things. He drew up a design for a bantam automobile with three-point suspension and a removable engine in the rear. He considered sending the plan to Paris Singer, but never got around to it.

He developed a new photoengraving process he thought would

revolutionize the printing industry. He even experimented with stereoptic projection. His favorite (and most elaborate) invention was a flying machine which combined the advantages of the airplane with those of the helicopter. Preston found himself fascinated with a young inventor named Henry Berliner, who made headlines in 1922 by demonstrating a vertical-lift machine for the U.S. Navy. Eventually, Preston designed his own, taking the idea a step further. "It can rise vertically from the ground," he wrote at the time, "and, at the desired height, fly with great speed in a horizontal direction. When it is desired to land, or if the motors should accidentally stop, this machine will descend vertically at the approximate rate of five feet per second. It will also take off or land in the usual manner of an airplane."

In illustration, the contraption featured two engines mounted on the struts of revolving airfoils, under which hung a wingless body powered by still another engine. He was very proud of it and wanted to build a prototype, but, again, never got around to it. Curiously, his main interest was usually wrapped in the actual creation of a particular object, and once the creation process was complete, he lost the interest in pushing it further. He seemed to be searching for the one great and magnificent invention—whatever it might be—that would sell itself, make his name, and seal his fortune. Nothing less would do.

Estelle put up with this for nearly two years. Preston involved himself deeply in his "work," but there would be weeks when absolutely nothing would happen. A procrastinator who functioned on inspiration alone, Preston accomplished little without a regular routine or direct supervision. At the estate he had neither. Estelle didn't care—the money kept coming and Preston was more accessible when not working on a project—but, after a while, things never seemed to change. One day, however pleasant it was, was exactly the same as the next; truly an idyllic existence.

Mary finally gave up the shop in Manhattan and took a lovely little cottage in nearby Woodstock. As time passed, the void between her and Preston healed and Estelle visited her often. The two actually became good friends, and young Estelle would listen for hours to her mother-in-law's fanciful anecdotes. Her adventures with Isadora Duncan and her circle fascinated Estelle—their zest for living, their freedom from responsibility that allowed each day to be different from the last. Estelle thought of these things as she observed Preston at work on one of his silly designs. There were piles of neatly inked drawings lying about the house, the text written in the curlicue style he had acquired at the Lycée Janson. He had never sold a one, and it definitely appeared that he would be happy to sit and draw for the rest of his life.

Estelle's restlessness grew, completely escaping Preston's notice. And then, finally, on the morning of March 17, 1927, she awoke and told him—quite impulsively it seemed—that she no longer loved him.

Preston was astounded. It was a greater shock than the night his father had told him he wasn't really his father. Preston sat for a moment dumbstruck, not fully comprehending the magnitude of what she was telling him. Was she kidding? She certainly appeared earnest. And then, exactly as on that night in Glencoe, he began to cry. Estelle offered little comfort. What should he say? What should he do? He tried to think as clearly as possible. If she no longer loved him, then she no longer wanted him. And he was too proud to remain where he was no longer wanted. He was, after all, a gentleman. Preston regained his composure and told Estelle that if she no longer loved him, then it would be immoral for him to remain any longer. He packed with great dispatch and left for Chicago that same morning.

". . . I nearly died," he later wrote. "It wasn't that I loved my first wife any more than the three others, it was just that it was my first marriage . . . and I had a child-like faith in the institution. At the time, my feelings were swan-like, or wolf-like, if you are familiar with the extraordinarily correct behavior of these animals. I didn't even like to dance with another woman and feel her breasts squashed up against me.

"It wasn't that it had so much to do with sex because the Lord knows oxen don't have any sex life, yet they become so attached to each other that if one dies from an accident the other dies shortly thereafter of grief. Though it may sound corny, two people actually *do* become one in a true marriage and that's why it works. Because nobody can stand living with anybody else. Fish and guests stink after three days they say, but your wife isn't a guest but definitely a part of you—your other half for better or for worse no matter how naif this sounds and you die without her.

"I was already dead inside, I thought, so I decided to go down to the lake that night and get it over with . . . and at that exact instant I heard a blood-freezing scream and a mason who had been working on the sixteenth floor of the Ambassador East passed within six feet of the window where I was standing and crunched on the sidewalk below me. All ideas of suicide left me permanently and I went back to New York."

In New York, his mother poured him a tumblerful of bathtub gin. He examined it carefully. "I wonder if I really ought to drink that," he said, "because I haven't eaten anything yet today and if I take that on an empty stomach I might feel it."

"If you don't want to feel it," Mary asked him, "then why bother?"

5.

After two years of marriage and invention in Yorktown Heights, Preston Sturges seemed lost in Manhattan. He gravitated between New York and Chicago. Estelle was gone; the Maison Desti defunct; there was no money other than the allowance from his father. The fact that he was approaching thirty depressed him. He tried working on some inventions, but nothing seemed to jell. Mary made plans to return to Isadora in Paris, and, through with the Maison Desti, offered to return what was left of it—a few cases of creams and rouges—to Preston for good. Solomon, desperate to get him moving in a positive direction, volunteered the capital to lease a storefront and buy some used fixtures, but Preston, only marginally interested, went to shows and did little about the family business. Solomon soon tired of sending money. Preston thought it would be a good idea to spend Christmas with him, and suggested as much in a letter. Solomon wired back that it seemed like a waste of money, but to come ahead.

Preston was going to need some new clothes if he was going to get something going, he decided. He didn't want to ask outright for a new suit, but his father had always seen to it that he was well and expensively clothed.

"For me Chicago has always had the magical attributes of wealth, security, gaiety, and good food," Preston once said, "which all together made for what the Germans called *Gemütlichkeit*. However poor I might be in New York, scratching myself in a three-dollars-a-week room, out in Bagdad-by-the-Lake I was a member of one of the founding families. . . . During my visits, if our apartment at 20 East Goethe Street was full, Father would get me a wonderful room and bath at the University Club on Monroe Street, then give me charge accounts in all of his favorite restaurants; De Jonghes, the Blackstone, the Red Star Inn, the Tally Ho, way high up overlooking Michigan Avenue, the Bismarck Gardens, and a lot of others I can't remember. As if all this wasn't enough to spoil me rotten, he allowed me to have my suits made at his tailor's, the Stevenson Company, at the ridiculous figure of two hundred and twenty-five dollars each, and shoes at the Moberg Brothers at fifty-five dollars a pair . . . at a time when you could get fine suits for thirty-five dollars and shoes for five dollars. Stuffed with all these expensive meals, and draped in all this finery, I would stagger back to my three-dollars-a-week room in New York to recuperate."

Preston was qualified to do essentially nothing. Worse still, nothing seemed to interest him. It was as if Estelle had completely pulled the rug out from under him. At one time, he had wanted to be a stockbroker like his father, and have a seat on the New York Stock Exchange. Solomon discouraged the idea; in fact, he had a very poor opinion of stockbroking in general and, at the end of his life, said that he had never been anything but a betting commissioner. Nonetheless, in 1916 Preston had worked briefly as a runner for F. B. Keech & Company in New York—long enough to make it apparent that he had absolutely no talent for the financial world. More and more he became subject to black bouts of depression, fueled by insecurity and an overwhelming sense of uselessness.

In Chicago, Solomon Sturges studied his son with disgust. How much lower could he sink before something would click in the boy's mind and he would rejoin the human race? There was such promise in this young man, but he seemed so richly endowed with his mother's lack of direction.

"You'd better go down to my tailor first thing in the morning," he told Preston predictably, "and order yourself a couple of suits." That next morning, however, Preston began to feel ill. At first it felt like nothing more than mild gas pains—after all, he hadn't been eating that well. But gradually it got worse. Fearfully, he diagnosed appendicitis. And the cost of an operation would mean no suits. Preston decided to tough it out—at least until he finished at the tailor's. There he felt nauseous; he began to sweat, vomiting all over the fitting room. When he started home, the ache in his side grew worse still. At home, he phoned his father, who sent a doctor, who detected no fever and prescribed only bicarbonate of soda. For the next week he took bicarbonate of soda until he could no longer walk. Finally, the day before Christmas, he struggled to the phone and told his father he was dying. He then collapsed on the living room floor. His father and the doctor found him and called for an ambulance. By the time Preston reached an operating table at Chicago Presbyterian Hospital his appendix had burst. Peritonitis set in: the surgery took six hours, the recovery six weeks.

Stuck in his off-white, semiprivate room, Preston had plenty of time for thought. He had come close to death and it frightened him. What would have happened had he died? he wondered. His father and mother would have grieved, but would anyone else?

Probably not. He had contributed nothing to society; he was a failed inventor, a failed businessman, a failed husband. And what were his plans? To continue aimlessly? To marry again? Didn't he have something he might turn his talents to?

Preston read quite a bit. His father visited daily, bringing an assortment of books, newspapers, and magazines. And some of Solomon's friends sent notes of good cheer. One sent Preston Irvin S. Cobb's humorous essay "Speaking of Operations—." Since its publication in 1915, the slender volume had become a standard cheer-me-up for surgery victims. It was quick, easy reading and very funny.

Preston began to envision something more than the printed pages. As drama it would be marvelous. He could see the hapless patient already. The humiliation of it all, the silliness and the boredom. It could make a very funny play.

In bed, Preston could either eat, sleep, read, or write. Of the four, writing was obviously the most productive. He rolled the idea of a play around in his mind. God knows he'd been to enough of them. Was he up to the task of writing a play based on "Speaking of Operations—"? Unquestionably. He was, after all, an inventor. And plays were inventions. More to the point, he knew he was stuck there for at least a month . . . it would cost him nothing to try.

When Solomon next came to visit, Preston announced he had decided to invent a play based upon the little Cobb book. Preston asked his father for a few choice volumes on the art of playwriting. Solomon returned the next day with several tomes—among them a book titled *A Study of the Drama* by Columbia University's James Brander Matthews. Preston scanned the other texts but read the Matthews cover to cover. It was "splendidly lucid and sane theatrical advice."

Preston developed an admirable regimen and *Speaking of Operations* took shape quickly. Before long, it had become a lavish musical; a sort of operetta, replete with dancing patients, singing anesthetists, and a buxom chorus in stylish nurse's uniforms. It began to look like a masterpiece to Preston—as compelling an entertainment as had ever been conceived for the stage. He didn't bother to read it until he was halfway through. He began with Act I, and read clear through, picturing specific actors in specific roles and imagining the approximate tempos of the songs. When he finished he was dumbfounded: the transitions were sloppy, his dialogue flat. There was no conviction in it, no matter how ridiculous the whole thing was supposed to be. It was, after all, a musical comedy about abdominal surgery.

Preston went back and tried to make repairs. Again the opening, again the diagnosis, again the hospital. Soon he was mired in what he had once perceived to be perfect. Still he kept at it.

When he was released from the hospital in mid-February, Preston took the Cobb script home with him. After rereading the Matthews book, he sat down for a final review of his material. Sober, clearheaded, he reached a conclusive verdict: he had written a pile of absolute trash.

Unfinished, Preston Sturges' first play was tossed into the waste can. He wrote the episode off as a side effect of the ether. Another failure; again no aptitude.

Sturges brooded a few days, then returned to New York. He decided once more to try his luck at songwriting. NOTHING was simpler than songwriting. All a man had to do was sit at the piano and poke at a simple sequence of keys until a melody emerged that he hadn't heard before. Then, rhyme some words about love lost or found and hope somebody liked it. Since his skills at the piano were essentially nonexistent, Sturges responded to a newspaper ad for a piano course called "Piano Bill," which consisted of numbered keys on a chart propped atop the keyboard. With "Piano Bill," Sturges learned to play by ear. But he still couldn't read or write music, and, finally, with vague melodies swimming in his head, Sturges joined forces with an arranger named Sammy Grossman and wrote several songs of questionable merit.

Sturges and Grossman printed up elegant business cards and set about selling their catalogue. Louis Bernstein, of Shapiro, Bernstein & Company, greeted them with typical enthusiasm. "Now that you're in," he moaned, "let's have it," whereupon Sturges and Grossman launched into a spirited performance of their song "Smilin'."

"Another of those goddamned cheer-up songs," concluded Bernstein. "They've almost ruined the business already." Sturges and Grossman tried another. And another. In parting, Bernstein offered some undeniable wisdom. "They're amateurish," he said, "and you won't know *why* they're amateurish, because *you're* amateurs."

Met with similar enthusiasm elsewhere, the team soon dissolved. Sturges, however, kept at it. One of the publishers he accosted was Ted Snyder, author of "My Wife's Gone to the Country, Hurrah, Hurrah," and the man who gave Irving Berlin his start. Snyder was a bit more helpful than the others.

"This is terrible," said Snyder of "Smilin'." "You don't know anything about writing tunes, but I think you have a talent for writing lyrics—that is, short sentences." Every night for six weeks, Snyder and Sturges had dinner together. Snyder schooled Sturges in the art of "wedding the words to the music," and "pointing" his lyrics for optimum effect. As an exercise, Snyder wrote the music and Sturges composed the lyrics for a song titled "My Cradle of Dreams."

The pupil's lyrics went like this:

> There's a nest
> Not so far away,
> Where I rest
> At the end of day
> Heaven-blessed,
> It's my cradle of dreams,
> Small and white
> Little treasure-chest
> of delight,
> All I love the best
> Waits tonight
> In my cradle of dreams.

When the song was finished, Snyder pronounced Sturges a professional. "You may not be any good," he qualified, "but you are a professional."

Encouraged, Sturges went on to write such musical delights as "Oh, Minnie," "Asia Minor Blues," and "Maybe You'll Be My Baby." Not one was published.

Back in Chicago, Sturges began seeing a well-known stage actress whom he had first met in New York. He was a songwriter —albeit unpublished—and she thought he made an attractive escort. He was tall, with curly black hair, a pencil-thin moustache, and a richly pleasing voice that might have made him a wonderful radio announcer. She evidently didn't take him very seriously, and Sturges found their relative incomes to be a source of great embarrassment. He was quick, an excellent conversationalist, charming, with superlative manners, but she was the one making several hundred dollars a week. Sturges was older than she, but he lived in his father's home, surviving on an allowance until his first song was published. It was something of a masochistic relationship, but after all, he had lived on Estelle's income for all those years.

Sturges and this woman fought frequently. She was a master of the put-down and would attack whenever her ego needed bolstering. He was, after all, a bum in the eyes of his father, a useless inventor, and a terrible songwriter. These truths kept him in his place.

What tortured Sturges was the knowledge that he *was* clever and that he *did* have potential. He just couldn't seem to exploit his qualities successfully. He suspected that songwriting was a lazy man's way to wealth, but he did honestly believe that he was a gifted lyricist and that it would only be a matter of time before his struggling paid off. He was twenty-nine; just how long would he have to wait? Her name was a matter of news. He longed for a little of the public attention she received. Her monthly income could extend well past his own life's earnings.

One night an especially vicious argument took place. She had treated him badly, and, damn it, he was sick of it. He gave her a berating as brutal as he could make it. This was the end, she thought, and returned the fire with an imaginatively galling lie.

Had she been seeing him because she liked him, or had some regard for his talents and intellect? Not at all. He was a fool. In fact, she found him "painfully insipid" and merely desired first-hand knowledge of just "how dull a human being could actually be." She was writing a play, she told him, in which the main character was the "champion bore of all time." She then thanked him for being an excellent guinea pig.

Unknowingly, she struck a particularly sore point: he had tried writing a play, and, like everything else, had failed at it. Now *she* was writing a play and using him for research. Sturges paced the floor, his mind white with rage. "All right," he said finally, aiming a quivering finger at her nose. "If *you* can write a play, *I* can write a play. And I'll tell you one thing: my play will be *better* and my play will be produced *first!*"

With that, he stormed back to his room on East Goethe Street and wrote the entire third act of a play in one sitting. He even decided upon a title—*The Guinea Pig.*

Within a matter of days, the couple drifted back together, all presumably forgotten. Preston continued to bat away at his play, ignoring the third act, but working out the first two with great difficulty. He spent two months on the setup, fueling himself with the Matthews book and the suspicion that his girlfriend had no intention of writing a play. Something drove him on—he worked mornings, afternoons, sometimes past midnight. He had only the slightest of plots, with everything seemingly concentrated in the last act. Slowly, he began to suspect that the drama would come from the *characters* he created, not the *situations*. This clearly fit with what Professor Matthews called "the sole law of the drama, the one obligation which all writers for the stage must accept." Simply stated, "Some one central character *wants* something; and this exercise of volition is the mainspring of the action." Appropriately, Preston designed three characters who wanted something: two young playwrights—a girl who wanted experience and a boy who wanted the girl—and a Jewish fur dealer-turned-producer named Sam Small, who wanted a play. Sturges wrote the boy and girl parts fairly straight, but drew upon some of the blustery, thickly accented professors he had known in Europe for the character of Small. He suspected that although the story he wanted to tell was about the boy and girl, it was the Sam Small character that would provide the entertainment—the laughs that would make the play a commercial success.

Finally the job was done. It had taken forever and still it seemed rough. Sturges was no longer sure whether it was funny or involving or even worth a damn. The lines seemed funny the first few readings, and then began to sour. Would they seem fresh to others?

One night he screwed up enough courage to show the play to the woman who had inspired it, not so much to demonstrate its quality but simply to show that it had indeed been done, and that the incident was certainly not forgotten. He explained as much, although not quite so humbly. "Would you care to read it?" he asked.

"Nonsense," she purred. "I never read plays by beginners. They're just too awful and I like you too much to spoil our relationship over such a matter."

"Oh, go ahead," he urged. "Just a couple of pages."

Grudgingly, she accepted the script, read awhile, and said nothing. She continued to read. When she finished Act I, she sat dumbfounded. "Preston," she said at last, "this dialogue—it's like champagne!"

Sturges gloated. "And it *will* be produced," he told her.

6.

Brander Matthews' book was a revelation. Never before had Preston Sturges thought about the playmaking process in such clear and concise terms; Matthews expressed the mechanics in such a manner as to make the playwright's job appear deceptively simple. With a firm grasp of the concepts Matthews held dear, anyone with a good, inventive imagination could write a successful play. And Sturges knew he was endowed with such an imagination. He read and reread *A Study of the Drama*, adopting many of its attitudes as his own.

Matthews was an exponent of the popular theatre, and his book was loaded with references to audience acceptability and influence. "The true dramatic poet," insisted Matthews, "would never hesitate to adopt Molière's statement of his own practice: 'I accept easily enough the decisions of the multitude, and I hold it as difficult to assail a work which the public approves as to defend one which it condemns.'"

So much for artistic triumph. Sturges would not only have to write a good play; he would have to write a hit. But so much the better: he was a man in search of a livelihood, and he was now to believe that the truly successful playwright was a man of the box office, not of the critics. Continuing on, Matthews addressed himself to the "law of drama" as portraying a character that *wants* something, and then divided the law into several "species." When the obstacles are insurmountable and the struggle is likely to end in death, one has tragedy. If the obstacles are not insurmountable, one has serious drama without an inevitably fatal ending. Comedy results when the conditions of the struggle are equalized and two human wills are set in opposition. And if the obstacle is nothing more than an absurdity of custom, the comedy becomes a farce.

Sturges studied *The Guinea Pig* with these thoughts in mind, allowing that the germ of his play was nothing more than the simple rejection he experienced at the hands of his girlfriend. Ideally, he wished to strive for both comedic and dramatic effects, and was basing the action of the entire play upon the third act, in which he himself had more or less participated. Victor Hugo had written that there are three classes of theatre spectators—the "main body of spectators who demand action; women, who desire emotion; and thinkers who look for character." Sturges was long on emotion and character, but painfully lacking in the action department. His characters were static and this worried him. Ultimately he found himself more concerned with pleasing Professor Matthews than in developing his own dramatic instincts based upon the book's basic truths. Matthews quoted the elder Dumas on the secret of dramatic success: make "the first act clear, the last act short, and all the acts interesting." For the time being, Sturges would concentrate on making his play interesting.

The problem with *The Guinea Pig* was twofold: it was a beginner's play, with a beginner's sense of structure and, like so many beginners' plays, it was about a struggling young playwright; moreover, it had been written out of spite for a personal reason that took precedence over entertainment value. Sturges wanted to rub this woman's nose in it, to show her just how shabbily she had treated him. The third act—written in one sitting in a haze of anger—featured very little outright comedy. He had a woman who, for reasons he would manufacture later, knows nothing of love and yet Small, her producer, wants her to dramatize a best seller, a love story. So she latches onto the boy in the story, takes him to bed with her, then drops him when she has what she believes she needs.

In the third act, the boy tells her that he has written a play "about a girl who told a fellow she loved him . . . and then said she didn't." The title, he tells her, is *The Spider and the Fly*, at which point she acknowledges the crime. "You're so sweet, Wil," Sturges has her say. "You know I wouldn't hurt you; but I had to make the experiment. . . . I never had any romance in my life . . . or any love. . . . I didn't know how sweet a young man could be. . . . I was . . . I was like a scientist, making an experiment, that's all."

The two fall genuinely in love with a fatherly Small in the background to usher them off. It wasn't especially funny and, at first, Sturges wasn't even sure it was a comedy he was writing. *The Guinea Pig* took shape with its first two acts. As it did so, the third act seemed only more incongruous. And not necessarily short.

Whatever uncertainties existed in the author's mind about the overall quality of his play were overridden by the fact that *The Guinea Pig* was all he had. It might be awful, he conceded privately, but he suspected it wasn't and saw no harm in pushing it. It suited *him*; at the moment that was all that mattered.

Sturges borrowed enough money from his father to return to New York. He knew nothing about the art of marketing a play, but there had to be at least *one* producer—with all the hundreds of plays produced each year—who would concede the quality of his work. He would submit the play to anyone who would read it. But who would be most likely to produce a new playwright's first work?

He checked around. He talked with readers, agents, actors, producers, even a few playwrights. He found them in and near theatres, in restaurants, in speakeasies, and they all told him the same thing: see the play performed. Find a repertory company: maybe a college group. Offer to let them do the play gratis. Then watch it in front of an audience . . . and save the notices. Is it funny? Does it sustain itself? Do audiences like it? Talk to them. Would they pay to see it on Broadway?

The advice made sense, in keeping with Matthews' test of public acceptance. Sturges began calling on semiprofessional groups, outfits anxious for new material that could give the modest *Guinea Pig* a respectable mounting. Within days he had suitable company: the Wharf Players of Provincetown, Massachusetts, buried deeply in their 1928 season. He had to borrow additional money to get there, and once he arrived, had to stay out of director Louis Leon Hall's way. Hall was the man whose enthusiasm got the play produced; Sturges had definite ideas how things should be done, but he knew enough not to antagonize the director or the players, and went so far as to observe under a pseudonym. As "Peter Jackson" he helped build the sets, duplicate the scripts (Hall fortunately refrained from demanding changes), and design a long pink cardboard flyer that read:

SEE
PIG!
   it's
humorous
a hummer!

   you go
to nite 8:30

   see
THE GUINEA
   PIG

by Preston Sturges

at the WHARF
THEATRE . . .

"ADMIS" 75¢

Sturges passed these out on local sidewalks. It was the middle of summer, 1928, but he attached little significance to the fact that his play opened on Friday, the thirteenth of July. That night he got his first taste of being a playwright in the back of a crowded theatre. The man playing Small, a local actor named Ralph Morehouse, was a little hammy, thought Sturges, but he seemed to know what the Provincetown audiences responded to. He pulled out lines like "It's cold wit frizzing. Like two polar bears spooning on a cake of ice" and ". . . such HORSEREDISH I never read before" like large clumps of taffy. Small was funny in the way he approached the language, not necessarily in what he said. He was the catalyst holding the story together, making it work: if the audience liked Small they liked *The Guinea Pig*.

On opening night, Sturges discovered he had written the same cue twice when a scene from Act II was repeated in the middle of Act III. Otherwise, the performance went wonderfully well. The local notices, such as they were, were kind, and the laughter and applause absolutely intoxicating. For the first time in his adult life, Sturges knew he had created something unique and people were telling him so. His inventions were one thing, but they were never placed before the public for approval or rejection. The same for his songs. But now he had written a full-length play and seen it performed before an actual audience. And they had laughed where he had wanted them to laugh. It was a position of magnificent power: the ability to manipulate people and their emotions. Sturges knew then for certain what he would do with the rest of his life; what the fates wanted of him. He had to get his play on Broadway—the theatrical showcase of the United States. His success would be cemented there, his achievement legitimized to the fullest. It was to become an obsession.

The Guinea Pig ran a week in Provincetown. When it ended, there were handshakes and thanks all around, but no money. Sturges left his watch with his Provincetown landlady in lieu of $14 rent and returned to Manhattan. With him went the scripts and an envelope of press clippings. He had no idea what his next move would be.

Back in Manhattan, Sturges headed immediately for Pirolle's, a small theatre district restaurant run by a dapper little man named Alexis A. Pillet. Pillet managed an excellent restaurant and had a weakness for theatrical people between jobs. Countless meals at Pirolle's were eaten "on the cuff," and Sturges had already consumed his fair share. He added one more to the number while contemplating his next move.

At another table sat actor Georges Renavent, whom Sturges knew casually. "I've just seen my first play produced," Sturges told him, "and it's very funny." To be of help, Renavent thought he knew of a job: the actor was working for producer Brock Pemberton, who was presiding at that moment over the "rather hectic" rehearsals of a new play titled *Goin' Home*. Renavent thought

Pemberton might be able to use an assistant stage manager. Would Sturges be interested?

Renavent returned to the theatre with Sturges in tow and introduced him to Brock Pemberton. "He needs a job," the actor told him, "and will work for almost anything." On the basis of that glowing recommendation, Sturges was hired. Already, thoughts of presenting *The Guinea Pig* to Pemberton swam in Sturges' mind.

Although a virginal Broadway figure, Sturges, fueled by Brander Matthews' axioms, soon became insufferable. Pemberton found him talking and acting like a "founder of Equity and a charter member of the Dramatists Guild." One of the nicer adjectives applied to Sturges was "precocious."

"Handling the marching troops and other off and on-stage effects of *Goin' Home* was no mean trick of stage management," the producer later wrote. "So expert did Mr. Sturges become in his new job that when Jack Gilchrist, No. 1 Stage Manager, could not fill the post when it came time to produce *Hotbed*, the newcomer was assigned the task. Then, as there seemed to be no limit to his versatility, he assumed a bit in the first act." Pemberton identified Sturges as the "rather chubby-faced young man who mumbled something through a French window after he had batted a baseball through it."

Sturges earned $85 a week on *Hotbed*. *The Guinea Pig* acquired a handsome black binding and gilt title. Pemberton's play reader didn't especially like it, and Pemberton's associate, actress Antoinette Perry, called it "the basis of good comedy on which work should be done." Pemberton himself never read it completely.

The Guinea Pig needed no work, Sturges insisted. He had heard those people in Provincetown with his own ears. The play worked beautifully in its present form and there would be no "improvements." Win or lose, Sturges knew he needed faith in his work to survive. If something was wrong with *The Guinea Pig*, something was wrong with Sturges the playwright. And playwriting was all Sturges had left; his only hope.

When *Hotbed* closed, Sturges asked Pemberton for a letter of recommendation. Said the producer, in acquiescence, "Now that you've had a taste of the theatre, you'll probably never do an honest day's work as long as you live."

Jack Gilchrist, Pemberton's other stage manager, was also an aspiring playwright. Sturges read Gilchrist's stuff and Gilchrist read *The Guinea Pig*. Each told the other how magnificently talented he was, how soon it would be that something of his got produced and hit it big, etc. Sturges, however, disliked contemplating the sizable number of other budding playwrights in New York City and consciously avoided them. Their sheer numbers depressed him, reminding him of the slight chance he had of actually doing the thing he wanted to do. Gilchrist he considered no threat; his work was inconspicuous at best. But what of the others scrambling for the attention of producers and readers?

Sturges and Gilchrist formed the "Broken-Down Stage Managers' Club," which met nightly, after performances, at Child's on Broadway. Child's was a cafeteria in the basement of the new Paramount building, a centrally located hangout for a tremendous number of theatrical people. There, Sturges and Gilchrist could mix socially with those who could read and reject their crumpled manuscripts, though one of these people proved to be just what Sturges and *The Guinea Pig* needed. One night he met a successful lawyer-turned-producer named Charles H. Abramson. Any white water that existed on Broadway was negotiable by Charley Abramson. He was well known, a common target for unproduced writers, albeit a genial and willing audience. Sturges heard this and one night offered *The Guinea Pig* to Abramson over midnight coffee. "I wrote it on a dare with a girl," he told him. "It's very funny." Abramson, typically, read it the same night.

Sturges followed up his submission gingerly. He was back the next night at Child's. And there again was Abramson.

Abramson was candid. "I think it needs work," he told Sturges. "Especially the third act." Sturges stiffened. He had no intention of altering it, *especially* the third act. In any event, Abramson confided, he was not interested in producing *The Guinea Pig* but felt that its author had talent and he wished him well.

Sturges lingered. He had been wondering if it was possible to produce the play himself. Casually, he asked Abramson how much money he thought it would take to produce *The Guinea Pig* on Broadway. Probably $15,000, the producer replied. Sturges persisted. Was that the *absolute minimum?* Abramson shook his head. "Not necessarily," he said. "You want the absolute minimum?"

Abramson thumbed the manuscript a moment. "Now mind you," he qualified, "I know a lot of tricks and short cuts in this business. I'm not saying that a complete novice could do it for this."

"Understood."

"But if *I* were doing it, I could probably do it for . . . $2500."

That was all Sturges needed. From that moment on, he looked for backers as well as producers; patrons of the arts with $2500 to invest. One day, he mentioned the sum to the hostess of a dinner party and she immediately wrote him a check; that night he zoomed back to Child's and confronted Abramson once more.

"Mr. Sturges, I told you I wasn't interested in producing your play," he said patiently. No, no, Sturges said, he wasn't asking him to *produce* it, but merely to help provide some direction. Abramson had said he could produce *The Guinea Pig* for $2500. Could he please say how?

Abramson liked Preston Sturges and admired his drive. "Okay," said Abramson, "I'll help you. What have you got to work with?"

Sturges proudly displayed the check.

"Go to the bank tomorrow and see if it's good. Then come see me at my office."

The check was good and Sturges appeared at Abramson's office promptly at ten. Abramson's first task was to convince his new friend that a Broadway opening was out of the question.

"I honestly didn't think it was good enough for Broadway," he later revealed. "The idea was to showcase a new writing talent."

This took some doing. Broadway was Sturges' dream for *The Guinea Pig*, but Abramson saw the whole plan more shrewdly than the playwright. A Broadway theatre—even a small one—was out of the question for $2500. It would be tough enough to get a good theatre *off* Broadway, but he thought he had an angle.

Abramson had two friends, the Leoni Brothers, who ran an Italian restaurant on 48th Street. Next to their establishment was the little Totten Theatre, a three-hundred-seat house that had enjoyed, up to that time, an unbroken string of failures. It was almost a jinx house, and when the Leoni Brothers acquired the place—almost by default—they were somewhat unsure of what exactly to do with it. Abramson went to them, worked out a percentage deal, and proposed the theatre's name be changed to the President, after the hotel across from it. *The Guinea Pig* got rolling.

Next came the establishment of a corporation to produce the play. Abramson, a lawyer, knew his way through such arrangements. Twenty-five percent of the stock in The Guinea Pig, Inc., was given to the scene builder in exchange for the play's two modest sets. There were parts for eight actors, and Abramson showed Sturges how to hire them without posting much money for bonds. Finally, Sturges and Abramson were able to secure the services of *Potash and Perlmutter*'s Alexander Carr—a popular stage and screen star used to earning $2500 a week—for a modest salary, 10% of the gross, and delinquent hotel bills amounting to $750. Carr was bad with money, which was good for them.

Rehearsals began in mid-December, 1928, with Walter Greenough (an actor from *Hotbed*) directing. Sturges appointed Jack Gilchrist stage manager and himself producer. Charley Abramson checked in daily, helping to keep the production on an even keel, but enjoying no official title. He wished to keep his distance, but did everything in his power to ensure the play's success.

Carr, who did wonders with the Sam Small part, showed Sturges how to "point" his dialogue as one might "point" song lyrics. Some lines were rewritten. In the first act, the girl Catherine describes her ex-husband: fat, old, and drunk. "I admired his writings," she says finally. "Isn't it silly? He had a brilliant mind."

"No, dearie," replies Small. "He was a damn fool. Excuse me to contradict you." Carr cringed at such lines. Pointed, the line would read, "Excuse me to contradict you . . . but he was a damn fool." Sturges caught on quickly. He had been through this with Ted Snyder.

The production ran through two sets of boys and girls before settling upon John Ferguson and Mary Carroll. And then, just prior to the previews, the money ran out. The show was suddenly in danger of closing before it opened; the problem was to find a way to get some performances in front of an audience without cost. At once, Sturges had an inspiration: during his tenure near Yorktown Heights, he had attended summer shows at the Frank A. Vanderlip estate in Scarborough. He wondered if that wealthy suburban community would respond to the novelty of a holiday preview in the dead of winter. Sturges investigated, and was welcomed with open arms. He got the theatre for two nights for only $60 with the gardeners from the estate thrown in as stagehands. Furnishings were loaned from the mansion itself, and the place was packed both nights. The laughs were where he had left them in Province-town and, once again, he was buoyed by the audience.

The New York opening was scheduled for Christmas week, and then postponed at the last minute. Abramson knew Christmas week would be a lousy time for a small play to open and argued for its postponement until a time when there would be much less competition for attention. Two weeks later, on Monday, January 7, 1929, *The Guinea Pig* opened in New York. The directory listing read:

The Guinea Pig
A Comedy by Preston Sturges
The trials of an authoress who aspires to
dramaturgy.

All the major critics, returning to work after the hectic Christmas season, were there. The house was packed, and the response was generous. In a season of overblown revues and pretentious dramas, *The Guinea Pig* was as modest and pleasing as a light dessert at a holiday banquet.

The *Evening World:* "As a first effort, THE GUINEA PIG is rather promising. However, it gives vivid evidence of being a first effort. Substantiality of story is lacking; in fact, the play affords Mr. Carr opportunity for only one scene that hits home."

The *Telegram:* ". . . 1929's first new comedy success in this humble person's opinion. The play was the perfect vehicle for the veteran Alexander Carr, and to the delight of a capacity audience, he made the most of it."

The *Herald Tribune:* "Out of the minor tribulations of a theatrical producer, a woman playwright, and a gawky youth, Preston Sturges has fashioned an entertaining and at times moving drama and in his role as producer Mr. Sturges has equipped the play with a uniformly competent cast and not unpleasant settings."

The *Sun:* "Mr. Sturges writes with a light comedy touch, and such experienced players as Mr. Carr and Miss Carroll carry the action along in a more than satisfactory manner."

Sturges bought a set of scrapbooks and carefully pasted into them everything printed anywhere about *The Guinea Pig:* reviews, press releases, ticket stubs, even ads—rows of the same identical one-inch-by-two-column ad with the little comic guinea pig drawn by Sturges himself. In a place of honor he pasted his favorite notice: that of *Times* drama critic George S. Kaufman.

"An uncertain little comedy," wrote Kaufman, ". . . miles from sure about where it is going and how it is going to get there, but with quite a little simple and entertaining humor in it, and so completely unpretentious that time and again you are drawn to it."

The clippings filled seventy pages by the time the sixteen-week run had ended. Sturges then took the show to Philadelphia for another two. *The Guinea Pig* simply could not sustain itself in New York. Sturges knew the theatre's location and reputation might be a problem, or even the title. At one point, he sponsored a contest in the local papers to generate a new one. The winner was *Passion Preferred* and under that title it moved to Philadelphia. The final closing depressed him, but Charley Abramson knew better. *The Guinea Pig* was only a first step, and a respectable one at that. From it, Sturges earned a producer's salary of only $50 a week. But he had also earned a name, and something of a reputation. Although *The Guinea Pig* wouldn't ensure his fortune, it would open a tremendous number of doors. His stuff would be read, and he had learned much about the theatre. All it took was another play . . . a better, stronger play. At the bottom of the seventieth page of his scrapbook he wrote, "Thus endeth the first lesson."

Sturges hopped aboard a touring company of *Frankie and Johnnie* as an actor and assistant stage manager. He stayed with the show until it took him to Chicago, where the police closed it in June. He had a new idea fermenting in his mind, and needed time to sort things out. He took his scrapbooks to his father's home on East Goethe Street and began to work.

"The day after the show closed," he wrote Charley Abramson, "I went to work on my new play. It's a 'Wow,' said he modestly. Only six more pages to do. It will be finished by the time you receive this. And in SIX WORKING DAYS!"

He wrote next to Brock Pemberton:

"Dear Boss, get excited, will you? My new play has only six more pages to go!"

7.

"In every act," wrote Brander Matthews, "there is often a startling disproportion between the exciting cause and the ultimate result. We might almost liken the artist to the oyster which is moved by a grain of sand to produce a pearl of great price."

The original title of Preston Sturges' second play was *Come, Come Isabelle*, but the title bothered him, and it wouldn't be the one he would send it out under. In a way, it was an even slighter work than *The Guinea Pig*, his only motivation for writing it being his need for a second play and his wish to write something for his friend Georges Renavent. But this time, Sturges set out from the start to write a comedy: a group of amusing characters in amusing surroundings doing amusing things. Sturges refused to consider his creation's frailties for fear of destroying the momentum *The Guinea Pig* had established. The idea of a screwball comedy set in a speakeasy percolated in his mind while on tour with *Frankie and Johnnie*. For Renavent, a specialist in continentals, Sturges imagined a foreign-born cad winning the girl from her clean-cut New Jersey boyfriend: a direct defiance of American theatrical convention.

For posterity, the author kept a diary chronicling his daily progression.

"JUNE 26, 1929: Got letter from Pemberton asking me to send on play as soon as it was finished. Will send carbon copy right away. Later: Did so."

Solomon Sturges was genuinely worried about his son. Granted, he had been moderately successful with his first play, but it seemed that minimal success had gone to his head. He had become cocky and almost insufferably confident. The elder Sturges considered such a case of self-induced hypnosis unhealthy. When Preston arrived in Chicago with *Frankie and Johnnie*, he told his father that he would complete his new play in exactly thirty days. He would then send it to Brock Pemberton, who would immediately produce it on Broadway. Furthermore, it would make his name in New York, and ensure his place in theatrical history. *In thirty days.* That was bad enough, but nine days later, Preston announced that his masterpiece was *finished* and he was preparing to mail it to New York. Pemberton's letter arrived the next day and off it went. The new title was derived from an adolescent exchange Sturges recalled in which he was desperately interested in luring a presumably innocent young girl to his room. Imagining himself the sophisticated bounder he was sure all males of similar background were, he minced no words when she hesitated and then asked, "Just what are your intentions toward me?"

"Strictly dishonorable," leered Sturges.

Sturges calculated that Pemberton would have time to receive the play, read it, recover from its overwhelming comedic impact, and wire his hearty congratulations by the following Saturday morning.

Solomon's irritation rose to the surface. "Will you stop jinxing everything?" he snapped. The boy was thirty-one years old and acting like a child. Solomon decided he should make a special point to be at home that next Saturday, maybe to take a little hot air out of his son's sails.

Preston stood firm. Saturday arrived, and both men remained at home. The clock ticked loudly and the house was uncomfortably quiet. Within one hour of noon, the doorbell rang. Preston threw open the door triumphantly: to the mailman returning the manuscript, marked INSUFFICIENT POSTAGE.

"JUNE 30: Diary: prepare for a surprise.

"To-day, beginning at 9 A.M., I planned the sets and then did 18 pages of the first act of *Recapture*. Some very funny stuff and some moving stuff. I think it's going to be a fine play. Intend to keep my schedule, 5 a day, as before. F. 6 P.M."

"JULY 1: Changed second act set plan, then finished Act I, 37 pages. Did 19 to-day. Some good stuff. Schedule calls for 10 completed and I've done 37. Am I, perhaps, learning to write? Finished 6 P.M.

"Pemberton probably received *Strictly Dishonorable* this morning."

Things were definitely starting to fall into place.

"JULY 2: Telegram received to-day:

"'Congratulations if you are willing to do a little work think you have fine commercial property first act one hundred per cent, second and third skimpy need developing play ten minutes too short but contains worlds swell material can you come for conference and when would like to try for August production. BROCK PEMBERTON.'"

Sturges saw no need to hurry; he knew exactly where the play needed work: page 23 in Act II and page 13 in Act III. The rest was fine. Accordingly, he lingered in Chicago another six days, time enough to complete a good portion of *Recapture*. Finally, he boarded the Lake Shore Limited with the cool aplomb any successful playwright would exude en route to New York. Production would be a matter of little concern: he would simply rent an apartment, visit Pemberton's rehearsals occasionally, write during the daytime, and enjoy his newfound status around town. Not a bad life, though sorely overdue. He had finally redeemed himself, or so it seemed. The meeting with Pemberton didn't go well.

"By offering an immediate production if he would do some work on the comedy," wrote the producer, "a few more scenes were forthcoming, and then by threatening postponement if further scenes were not written, a tentative draft was reached. With this and the understanding that the remainder of the ninety-eight pages other than page 23 in Act Two and page 13 in Act Three would be worked on as the actors developed their characters, rehearsals were begun. The happenings of those three weeks of rehearsal and one week of out-of-town performances are, as someone once said, and likewise literally, nobody's business."

Sturges was unsettled, to say the least, by Pemberton's insistence upon a total rewrite. Just what did the man want? The two fought constantly during rehearsals, Pemberton insisting, Sturges resisting.

The core of the play was the hero's—opera star Count Di Ruvo's—pursuit of the naïve heroine, one Isabelle Parry. The surrounding material amounted to little more than the boozy goings-on within an Italian speakeasy on West 49th Street. Sturges, however, had five sturdy characters, and it was those five that made the play: Isabelle; the Count; Isabelle's boyfriend, Henry Greene; Judge Dempsey, a chronic patron of the speakeasy; and Patrolman Mulligan, the local cop. All five were vividly conceived and, if cast effectively, would carry the slight plot. Here is where Brock Pemberton's talent lay: one of the things that convinced him to do *Strictly Dishonorable* was the fact that he knew exactly whom he could get to play Judge Dempsey and Patrolman Mulligan. Actor Carl Anthony was born to play the judge, a boozy Thomas Mitchell type; and Edward J. McNamara had built an entire career out of playing dumb Irish cops like Mulligan. Pemberton breathed easier when their contracts were signed.

Anthony and McNamara were joined by Muriel Kirkland as Isabelle, Louis Jean Heydt as the boyfriend Greene, and Tullio Carminati as the Count. Georges Renavent, by this time, was in California making movies.

During rehearsals, it would be charitable to note, Sturges and Pemberton were occasionally not on speaking terms. The rehearsals themselves were conducted in a madhouse atmosphere, with much actual rewriting done on the spot. "A play, as produced, is rarely the work of one individual," Sturges later acknowledged. "During the rehearsal period, suggestions are accepted from everyone within shouting distance. Many of those suggestions are excellent, and all of them are used."

In the case of *Strictly Dishonorable*, many single lines—all good laughs—came out of rehearsals. Sturges' personal favorite was suggested by actor McNamara: Isabelle, in a scene in the speakeasy, speaks up when Mulligan is preparing to enjoy a drink. "But policemen never drink on duty!" she says.

Replies Mulligan, "It just seems like never."

The rehearsal process was healthy for *Strictly Dishonorable*. But Pemberton monkeyed with too much of it, Sturges felt, objecting to things that weren't objectionable and insisting upon the rewriting of things that didn't need rewriting. If the play was so fine when he first submitted it to Pemberton, then what was all this mindless meddling about? Pemberton needed to contribute, Sturges figured, but he was ruining the play, and when it flopped, would Pemberton be blamed? A little, maybe, but it would be the hapless playwright whose delicate career would be damaged. Pemberton forced the reshaping of *Strictly Dishonorable* to such a degree, in fact, that when it opened at the Avon Theatre on September 18, 1929, Sturges was convinced that it had been ruined. He stood at the back of the theatre, chain-smoking cigarettes, and thinking every line out of an actor's mouth was more banal than the last. Since Sturges wrote through character, he rarely produced the clean, quotable one-liners that demand instantaneous responses from a cold audience. *Strictly Dishonorable* took a few minutes to warm up, but it was more than Sturges could stand.

After about ten minutes, frustrated, disgusted, wet with embarrassment, Sturges bolted from the theatre and marched into a local speakeasy, where he proceeded to get drunker than at any other time in his life.

The performance went exceedingly well, just as Pemberton had said it would. The actors performed beautifully, and the great good humor that permeated the piece worked superbly. The dialogue, from the mouths of masters, was slick and bright. A pace developed (carefully bestowed by director Pemberton), and carried the play along effortlessly. Anthony and McNamara scored heaviest of all, as Pemberton had again predicted. Sturges had written them some beautifully inconsequential exchanges.

JUDGE: Would you like a little drink, Mulligan?

MULLIGAN: Shure, your honor, an' me tongue is like blottin' paper, but I never touch a drop whilst pursuin' a criminal.

JUDGE: And a very good rule, too. How about a little ginger ale, out of a non-refillable bottle? That's what I'm having.

MULLIGAN: Oh, ginger ale! With pleasure, your honor.
   (The JUDGE pours two stiff drinks.)
MULLIGAN: Well, here's to Prohibition, sor: a noble law.
JUDGE: Experiment.
MULLIGAN: Whatever it is.
   (They drink.)
MULLIGAN: And what a wonderful improvement they've made in
   these soft drinks since the law went in.

The material and the actors melded perfectly, complementing each other as would befit the tailored job the play had become. When it was over, the audience gave the company a standing ovation. Pemberton and Antoinette Perry took bows, but the author was nowhere to be found. Miserably, Sturges sat not far away, looped beyond all reason and brooding over the six months' rent he owed and his sizably outstanding tab at Pirolle's. Pemberton, the bastard, had ruined him for good.

Sturges waddled back to his apartment about 3:00 A.M. and collapsed onto the bed. He didn't stir until midmorning, when Charley Ambramson came pounding on his door, his arms loaded with the morning editions of the big dailies.

Groggily, Sturges tried to focus on the newsprint held before him. ". . . Refreshing, stimulating, exhilarating. An utterly joyful little comedy . . .", said John Mason Brown in the *Post*. Sturges tried his best to comprehend. The *Times* was folded to Brooks Atkinson's review.

Sturges read the first words carefully: "Out of the slightly balmy civilization that has grown up around the more homelike and deferential speakeasies, Preston Sturges has written a well-nigh perfect comedy in *Strictly Dishonorable*, put on at the Avon last evening. After the sparkle of the first act we all held our collective breaths for fear the second act might destroy it. But the second act did not falter, nor the third; and by the time the final curtain had dropped on as well-turned a phrase as a gourmet could ask for, it was certain that a fresh talent for gay, buoyant comedy had come into the theatre."

Sturges began to pull himself together. The phone rang. A friend requested a pair of tickets, and Sturges groggily phoned Brock Pemberton to relay the order. "You poor fool," said Pemberton, "we're sold out and have turned away fifteen hundred people!"

Strictly Dishonorable settled into the Avon for a long run. It spawned companies as far away as Berlin. It won for Sturges the Magrue Prize of the Dramatists Guild of the Authors' League of America. Tickets were scalped for $60 a pair.

Sturges rationalized the play's success by noting that good comedies were in precious short supply. The movies had taken a chunk not only of business but also of talent from Broadway, and talking pictures threatened to do still more harm.

"Comedies are the one salvation of the drama today," Sturges wrote in *Panorama*. "The moving pictures can do melodrama, crime plays, and detective stories far better than they can be given on the legitimate stage. To write a straight comedy is pretty much of a stunt. We can use so few characters and so few sets. The comedy, therefore, depends more on its dialogue than on its movement. Whereas the movies can beat us on movement, we have them on dialogue—and how!"

Sturges deplored the great talent drain and swore that he would not become part of it. He considered himself best suited to writing dialogue—not action—and it looked as if the movies needed just the opposite. The few talking pictures he had seen had been terribly stilted affairs—actors clustered around hidden microphones—and he knew that the movies couldn't walk and talk at the same time. Dialogue was the key, he told himself. And he had a gift for writing it.

"Dialogue," Sturges told an interviewer, "consists of the bright things you would have liked to have said, except you didn't think of them in time."

8.

Overnight, *Strictly Dishonorable* made Preston Sturges one of the hottest new playwrights in America. His picture appeared in the drama section of every major daily on the East Coast. His first week's royalty check was for $1500.

"It is a pleasure to announce the first crocus of civilization to appear in the new season," wrote Robert Benchley in *The New Yorker*. "If, when the season fades, there has been one other as nice as this, it will have been a good season for me. I have a feeling that if there *is* another, Mr. Sturges will have written it."

Sturges was delighted with the attention. He hired a clipping service and preserved every piece of newsprint bearing his name. Ads, photos, criticisms, gossip columns, anything. He bought still more scrapbooks, and hired Jack Gilchrist's wife, Bianca, a dark woman of Jewish descent, as his secretary. Initially, her job was to paste these various bits and pieces neatly into the green scrapbooks, and then to peruse the newspapers herself, lest the clipping service might miss something. Sturges had put up with too many years of obscurity and failure not to savor fully all this praise. He had been conditioned for so long, in so many ways, to expect a minimum return on anything he did, no matter how well he had done it, that he found it almost impossible to accept the fact that he was successful. What was it about *Strictly Dishonorable* that made the difference? In the back of his mind, he feared it was Brock Pemberton, Pemberton who had forced the rewrite that was now so successful. The *Strictly Dishonorable* selling out nightly at the Avon was *not* the *Strictly Dishonorable* that Sturges had first written. Could he do it again? Could he write a hit without Pemberton?

Sturges joked about keeping the scrapbooks as "evidence," and thought, in lighter moments, that his problem had been a common one among artists: the thrill of creation. Salesmanship and marketing savvy were of little interest to him, but he knew that promotion was a good portion of any real success story. That, Charley Abramson told him, was what Brock Pemberton had contributed—not the play, but the moxie to raise the money to produce it, and the skill and energy to sell it when the time came. Sturges bought that grudgingly, but, still leery of success, spent his money carefully. It would be up to him not to panic and lose his footing if *Recapture* failed to measure up. He swore he would never borrow another dime from his father, and would sustain himself, no matter what.

Sturges took a comfortable apartment at 603 Fifth Avenue, inviting Charley Abramson to share it with him. He scrupulously paid his debts—including his rent in Provincetown and the tab at Pirolle's—and then sent $15,000 to his father to invest for him. He accounted for every dime, purchasing exactly one new overcoat and a $250 automobile, model 1922. And he worked feverishly. "When you haven't worked in thirty years," he wrote his father, "you have quite a lot of accumulated energy."

Sturges not only wrote, but set up a small downtown factory in which to build a steam engine he had once designed. "He spent a fortune there and had all these boilers," said Charley Abramson. He was also offered screen adaptation jobs for Paramount Astoria. The money was good but the work didn't interest him; he did only two. Instead, he sold off the Desti cosmetics. "He had a closet full of powders and lipsticks," recalled Charley, "and some of the customers—the Reinhardts and the old social families who were customers of his mother—would send their chauffeurs or butlers to buy the product." Soon, a Chicago company of *Strictly Dishonorable* was in the works, but Sturges paid scant attention. *Recapture* was all he could think of.

The great market crash of 1929 severely undermined Sturges' resolve to save and invest. His $15,000 disappeared and his father, although not ruined, was hurt badly. To a degree, Solomon Sturges had anticipated the crash and did what he could to protect himself. His business never recovered, but he remained afloat, and for that he was thankful. So much for securities, thought Preston. He might just as well have set a match to that money. At Christmas, 1929, he broke training and spent an entire week's royalties on Christmas presents. In mid-January, in anticipation of his new play's opening, he paid $25,000 for a fifty-two-foot cruiser, the first of several boats he would own. He named the craft *Recapture*.

The play *Recapture* was a curious blend of comedy and drama for which Brock Pemberton could muster little enthusiasm. Sturges had reverted to the days of *The Guinea Pig*, drawing upon his private life for inspiration. *Recapture* was modeled on his romance with Estelle Mudge and (as in *The Guinea Pig*) personal elements got in the way of the master narrative. It has been likened to *Private Lives* with an unhappy ending, and both Pemberton and Abramson tried desperately to talk him out of it.

If anything, Sturges was out to prove it was *he* who had ensured the success of *Strictly Dishonorable*, not Pemberton. Pemberton simply wanted another comedy, but Sturges insisted upon flexing both his creative and commercial muscles. The critics would expect another comedy, too. Also the public, but if he could win the critics, he'd have a chance at another hit. Imagine! Two Sturges plays running on Broadway at the same time! The thought intoxicated him. Sturges was proud to acknowledge that *Recapture* had a great deal of drama in it, and those who recognized his name might be put off by the idea of a romantic comedy-drama with an unhappy ending. But critics were paid to see past such limited expectations, and would surely applaud its quality.

Sturges secretly hoped that Brock Pemberton would pass on *Recapture*, so he could show a certain degree of independence. Pemberton predicted disaster, and Sturges wanted badly to prove him wrong. Ultimately, Pemberton did decline it, staunchly maintaining that another comedy would be the wisest thing to follow the hit comedy of the season. His reputation was critical to his future, Pemberton warned, but Sturges simply wouldn't listen. If *Recapture* were to fail, it would fail as a product of Sturges the playwright, not Sturges the collaborator. He no longer needed Brock Pemberton.

Sturges had no trouble in securing a producer for *Recapture*. With *Strictly Dishonorable* running, backers were plentiful. Producer A. H. ("Al") Woods, who had done *Frankie and Johnnie* with Sturges, wanted to do it very badly. A shrewd businessman, Woods knew what the public would buy. His forte was melodrama and farce, and he had done the *Potash and Perlmutter* series. But Al Woods aspired to more prestigious productions as well, having successfully brought *The Green Hat* to Broadway in 1925.

Woods made Sturges an extravagant offer: a flat 10% of the gross. An author's standard weekly income (and what Sturges was getting at the time) was 5% of the first $5000 gross, 7% of the next $2000, and *then* 10% of the gross in excess of $7000. The deal was sealed with a handshake; *Recapture* would open in January.

Much fuss was made about *Recapture*'s arrival. It was certainly the first true *event* of the new year. Woods leased the Eltinge Theatre and engaged a fine cast headed by Glenda Farrell, Melvyn Douglas as the divorced husband trying to recapture the love of his ex-wife, and Ann Andrews as the ex-wife who knows she can never love so rapturously again. Director/playwright Don Mullally directed with competence, and when *Recapture* opened on January 29, 1930, the play itself was the problem, nothing else. Sturges had composed a giddy first act of reunion in the lobby of a Vichy hotel, a second act of indecision over a relationship thought dead, and a third act of separation that ends with the heavy-handed death of the ex-wife in their hotel's rickety elevator.

Structurally, *Recapture* was a mess, neither comedy nor drama but an uneasy blending of both. J. Brooks Atkinson's notice in the *Times*, undoubtedly the best notice *Recapture* received, acknowledged that the play was the work of an "unusual talent in play composition," and "a very clever young man."

"If Mr. Sturges had persuaded himself to keep *Recapture* in the spirit of comedy throughout," wrote Atkinson, "he would have spared himself the solemn pronunciamentos on love for which he has little talent, and he would have made his actors' lot more continuously happy."

Recapture, resoundingly thrashed by the critics, stood little chance of surviving past the advance sales. Sturges told himself they were expecting *Strictly Dishonorable* Part II; that Pemberton, on that count, was right.

"*Recapture* received the most violently destructive notices I have seen in years," Sturges wrote to his father the day after the opening. "The critics boiled me in oil and then danced a swan song on my corpse. However, their combined efforts have cleared the atmosphere and from the next play they will expect nothing and I may be able to surprise them a little. It was a perfectly natural reaction on the part of the critical faculty. *Recapture* is not a bad play, but I took a few liberties with the dramatic construction which they might have forgiven O'Neill but which, in me, they considered only impudence."

The impudence of *Recapture*'s construction was inconsequential compared to the next project Sturges had lined up. In the not-so-distant days when Sturges regarded himself as an up-and-coming songwriter, he had met a French composer named H. Maurice Jacquet. Jacquet also had plans for conquering New York, and both *Strictly Dishonorable* and Jacquet's show, *Silver Swan*, opened within ten weeks of each other. The Sturges play was a remarkable success and the Jacquet show, an expensive operetta, a miserable flop. Knowing Sturges' weak spot for things musical, Jacquet salvaged *Silver Swan*'s scenery, costumes, and orchestrations. He then went to Sturges and painted an elaborate picture of a new bargain-rate operetta, written by Sturges and paid for, in part, by the hapless backers of *Silver Swan*. It was too much for Sturges to refuse. This was December 1929, and all anybody wanted from him, it seemed, was another comedy. *Strictly Dishonorable* was doing wonderful business, *Recapture* hadn't yet opened, and Sturges was feeling a rush of confidence. In fact, only weeks before, "My Cradle of Dreams" had finally been accepted for publication—on the very same day the contracts for *Strictly*

Dishonorable were signed. An operetta? Just the right idea, at just the right moment. The problem with *Silver Swan* throughout, Sturges decided, was easily correctable. The sets and costumes were perfect, and there was nothing wrong with Jacquet's music or the costly orchestrations. The *words* needed changing, that was all. Sturges hesitated, but not for long. The cost would be minimal; he could back it himself, if necessary. Around the sets and costumes he could write a new libretto; within the music and orchestrations he could write new lyrics. The limitations would prove a challenge, but, in a sense, Sturges was only being asked to doctor *Silver Swan*. He would not have to create from scratch, he would simply modify and improve. The elaborate project sounded like tremendous fun; he decided to go to work as soon as *Recapture* was in production.

When Charley Abramson heard of the scheme he was outraged. "It's hard enough to write a show without any restrictions whatsoever," he argued. "How do you write for a piece of scenery?" Sturges, however, had made up his mind. In fact, he preceeded to make arrangements to write the show in Palm Beach, at the home of his friend Paris Singer. He needed to get away from New York and the self-styled experts who were now trying to advise him. Most thought *Silver Swan*—or whatever he intended to call it—was doomed from the start. Sturges found the negative atmosphere an impossible one in which to work. So he would go to Florida, rest, and write.

When *Recapture* flopped overwhelmingly, the threat of the *Silver Swan* scheme intensified. Sturges had lost one game and was preparing to lose another. Abramson worked on him further but Sturges would concede nothing; besides, he had already committed himself.

Recapture's failure was more of a blow to Sturges than he let on. More than ever now, Sturges felt the need to prove himself a second time—to prove that *Strictly Dishonorable* was no Pemberton-induced fluke. But at such a critical time, when most playwrights would have retreated to the safety of another comedy, Sturges found himself saddled with a project as eccentric as the *Silver Swan* rewrite. It worried him, but he also knew that any chance at success would depend upon his approach to the thing as well as his attitude. For better or for worse, *Silver Swan* was it. Anxious to get *Silver Swan* over with, he was at the same time looking forward to the challenge the project presented. Could he indeed write the lyrics as well as the libretto? Could he rise above the Tin Pan Alley stuff he had written before?

Strictly Dishonorable was set to open in Chicago on February 10, but after *Recapture* Sturges decided to get out of town as quickly as possible. He was genuinely torn, as he would love to host his father and his friends on opening night, but he could stand the wait for *Silver Swan* no longer. Preston wrote his regrets; the day the biggest hit comedy of 1929 opened before Solomon Sturges and twenty-three prominent friends in Chicago, its author boarded a train to Palm Beach to try to salvage his flagging career.

9.

Eleanor Post Hutton was the stepdaughter of financier Edward F. Hutton and the granddaughter of C. W. Post, the cereal magnate of Battle Creek, Michigan. She was an attractive twenty, and when Preston Sturges first saw her on the train to Palm Beach (where her family maintained a winter home), he remembered meeting her a couple of months earlier at a dinner party in Manhattan. The journey to Florida was a dull affair, and since Sturges didn't care to work on the train, he approached the Hutton girl and the two spent the rest of the trip charming each other—Sturges by telling her all about *Strictly Dishonorable* and the show he was about to write; Hutton by listening.

Indeed, so charmed was Eleanor Hutton by Sturges, appealingly older and more worldly than the men to whom she usually found herself exposed, that she invited him to stay at the Hutton estate—rather than Paris Singer's or the Everglades Club—and to rewrite *Silver Swan* there. Sturges, in turn, was delighted to accept. Eleanor was younger than the women he usually saw and, in many ways, wonderfully naïve. She seemed genuinely impressed with his talents and found the story of his struggles fascinating.

"She was twenty," shrugged Charley Abramson. "He was a fascinating guy."

Sturges spent the next ten days in Palm Beach doing more courting than writing. Eleanor Hutton came along at a time when Sturges desperately needed someone supportive and, in a sense, distractive. Eleanor laughed at his jokes and witticisms and told him fervently and repeatedly what a great playwright he was and what a hit the operetta would be. After ten days of bolstered spirit and stroked ego, Sturges approached her stepfather. The two closeted themselves in the library, where Sturges opted for the direct approach.

"I'm going to marry Eleanor," he blurted, uncomfortably aware he was speaking to the founder of E. F. Hutton & Company and the Chairman of the Board of General Foods.

Hutton stiffened. "Mr. Sturges; you can't marry Eleanor. First, you haven't known her long enough, and second, you can't *afford* to marry a girl like Eleanor."

"Why not?" Sturges protested. "I've got a hit play and an income of fifteen hundred a week!"*

"For her that's pin money," said Mr. Hutton patiently.

Sturges got nowhere with the old man, and Eleanor fared no better with her mother. Preston was a successful playwright, from a good family, with a very respectable earned income, she boasted. "He even owns a yacht."

"How large?" asked Mrs. Hutton, the former Marjorie Post, daughter of C. W.

"Fifty-two feet," Eleanor replied.

"My dear," her mother corrected, "you mean a *yawl*."

Despite the Hutton family's refusal to take him seriously, Sturges pursued the hand of Eleanor with dogged determination. His intention to marry her took its place alongside his intention to write Jacquet's operetta—however reckless the obsession seemed. Opposition only strengthened his resolve and stubbornness.

"There are a few heart complications in the offing," wrote Sturges to his father on March 18. "I fell in love with Eleanor Hutton, the step-daughter of Edward F. Hutton. She liked me too and we wanted to get married on the 3rd of June. The family promptly decided that I was a fortune hunter, a bum, a drunkard, and everything else they could think of to say. Hutton had detectives put on my trail to dig me up a bad reputation, if possible but so far, they haven't succeeded. They have promised to cut Eleanor off without a cent if she marries me without their consent, and when I still wanted to marry her, it knocked the fortune hunter theory for a loop. They also object to the fact that I was divorced, although her mother has been too. They also feel that the difference in our ages is an insurmountable barrier, although I don't think my eleven years' seniority makes it exactly a May-December romance."

The Hutton family steadfastly refused to condone the marriage and then, in desperation, asked that Eleanor wait at least a year. Finally, on Saturday, April 12, 1930, the couple eloped to Bedford Hills, New York, where they were married by a justice of the peace. From there they visited the bride's uncle at Cornwall-on-Hudson and then motored directly to Mary Desti's home in Woodstock, where they spent the remainder of the weekend.

The papers had the story by Monday morning and played it for all it was worth. It was front-page news in the New York *Times*,

---

*In addition, the motion picture rights to *Strictly Dishonorable* had recently sold for $125,000.

headlined ELEANOR HUTTON ELOPES WITH PLAYWRIGHT; WEDS PRESTON STURGES OVER PARENTS' PROTEST.

Gushed the *Times*, "For several weeks the probability of Miss Hutton's marriage to Mr. Sturges has been a subject of discussion in society circles. It was known that both Miss Hutton's mother and her step-father, Edward F. Hutton, were opposed to the match. But it was also known that she was determined to marry with or without her parents' consent."

Both Sturges and his new bride were somewhat surprised by the amount of attention their elopement received, though Sturges seemed to enjoy it. The couple quickly returned to Manhattan, where Sturges confronted the press at the apartment he and Charley Abramson had been sharing at 603 Fifth Avenue.

The honeymoon, Sturges said, would be spent on his little cruiser, *Recapture*, which was being put in shape. He described it as a "fifty-two-foot motor boat." They would start on the trip in two weeks, without any particular destination. "Just sort of wander along," he drawled.

In the wake of Isadora Duncan's tragic death, Mary Desti's health had begun to deteriorate. After accompanying the dancer's young pupils to Russia for performances in 1927 and making arrangements for an American tour for the Isadora Duncan School, she became ill from what she considered merely fatigue. Returning to Paris, however, she could "scarcely get up mornings," and after learning of her son's appendicitis operation, boarded the first available ship for America.

In New York, Mary's condition was diagnosed as myelogenous leukemia, an especially mysterious form of cancer. A publisher approached Mary to write a book about her life with Isadora—the dancer's last years—but she wondered whether she could ever complete such a project.

"By now my health was becoming alarming and I feared I would be unable to do any serious work," she wrote. "Almost immediately I broke down completely, the doctors despairing of ever curing me. Each day I grew weaker and weaker, until, towards the last, I could no longer move. It was believed the shock and strain of Isadora's death had brought on this condition."

Mary was taken to Memorial Hospital at 106th Street and Central Park West and assigned a secretary to transcribe her recollections. The resulting volume, published in 1929, was hyperbolic, to say the least. ("From far antiquity came Isadora bringing to moderns all the grace of movement, suppleness of body, charm and lightness of raiment, long sealed in the secret archives of sculptural Greece," reads the opening sentence.)

By early 1930, the disease in remission, Mary could, with a generous allowance from Preston, function independently, dividing her time between her cottage in Woodstock and a studio directly below her son's apartment on Fifth Avenue.

"Mother is not well," Preston wrote his father, "and, frankly, I have small hopes of her ever recovering. I paid up her back rent and hereafter I will pay her rent each month outside of the allowance so she won't have to worry about that any more."

The honeymoon Sturges had announced was postponed indefinitely; with Mary's failing health and the need to complete the operetta, he found his time consistently monopolized. Charley Abramson moved out of 603 and Eleanor moved in with trunks of clothes.

Richard "Dickie" Hale, Temple Duncan's first husband, was one of the first friends to dine with the new couple. He could perceive problems even then:

"I'm not being disloyal to Preston when I tell you I thought he was making a big mistake; he was cracking a whip over Eleanor. Partly for my benefit and partly for hers.

"They had set up a closet for her clothes (and you can imagine the clothes this girl had—arctic dress, Palm Beach, traveling); it was all neatly arranged and she had on a kitchen apron and she fixed the dinner. All was fine until it was time to make the coffee. Eleanor said, 'Oh darling, would you make the coffee? You know I make dreadful coffee.' And Preston said, 'Well it's time you learned! You do it!' And she did."

For all of Preston's professed love for Eleanor, he found it difficult to take his wife very seriously. She was simply too young; she seemed to demand too much of his time and attention. When working, or with friends, he expected her to remain silently at his side—to speak when spoken to. He had not married a competitor —despite her wealth and heritage—and stoutly resisted her attempts to balance the relationship. The infatuation weakened as she struggled to make the marriage work.

Said Dickie Hale, "She was such a sweet, lovely girl, really. And devoted to him."

Sturges' seeming indifference was fueled by his work on the operetta, which had by now become a burden rather than a lark. Restricted by the conditions of the production and by the logistical problems of such an elaborate show, he found it almost impossible to attract backers.

Sturges' intentions toward the show were never clear; principally, it seemed, he wished merely to prove he could do it. Any attempt at satirical burlesque became garbled in transmission. What emerged was a commonly plotted operetta, about a mythical Germanic kingdom in which a prince and a princess fall in love but are prevented from marrying for reasons of state, peppered with only occasional hints of satire and lighthearted romance (the mythical kingdom was called Magnesia). Sturges was decidedly out of his element, whether he cared to admit it or not.

The libretto was completed in July of 1930, which Sturges called *The Well of Romance*. Charley Abramson was first to read the script and was appalled by its mediocrity. As he had done since the idea's inception, he immediately tried to convince Preston to abandon it, to no avail. The show was anything but extraordinary, Abramson argued, and would be very expensive to produce. In addition, after *Recapture*, Sturges was no longer in a position to get financing on the basis of his name alone.

Still, Sturges found it impossible to accept the idea he was good only as a humorist. To survive as a playwright, it would be necessary for him to deal with a variety of things—musicals, tragedies, all the brands of entertainment commonly offered up on Broadway. The idea of being pigeonholed as a writer of endless *Strictly Dishonorables* must have frightened him, for without the theatre, he truly had nothing. He was nagged also by the recurring thought that comedy was somehow less important—more frivolous—than drama. Less significant . . . non-lasting . . . forgettable. That *Strictly Dishonorable* was one of the great popular hits of the twenties didn't seem to matter. When the Pulitzers and the critics' laurels were awarded, they always went to the dramas —the *Strange Interludes* and *Street Scenes*—the *significant, lasting* works of the theatre. Sturges often found himself defensive about being a writer of comedy, even when common sense told him there were no apologies necessary. His clear and repeated conviction was that of Brander Matthews: that all *good* theatre was equal, in spite of what the critics might say. Still, he wanted to prove, to himself as much as to others, that he was capable of writing in most any genre . . . and that he wrote comedies through choice and not desperation.

When *The Well of Romance* was repeatedly met with disinterest or revulsion, Sturges once more contemplated producing the show himself. Initially, he wanted Charley and Eleanor to split the costs, but Charley, by now, thought the idea insane. "You haven't got a chance," he told Preston frankly. Privately, he told Eleanor, "Don't put a dime in it."

But Eleanor appreciated its personal importance, if not its slight worth, and decided she should back the show in total, as a wedding gift, with a portion of the inheritance her grandfather had willed her. The money was due her in December, on the occasion of her twenty-first birthday.

Predictably, Sturges couldn't wait until December. Eagerly, upon the promise of Eleanor's aid, he shoveled every last dime they had—to the eventual tune of $64,000—into the production of *The Well of Romance.*

A firm believer in pageantry and color, Sturges modified the costumes and existing sets. A "Continental Male Chorus" was engaged to sing a sort of football cheer song called "Hail the King!" Two men in a cow skin constituted the royal mascot. For the leads, the Princess and the Poet Prince, Sturges engaged Norma Terris and Howard Marsh, the original Magnolia and Gaylord fresh from Ziegfeld's historic production of *Show Boat*. He hired a director (playwright J. Harry Benrimo) and a producer (G. W. McGregor), neither of them with any previous experience in light opera. Sturges then leased the Craig Theatre and prepared to do battle.

The sorry spectacle debuted on Friday, November 7, 1930. Nothing in particular went wrong, but Sturges could see from the start the audience had neither interest nor empathy for the characters he had written. *The Well of Romance* was a big, costly vacuum of a show, devoid of any distinct or appealing character. The playwright's distraction was evident. The headline for the *Times* review of the next morning read "WELL OF ROMANCE" OF FAMILIAR MOLD. The reviews weren't especially bad; the show was simply nothing to get excited about. The audience response on opening night was polite; before the second act had begun, Sturges knew he had written another flop.

All this did little to help the unsteady new marriage. Eleanor realized the show was no good and that they were now, in effect, broke—except for Preston's dwindling percentage of *Strictly Dishonorable*. The apartment at 603 Fifth Avenue grew smaller and Eleanor and Preston began getting on each other's nerves. Eleanor's closet full of expensive clothes irritated her husband. His friends were in often and the lack of proper space became a serious issue. When some money finally did come through—not without protest from the bride's grandmother—they moved.

The Sturgeses found themselves a townhouse at 125 East 54th Street that was as large as 603 Fifth Avenue was small. A marble staircase at street level led to a living room two stories high. Eleanor's bath and bedroom were on the next level, and the master bedroom was directly above that. With quarters for twelve servants, there were twenty-eight rooms in all.

Now with too much room, the void grew wider still. Sturges spent his time working or with cronies like Dickie Hale and Charley Abramson, leaving Eleanor to run a household on a budget of sorts. This especially was difficult for her—always before having had all the money she needed. Preston's taking her for granted hurt her terribly. Eventually, with the surplus of empty rooms, she invited Charley to come live with them. He did, although not in a room of his own. He simply moved another bed into Preston's master bedroom.

Sturges and Abramson spent entire nights talking business. It became apparent to Eleanor she could never command her husband's respect the way Charley could. She was too young, too inexperienced, too . . . female. Women were difficult to understand; unpredictable, flighty, overly emotional. Preston had trusted a woman's lifelong commitment to him only once—when he married Estelle Mudge—and when that blew up he almost killed himself. Never again would he allow himself a relationship like that one.

As his mother's condition worsened, Preston spent more time with her, hiring a nurse to attend her and watching her slowly, painfully disintegrate.

Toward the end she spent most of her time in a special bed Preston had bought for her, sunk deeply into its makings and angled so that she could watch the traffic along Fifth Avenue. It was there that she died—shrunken to ninety-eight pounds of her former bulk—at dusk on Tuesday, April 21, 1931.

"I know you haven't always approved of what I've done," she told her son before she died, "but I was only trying to find happiness." She was cremated, having expressed the desire that her ashes be scattered on the waters between New York and Paris. Preston planned to do just that during his next voyage to Europe.

Eleanor remained with Preston through the ordeal of his mother's death, but he had grown impossible to live with. He couldn't write—couldn't concentrate—the concern for his mother and the pressure of two flops weighed heavily on his mind. The marriage ran a year but took almost two to unravel. Eleanor, a Catholic, was not anxious for a divorce, but felt she had to get away. In June of 1931 she sailed aboard the M.S. *Saturina* for a tour of Europe that would land her, on August 1, in Paris to study opera. Preston agreed to the separation and was hopeful.

"I love my wife with all my heart and soul," Preston wrote his father. "We had a terrible year . . . in a tiny apartment, and we had got very much on each other's nerves . . . we decided to separate a few months to SAVE our marriage. I was terribly unhappy when Eleanor first sailed. . . . I thought we'd reached the end although she told me I was a fool . . . now I think we're going to be all right."

Preston's faculty for composition lurched into motion like the rusted gears of an old tractor. It was hard to think; there would be no writing another *Strictly Dishonorable* in only six days. He toyed with a bedroom farce he called *Unfaithfully Yours*, and then abandoned it in favor of a mild little comedy about the mistaken winner of a slogan contest. He called the play *A Cup of Coffee*, a comedy with absolutely no tragedy or music in it whatsoever. He thought it a fine piece of work, charming but perhaps too fragile for Broadway.

He toiled carefully on *Cup of Coffee* but his heart wasn't in it. Preoccupied with his unsettled personal life, he tried to discipline himself, but truly didn't give a damn. He ate excessively and ballooned to 209 pounds, complementing his rotund physique with a long, flowing moustache he said "makes me look fifty years older."

The taxi-dance hall, or dime-a-dance palace, was then at its peak. Bored that summer, Sturges got into the habit of patronizing such harmless establishments. One night at Tony's, a favorite restaurant on West 52nd Street, a reporter friend of Sturges' warned him that one of the tabloids had stationed a reporter and photographer at a dance joint he frequented, hoping to snap a picture of Eleanor Hutton's husband in the arms of a taxi dancer.

Incensed, yet concerned that the news might somehow get to Eleanor, Sturges told Charley Abramson what he had heard.

Abramson shrugged. "An author can go anywhere in search of material," he said.

Charley was right; all Preston had to do was write a play about the dance halls. He completed *A Cup of Coffee* and settled down to write himself a dance hall romance. The idea grew on him.

Sturges drafted two relatively predictable characters: an ignorant, ill-bred but beautiful taxi dancer; and a millionaire, in this case the owner of the property on which the dance hall sits. He has them meet, fall in love, even marry. Again Sturges found himself dragged into the twilight world between comedy and drama and, again, he resisted writing a straight comedy.

A Cup of Coffee was sent out and confirmed Sturges' fears for it. There were some nice comments but nobody wanted to chance it. Sturges threw the entire weight of his enthusiasm behind the dance hall tale.

"I have been working very hard and have completed *Consider the Lily*," he wrote his father on September 9. "I sent out the other play, *A Cup of Coffee*, but I can't say it caused any particular stir as no one has yet come forth who wanted to produce it. However, that doesn't really matter because it was an excellent exercise in writing and in discipline. I worked very hard on it and dug up so many ideas that by the time I came to *Consider The Lily* I was in full swing. The latter play took sixteen days to write and has 'stood on his ear' everyone who has read it. Everybody who has seen it has offered to produce it immediately and I have several offers from people who have only heard about it. It's a good play and I think you'll enjoy it. The story is one year of the life of a little New York girl. We meet her as a taxi dancer and leave her a year later beautifully arrayed and the mistress of a multimillionaire. The story has no moral but a lot of drama and fun. It's all fire and ice."

Sturges was at the point in his career where another flop could kill him off. *Strictly Dishonorable* would not run much longer and then, once more, he would be financially dependent upon his wife. He wrote Eleanor, imploring her to return to him, but declined to go to Paris himself. *Consider the Lily* comprised his entire career. He seemed to have another hit on his hands; he had to devote his full attention to it. Still, Sturges brooded over the state of his marriage, his wife's estrangement interfering more and more with his efforts to sell his play. The uncertainty gnawed at him. Finally, one day in October, he could stand it no longer.

Irritated, impatient, yet oddly repentant, Sturges sailed for Paris to return his wife to his side. "I've thought out a lot of things during this summer," he told his father, "and I'm going to be a much nicer husband than I was before. I used to think of myself as the proprietor . . . very foolish I know . . . but I'm all over that. From now on I ask only to be the Favorite Man . . . a sort of Lover-in-Law. If you figure this out, you'll see it has far-reaching effects. It means that one cannot sit back and rest on one's laurels, but on the contrary continue to put the best foot forward and be at least as gentle and nice to one's wife as one was to one's fiancee. However well everyone else may know all this, for me it has been a discovery."

Eleanor received her husband coolly. She relished being in control of the situation. Preston wanted her back, but she was enjoying the first real independence she had known in her young life. There was still some feeling for Preston, but it was tempered with the adoration of an endless string of single men she had met in Europe. The competition made her seem all the more inaccessible to Preston, and therefore all the more desirable. Instead of the confrontation Preston envisioned when he first arrived in France, he dutifully took his place among the other pursuers and set about trying to win her back.

"I have done and said every single thing I intended not to say since my arrival here," he wrote to Charley Abramson, ". . . I'm terribly in love . . . but if you could only see her, Charley, she is unbelievably beautiful and smart. Every man in Europe is in love with her and wants her to divorce me and marry him. I can't swing a cat without hitting a rival, and frankly I don't blame them all. Rumors are rife—but they're all horsefeathers. As you know, neither of us can be seen with anyone without a reporter having a hemorrhage—and it means nothing. Eleanor has conducted herself admirably. With every Prince, Lord, millionaire and fortune hunter over here pursuing her, she has been completely fine, dear and honorable—I worship her.

"At last, the other night, I found words to describe her as I think of her. We were in a delightful restaurant. A gypsy orchestra was playing and I said:

> 'A thousand poets dreamed for
> a thousand years—
> and then you were born.' "

Sturges begged her to return with him, but respecting her wish to continue her musical studies, left in late October with a renewed sense of commitment and security. Now there was an additional reason for *Consider the Lily* to be a success—to renew the Sturges reputation and somehow to justify Eleanor's continued devotion to him.

In New York, Sturges quickly struck a deal with A. C. "Blumey" Blumenthal, a dexterous businessman with great faith in the new play. Sturges retitled it *Child of Manhattan*. Playwright Howard Lindsay (*Anything Goes, Life with Father*) was engaged to direct and Reginald Owen, Dorothy Hall, and Douglas Dumbrille were cast as the leads. Sturges kept a steady stream of letters floating between Manhattan and Paris, informing Eleanor of every event of casting and production.

On March 1, 1932, *Child of Manhattan* opened at the Fulton Theatre in New York City. The playwright was honored by the presence of Mayor James J. Walker, Earl Carroll, Mary Pickford, Sir William Wiseman, Otto Kahn, Bert Lytell, Grace and Helen Menken, Billie Dove, Ada May, Millard Webb, Lee Shubert, Pola Negri, Elsie Janis, Isabele Leighton, Gus Edwards, Jesse Lasky, Mrs. Leslie Howard, Al Woods, Nancy Carroll, Mary Eaton, Hiram Bloomingdale, Ernst Lubitsch, Lewis Milestone, Fannie Ward, Mr. Leon Schinasi, Mr. and Mrs. Adolph Zukor, Jack Warner, Arthur Hopkins, Peggy Hopkins Joyce, Billy Leeds, and Alfred E. Smith.

The reviews the next morning were brutal. Wrote Sturges later of his clippings, "I had concocted, it appeared, an evening of 'sheer trash.' According to another pal, I had promulgated a little ditty 'as deeply offensive as any ten editions of the low-jinks of the Freres Minsky.' My talents, if any, I read, 'lie in the direction of forcing poor actors to mispronounce the English language into poor jokes such as Greenpernt for Green Point, Ersters for Oysters, Erl for Oil etc., ad nauseam.' The critic spelled it nauseum, like museum, but I knew what he meant.

"Dipping further into that happy morning, I rejoice in little jewels like 'Coarseness and cheapness of thought and expression in the theatre.' 'Concerned with vulgarity,' 'Buckity-buckity downhill into bathos and sweetish bosh,' 'Tawdry gags and nonplussing commonplace,' 'As silly as it is trite,' *Time*, March 14th, 1932, etc., etc.

"In fact, I have only to close my eyes, stick a pin into any part of any page of that scrap book, and spear myself a free insult. As you may have gathered, I had a flop."

If ever Preston needed the love and support of his wife, it was immediately after the failure of *Child of Manhattan*. As soon as the notices were in, Sturges, completely broke, borrowed $2000 from Blumenthal against the picture rights to the play and left for Paris to be with Eleanor.

The year of neglect and the months of separation had taken their toll on the marriage. Eleanor was now completely disinterested in salvaging the union and, in fact, asked him how much he would "take" to give her a divorce. The question fried his Victorian sense of chivalry to a crisp. Alone, rejected by his audience and now his wife, Sturges regarded her coldly. She owed him a substantial sum of money—$100,000 he figured—what with the house on 54th Street and the money he had sunk into *Well of Romance*, but he was loath to mention it.

Instead, he said simply, "It will cost you one courteous request, madame, and a polite thank-you when it is all over."

It was exactly what he got, minus the thank-you. Upon his return to New York, he discovered he could communicate with Eleanor only through her lawyers; she would speak to him no longer.

Child of Manhattan limped along for eighty-seven performances, changing theatres and unpaid cast members as it went. Blumenthal took a bath with the production, cursing Sturges resoundingly for leaving the show when it still obviously needed work. Surprisingly, he was able to effect a movie sale to Columbia Pictures for $40,000. Sturges, occupied with his marital problems, had let the deadline for repaying the loan pass and ended up with only the $2000 he had borrowed.

"The Doctors of the Drama had the final say," wrote Sturges. "Like Moliere's physicians, they could not cure but they could kill. A few exceptions have occurred, of course—patients like *Abie's Irish Rose* and *Tobacco Road* outlived their doctors—but nothing like that ever happened to me. When they killed me I stayed dead. And the deadest I ever was was on that beautiful morning of March 3rd, 1932, with the sun streaming in through the windows of my five-story house, picking out the awful reviews that surrounded me like obituaries piled into a funeral pyre. My twelve servants chattered gaily in the distance, the gas furnace hissed happily in the cellar at about a dollar a hiss, and the birds in the Ailanthus trees sang gaily in the back yard."

His final words on the subject of his marriage came several months later in a letter to Estelle. Eleanor's lawyers had arranged for an annulment on the grounds that Estelle's Mexican divorce was invalid in the state of New York.

"I think it was a very good thing that Eleanor and I parted," he wrote. "We loved each other very sincerely, but disliked each other so much, because of dissimilarity of tastes, education, and ideals, that there was no hope for us. I'm quite reconciled to the turn of events and, though my heart is a little sad, my head is shouting 'hooray.'"

Preston Sturges' star had, for the moment, sunk deep into the Atlantic. The critics bemoaned his failure to live up to his early promise. The sizable fortune he had collected in royalties had completely—and, to him, inexplicably—dissolved. It was doubtful his name could ever again carry another production to success.

10.

November 5th
1 9 3 1

My dear Mr. Laemmle:

I have just seen the celluloid version of *Strictly Dishonorable* and want to tell you how disappointed I am. I thought the screen play would begin in a colonial mansion with sixty-four columns and an army of liveried flunkeys and progress luxuriously through Roman baths, gin parties, and Roman baths to a thrilling automobile chase ending on a mountain top with the golden dawn bathing the features of the two lovers ensorcelled by each other's beauty.

That is what I expected. Instead, I saw only my play. Granted that you did it beautifully; granted that your cast is magnificent; granted that you used taste and discretion; and granted that little Sidney Fox can charm the birds out of the trees and back again, your production left me sad and disillusioned.

I arrived in the projection room with a very superior feeling and a carp in each pocket and presently found myself deeply interested and admiring my own play. Nothing could be lower than this. I am greatly disappointed.

Cordially yours,
Preston Sturges

Preston Sturges' first brush with the motion picture industry occurred hot on the heels of his success with *Strictly Dishonorable*. Paramount had a studio in Astoria, Queens, on Long Island, in which rather lifeless, studio-bound talkies were made with the talents of the Broadway stage and Hollywood regulars who felt like working on the East Coast. Walter Wanger, who had produced for the London stage and served as assistant to Jesse L. Lasky, was in charge of production. During the days of the silent film, Wanger could keep several productions filming simultaneously in the one massive studio ringed with administrative and production offices. With the coming of synchronous sound, though, production slowed and became infinitely more complex. Dialogue no longer appeared on neatly lettered cards; instead it was actually heard from the mouths of the performers. The microphones were sensitive and static; silent film actors, trained in pantomine and exaggeration, hired voice coaches and were given dialogue directors. Those with bad voices or no sensitivity to the spoken word were quickly dropped; the others adapted accordingly.

To indulge the "talkies," the film industry turned to the stage, Broadway in particular, for people experienced in the recitation of dialogue. Actors like Fredric March and Spencer Tracy, writers like Ben Hecht and George S. Kaufman, directors like George Cukor and Rouben Mamoulian. Those who could be persuaded were brought to Hollywood. Those who could not (i.e. the Marx Brothers) filmed at Astoria during the day and appeared on the New York stage at night.

All the currently successful playwrights were offered work, and Sturges was no exception. He didn't seek movie work, however, and had trouble taking it seriously. Movies played for two days apiece in places like Rawlins, Wyoming; they didn't give Pulitzer prizes for movies.

Of course, a lot of the pictures being produced at that time were based upon plays—from classics like *The Taming of the Shrew* (with Mary Pickford and Douglas Fairbanks, no less) to current hits like *Journey's End* and *Holiday*. In November of 1929, Wanger offered Sturges $1000 a week to occasionally adapt a play for the screen. Sturges was busy with *Recapture*, but the offer was just too tempting. The work was not difficult and the money was good. October 29, the infamous "Black Tuesday" of the 1929 stock market crash, had just occurred; to reject Wanger's offer would be true insanity.

Temporarily, Sturges put *Recapture* aside and turned his attentions to the play *The Big Pond*, which was to commence shooting in just a few weeks. At least two other writers had worked on the project, and neither had produced a satisfactory script. Sturges read the play (which he had seen the year before) as well as the material his predecessors had produced, primarily to get an idea of the format he was expected to use. Happily, *The Big Pond* was to star Maurice Chevalier, which gave Sturges an excuse to do just about anything he wished with it. He did an almost complete rewrite, molding the material to fit Chevalier's personality like a glove. Still, the task seemed too simple, and when he turned in his completed draft, the entire job had taken only two weeks. Wanger, of course, was delighted.

The Big Pond was rushed into production and Sturges was tendered another play to adapt, *The Best People*. The plot for this one was wonderfully ironic in that it concerned a wealthy family's objections to their daughter's marrying a commoner. Having learned since finishing *The Big Pond* that the average time to complete a screenplay was *ten* weeks and not two, Sturges took his time with *The Best People* and finished not long before meeting Eleanor Hutton and going to Palm Beach.

Movies annoyed Preston Sturges. He tended to look down upon them from high atop his perch at the Avon Theatre, but the money—he had to admit—was very good. Twelve thousand dollars for what amounted to a month's casual labor was more than even *Strictly Dishonorable* brought him. But no, he was a playwright, and the eminence the playwright enjoyed in the playmaking process was all-important. Movies took writers in like vampires, charming their victims, feeding them well, dressing them carefully, and robbing them of their souls. There was little individuality in the talking picture, Sturges felt, principally because writers were not accorded the positions they rightfully deserved. Talking film was a producer's medium, and—to some extent—a director's.

A case in point was the work Sturges himself had done for Paramount. He had prepared complete shooting scripts for both *The Big Pond* and *The Best People** but his credits on the finished films were merely for "dialogue" and the total writing credits were shared among three different writers in each case. Not that he necessarily did straight transcriptions of the plays in question (he didn't). Not that the films differed considerably from his scripts (they didn't). *The Big Pond*, in fact, began shooting only days after Sturges had turned the script in.

The question was one of creative sovereignty. Most Hollywood producers—and their New York counterparts—seemed sold on the concept of multiple writers, convinced that a writer capable of composing single-handedly for the stage was equally incapable of doing the same job for the screen. Writers in the picture business were considered hacks. Men of fine talent were pigeonholed as specialists, working exclusively on love scenes, or slick comic banter, or murder mysteries. Scripts were built and refined in pieces, as one might design a house or an automobile.

Sturges held a dim view of collaboration and steadfastly refused to engage in such work. "The results of collaboration have never equaled the results of single effort," he once told an interviewer, "although they probably resulted in more output . . . each loafer prodding the other on."

Things were somewhat different on the East Coast than in Hollywood in the sense that a talent involved at Astoria could also work on the Broadway stage. In California, however, there was no

---

*Released as *Fast and Loose* (1930).

theatre district to speak of and one became the sole property of one's studio by virtue of geography. Opulent homes, plush offices, and regular paychecks had robbed New York of more than one popular actor, accomplished writer, or talented director. Sturges disdained such goings-on, but as the money and opportunities in New York grew scarcer, at least for him, Hollywood became less of an option than a matter of necessity. By 1932, East Coast production had dwindled greatly in favor of California—where the stages were larger, the exteriors more accessible, and the weather more temperate. If Sturges went to Hollywood, he decided, it would be merely to recoup his fortunes and prepare another assault on Broadway. New York was decidedly his natural habitat, and stories of regular hours and ten o'clock bedtimes made him shudder. He would remain no longer than absolutely necessary—provided, of course, that he could get a job.

Early in 1932, Carl Laemmle, the patriarchal founder and president of Universal Pictures Corporation, sent Sturges a letter. Pleased with the results of his company's film version of *Strictly Dishonorable*, and somewhat amused by the limited correspondence he had enjoyed with the playwright, Mr. Laemmle made an inquiry. What properties did Mr. Sturges consider to be his finest? What properties would, in his estimation, make successful moving pictures? Universal would like to discuss them.

Sturges' "trunk" at the time consisted of fragments of *Unfaithfully Yours*, a farce of little consequence; and *A Cup of Coffee*. The latter was the one Sturges decided that Universal needed, and its subsequent submission paved the way to its author's engagement as a screenwriter.

Sturges flew to Los Angeles in September of 1932. Bianca Gilchrist, his personal secretary, chose to accompany him. Following in Sturges' Lincoln were two New York cronies being imported for the duration. Sturges planned to stay just long enough to retire some outstanding debts. He maintained his apartment in Manhattan, and his boat as well. A call from New York would return him immediately, but no such calls were to be forthcoming. He rented a house on Ivar Avenue in a not very fashionable neighborhood near Columbia, RKO, and Paramount. His brief stay in California was to last twenty years.

Sturges was assigned his own little office on the enormous Universal lot in the San Fernando Valley. Within days, he had his first assignment. The Laemmles were evidently convinced—as was Sturges—that he could do anything. They therefore asked him to tackle a screenplay that had thwarted eight previous attempts— *The Invisible Man*.

Carl Laemmle, Jr., the studio's twenty-four-year-old production chief, told Sturges to ignore the original story by H. G. Wells, as it stunk. Sturges pleasantly abided by the directive, unaware that the resulting approach to the material was exactly the same one that had gotten the project's other writers into trouble. He quickly conceived an elaborate scenario of revenge set in Central Europe and Russia. Wells' comfortably English principals, with names like Griffin, Kemp, and Hall, were replaced by characters called Leonid, Septimus, and Sarkov. This *Invisible Man* would retain nothing more from the original than the title itself.

The script progressed with relative ease. Sturges considered the assignment lightweight, but enjoyable and—in its own modest way—satisfying. He took the trouble to become acquainted with a good cross section of the Universal employees and to formulate shrewd impressions of operational and political situations. Junior Laemmle lunched with his new writer on occasion and commended the first pages of script that filtered from Sturges' office. Universal's new star property was character actor Boris Karloff, who had gained stature early in the year as the menacing, oddly sympathetic creature of their hit horror picture *Frankenstein*. Junior, at wit's end developing suitable follow-ups to that film, was anxious to put *The Invisible Man* into production as soon as possible. After Sturges began work on his script, Laemmle brought *Frankenstein*'s celebrated director, James Whale, onto the project. Daily memos were issued to both men in an effort to spur progress. Sturges obliged, carefully structuring Karloff's part for maximum impact with the skill of a master dramatist. He took a gaily flippant attitude toward Laemmle's fussy communications and, on more than one occasion, signed memos to the producer and Whale, "Yours for bigger and better goosepimples."

"I am making Karloff's part in *The Invisible Man* just as important as I possibly can," Sturges wrote to Laemmle. "The strange thing about these horror characters is that their effectiveness grows in inverse ratio to the amount of time we see them. Familiarity breeds contempt and too much gruesomeness becomes funny. Karloff will curl your back hair in every scene I've got him in to date, and you ain't seen nothin' yet."

When finished, *The Invisible Man* was a fine piece of screenwriting that bore only passing resemblance to the Wells story. Whale chose to try again, using this time his friend, playwright R. C. Sherriff. Said Sturges, "I turned in an excellent hair-raiser in eight weeks. As my option came up the next day, calling for a $250.00 raise and a year's employment, I was fired without further frills."

Sturges, however, remained in his studio bungalow, undaunted, doing three weeks' complimentary work on a Slim Summerville/

ZaSu Pitts comedy called *Happy Dollars*,* lunching with Junior, and preparing an original screen story he called *The Power and the Glory*. He prided himself on maintaining an exceptionally fine relationship with his former employers, and considered the good-will gestures he made to be prudent investments toward a future in Hollywood that might not be as soft (or as brief) as he had initially anticipated.

"I hope that this bread cast upon the waters will return as ham sandwiches," he said.

California depressed Sturges. He missed New York, his friends, and the theatre—no matter how fickle. He wondered if he would ever again enjoy the triumph of another *Strictly Dishonorable* or if he had a future in the motion picture industry. He saw little difference between writing for the movies and writing for the stage, other than prevailing industry attitudes toward writers like himself. He wanted to fight those attitudes, bend the film industry to his own terms, rather than adapt himself to theirs. Sturges decided to write a play for the studios as he would for the stage. He would complete it on spec and sell it to the highest bidder—calling the shots and maintaining as much creative control as possible. It was an idea nothing short of revolutionary.

"I like it out here very much," Sturges wrote to Charley Abramson, "but it's very God Damned far away from everything. If I work out my new system of writing continuities on my own time and selling them later, I will be able to write them wherever I like, which is not so lousy an idea. Can you see it? The spring in Paris, the summer on my boat, the fall in New York, and the winter in Palm Beach. Then three days in California to sign new contracts. This would satisfy me I think. However don't mention a word of it as I do nothing but rave about the beauties of this joint, which really is like Bridgeport with palm trees, only Bridgeport is greener and it has Fairchild in its outskirts, and it's only two hours from New York. California is all right for Californians. The people who rave about it are the people who came from someplace worse."

---

*Released as *They Just Had to Get Married* (1933).

11.

While married to Eleanor Hutton, Preston Sturges had been fascinated by tales of her grandfather C. W. Post, the millionaire founder of the Postum Cereal Company (later General Foods), who died when Eleanor was only three. Post was a powerful, dynamic individual who built a sales career in "agricultural implements" into a $20-million estate; a rancher, inventor, and renowned art collector who, at age fifty-five, shot and killed himself at his winter home in Santa Barbara.

The stories stuck with Sturges, nagging at him. He applied the implications of such a life to his own experience. Had the money he made from *Strictly Dishonorable* brought him happiness? Not necessarily; most of it was gone by 1932. Had the home on East 54th Street been any more comfortable or desirable than 603 Fifth Avenue? No, it never suited him as it had his wife. Sturges wore success like an ill-fitting suit. "He was very careless with money," said Charley Abramson. "He was interested only in doing things. Money was just a tool to him." The fabulous sums had enabled him to tinker with steam engines, buy a boat and presents for his friends. What was left was an anathema to creativity. "Men of intelligence need very little," Sturges once noted, "and writers have always worked better hungry. . . ."

Somehow, Sturges suspected, the story of Post—or a character *like* Post—would appeal to Depression-era audiences, who were now, more than ever, both suspicious and envious of the rich and powerful. The idea that such a life could end in such despair would fascinate most anyone. That self-destructive urge in all humans suggested there were those who, through desperation or undeniable ingenuity, moved beyond their intended caste in life, hence suffering a natural inability to cope with their achievements. Maybe Post simply wasn't meant to achieve the things he did; maybe he bolted from the place he was meant to hold in life and was punished for his temerity.

Naturally rich people didn't interest Sturges much—except perhaps as subjects for ridicule. Sturges counted himself among those who enjoyed wealth as a condition of life, not as a way of life. In and of itself, money was a dull commodity. One must *care* about money, Sturges concluded, and cultivate it; that was the ultimate difference between those who handled it well and those who did not. It might well be the theme of the screenplay he would write; a screenplay based loosely upon the life of Charles William Post of Battle Creek.

But as Sturges began to formulate the story of his fictional tycoon, he encountered structural problems. How could he present such a story? A straight narrative beginning in poverty, peaking with success, and then degenerating into self-destruction seemed both unimaginative and inappropriate. He had to grab the audience at the start; what was the angle, the natural point of interest, the thing that fascinated Sturges so? The suicide, of course. It must be the first and overriding point of the entire film: that this man had shot himself in spite of what he had and what he had achieved. What in the world drove him to it? *That* was the crux of the story in Sturges' mind and he was sure it was what the audience would respond to also.

But then Sturges carried this reasoning one step further. He had not heard the story of C. W. Post in one concise, chronologically correct installment. It was all secondhand information, consumed in scattered bits and pieces. First the suicide, then the first marriage, then his illness, then his childhood. The bits and pieces of his life were jumbled in a crazy-quilt manner and, yet, they all made perfect sense. What if Sturges constructed his film in a like manner, pulling the audience back and forth in time as one thought dovetailed into another? Suppose Eleanor were telling the story? Could they follow? He didn't know. And how to present such a construction? Again, he didn't know.

Sturges spent a good two months working out the structure of his play, which he titled *The Power and the Glory*. It took form as a recollection—a give-and-take—between the central character's oldest friend and that friend's wife, opening on the day of the character's funeral, quickly reverting to childhood (where the two friends first meet), then moving back and forth in time as the monologue leads.

The friend, Henry, tells the story in rebuttal to his wife's obvious dislike of Tom Garner on the day of his funeral. Henry, it seems, knows the complete story behind the suicide of Tom's first wife and the failure of his second marriage.

Presently, we meet Tom Garner, the president of a large and successful railroad. He is in the process of bullying his board of directors into purchasing another line—a deal he has, in fact, already consummated. Here Tom is established as a tough, resourceful, even admirable streetfighter of a businessman, obviously where he is through hard work and raw, undeniable talent. This is a man Sturges admires greatly, a man whose natural place is where he is at the moment.

From there, Sturges pulled the story back in time to the meeting between Tom and his first wife, Sally. He then jumped forward to contrast that scene with Tom's first meeting with Eve, the daughter of the president of his new subsidiary, with whom he engages in an affair. Back and forth, back and forth. Sally is old, having prodded Tom to success and now regretting it. Tom, a cold shadow of his former self, tells her he loves the younger Eve and plans to marry her. Sally leaves in a daze and walks in front of a bus.

Throughout, these vignettes are tied together by Henry's sympathetic narration. Like Post, Tom is an antiunionist whose confrontation with his striking employees is one of the highlights of the play. But Tom's life goes sour as he becomes almost sedentary in his position. As C. W. Post's health failed, so does Tom Garner's second marriage. His young wife has obvious contempt for the old man to whom she is married. She enters into an affair with Tom's own son—whose prayerful birth we have witnessed earlier—and gives birth to a baby boy. Tom realizes what has happened, and, in an emotional confrontation with his son, shoots himself dead.

The Power and the Glory was the American success story gone sour; wealth and happiness as the prelude to tragedy. Fate as the eternal and ultimate control. It was Sturges' personal scenario of success—success for a man not meant to strive for the things he did. The talking screen had no precedent for such a cynical, fatalistic yarn, especially in the darkest days of the Great Depression. Sturges was torn with uncertainties—would the story sell? Would the story work the way he had structured it? Was Henry's voice-over explicit enough?

Sturges was approximately one third finished with his "play" when one night at a party he met a man called Hector Turnbull. Turnbull was story editor and associate producer to Jesse L. Lasky at the Fox studios, and during the course of his conversation with Sturges, *The Power and the Glory* was mentioned. Turnbull was genuinely impressed by the unique nature of the story and offered to arrange a conference with Lasky, one of the founding fathers of Paramount, who had recently joined Fox as an independent producer.

Whether Depression audiences of 1933 were ready for a film that began with a funeral and ended with one was not a question that concerned Lasky. Tasteful, respected, one of the absolute giants of Hollywood, he was solely concerned with making a fine motion picture. Sturges related the projected content of *The Power and the Glory* (while carefully outlining the convoluted structure of the piece) in a cordial meeting. Sturges liked Lasky, was impressed with his approach, but intended to hold fast to his determination to sell the script on a percentage basis.

Lasky was impressed enough to ask if Sturges would prepare a "treatment"—a five- or ten-page summary of the play in short story form—but Sturges was too deep into its actual composition to bother with such nonsense and politely demurred. The complexities of the structure, Sturges explained, designed specifically for the motion picture medium, would be difficult to convey in another format. He could not—he would not—furnish a treatment of *The Power and the Glory*. But he could furnish a complete script: a *shooting* script.

Lasky was understandably taken aback; he wondered if Sturges even knew what a shooting script looked like. "I knew if it had any merit," Lasky later wrote, "I could put a team of two or four or a half-dozen skilled film writers on it to develop the basic idea in a manner suitable to the film medium."

Sturges returned to his office at Universal and completed his play in less than a month. Lasky then read the script with understandable skepticism.

"I was astonished," he later said. "It was the most perfect script I'd ever seen."

Terms were discussed. Assured by Lasky that his play would be treated with respect and admiration, and that the author would have a significant voice in every facet of its production, Sturges proceeded to sell *The Power and the Glory* to Lasky and Fox as he would any other play of his—by percentage. It was revolutionary; unheard of in Hollywood. Lasky, however, agreed.

The screenplay was readied for production after one three-hour story conference. "We tried to find something in the script to change," said Lasky, "but could not find a word or situation. Imagine a producer accepting a script from an author and not being able to make ONE CHANGE."

Both Lasky and director William K. Howard concurred: *The Power and the Glory* should be filmed *exactly* as written.*

Jesse Lasky, convinced that he had one of the year's biggest films, handled it admirably. News of the writer's unique deal spread quickly, though, creating a surprising amount of alarm within the industry's power circles. They feared—rightly or wrongly—that if *The Power and the Glory* were a hit, percentage

---

*Some minor changes were made in the film after a first preview in mid-June of 1933, primarily to correct structural problems that seemed to confuse audiences during the film's second half. Verbal references to an incestuous relationship between Tom Garner's first son and the son's stepmother were also removed, somewhat altering the picture's final moments.

deals would become fashionable for other writers, not to mention possible restrictions being placed upon producers in altering their works. The controversy reached its zenith in February 1933, when *The Hollywood Reporter* printed an editorial on the subject by B. P. Schulberg, former general manager of Paramount's West Coast production. Schulberg took Lasky to task for permitting a writer—*any* writer—such a deal, and blasted an earlier *Reporter* editorial that suggested that the percentage deal and the practice of allowing original screenwriting to stand unaltered might constitute a cure for most all bad screenwriting. Sturges read this tirade with amusement, but nonetheless felt the need to respond. On March 2, he addressed a letter to the editor of the *Reporter* which amounted to a statement of the principles by which he intended to function in Hollywood.

"Three months ago," he wrote, "having nothing to do, I sat down and started work on *The Power and the Glory*, an original screenplay. I had had the idea for a couple of years and had wanted to write it for some time. In fact, I came to Hollywood for the especial purpose of writing it.

"Six weeks ago I took the completed script to Jesse Lasky. It was the final job, the shooting continuity, because that is the way I wrote it in the first place. Mr. Lasky said he would like to produce it and asked me how much I wanted for it. I said that producers weren't accustomed to paying large amounts for original screen material and as I valued this script pretty highly, he'd better give me a percentage of the gross. He asked me how highly I valued it for an outright buy and I said, '$62,475.' So he smiled and then we talked some more about a percentage of the gross and made the following dicker: that I was to get 3½% of the first $500,000, 5% of the next $500,000 and 7% of anything over a million, if and when. To keep me from starving to death in the meantime he gave me a $17,500 advance and that was that.

"The transaction, from the first to that last, has been simple, logical, and pleasant; but for some reason it has attracted a certain amount of comment.

"Came first an editorial remarking upon the fact that the script was to be shot exactly as it was written. I don't see anything particularly astonishing in this when it is remembered that it was a finished job intended to be translated into celluloid rather than a brief succession of nebulous ideas intended for use as ammunition in a series of debates, i.e. a treatment. Mr. Lasky liked the script all right and so did Mr. Howard, the director. I wanted to make a few changes, but they wouldn't let me.

"Came next a long and solemn article by an executive of great importance. His name does not matter here, so I will refer to him simply as My Learned Opponent. In not a few well-chosen words he lays bare the fallacy of the Lasky-Sturges contract and sounds a somber warning to authors against sharing in 'doubtful profits.' He will be relieved to learn that my arrangement calls for a percentage of the gross. I feel the way he does about profits, but they tell me there is usually a gross of some sort. Enough of vulgar rewards, however, let us consider the method of writing. The Learned Opponent has a good deal to say about this and none of it is hopeful.

"After sending us his good wishes, which we reciprocate, he unbosoms himself of the belief that from two to eight authors working together on a single script are better than one. Now, if eight are better than one, eighty are better than eight, eight hundred are better than eighty, eight thousand are etc., etc. I for one can think of no surer way of stamping out originality, initiative, pride of achievement, and quality. You can't play football with a thought. The ideal talking picture would result from the alliance of painting, literature, and music. Considering these arts, no famous collaborations spring into mind, excepting, perhaps, the Bible. Barring a few sequences this would make a dull epic.

"Later in his epistle, The Learned Opponent finds it obvious that the same writer cannot tear off a great emotional scene and a great comedy scene. Agreeing with him to the extent of the word 'great,' I agree no further. Entirely apart from the fact that writers transmit emotions through words and that sad emotions are no more difficult to transmit than funny ones, there is the other fact that, without a sense of humor, a writer's sad scenes might easily become ludicrous and, without a sense of pathos, his funny scenes would not be very funny. Writers as double-jointed as all this are: Shakespeare, Tolstoy, Noel Coward, Owen Davis, all of the Authors' League, and the members of the writer's club in Hollywood, to name but a few.

"Nearing the end, the gentleman takes all supervisors to his bosom, pats them on the back, and tosses off the conviction that they write at least as well as writers, that they are, in fact, interchangeable with the latter. Having read his article carefully, I doubt this statement, but I may be mistaken.

"Saying which, I will retire into a vacuum and start work on another epic. It is called *The Concert*. The price is $62,475.'"

The Power and the Glory was readied for production with a starting date set for late February of 1933. There were industry oracles who predicted the film would never be made, what with that screwy writer's deal and the convoluted story line, and Sturges feared they could be right. There was talk beyond Schulberg's letter in the *Reporter* about what the picture might do to the industry's top screenwriters if it were a hit, that they would all probably want percentages and editorial approval and the like.

Sturges suspected—probably correctly—that he was immensely fortunate to have submitted the script to Lasky first; indeed that he and Lasky had connected at all. It was likely most other producers in town—like B. P. Schulberg for instance—would have laughed at such a script. Imagine! Telling a story with scenes in no sort of chronological order! Even if he *were* able to sell it to a major studio, it was doubtful the executives would have left it alone. Certainly they would have taken it apart and put it back together chronologically. And certainly they would have given it to another writer or two to diddle it up in some manner or another. And even if they did respect its worth and promised to leave it alone, who ever would have even considered giving Sturges a percentage of the gross—something not done even with the likes of Ben Hecht or Robert Riskin.

Eagerly, Sturges awaited the signing of his contract. The starting date was set for February 27, but the fifteenth came and went with no formalized agreement. Lasky told him not to worry, but Sturges hadn't earned any income since being let out of his contract with Universal. "I don't mind telling you in strict confidence," he wrote to Charley Abramson, "that I sold this play JUST IN TIME." The starting date grew closer and still no contract. Had someone gotten to Lasky or old man Fox? Sturges worried. Was his percentage deal too dangerous to the natural order of things? Maybe Lasky had had second thoughts about the story itself—the structure and dramatic content.

The week of the twentieth, a two-week postponement was announced. Still no contract. Patience, he was told, the lawyers were still haggling. On March 4, Franklin Roosevelt entered the White House and suddenly all seemed lost. Bank holidays were declared amid speculation concerning the very survival of the motion picture industry. "Cash only" rental policies were instigated; theatre chains threatened closures. As the architects of the New Deal worked away in Washington, only M-G-M seemed secure. The other companies—notably Universal and Fox—were on shaky financial footing. Warner Bros. alone reported losses in excess of $14 million.

Amazingly, the lawyers stopped haggling and Sturges was told he could come in to sign his agreement and collect his check. Then, quite suddenly, a legal holiday was declared in California . . . no contracts or checks could be signed. Word got around that the major studios were asking their employees to accept pay cuts of 50% for the duration of the crisis. Sturges worried they would try to chisel his advance. He then discovered an error in his checkbook that meant his account was overdrawn.

Four days later, the national bank holiday went into effect. Sturges began plotting to return to New York—if he could get there. But why should the theatre do any better in such a situation than the film industry? The trades reported heavy union opposition to the pay cuts and that studios were going to close for three months. Rumors were that Fox was sunk for good.

The storm, however, cleared in a space of two weeks and when the banks reopened and Roosevelt seemed firmly in control, Sturges was an emotional wreck. Finally, Jesse Lasky phoned to say that production on *The Power and the Glory* would commence in a week's time. "I almost kissed him over the telephone," Sturges said. He signed the contracts and collected his check the following day.

Word was already out that *The Power and the Glory* would be one of the major films of 1933. Lasky and director Bill Howard shrewdly assembled an impeccable cast: the leads were Spencer Tracy, a Fox contract player who had recently received considerable attention in Warners' *20,000 Years in Sing Sing*, and Colleen Moore, the gifted silent star and light comedienne, who jumped at the opportunity to prove she was also a superb dramatic actress. *The Power and the Glory* was to be one of the first of Tracy's remarkable string of classics, and one of the last for Moore.

James Wong Howe, who started with Lasky as a cutter's assistant and slateboy in the late teens, was set as cinematographer, and Sturges, fascinated with the moviemaking process and the idea that he might himself one day both write *and* direct feature films, volunteered to serve as Howard's dialogue director with an eye toward learning as much as possible. Shooting began on March 23, 1933, and continued into early May.

Sturges delighted in shattering local tradition in having the writer on the set during filming. He knew his arrangement made him the subject of much talk and the entire business pleased him no end.

"In my whole career I never saw a writer," said Colleen Moore. "They told me they existed, but Preston was the first actually on the set . . . all day long, utterly fascinated by motion picture technique and direction as opposed to stage direction."

The part of Tom Garner was an actor's dream, and Tracy played it for all it was worth. Wrote William Troy in *The Nation*, "Spencer Tracy's railroad president is one of the fullest characterizations ever achieved on the screen."

Sturges felt sure that if he and Tracy could sell Garner as a populist hero—a man of little formal education who achieved his success with street sense and moxie and was at constant odds with the power elite—then the film would have a good chance at finding its audience. The big question seemed to be not so much over content as structure. The uncertainty nagged everyone on the picture—could audiences in Middle America follow a story so radically constructed? Sturges thought he had himself covered with the narration-over-action technique in which all the character voices for particular scenes were provided by Henry, the narrator, whom we meet at the very beginning. A good example of the technique is the scene of Tracy's hilltop proposal to Moore, Tracy being the ignorant mountain boy and Moore being the local schoolteacher who is teaching him to read.

"There wasn't any higher to go," says Henry as we see Tracy and Moore climbing to the top of a hill, "so something *had* to happen. They looked around at the view (Tracy and Moore scan the scene) and it sure was a pretty sight. On one side was the valley they'd just come from with its little houses and railroad tracks, straight and shiny, reaching away beyond the hills. On the other side were the *real* mountains and Sally thanked the Lord he hadn't taken them up one of those. The sun was almost set, the mist was rolling up. (Tracy and Moore stand awkwardly and eye each other.) It got to be chilly; something had to be done. So he looked at her with a terrible expression on his face (Tracy contorts his features) and his hands opened and closed (Tracy's hands open and close), then he screwed his eyes shut (Tracy shuts his eyes tightly), counted one, two, three (Tracy does so), and said, 'Will you marry me?' (Tracy mouths the line). And she said, 'Of course I will, darling,' (Moore mouths these words also) and they kissed each other a little scared (Tracy and Moore embrace). And then she said, 'But Tom . . . couldn't you have asked me at the FOOT of the mountain?' " (Moore mouths the line and the scene ends.)

"It is neither a silent film nor a talking film," Sturges explained in a letter to his father, "but rather a combination. It embodies the action of a silent picture, the reality of voice, and the storytelling economy and richness of characterization of a novel." Lasky and Sturges dubbed *The Power and the Glory* a "narrative picture." The Fox publicity people then coined the word "Narratage," which the two men immediately embraced.

The film was finished on schedule and previewed before a theatre audience in mid-June. Some of the concern for the picture's structure was justified. "The first half of the picture went magnificently," said Sturges, "but the storytelling method was a little too wild for the average audience to grasp and the latter half of the picture went wrong in several spots. We have been busy correcting this and the arguments and conferences have been endless."

The changes weren't extensive though and *The Power and the Glory* was a sensation even before it was released. It was enthusiastically received at a Fox sales convention in Atlantic City that summer, where the Fox executive circle declared it a "box-office smash."

"Mr. Lasky and all the people at the Fox studio say it is the greatest picture ever made in Hollywood," Sturges wrote to his father, "but I, for one, will wait and see what the audience will say about it."

The world premiere engagement opened at the Gaiety Theatre on Broadway on August 16, 1933. The reviews rivaled those of *Strictly Dishonorable* in their praise:

Rose Pelswick, New York *Mirror:* "It is a gripping and fascinating film."

John Alicoate, *Film Daily:* "Unmistakably a great picture."

Kate Cameron, New York *Daily News:* ". . . deserves to be placed among the most distinguished pictures of the year."

Carol Frink, Chicago *Herald and Examiner:* ". . . an unusual picture of great beauty."

In New York City, *The Power and the Glory* did better opening business than had Fox's *Cavalcade.** People stood in long lines to pay $1.65 apiece to see it. Extra matinees were scheduled on the weekends. By all standards, it looked as if the doomsayers and skeptics and B. P. Schulberg were all wrong. *The Power and the Glory* seemed destined for a remarkable commercial success. It looked like a hit.

But it wasn't.

The business it did in Manhattan was not repeated in its road show engagements elsewhere. Perhaps it was the unique construction of the film. Maybe Tom Garner wasn't a hero with whom audiences of the time could identify. It might simply have been a matter of a fine, but dark and depressing, picture to which audiences simply didn't care to subject themselves.

"Nobody wanted to see a story of futility," suggested Colleen Moore. "It was futile. Everyone was saying, 'Just give me something to take me out of myself. I want to laugh.' There were no jobs; there were bread lines. A picture that was depressing—and *The Power and the Glory* was depressing if you were trying to communicate with it—could never make any money."

The Power and the Glory ultimately grossed about one million dollars and disappeared. It was never reissued. A few years later, generally forgotten, the negative and master lavender were destroyed in a New York fire.

---

*Written by Noel Coward and directed by Frank Lloyd. It ultimately won the Academy Award for Best Production of the year.

12.

The temporary nature of Preston Sturges' stay in Hollywood dissolved with his Universal contract. He could no longer blithely remove himself after knocking off a few *Invisible Man*s. With *The Power and the Glory*, miles beyond most screenplays in the marketplace, he had created a remarkable document of the talking screen. He would have to remain and take advantage of whatever opportunities that film afforded.

Fittingly, Sturges decided he needed a larger place if he was going to stay awhile, nothing quite so ostentatious as 125 East 54th Street, but something more permanent than the temporary quarters he had rented on Ivar.

In time, Sturges settled on a place in the Hollywood Hills on Bryn Mawr Drive, which he rented from a Dr. Bert Woolfan. He then had built for himself a seagoing schooner he called *The Destiny* and took to sailing on a semiregular basis.

Sturges generally remained aloof from other writers in Hollywood. They were solitary types, given to bouts of insecurity and self-doubt; Sturges saw these same qualities in himself. He chose friends, therefore, who posed little threat to him: people who weren't writers, people who weren't aiming for the same goals as he. Often, his friends were completely outside of the motion picture industry, which created a reputation for him as a loner. Since he didn't mix well with people within the industry, this label was indeed appropriate. Sturges enjoyed people around him, so long as they were people of his own choosing. He tended to be extremely possessive of the people he cared for; he placed a high value on their loyalty.

"He had a great inferiority complex, I think," said one close associate. "He just felt he wasn't good enough. He had an ego but an inferiority complex at the same time. So he had the security of little people around him. They were people who didn't threaten him. And the big people in Hollywood probably threatened him. . . . He would have made a great feudal baron."

One of the people Sturges brought from New York with him

was an old photographer who had shot some portraits for *The Guinea Pig*. Sturges established a little studio for him in the house on Ivar and equipped it impressively. Indulging his inventor's instincts, Sturges occasionally tinkered with the equipment much as a father might play with his child's trains. In a dispatch to Charley Abramson he bragged about their making "extraordinarily good enlargements from moving picture film which cuts the cost down to nothing, besides being rapid, practical, and permitting us to use a camera about the size of seven packages of cigarettes piled on top of each other." The photographer—Arnold Shroeder—passed out business cards identifying himself as "Dr. Shroeder, the painless photographer." He proudly did $66 in his first month in business.

Sturges brought Dr. Woolfan into his life one night when Shroeder plunged his car over a little precipice while negotiating his way to the house on Bryn Mawr. He was thrown some thirty feet and almost killed. Sturges always credited Woolfan—whom he called "Bertie"—with saving Shroeder's life, a somewhat dubious feat considering the patient functioned as little more than a vegetable for the rest of his life. Sturges took personal charge of his care, paid all costs, and continued to support him until Shroeder's death in the late forties.

Woolfan was a popular general practitioner in the Hollywood area; a not especially big man with sad bloodhound eyes and a face reminiscent of C. Aubrey Smith. Sturges admired his dramatic treatment of patient Shroeder on the night of the accident. "Get out of here!" he roared at Sturges, slamming the door in his face. "I'm not giving up on the old man yet!" When the doctor finished, Sturges took his hand and shook it vigorously. "I want to be your friend," he said carefully, "and I would like you to be my friend. I would like to call you by your first name. And I would like to meet your wife."

The doctor was immensely flattered, as was his wife, the former silent screen actress Priscilla Bonner. A lifelong friendship was born. "From then on," said Priscilla Woolfan, "he *owned* us."

The hub of Sturges' small society was undoubtedly Bianca Gilchrist. Bianca had a Ph.D., spoke three languages fluently, and was possessed of an atomic temper.

To Sturges, a good temper was essential to a healthy human being. But Bianca's violent furies often went beyond robust good health. Once, during a routinely noisy argument, she slammed a windowed door in Preston's face. By reflex, he jammed his arm through the approaching glass and severed three arteries. On another occasion, en route to *The Destiny*, the couple became embroiled in a heated debate that Bianca sought to punctuate by removing her left shoe and beating Preston over the head with it.

Finding it difficult to drive under such conditions, he, in turn, swung his right arm into her face and managed to break her nose. Bianca later proclaimed how delighted she was at the opportunity to have her traditionally Jewish nose reshaped into the more demure specimen she wore thereafter.

"Bianca was a very smart woman," said Priscilla Woolfan, "and a woman with a lot of energy and drive. She'd push Preston; make him work. 'But one has to live a little,' he would say. Bianca stood up to him."

Sturges and Gilchrist made a volatile couple; probably a little too volatile to form a good marriage. "He'd never marry her," said Priscilla definitely. She was obviously an exciting mate, but also wearing and not always supportive. Such women made fine lovers but lousy wives, Sturges seemed to feel. His wives had been more docile women, with their ingrained femininity and Catholic backgrounds. But Bianca, certainly a favorite, stuck with him throughout his formative years in Hollywood.

Sturges was elated with the initial reception of his screenplay for *The Power and the Glory*. Immediately, he embarked upon another, working nights during the shooting of the Lasky picture in hopes of passing the first draft around just as the reception of the completed film was assured.

Having generated such fascination with a truly jaundiced view of a successful man, Sturges addressed the theme once again. His subject this time was a fictional politician drawn from his years in Chicago and stories of William "Old Bill" Sulzer, former governor of the state of New York and a veteran Tammany politician, who found himself impeached when gubernatorial concern for the state began to interfere with the workings of the Democratic machine. Sturges also remembered his talks with Andy McCrery, a neighbor in Westchester County, whose brutal death in 1929 was assured by his failure to meet the payments on a city magistracy he had purchased. It was he who told Sturges how Tammany got out the vote in bad weather, how repeat voters were used, and how influence was routinely bought and sold. Again, Sturges found himself intrigued by men like Sulzer and McCrery, men who achieved their positions through cooperation and obedience and then suddenly began to see themselves as being beyond the circumstances that made them what they were. Sturges recalled an office boy named to a dummy board of directors of the Maison Desti by his late mother. Suddenly apprised of his apparent eminence, the youth proceeded to take charge of the business with such zeal as to remonstrate with Madame Desti herself about the proper conduct of business. Considering Mary's admittedly poor business sense, the boy's remarks were no doubt appropriate, as his concerns lay first and foremost with the corporate well-being. Nonetheless, the boy quickly found himself out of a job. The simple moral: Good Intentions Are Not Enough.

Examining this situation from the standpoint of an outsider, Sturges found the idea appropriately cynical. The theme in many ways complemented *The Power and the Glory*, and Sturges entertained ideas of multiple films examining the American success syndrome; a classical trilogy perhaps, a string of prestigious films to span comfortably the gap between Hollywood and Broadway. He called his first draft *The Vagrant*, which he completed in mid-July of 1933.

Since Sturges had successfully achieved a percentage deal for *The Power and the Glory*, he set out to sell his next play on the condition that he also be engaged to direct it. This, he felt, was only reasonable considering the amount of thought and effort he put into one of his scripts. Who could better define the intentions of the original author than the author himself? Sturges' concern was in preserving the integrity of his work, an integrity that could be seriously undermined by another director's careless deletion or misinterpretation. And—almost surprisingly, considering his limited experience—there was some very definite interest on the part of at least two studios. Naturally, Fox was interested; but so was Warner Bros., the studio perhaps most adept at turning out pictures about gangsters and crooked politicians. *Public Enemy, Little Caesar, I Am a Fugitive from a Chain Gang,* and even Tracy's *20,000 Years in Sing Sing* were all made at Warners'. A tentative fee was discussed: $15,000. Not much, but it was a chance for Sturges to prove his worth with a relatively inexpensive picture. If he did well, if he brought his film in on time and budget and received good notices, the job would pay dividends for years to come. Obviously no studio was going to entrust a $500,000 picture to a complete novice; the fee was quite acceptable, Sturges told them.

Unfortunately, the rave notices for *The Power and the Glory* could not hide its generally poor showing at the box office. Broadway was crazy about it; it died like a dog in most other engagements.

Once again, Sturges found himself cursed with the stench of a flop. A well-known flop. Any company engaging him would not be doing so for the money he had made for Fox. Warner Bros. suddenly cooled to the idea of *The Vagrant*. Political pictures were commercial death, anyway. Sturges—people suspected—was a fine writer who had absolutely no idea what audiences would buy tickets to see. *The Vagrant* might well be another *Power and the Glory*—good, not a money-maker.

The windfall from *The Power and the Glory* never happened; he was also unsuccessful in his efforts to get the play published as an interesting example of the screenwriter's art.

Sturges made the rounds of the other studios with *The Vagrant* in hand, but to little effect. Fox, Universal, Warners', RKO, Paramount—there wasn't much interest anywhere. Sturges signed with the William Morris office and finally, in desperation, accepted a staff position at M-G-M for a straight $1000 a week. Little is known of this assocation, other than the fact that Sturges reported directly to producer Irving G. Thalberg, one of the industry's few bona fide geniuses. Thalberg's taste and sense of audience were unquestioned and his ability to troubleshoot defective scripts and pictures legendary. Thalberg evidently engaged Sturges on the basis of *The Power and the Glory*—which he had admired—but Thalberg was well known for his casual use of multiple writers: "ditch diggers," as he called them, to work out basic ideas, and then structure and dialogue specialists to work to the producer's own specifications. Predictably, Sturges didn't fit well into this matrix and was summarily released after eight weeks.

Sturges left Metro on a Thursday evening in November of 1933, spent a painfully restless night in bed—wondering, in the pit of the Depression, whether he would ever write again—and was then offered a new job the next morning. Directly from Thalberg, Sturges bounced into the arms of Columbia's Harry Cohn—an explosive and vulgar man who hadn't seen *The Power and the Glory* but knew Preston Sturges as the author of *Strictly Dishonorable*, which had done well for Laemmle, and of *Child of Manhattan*, which Columbia had filmed late the previous year. Cohn agreed to Sturges' now established rate of $1000 a week and put him to work on Hecht and MacArthur's screwball comedy *Twentieth Century*, the Broadway hit that Cohn had recently acquired for actor John Barrymore. Cohn wanted no part of *The Vagrant* or, for that matter, Sturges as a director. Cohn, however, ran his studio on guts and instinct and Sturges sensed that if he could prove himself to his new boss, he might be given a chance to do *The Vagrant*. The idea also appealed to him that he would be a relatively large fish in a relatively small pond . . . like Cohn's wonder boy Frank Capra. Columbia was one step above Poverty Row, churning out scores of cheap melodramas and an occasional "A" production from Capra or free-lancers like John Ford and Howard Hawks.

Sturges dove into *Twentieth Century* as if it were his last chance at Hollywood (he suspected it might be), but Cohn had an opportunity to borrow Elissa Landi from Fox and was looking for something to put her in. Sturges took the cue and four days into his Columbia engagement presented Cohn with a treatment for a drama he called *Matrix*. Since he had not read any of Sturges' work on *Twentieth Century*, Cohn was incredulous: here was an odd, dark story of a woman who marries an incredible jerk of a man to satisfy her mothering instincts. To Cohn, it wasn't interesting and certainly not funny. All that occurred to him was that he had hired a onetime comedy writer who now imagined himself a tragedian; certainly not the kind of man to whom he was willing to entrust *Twentieth Century*. Without further comment, Sturges was fired.

Three more days passed, then Sturges did two weeks' work at Universal on an adaptation of *Imitation of Life*, little of which was ultimately used. John Stahl, the director, wasn't interested in Sturges scripting the film (Stahl had directed Laemmle's version of *Strictly Dishonorable*) and chose William Hurlbut instead. As 1933 drew to a close—the year of *The Power and the Glory*—Sturges was out of work . . . out of money . . . and seemingly out of opportunities.

Reaching, Sturges returned to Jesse Lasky and tried to sell him on the idea of "redialoguing" a picture Lasky was preparing called *The Worst Woman in Paris*. "Dialogue is the flavor of a talking picture," he memoed the producer. "Mediocre speeches will ruin the story as sure as bad cooking will ruin good food. I believe good dialogue is the cheapest insurance a producer can buy. It makes good material magnificent and average material at least presentable. It's like good tailoring. When Shakespeare wrote *Abie's Irish Rose*, he used different dialogue and called it *Romeo and Juliet*."

Lasky, with thanks, declined.

Sturges, with a more mercenary approach, desperately sniffed the wind for virtually any producer who would meet his price. Perversely, the next producer to come through was his old nemesis Ben Schulberg. Schulberg, preparing a frothy vehicle for Sylvia Sidney based upon a *Ladies' Home Journal* story called "Thirty Day Princess," kept Sturges on the picture just long enough to humiliate him. Predictably, the two men clashed, exchanging hostile memos for several weeks. The battle they had once fought in the pages of *The Hollywood Reporter* was restaged almost verbatim, Sturges again asserting that multiple writing credits robbed writers of the "pride of achievement," and that the policy was artistically foolish at best. Schulberg's response was simply to assign another writer to the project. This time, when the film was released, there were not just three credits for writing but *four*. Sturges fumed at Schulberg's cavalier treatment of his material, estimating only about 10% of the film was his. Regardless, he fought for screen credit with the other three, figuring it would do him more good to have his name on ten bad pictures than none at all. Schulberg said he thought Sturges "selfish," to which Sturges responded, "When and if I care so little about my work that I become unselfish, I will no longer be worth the fancy prices I am receiving at the moment."

Sturges was at wit's end by the time he was offered Samuel Goldwyn's production of the Tolstoy novel *Resurrection*, at the behest of director Rouben Mamoulian. Goldwyn was anxious for a good picture to spotlight his "Russian Garbo," Anna Sten, who had made an unmomentous American debut in the producer's recently completed *Nana*. By the time Mamoulian came onto the film, Goldwyn had already commissioned two scripts (one by Maxwell Anderson, another by Leonard Praskins) that were deemed both expensive and unacceptable. Sturges caught wind of this and, although he was hardly in a position to be choosy, upped his asking price to $1500 a week on the theory that, in Hollywood, one was only as good as one's last price.

Goldwyn was decidedly leery of Sturges—"Sturgeon," as he sometimes referred to him—but met his price on Mamoulian's assurances that he was indeed the man for the job. "He had a great feel for it . . ." Mamoulian recalled, "and it was a very harmonious, creative relationship."

Mamoulian, a Russian émigré, worked closely with Sturges to ensure as much authenticity as possible. For this he emphasized attitudes and atmosphere over details of expression and dialogue, which were distinctly American. Sturges respected the novel in broad strokes, knowing that to squeeze Tolstoy into an eighty-four-minute movie would invite disaster. "To condense Tolstoy is an enormous task in any case," Mamoulian affirmed. "It was a tough job. You're *never* completely successful."

Getting Sten's character, Katusha the peasant girl, and Prince Dmitri—played by Fredric March—together was a task to be accomplished with all possible haste: their affair spans an entire decade. Sturges resorted to a trick he had practiced since *The Guinea Pig* of "hooking" his dialogue—impregnating each speech with something upon which the other character can comment, a "hook" on which another character can hang a response. Usually, Sturges accomplished this by giving his lead character an assertion of some sort; an ideal or dogma that comfortably serves to round out character while at the same time developing necessary interrelationships. For *Resurrection* he saw Dmitri as a bumbling young idealist home from the university who spouts on about his classless society *ad nauseam*. His two aunts of course pooh-pooh the very thought, and, presently, Dmitri takes his case to Katusha in the barnyard.

Sturges, with Bianca at the typewriter, would dictate such scenes pacing restlessly in his office. Given that Dmitri wants to tell Katusha about a book called *Land and Freedom*, Sturges would close his eyes and invent the exchange between them by taking both parts. In deep tones he'd impersonate the Prince saying, "The government has suppressed it! I've met Simonson the author—

he's a great thinker. The police are after him!" Then Sturges would pause and imagine himself as the peasant girl. Picking up the "hook"—*The police are after him*—he would then raise his voice and with wide-eyed innocence ask. "Is it an immoral book?" To which Dmitri would reply, "It's the most moral book ever written! It says that all people are equal and that the land should belong to everyone."

Sturges could dictate reams of dialogue in this manner, his only problem coming later in the editing down of trivial byplay for pacing. As he worked rapidly, he was much more economical a choice than either of the two costly writers who had preceded him. In ten working days Sturges churned out fifty pages, in contrast to the six months that had been charged to the screenplay thus far. Nonetheless, Goldwyn watched costs, anxious to move into production.

"When can we get rid of this fellow Sturgeon?" Goldwyn demanded in his high, nasal accent. Mamoulian held the mogul at bay for several weeks while Sturges slugged his way through the awkward transitions of Dmitri into a proper member of the Russian aristocracy and Katusha into a common prostitute, a task that the novel took four hundred pages to achieve. The behavior of March's character bothered Goldwyn, and Sturges wondered if Goldwyn had ever troubled himself to read the novel. "This Dmitri," Goldwyn complained. "He is a horse's ass!"

Still, Mamoulian could find little fault with the draft Sturges turned in. ". . . I do remember when we got through with the script I had trouble with an important love scene," he qualified. "And somehow Preston didn't come up with the right scene there. So I got Thornton Wilder and he did this scene."

When Goldwyn was finally free to fire Sturges, he did so, said Sturges, "with great alacrity."

Resurrection, retitled *We Live Again*, was released in November of 1934. Annoyingly, Sturges noted the single screenplay credit he felt rightfully his debased by the names of Anderson and Praskins under the nebulous heading "Adaptation." It was, though, after *We Live Again* that Sturges returned to Universal under an agreement calling for his new rate of $1500 a week. All of a sudden, after the *Invisible Man* debacle, he was once more in demand at his home studio, a situation that pleased him very much. The lot was roomy and the atmosphere decidedly familial. Sturges now thought his best chance to become a writer-director was at Universal. At last he could feel the beginning of a great upswing in his career.

13.

The Hollywood studios, who derived a good 40% of their revenues from foreign sources, were notoriously unwilling to do much importing of their own. A chunk of top-flight British product appeared in America, but foreign-language films were a special problem since the coming of sound and the process of subtitling or dubbing a film for the American market was both awkward and expensive. Hollywood preferred to import the filmmakers themselves, or to appropriate the stories for remaking with English-speaking casts.

The Laemmles had acquired to rights to make an English-language version of *Fanny*, the middle part of what ultimately became a trilogy of character studies on the Marseilles waterfront. Marius, Fanny's lover, was the subject first of a 1929 play of the same name, and then a 1931 French film written and produced by Marcel Pagnol and directed by Alexander Korda. The film was an immediate and resounding success in Europe and the following year Pagnol made *Fanny*, also in French. It was in fact a distillation of these two plays that Universal sought to make.

Preston Sturges, with his European background and excellent command of the French language, was an obvious choice to domesticate the regional dialect and adapt the story to popular tastes; *We Live Again* was a job widely admired. Junior Laemmle augmented his participation with director William Wyler and producer Henry Henigson. Sturges knew Henigson, a clever and somewhat intellectual man, from his previous work at Universal: Henigson had been associate producer on both *They Just Had to Get Married* and *Imitation of Life*. Wyler, on the other hand, was family—a second cousin to Junior imported from France, who was getting his first "A" pictures after an apprenticeship in foreign publicity and "B" Westerns. Like Preston, Wyler was educated in Switzerland and France, and the two men liked each other instantly.

Eagerly, the three set to work in the spring of 1934, Universal going so far as to bring out a newcomer named Jane Wyatt to play the title role. But early on there were problems with the story. The plot concerned Fanny's seduction and impregnation by the seagoing Marius and the fuss created over giving a proper name to the unborn child. The problems would not have been considered insurmountable had not the Catholic Legion of Decency begun a well-publicized crusade against movie immorality. The apparent effect would be to give teeth to the old Motion Picture Producers and Distributors of America (MPPDA) Production Code, and to restrict severely the ability of producers to depict certain stories on American screens. The industry sought to strengthen the code against any movements toward a government-imposed censorship. Aimed most obviously at Mae West and her animated counterpart Betty Boop, the result was a reconsideration of all things questionable, and this, in the spring of 1934, certainly included *Fanny*. There were also internal rumblings. Junior was at odds with the New York salespeople and *Fanny* was a pet project of his. If the costly *Fanny* were made and then became mired in censorship debates, the effect could be a smudge on the Universal globe, an expensive pile of bad publicity at a time when the company was in a precarious fiscal position.

Sturges felt he could circumnavigate these problems, but his confidence was solitary. Within weeks the project was shelved. Wyatt's debut was shunted to James Whale's *One More River* and Sturges made his disappointment known.

Almost immediately, though, the trio was shifted from the stillborn *Fanny* to a second assignment. Universal had acquired the Molnár comedy *The Good Fairy* after its respectable Broadway run with Helen Hayes and was now eyeing it as a showcase for the up-and-coming Margaret Sullavan. Sullavan, who—ironically—first came to notice as Isabelle in a touring company of *Strictly Dishonorable*, had just finished *Little Man, What Now?* for Frank Borzage and Junior was hopeful he could get *The Good Fairy* into production by the end of summer.

Sturges watched Sullavan in the new film with fascination. He could see a marvelous naïveté; a grand potential for a vulnerability and innocence in some ways contrary to the blithely manipulative heroine of the play. He discussed the possibilities with Wyler—himself extraordinarily taken with the actress—and was of a mind to alter the play to Sullavan's benefit in any way he pleased. Wyler agreed and in several days, Sturges had set about softening the play considerably. He built the innocence of Sullavan's character by placing her in an orphanage and taking the opportunity to inject some early slapstick. For Sturges, this picture was his first chance at outright comedy since *Strictly Dishonorable* and what he intended to write bore only a passing resemblance to the play; it is doubtful, in fact, that one line of Molnár dialogue survives in the finished product. Sturges sought to create a tug-of-war between the various male elements of the piece, through which the girl wanders with unsullied virtue.

As if to declare the piece uniquely his, he made wholesale alterations of character names and personalities: the girl, Lu, became Luisa Ginglebusher, a name perfectly befitting a girl who would spend most of her youth in an institution for the unwanted; Kellner, the girl's apparent husband-to-be in the play, became the raucous and fatherly Detlaff. Sturges chiseled the age of Dr. Sporum, the lawyer Lu picks from the phone book to be the beneficiary of her good deed, for actor Herbert Marshall, with whom Sullavan had to wind up at story's end. Page by page, scene by scene, Sturges wrote *The Good Fairy* almost from scratch. In the process, he tailored every line of dialogue to Sullavan's lilting voice. "She had a marvelous voice," said Wyler, "something very peculiar in the voice that was very attractive."

Henry Henigson, to his credit, did not meddle in the writing of *The Good Fairy*. He was respectful of Sturges' talents and after reading *A Cup of Coffee*, became a strong advocate of Universal's making the picture and—even better—of Sturges' directing it. His lobbying paid off nicely:

"Things are going pretty well here," Sturges wrote to Charley Abramson on June 15, "and with a little luck I should be all right. You always said I would get something sooner or later for the effort I put into *A Cup of Coffee*, and you seem to be right as Universal have already paid me $4000 on account with $5000 to come when the script is finished and $6000 to come for directing it, not counting the chance it gives me to direct, which is worth a great deal of money."

Impatiently, Sturges hurried to finish *The Good Fairy*, but the filming didn't go smoothly. The problems created by completely restructuring the play slowed its progress. Sturges' concept skillfully moved an unfilmable story past the Breen office with little objection, but the character sometimes came out a little too naïve for her own good. Sullavan, a difficult and headstrong woman with ideas of her own about Luisa, stoutly refused some of the words Wyler and Sturges fed her (lines like "Oh, isn't this wonderful?" hit the wide-eyed wonderment at the big city angle just a little too hard, she felt). So when shooting began—in October of 1934—the script was still not finished to anyone's satisfaction and Sturges found himself stuck on the film throughout production.

The film was important to Wyler and he liked the character Sturges had developed, but the *The Good Fairy* was not a happy experience. With Sullavan, Wyler was constantly at odds; nothing he could say or do pleased her. There were marathon rewrites on the set itself. But Sturges knew his place and was careful to keep to his script. "He enjoyed being on the set," Wyler recalled, "but I had no idea he had ambitions to be a director. He never said so; never did anything." Wyler would have approved of his friend's goal, though. "If anyone had asked me," said Wyler, "I would have said, 'Yes, I think he'd make a good director.'"

Production crawled on. Wyler's fights with Sullavan began to show in the rushes—the lines and the worn expressions were especially apparent in the close-ups—and Wyler finally decided to force a showdown. The two went to dinner one night, growing friendlier in the days following. Indeed, he confided to Sturges, he was growing very fond of her. "He was a great talker," said Wyler. "He was not as good a listener as he was a talker, but that was okay because I'm a better listener than I am a talker." One night Wyler asked, "What would you say if I got married to Maggie?"

"I'd say she's not marrying you for your money," Sturges replied.

One weekend in late November of 1934, with two weeks' work on the picture yet to be shot, Wyler and Sullavan flew to Yuma, Arizona, and were married by a justice of the peace. The film finished in relative calm and Sturges was free for *A Cup of Coffee* by the first of the new year.

In January *The Good Fairy* was released to essentially fine notices and became a sizable hit. It was the first time Sturges had had a screenplay credit to himself since *The Power and the Glory*. Now he had a hit comedy on his hands that was almost entirely his own. All that remained now was to get another original filmed. Intact.

A Cup of Coffee adapted well to motion pictures. The film could be made cheaply—on three or four modest sets, if need be—and Sturges chose to keep it that way in case money proved a problem. He made it a point to see all the new Universal releases and couldn't fathom—considering their overall quality—why it was seemingly so easy for directors like Stuart Walker and Harry Lachman to make pictures and so hard for him. He saw *Imitation of Life*, which the great John Stahl had directed, and pronounced it a "very bad picture," noting that very little of his adaptation was used.

"Most of the directors out here are the biggest bluffers and four-flushers that ever lived," Sturges told a friend. "I do not intend to be like them."

He organized a ten-to-fifteen-member bowling team at Universal and played in Beverly Hills on Wednesday nights. The group included editors and secretaries and Sturges was naturally the center of attention. He made friends and worked diligently on his script and had it ready to shoot by the middle of February. But Henry Henigson was growing dissatisfied under the political turbulence that engulfed Universal during its last year under Laemmle control. It looked as if he might soon leave for another studio. Sturges could sense trouble when *A Cup of Coffee* was delayed and he was then asked to "fix up" the script for an elaborate biography of "Diamond Jim" Brady. Sturges asked as a condition that his rate be upped to $2500 a week for the duration of the job. This the studio agreed to, figuring it would take Sturges no more than four weeks to whip the film into shape.

Sturges knew little of the real Diamond Jim, and began by reading the studio's source material, a newly published biography by Parker Morell. The book was a revelation for him: beforehand, Sturges had considered a relatively straight translation of Brady's life, following the first-draft screenplay by Harry Clork and Doris Malloy. As he read though, Sturges began to see Brady as a modern folk hero quite genuinely struck from the same mold as his own Tom Garner or the politician O'Hara from the unproduced *Vagrant*.

Diamond Jim Brady was born in Atlantic City in the middle of the nineteenth century and educated in the local public school system. He began work as a messenger boy for the New York Central Railroad and subsequently climbed to the position of dispatcher and, ultimately, mechanician. From there he jumped into sales, landing first a position with a manufacturer of railroad equipment called Maxwell & Moore, and later promoting the manufacture and sale of a metal-cutting "hack" saw which entered into widespread use. Brady capped his sales career with what became the Standard Car Company, makers of pressed-steel rail cars. His repute as a salesman of such equipment became nation-wide. Single contracts routinely amounted to millions, and his commissions amassed him a considerable fortune.

But unlike Garner of *The Power and the Glory*, Brady was a wholly likable man who became a world-famous philanthropist and party-goer. Said a close friend on the occasion of Brady's death, "Jim Brady was one of the greatest men this country has produced. Not only as a salesman, but as a real man. There never was an appeal made to him for money or clothes by man or woman to which he did not respond. . . . He never touched liquor, tobacco, tea, or coffee, but he certainly was an eater, being particularly fond of sweets. I have seen him eat a pound of candy in five minutes."

Sturges quickly jettisoned the Clork/Malloy script and started over from scratch. He outlined Brady's life and career, but merely for reference. Instead of allowing Morell's book to dictate the story, Sturges treated Brady as a fictional character with the attributes of the real man. In being true to the character of Diamond Jim, Sturges felt free to alter the various events of his life as the drama required. Brady throughout would remain Brady, but he would be Brady as Sturges, rather than Morell, understood him. Once the character lived and breathed in Sturges' mind, he could close his eyes and imagine himself in any situation and respond as Diamond Jim.

This was all well and fine, but the studio had asked for a "fix-up" and not a whole new approach. They had the perfect man to play Brady in Edward Arnold, a rotund character actor with much stage experience and some popularity in films whom the Laemmles felt had potential as a major star. Also cast were Jean Arthur, Binnie Barnes, and Cesar Romero and they were set to go in just a few weeks. Sturges could not be dissuaded from his approach, however, and found an ally in the film's director, Paramount's Eddie Sutherland. Sutherland was enthused with the Sturges rewrite and proclaimed his willingness to begin shooting while Sturges worked away. *Diamond Jim* was planned as an elaborate period piece with a budget approaching $1 million. The studio was loath to wait indefinitely while Sturges and Sutherland nitpicked the book. The go-ahead was given and *Diamond Jim* began shooting with exactly seventeen pages of screenplay.

Sturges began with his hero's birth and an unremarkable youth that ends—prematurely—with the death of his mother when he is only ten. Soon, Brady, like Garner, is working his way up from the bottom of the railroad industry, developing into the flamboyant salesman he became.

To Sturges, Brady was an essentially good-hearted man who never quite recovered from the loss of his mother. His loves are more like infatuations, and he lives as if his mother is watching over and approving his every action. He remains aloof from alcohol and tobacco and finds an outlet for his energies in the work he does and the food he consumes. As he grows wealthier, he spends his money as well—for charitable endowments of all kinds and for jewels. He is loved, but platonically, as he himself loves. Sturges built for him a wide, costly abyss of a life from which no lasting happiness could be derived.

Sturges, as with *The Good Fairy*, was on the set often. He would be called upon to sharpen scenes and modify dialogue as the need arose. Sutherland found Edward Arnold to be a large, directionless slate of an actor with no definite attitudes toward the man he was playing and consistently dependent upon detailed direction. Often, Sutherland would formulate the emphasis of a particular scene in conference with Sturges before speaking with his star.

The primary opposition Sturges and Sutherland encountered was over the film's ending. Sturges envisioned Brady—like Garner —a suicide, and had concocted an ingenious and fitting way of accomplishing it. The real Brady suffered from stomach problems for most of his life and when he died, in Atlantic City in 1917, obituaries stated it was of a heart attack and ill health "superinduced by acute indigestion." Sturges therefore wrote a chilling ending in which the pitiful millionaire broods away in his palatial home—burning the IOUs that will never be paid and then walking off into a final orgy of food in which he will—quite literally—eat himself to death.

The producer objected to the death scene, insisting an alternate ending be written. Both Sturges and Sutherland protested vigorously, arguing that the entire film—which they had shot in perfect sequence—pointed to that ending and any other would effectively ruin the picture. There was talk, in fact, of shooting both endings and letting the preview audiences decide, but finally reason prevailed and *Diamond Jim* was completed as Sturges intended.

The Brady job took much longer than had been anticipated. During filming, Henry Henigson solidified his plans to move and left with regrets in April of 1935. Sturges figured this was effectively the end of *A Cup of Coffee*—at least for the time being—but he wished his friend well. To Sturges, Henigson was a perfect producer. He attended to his responsibilities quietly and well and left the actual moviemaking to others; in short, he was a pleasure to work with. And since Henigson was moving to Paramount, there would undoubtedly be work there for Sturges also. In fact, Henigson talked about buying *A Cup of Coffee* from Universal and making it at his new studio. Sturges, certain the Laemmles were preparing to sell, was growing increasingly fearful that such a plan might indeed be necessary.

The strategy Sturges formulated would be to align himself with a major studio like Paramount and then to price himself into more expensive pictures. As he was able to command $2500 a week, his salary would be a bargaining tool to use when going after the director's job. If not, at least being so expensive would restrict the number of features that could afford him. He would therefore work a little less often but attract a better class of assignment.

He sat tight. He thought he should organize his personal affairs and began setting aside one fifth of anything he made to help meet his tax obligations. He also began looking for a house to buy, preferably again in the Hollywood Boulevard area. He dieted, dropping eighteen pounds, and wrote six new songs with his friend Ted Snyder. One of them, "Paris in the Evening," ended up in Willie Wyler's next picture, *The Gay Deception*.

Sturges received six offers on the strength of *Diamond Jim*. Of these, he accepted two from Universal. It was not that they interested him more than the others—they simply paid more money. He did some quick computations, figuring that if he could handle both *Spinster Dinner*, a Faith Baldwin story for Carole Lombard, and *Next Time We Love* for Maggie Sullavan, and write them both for job prices more or less simultaneously, he could set a record for screenwriters and earn—for a short time at least—the weekly rate of $7000.

*Spinster Dinner** was a comedy of sorts and *Next Time We Love* a misty soap opera. Sturges completed one script for each, turned them in, and gave them no further thought. He had something more important to occupy him, a musical comedy of his own invention. He quite honestly considered it one of the funniest stories yet contrived for the screen. Still, he suspected he might encounter trouble in pushing it along. It was about the moving picture business. And much of it was patterned after Universal itself.

---

*Released as *Love Before Breakfast* (1936).

14.

Universal needed a debut for the Hungarian singing star Marta Eggerth. Eggerth had done several pictures at UFA and, more recently, *Unfinished Symphony* for Gaumont-British. They had earned her quite a following in Europe, and it seemed certain Universal would sign her. Preston Sturges took advantage of the afterglow from *Diamond Jim* to sell Eddie Sutherland on the idea of an opera singer who is brought to Hollywood to make a picture. Sutherland owed the studio another film and thought the Eggerth idea a good one. Preliminary meetings were arranged with Sutherland, Sturges, studio manager Fred Meyer, and producer Paul Kohner. Sturges drafted a treatment, which he titled *Song of Joy*, and presented it for approval. He expected some rough going but certainly not the venomous response it generated.

Song of Joy sounded a lot more benign than it read. The head of the Apex Film Company is a Sam Small-type character called Adolph Apex. At the start of the story, Sturges has Apex huddled with his top production people when it is announced that the famous opera star Miss Lilly Pogany has arrived. Apex tells his assistant to give her a tour and a lunch and some flowers and get rid of her, but within moments he is advised that Miss Pogany has not come to visit but to make a picture, under contract, and that she is being paid $19,000 a week, starting immediately. What's more, Miss Pogany has only four weeks before she is to sing at La Scala; the picture has to be made in a month's time.

This information sends Apex into a fury, raging about his people's negligence, extravagance, boneheadedness, pigheadedness, and "the throwing away of money by the wagonload as opposed to the usual throwing away of it by the shovelful," which he is willing to overlook. It is then, of course, revealed that Apex himself hired her, and that there is no story for her to film.

Sutherland read the piece cautiously. He was not amused by the opening, nor by the contingent of yes-men and bumbling producers, directors, and writers who fall all over themselves to make an impromptu movie in only four weeks. When he finished, he announced in conference that he considered the whole thing a mistake and that the dialogue was "slapsticky and cheap and nothing like the work Mr. Sturges is capable of." Said Sutherland, "I am sure that making fun of producers, writers, etc. is not entertainment."

Sturges was shocked at the reception Sutherland—whom he considered an ally—accorded his new story. He had hoped that Universal, which had earlier made *Once in a Lifetime* with great style and good humor, would see nothing wrong with another swipe at the pomposity of the industry. In fact, Sturges pointed out, in *Once in a Lifetime* the comedy was drawn from the stupidity of the characters; in *Song of Joy*, the humor derived instead from the situation. Unmoved, Sutherland declared he was reluctant to make an expensive flop for Universal, which he felt sure *Song of Joy* would be. Sturges promptly took his case to Old Man Laemmle himself. Again he likened the story to *Once in a Lifetime*, carefully explaining the differences, and pleaded for Senior's intervention.

"It is fresh in concept," he memoed, "contains two of the most beautiful production numbers ever put into a picture, and cannot fail, with the assistance of the charming Miss Eggerth, to furnish thorough satisfaction and pleasure to those who see it." But Senior was in the midst of selling his studio, and had little time to intervene. Junior Laemmle, Sturges discovered, was more interested in getting his massive version of *Show Boat* into production and could not be bothered with *Song of Joy*, or, for that matter, *A Cup of Coffee*. The whole affair died a quiet death: Eggerth was not signed, and *Song of Joy* was added to the Sturges trunk.

For the moment, Sturges turned his creative energies to projects of a more personal nature. He finally released his apartment in New York and freely acknowledged he was settling in for a long stay in California. There were things about California he still didn't like—the early hours and the lack of good restaurants—but these were problems he felt he could correct in time. The opportunities were many and the money would help finance the innovations he felt necessary. Asked when he was going to write another play for the theatre, he replied, "I have never stopped writing plays. This *is* the theatre."

One of the opportunities that came along was the chance to establish a workshop, a little inventor's haven similar to the one he had had in New York. Using some of his Universal money, he bankrolled a brother inventor.

The workshop was in nearby Wilmington and Sturges christened it "The Sturges Engineering Company." It consisted of one machinist, and the developer of an "extremely efficient, quiet, and vibrationless" diesel engine. The engine, which Sturges hoped eventually to manufacture, was of a design called "opposed piston." The explosion would occur between two pistons, forcing both outward at the same time.

The owner delighted in having his name on such an operation and was careful to work it into a conversation whenever possible. He called it his "machine shop" as in the sentence, "Oh, I can have *that* done in my machine shop!" It served to maintain his credentials as an inventor (though he considered writing itself a form of invention). He could talk at great length about the plans they had. The first engines, he said, would be for yachts and work boats. He even talked about bringing the *Recapture* out from the East Coast and having a prototype installed in it. If it proved to be as quiet as anticipated, he told friends, the new engine would be known as "The Silent Sturges."

Universal Pictures passed from Laemmle control in early March of 1936 and the new head of production, Sturges noted, was an "extremely stupid and inefficient moving picture producer called Charles R. Rogers." Rogers, formerly of Paramount, was not the least bit interested in Sturges' services, nor in any of his pending projects. The sale of the company knocked Sturges' directing plans "galley west," but he held steady, refusing an offer of $1500 a week from Metro (too little, he complained) and an "undesirable" job for Jesse Lasky.

Sturges kept both his Engineering Company and his life-style afloat by drawing on the money in his tax account. He even decided to purchase a home he had inspected on Ivar, not far from where he used to live and within walking distance of Paramount. The house was a rambling old woodframe structure that needed painting and remodeling and Sturges considered tearing it down and replacing it with something of his own design. It was the location he liked especially and the old Canary Island pines that sheltered the property. He then examined the building in greater detail and was soon commenting on its soundness and the fact that they just didn't build houses that well anymore, especially after he discovered cloth under the shingles. Gradually, the contents of the house on Bryn Mawr were transferred to 1917 Ivar and Sturges began to formulate his plans for remodeling.

Paramount finally beckoned, via Henigson, and Sturges dropped everything to answer the call. Henigson, assigned the task of developing a new Burns and Allen picture, wanted Sturges to take a crack at it. Certainly Sturges knew he could do better for himself than write for a couple of radio comics, but it was, after all, his chance at a staff position. He considered the problem carefully. What could he do with Burns and Allen, since they usually worked in tandem with other Paramount players and played characters like themselves? He would have to write routines for them, unless, of course, he could alter their characters drastically and treat them like actors. *A Cup of Coffee* wouldn't fit them and certainly not *Song of Joy*. Sturges found himself truly perplexed, but he had to establish he could handle just about anything. So Burns and Allen became a challenge. And he finally hit on an idea.

Sturges had long been attracted to the genre of bedroom farce. But his only stab at it, a play he wrote with Hugh Herbert in mind called *Unfaithfully Yours*, had never gotten off the ground. The dramatic weight of a good farce might well suit the comedy team and provide a challenge for the author that would extend beyond *Here Comes Cookie* or *College Holiday;* the delicate balancing of several separate stories with confused identities and the proper number of slamming doors and house detectives. One of the hardest of theatrical tricks to bring off—certainly one of the most complex, as pacing is everything. The writing of such entertainments is an exacting science, the skill rare, to be sure.

He prepared a treatment on spec: a classical bedroom farce he called *Hotel Haywire*. The intricate plot was developed specifically for a Paramount cast. Sturges allowed not only for Burns and Allen, but for Charlie Ruggles, Mary Boland, Fred MacMurray, and an ingenue of the producer's choosing. In 1933, Sturges switched from the large, impersonal William Morris Agency to an agent named Frank Orsatti. Orsatti was a round little man, a former bootlegger with whispered ties to organized crime and a close friendship with Louis B. Mayer. He had a reputation as a tough negotiator. Sturges' instructions to him were simple: get at least $2500 a week or a comparable job price and, down the line, a term contract.

As it turned out, Orsatti's job was not that difficult. Henigson sang Sturges' praises wherever he went. M-G-M, through Orsatti, was talking about a deal. Selznick-International was interested in a story. Even Sam Goldwyn asked when Sturges would be available. Paramount took the bait, agreeing that *Hotel Haywire* was perfect for them. The price was $17,500. At $2500 a week, that meant seven weeks' work; Sturges thought that adequate under the circumstances. With the basic plot and principal characters already worked out, the main challenge would be the writing of suitable routines for Burns and Allen. People were used to them every week on radio and Sturges grudgingly conceded that their exchanges would have to follow—at least to some extent—the established pattern. He spent several weeks studying their broadcasts and then composed—not without difficulty—five B&A routines for the film. He actually became quite good at it, joking that, if all else failed, he could always get work in radio.

For all its complexities, *Hotel Haywire* was an expert piece of work, delicately timed and a source of great pride to its creator. It was finished on schedule and Sturges hoped the result would bring him within range of a staff position.

Orsatti went to work promoting a straight two-year contract calling for $2750 a week for the first year and $3000 for the second. The studio was interested. Sturges himself blithely sat out the discussions, politely refusing other jobs, busily studying his new home. He made sketches of the decaying backyard, superimposing a pool, a brick barbecue, and a bathhouse. He contemplated new closets, new furniture, and even imagined rearranging the trees. Finally word came: the studio wouldn't go for more than $2500 to start, but the contract itself was the important thing and Sturges accepted it gleefully. A letter of agreement was dated August 13, 1936. The contract was drawn up and signed a month later.

Preston Sturges became an employee of Paramount Pictures on September 29, 1936. He was assigned a small office and given a secretary. He wondered how he could possibly interest someone in *A Cup of Coffee* or *Song of Joy*. Henigson was still enthused, but having problems with *Hotel Haywire:* Burns and Allen had become unavailable and the script was undergoing a rewrite. They did not ask Sturges to do it, however, as the film was now a lowly "B" and the budget couldn't stand the strain of any more of his time.

Sturges' first assignment was to producer Arthur Hornblow, Jr. Hornblow was a rather dapper and erudite man, short, balding, recently married to Myrna Loy. Sturges established a rapport with him through Hornblow's background in the New York theatre, where he had done some writing. Hornblow spent seven years as a supervisor with Goldwyn before joining Paramount, where he specialized in comedies; he had recently made *Ruggles of Red Gap*.

Hornblow had a story called *Easy Living*, written by Vera Caspary. He thought there might be something to it, given a sufficiently talented writer, and asked Sturges to give it some consideration. What Sturges read didn't especially amuse him. The Caspary story was a tiresome little chestnut about a poor girl who impulsively steals a mink coat and, draped in its finery, sees her life altered completely. One deception piles atop another and, in the end, her lies cost her the man she loves and she is left with nothing. Unimpressed, Sturges still thought he'd better make the best of it and not reject the first property offered him. He told Hornblow he might have an angle for it and secured permission to alter it as he pleased. Promptly, he junked the story—salvaging only the plot device of the mink coat—and began work on an original comedy he would nonetheless call *Easy Living*.

Building the story logically began with the girl and the mink coat, but Sturges didn't like the idea of her stealing it. Perhaps she might find it somewhere and try to return it . . . maybe it could just fall from the sky. But what kind of person would accidentally drop a mink coat out of a window and not instantly try to retrieve it? And the girl had to be the type that would return such valuable property—especially if its origin could so easily be traced.

So the coat had to be thrown purposely from a high window or a roof. Who would throw away a new mink coat? Someone agitated and wealthy enough not to care. It would follow that a person that rich would live in a high-rise. And the person the coat lands on is the heroine; the situation carries the action from there. All Sturges had to do then was develop his characters and see how they responded.

For Sturges, the best heroine was the one to whom things happen: Isabelle in *Strictly Dishonorable* or Luisa in the revamped *Good Fairy*. Chaos with the girl at the eye of the storm, a passive antagonist as he considered women to be. Against this character, which could be played by anyone from Carole Lombard to Claudette Colbert, Sturges imagined a bombastic player of the stock market. Someone of explosive temperament victimized by both his wife and his wealth. Long-suffering, surrounded by a myriad of ringing phones and kinetic secretaries. Frantic dialogue delivered at the top of the actors' lungs, action careening across the screen at breakneck speed, with liberal doses of slapstick. The process took time, but the emerging result proved worth the wait. Hornblow grew more delighted by the day. As Sturges composed and polished, the producer began to prepare for putting *Easy Living* onto film.

First came Mitchell Leisen, who was directing Hornblow's current picture, a remake of *Burlesque* titled *Swing High, Swing Low*. Leisen was, at the moment, Paramount's hottest director, but Sturges saw him as a bloated phony with whom he forced himself to get along. Leisen immediately started talking about cuts in the script, but Hornblow held him back and let Sturges proceed relatively unhindered. Together, Leisen and Hornblow cast the picture with only fleeting input from their writer. Sturges tailored his script for a few select character actors and suggested, with success, both Edward Arnold (as J. B. Ball, "the Bull of Broad Street") and Luis Alberni. Sturges had written a part into *Hotel Haywire* for Alberni, an expert at malaproping continentals, but when the film was scaled down after the loss of Burns and Allen, the part was dangerously inflated and given to Leo Carrillo.

Sturges worked on *Easy Living* well into 1937, confident that he was writing an absolute masterpiece of frantic comedy. Word got out that Leisen and Hornblow were indeed onto something special and congratulations were offered by people who knew the script only by reputation. Sturges, delighted, worried that Leisen was not the man to direct it. Privately, he resented the director, a fey and in some ways arrogant man who had been a costume designer and, for a while, DeMille's art director. Sturges, of course, felt that he himself was best qualified to direct *Easy Living*, but he bit his tongue, awaiting the chance he knew had to come eventually.

Easy Living began shooting in April of 1937, refined to the best of Sturges' abilities but without his further guidance. As a contract worker, he was already onto another assignment, a loan-out, ironically, to Henry Henigson.

Dissatisfied with Paramount and the problems with *Hotel Haywire*, Henigson left to work with Carl Laemmle, Jr., in a production deal at M-G-M. Junior, after a period of rest following the sale of Universal, decided he wanted to get back into production. He himself was no prize—as everyone in the industry knew—but he owned several properties that were in demand. One of these was the ill-fated *Fanny*. When the project dissolved at Universal in 1934, Junior hung on to it. After the studio was sold, he kept not only *Fanny*, but *The Amazing Dr. Clitterhouse* and a play called *Nine Officers*.

Laemmle eventually entered into a three-picture deal with Metro and set up shop in Culver City with Henigson in charge. The political atmosphere at Metro, however, was anything but cozy. Laemmle had incurred a lot of resentments during his years as production chief at Universal. Mayer's "family" was not at all hospitable and Junior was made to feel decidedly unwelcome. Before long, Laemmle withdrew, leaving Henigson and director James Whale holding the bag.

A writer, Ernest Vajda, had been engaged to write the *Fanny* script, based on the Pagnol trilogy and the fragments Sturges and Willie Wyler had left behind. Vajda did the best he could, but the screenplay still needed work. Henigson called for Sturges to do a final rewrite.

It was becoming apparent that Sturges would be working more consistently than ever before. The occasional flurries of nighttime work that he seemed to prefer got to be regular occurrences, and Bianca Gilchrist objected. Preston conceded a personal secretary was the answer and began looking for one.

Sturges disliked working at the studio. With conferences to attend, letters to write, and lunch to eat, it was difficult to concentrate on the work at hand. During the daytime he would arrive late, visit with friends, and then depart for an evening of dinner and relaxation. Usually, writing was the last thing attended to at night. A nocturnal creature by habit, Sturges learned as a child to rest when there was nothing happening, lest he should miss out on something .that was. And besides, he seemed to compose best after dark, well fed and slightly intoxicated.

Bianca could adapt herself to this regimen when necessary, but it was not fun night after night and Preston surely could now afford to hire somebody to take over. He scanned the classified ads in the trade papers, where people who wanted jobs as assistants and secretaries advertised. One day he found one that interested him enough to prompt him to call. The ad in *The Hollywood Reporter* offered an "Engineer/Secretary," a perfect combination.

Edwin Gillette possessed an engineering degree from Stanford University and an interest in the movies. He thought he wanted to get into the picture business but lacked a background. So he went to secretarial school and got a job with Standard Oil. But the work was boring. Soon he switched to a literary agent on the Sunset Strip, and then ran his ad.

Sturges liked the young man and offered him $25 a week. Not wishing to call him "Ed," or "Ted," or "Mr. Gillette," Sturges chose "Gilletti." It became the only name by which he was known in Sturges' circle.

Gilletti found his new boss quite different from what he expected a highly paid writer to be. Sturges' reluctance to work at the studio puzzled him, for it seemed the creative atmosphere was best there. Sturges would hear none of it. A confirmed day person, Gilletti preferred to work regular hours. But he said nothing and went along with the nightly routine. After a short while, it seemed that Gilletti was hired to be a companion as well as a secretary. With Sturges arriving late at the studio, Gilletti's work would often begin only after the boss had returned to Ivar.

"He hated to work," Gillette recalled. "He'd put it off as long as he could." Sturges would usually procrastinate by walking to the nearby Brown Derby for dinner. With Gilletti in tow, he'd take his time, enjoy several cocktails, and talk about anything that came to mind, save, of course, the work at hand. Occasionally, ideas would come to him, and Sturges would try these out on anyone handy, then file them away in his mind. Upon returning to the house, he might pilot his model train or repair to the game room, where he and Gilletti played pool. Finally, just when the new secretary was ready for bed, eleven or twelve o'clock or later, Sturges would say, "Well, let's knock off a page," and begin to compose.

Sturges would pace the floor or sit and drink coffee and dictate. "It was just awfully hard work," said Gilletti, "and it took him a long time. And the studio would go crazy prodding him just to get something out of him. He would wait weeks before he turned in a page. Sometimes they'd have to send one of their men out just to sit on the front step." Occasionally, Sturges would work for only an hour a night. Other times, especially when the pressure was on from the studio, he would work all night. At times like these he was capable of producing thirty or forty pages of material, often with little revision necessary. Then Gilletti would drag himself back to his apartment in Pasadena until the next evening.

Sturges was indifferent at best to the task of adapting *Fanny* and saw the job primarily as a favor to Henigson. The exhilaration he got from doing originals like *Easy Living* made those jobs the most important. The more he studied *Fanny*, the less sure he was of what to do with it.

Sturges halfheartedly trimmed *Fanny* to a series of blustery confrontations between Wallace Beery (who was certainly not up to the part of César) and Frank Morgan. The film was then made amid confusion and conflict between Beery and director James Whale. The project turned into a sorry mess which Sturges handled as quickly as possible. He then returned gratefully to Paramount.

Back at Paramount, he saw both *Hotel Haywire*, an abortion of his original screenplay (for which he nonetheless received sole credit), and *Easy Living*, which, he said, "left me cool." Leisen had done a workmanlike job, but the picture was simply not the airborne, fanciful comedy it should have been. There was no sense of pacing, other than what had been built into the dialogue.

"Leisen's more interested in the sets than the material," Sturges told Gilletti.

Sturges was next handed over to Cecil B. DeMille for work on a new picture called *The Buccaneer*, the story of the French pirate Jean Lafitte, and again Sturges seemed a logical choice. This opinion lasted until a story conference during which DeMille read aloud a scene Sturges had composed in which Napoleon conferred with his officers. Seated in a bathtub, the emperor did battle with a large map of Europe, mounted in the wall like a window shade, which refused to stay down. DeMille was incredulous. "He's made a comedian out of Napoleon!!" he exclaimed.

Sturges withdrew to busy himself with a new Jack Benny comedy, the premise for which came from a 1915 play called *Never Say Die*. The play's plot was the old confusion about a dying man who really isn't dying but thinks he is. That was all Sturges needed to develop quite a likable and atypical Benny vehicle in which the comedian would be cast as one "John Bennington Kidley," wealthy hypochondriac. (LADY WITH PINCE-NEZ: Is that Kidley of Kidley's little corn plasters? JEEPERS: Little Kidley Beans, if you don't mind, madam.)

Sturges settled in to a long summer working on *Never Say Die*. He set his story at a health resort in the Swiss Alps called Bad

Gaswasser ("Health from Mother Earth") where rich Americans bathed in heated mud and drank from a municipal fountain fed from a nearby laboratory. The hero's acidity test gets mixed up with that of a dog (similar names) and the delighted doctor tells him he has an acidity three times normal—that his body will actually digest itself in thirty days. With a personal fortune of some $20 million, Kidley becomes a popular man.

Sturges worked mostly on *Never Say Die* during the latter half of 1937, although he also was briefly involved in writing an all-star musical called *College Swing*. Such films were really of little interest to him, his conviction being that too much star power got in the way of characterization and story and therefore the entertainment. This film was projected to feature Burns and Allen, Ben Blue, Bob Hope, Charles Butterworth, John Payne, Martha Raye, Betty Grable, and Edward Everett Horton. Sturges worked listlessly and, before long, was allowed to return to *Never Say Die*.

The Benny script was finished around Christmastime of 1937. Facing a convenient holiday, steadily employed, Sturges began the extensive remodeling of his new home. The first order of business was the installation of a kidney-shaped swimming pool (before they were in vogue). In rapid succession, he then arranged for a new electrical heating and cooling system, a new kitchen of his own design, a new dining room, pantry, servants' quarters, a badminton court (instead of the obligatory tennis court), and a combination barbecue and bathhouse. When his next assignment came up, Sturges was casually rearranging the Canary Island pines he so loved.

As work on the house continued, Preston proposed to producer Paul Jones and production chief Bill LeBaron that he himself direct *Never Say Die* with Benny and Franciska Gaal in the leads. It was then he learned the picture would be postponed, for it looked as if Benny would be better off in a sequel to the popular *Artists and Models*. Instead, LeBaron assigned Sturges to a remake of *If I Were King;* he was, again, the perfect man for the job.

Paramount owned the rights to the time-honored play by Justin Huntly McCarthy, which had made a popular silent with William Farnum in 1920. The subject matter did appeal to Sturges: François Villon, the French poet, associated with criminal gangs, was several times imprisoned for homicide and robbery, and, in 1463, sentenced to hang. In turn mocking, ribald, and movingly pious, his poetry reflected a deep sense of fatalism and a constant preoccupation with death and decay.

The play itself was a creaky old thing, almost forty years old, based on an imaginary encounter between Villon and King Louis XI. In a tavern, the poet recites his contempt for the monarchy, witnessed—in disguise—by Louis himself. The punishment for such treachery is fanciful: Villon is given one week in the post of Grand Constable of France, the former occupant having been slain by Villon in a brawl. At the end of the week, Villon is to be executed.

McCarthy had peppered his play with nineteenth-century translations from such works as *Little Testament* and *Testament*, painting his hero somewhat whiter than reality and certainly more romantic. It was still a very serviceable legend; swashbucklers were in vogue at the time, Warners' having just finished *The Adventures of Robin Hood* and expecting it to dominate the summer season.

Sturges had his first meeting with producer-director Frank Lloyd, a veteran winner of the Academy Award, former actor and writer, maker of such films as *Cavalcade* and *Mutiny on the Bounty*, a tasteful, soft-spoken man who respected the basic premise of the play and loved the poetry which worked beautifully in the hands of a fine-enough actor. And Lloyd had a fine actor for the job: Ronald Colman. At forty-seven perhaps a trifle old, Colman was nonetheless an excellent choice for Villon, his voice the ideal instrument for the delivery of the character's dogma and verse. Sturges could easily see the potential in such a project, considering also that he had not before tackled a like piece of work. Flush with enthusiasm, in agreement with Lloyd on most points, Sturges steeped himself in Villonesque legend and set to work to create a classic—a thinking man's swashbuckler that would put Errol Flynn to shame.

Discounting Frank Lloyd's regard for the play, Sturges first set about to do his own translations of Villon's poetry and, in some cases, to fabricate his own.

Sturges dealt with the opening battle scenes efficiently, effectively, and yet he felt no need to linger.* As he saw *If I Were King*, the action would be minimal, essential only to the story. The poems would work as would the songs in a good musical. Sturges could hear Colman's wonderful, pipe-organ voice in perfect cadence with the words:

> If I were king—ah love, if I were king!
> What tributary nations would I bring
> To stoop before your scepter and to swear
> Allegiance to your lips and eyes and hair.
> Beneath your feet what treasures I would fling:
> The stars should be your pearls upon a string,
> The world a ruby for your finger ring,
> And you should have the sun and the moon to wear,
> If I were king . . .

---

*Director Lloyd chose to omit these early scenes from the finished film.

Against such lyrical beauty, Sturges placed a cackling, wicked witch of a Louis, deformed, brimming with evil humor. Basil Rathbone was chosen for the role, as complete a contrast to his usual suave villainy as could be imagined. Sturges' idea was to make Louis too funny to be unrelentingly evil, although he furnished Rathbone with some deliciously nasty lines. Entering his torture chamber early on, Louis pauses and sniffs the air. "Nasty smell in here . . . you'd almost think the cook had burned the roast."

Sturges fabricated a Villon poem and sent it to friends. "Villon didn't write this," he allowed, "but I pretend he did."

> O, Father Time, lay not thy frost
> Upon thy budding flower,
> On bitter seas of passion tossed,
> Forgive its tiny hour!
> And thou, Huguette, waste not thy heart
> Upon this juiceless mold,
> Ere all thy fragrant youth depart
> And leave thee useless . . . old.

The yellow draft of *If I Were King* was finished—with remarkable speed—by the first of February, 1938. Sturges then conferred with Lloyd and Ronald Colman and went back for revisions, which were completed in mid-April. All pronounced the final product a superb rendition of the Villon legend. Sturges was exceedingly proud of it himself, pleased to have had the opportunity of working with a man of Lloyd's talent. He took nothing away from the directors he respected—Mamoulian, Howard, Wyler, and now Lloyd—and wished that while he had to remain only a writer he could always work with men of their ilk. But it was not to be. As soon as he finished work on *If I Were King,* Sturges found himself back on loan-out to M-G-M for—of all things—another of those hateful all-star pictures. This one was an Eleanor Powell musical titled *Broadway Melody of 1939.* Sturges accepted his fate with reasonably good humor, noting that his salary had risen to $2750 a week and that being so high-priced, he could no longer expect to work on just anything. There were, after all, fewer $2 million pictures made than $300,000 ones.

As Sturges priced himself into more expensive pictures, so did he elevate himself into higher tax brackets. Always strapped for funds when March 15 rolled around, he considered taxation nothing more than armed robbery and treated the IRS people he encountered with polite contempt. Gilletti remembered a time when a tax man was scheduled to interview Sturges about some questionable deductions. The night before, Sturges took the receipts and papers in question and mixed them together in a large cardboard box. The result looked like nothing more than the debris

Mary Desti, 1898.

*Preston with Temple Duncan,
Bayreuth, 1904.*

At La Villa, Lausanne, c. 1913; Preston at extreme left.

As a pursuit pilot, Carlstrom Field, Arcadia, Florida, 1919; posing with his second wife, Eleanor, at Coney Island, c. 1930.

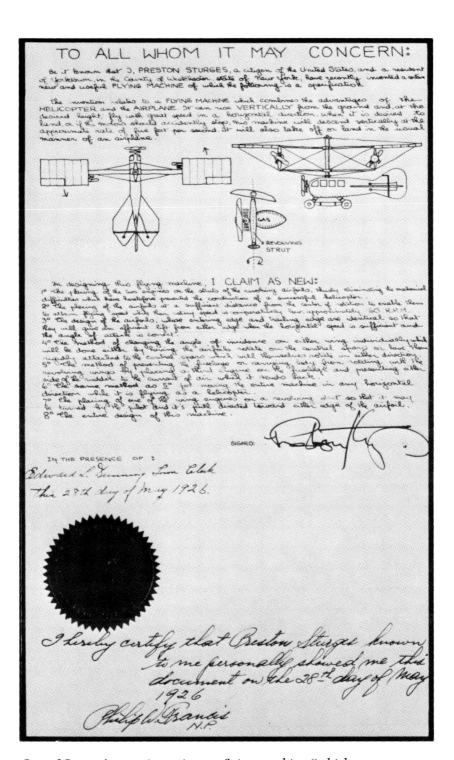

One of Sturges' many inventions: a flying machine "which combines the advantages of the helicopter and the airplane."
Department of Special Collections, Reasearch Library, UCLA.

Charles H. Abramson.

Scene from the New York production of Strictly Dishonorable *(1929). Left to right: Tullio Carminati, William Ricciardi, Edward J. McNamara, Muriel Kirkland, Lee Baker.* Theatre Collection, New York Public Library at Lincoln Center.

Eleanor Hutton with Sturges, 1930.

Sturges with director William K. Howard (left) and Jesse L. Lasky prior to the filming of The Power and the Glory *(1933).* Department of Special Collections, Research Library, UCLA.

CHRISTMAS
1934

Priscilla Bonner Woolfan.

On the set of The Good Fairy *in 1934. Left to right: actor Henry Hull,
Margaret Sullavan, Bianca Gilchrist, William Wyler, Sturges.*

Preston and Louise Sturges, 1938.

Preston with his father,
Solomon Sturges III,
Christmas, 1939.

As a staff writer at
Paramount, posing with a
model of the diesel engine
he helped build.

Casting The Great McGinty *with producer Paul Jones.*

On the set of McGinty *with Brian Donlevy.*

His pride and joy.

Sturges poses with assistant director George "Dink" Templeton on the Christmas in July *set (1940).*

A musical interlude on the Christmas in July *set: Dick Powell, Ernest Truex, Sturges, Ellen Drew, Harry Rosenthal.*

Sturges' cameo near the opening of Christmas in July *(1940).*

*An ad from the New York Sun; note the absence of billing for stars
Powell and Drew.* Department of Special Collections, Research Library,
UCLA.

Opposite: On the set of The Lady Eve *in 1940, director Mitchell Leisen,
Sturges, Barbara Stanwyck, Ernst Laemmle; testing a stunt for* The Lady
Eve.

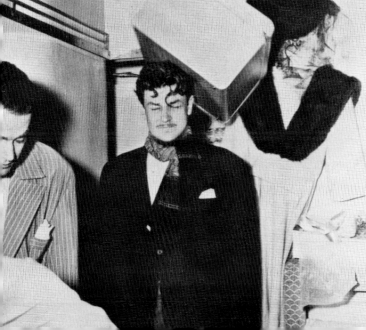

Accepting the Academy Award for The Great McGinty, *February, 1941.*

picked up after an especially wild party. "Really frustrated the guy," Gilletti reported.

The house was coming along nicely, though, and Preston wrote to his father in Chicago, urging him to come and live in California. "I expect to spend next year in jail for inability to pay income tax," he wrote, "and by the time I get out the garden should be very nice and green."

One hot summer day after the completion of *If I Were King*, Sturges lured his friend Ronald Colman out for a day aboard *The Destiny*. The actor found himself subjected to a running commentary on the state of the picture industry and what Sturges felt he could do to help things along. Said Sturges, "Ronnie, doesn't the fact that I have been a photographer, a painter, a playwright, a stage director, a lyricist, and a composer indicate beyond question that I must have the attributes of a motion picture director?"

"Absolutely and beyond question, Preston!"

"Then," asked Sturges, "will you make a picture with me?"

"As soon," Colman replied instantly, "as you've made *one* with someone else!"

15.

Ted Snyder retired from publishing in 1930 and brought his family to Los Angeles. There he opened a nightclub and lived comfortably on his ASCAP royalties. He and Sturges saw much of each other, the latter always grateful for the help Snyder had given him.

Sturges liked the idea of opening a restaurant of his own. The need seemed obvious; a place that didn't close at 10:00 P.M., serving more than just pie and coffee. Sturges preferred a late dinner and it seemed the places open the latest served the lousiest food. With his Paramount contract, he now had a steady cash flow and could afford to finance a place of his own. Owning a restaurant had special appeal—dating back to the days when young Preston ate daily at Ciro's in Deauville. In the late thirties, the dining scene in L.A. was not terribly impressive. Musso & Frank's was on Hollywood Boulevard; the Brown Derby on North Vine. The Trocadero had been on the Sunset Strip since 1934. Chasen's, on Beverly just east of Doheny, was very popular, but there was no Mocambo or Ciro's or Earl Carroll's as yet. The two entrepreneurs agreed that if Sturges put the money up, Snyder and his family would attend to the operation. Presently, the two began looking at possible sites on the Strip itself. There, at the corner of Sunset and Horn, they found an old house that could be had cheaply. They examined the building: it didn't look like a restaurant, but Sturges' mind set to work and he began painting an elaborate picture of the dining room and where the kitchen would go and how the entire building could be arranged. The old place had character, Sturges effused, and he quickly had his partner as interested as he. Both decided that it was a good and workable location and so they struck a deal with the owner and leased the place. The Snyder family went diligently to work and Sturges irregularly watched and advised. He told people about the new restaurant—*his* new restaurant—in precisely the same manner as had once heralded the birth of his machine shop. Nonetheless, the name of the new enterprise would be "Snyder's."

As Preston threw his spare time into things such as engineering companies and eateries, he had considerably less time to devote to Bianca Gilchrist. Especially now, with him working steadily for Paramount, their hours together were few. Bianca didn't accept the condition well and complained loudly that he took her for granted and that her principal function was to run the house and keep an eye on the workmen. Preston honestly saw nothing wrong with this because, after all, it was he who was bringing in the magnificent salary and he who had to attend to the matters of his screenplays and business enterprises. His pose as the Great Man in need of quiet and loving support did little to help. She grew madder by the day, tired of his apparent conviction that all women were created slaves.

"All day long, it's Bianca do this, Bianca do that!" she complained to Priscilla Woolfan. "I'm sick of it. I'm going to Mexico for a few weeks. I'll show him what it's like to be alone for a while!"

And one day, as Preston began work on a new script for producer Al Lewin, she left.

Preston was miserable. He moped about, listlessly, procrastinating on the film and wondering aloud what it would take to please her. She would come back and they would start again, he figured, but eventually, again, there'd be a blowup and a separation. He worried and reflected and then, all of a sudden, he was not quite so miserable. In Bianca's absence he began seeing another woman, indeed, the wife of another friend. At once, the old excitement was there again; the experience of a new relationship in the offing. And Bianca, at least for the moment, was quite forgotten.

Louise Tevis was ten years younger than Preston, born in Iowa, as complete a contrast to Bianca Gilchrist as could be imagined. Where Bianca was explosive, Louise was quiet, almost to the point of shyness. Bianca was Jewish; Louise, Catholic. Bianca was dark and exotic in appearance while Louise had a clean, all-American kind of beauty. She was calmly intellectual and better-read than Preston.

"Where Bianca was a fireball, a wildcat," said Priscilla, "Louise was like a cool cucumber. She had classic beauty. And Preston fell in love. He had stars in his eyes. The emotionalism that he was tired of and was worn out with in Bianca—this girl was just the opposite. He fell in love with her, but this was the real thing."

Louise had married into a prominent San Francisco family. Her husband was a stockbroker by trade, but poor at managing money. The couple lived mostly off an inheritance Tevis had, but he shared that wealth with his first wife, leaving himself and Louise with "very little." Even basic living expenses were difficult.

"You might say that we were professional house guests," Louise said.

In the Hollywood Hills, the Woolfans' Bryn Mawr house was situated roughly seventy-five feet above the home of Louise and Gordon Tevis. They had known Preston Sturges casually for five years.

Louise separated from her husband in 1938, taking a $30-a-month beach house and only occasionally joining him in town. On one such occasion, Louise was lured in with the promise of dinner at a Greek restaurant that served superlative Clams Bordelaise. When the night came, however, she found herself being driven in exactly the opposite direction.

Said Gordon Tevis innocently, "I forgot to tell you. I ran into Preston Sturges, who used to be our neighbor, and he has a restaurant on the Strip. It's the chef's night off and he's got an amateur cook working. He begged me to come up." Louise expressed her disgust, but Tevis was insistent.

Snyder's had not been open long, and had not developed the following Sturges had anticipated. On a Saturday evening the room was half full. Louise expected dull conversation and poor food. The food, however, wasn't as bad as it could have been. And Sturges hovered over them appreciatively. "He went out of his way to be extremely agreeable," remembered Louise. "At some point in the dinner, Preston asked me to dance . . . and we did not sit down for three and one half hours. After which I guess everyone decided the jig was up." Gordon Tevis fumed quietly but the years of relative insolvency had taken their toll. "He naturally didn't think well of it," said Louise.

Tevis conveniently lost his taste for Snyder's, but Preston tendered one dinner invitation after another. Louise came without him but still well chaperoned. "He had started a campaign of do-or-die," she said. "He was absolutely determined to marry me." During their third dinner together, Sturges proposed to her. She reminded him she was still married, but, yes, she conceded, she was as taken with him as he with her.

"He *glowed*," said Priscilla Woolfan. "He absolutely glowed. It was charming." He acted like the character in love in an animated cartoon, with hearts and flowers encircling his head, walking several inches off the ground. "I passed him going into Bert's office one day. He was behaving quite oddly. I said to Bert, 'What's the matter with Preston?' and Bert said, 'He's in love.'"

After that third dinner, Preston began to formulate an honorable approach to the problem of Louise's marriage. Gordon Tevis obviously wasn't madly in love with his wife, although, just as obviously, there was still some feeling there. And Preston *knew* Louise no longer loved him. How to go about it? Say nothing, and let Louise file for divorce? Or be direct, act like gentlemen, and discuss it in a mature manner?

"When Preston wanted to put on airs, there was nobody who could do a better job," said Priscilla. "He could become so elegant and so formal it was enchanting. . . . Preston had the most beautiful manners. It didn't matter what the occasion was—he knew how to handle it."

Sturges was a great one for a retinue. He enjoyed making an impressive entrance, to charm or intimidate the most unnerving of quarry. Priscilla continued, "Steve Brooks—dear Stevie—would always be just behind him and usually he would have a diplomatic case in his hand in case he'd have to take notes or anything. He was public relations, you know. Then there'd be a secretary or two. And then Leo the chauffeur and maybe one more."

Early on the day of his attack, Preston had his secretary phone Gordon Tevis to announce that "Mr. Preston Sturges" would like to call on him and inquire at what hour he might be received. Then, at exactly the appointed time, Sturges arrived at the Tevis home in chauffeured splendor, immaculately attired and with an escort of four. Exiting the car with great pomp and ceremony, he approached the bewildered Mr. Tevis.

"Sir," greeted Sturges, bowing deeply at the waist, "I have the *honor* of requesting the hand of your wife in marriage."

In Mexico, Bianca waited. A fortnight passed with no word from Hollywood. No frenzied attempts to find her. No six-page telegrams. No hastily arranged trips to reclaim her as with Eleanor Hutton. Nothing.

Bianca began to smell a rat. She packed her bags and headed back to L.A. By the time she arrived, Preston was in Reno, waiting with Louise the six weeks necessary for a divorce. Gilletti was there also, helping to maintain the pretense of working, but little writing actually got done. It was a time for romance, not work. "It was really a very tender love affair," Gilletti recalled.

With both Preston and Gilletti gone and the studio without a forwarding address, it fell upon Bertie Woolfan to break the news to Bianca. It was a task he approached with dread, but still Preston had asked him, and he treated the obligation with greater gravity than the episode deserved.

Louise and Preston were married in Reno on November 7, 1938. By the time they got back to 1917 Ivar, Bianca had vacated the premises, taking with her not only all of her own possessions, but some of Preston's also. "She took quite a few things of Preston's that she knew he especially liked," recalled Priscilla. "She was in a rage. Preston had some English hunting prints. They were valuable and beautifully framed and he prized them. I believe there were twelve and they were hung on the wall in a pattern. She took them. He also had some dinner service plates that were very expensive and very ornate and very beautiful. He was very proud of them. When he was going to have a sit-down dinner, there would always be a discussion: 'Shall I use my plates or shan't I?' They were his treasures and she took them also."

Preston wanted them back, but was terrified at the thought of facing Bianca. Instead, he called upon Bertie. "Tell Bianca I'll give her three hundred and fifty a month for life," he instructed. "I have an obligation toward her and I feel she's done a great deal for me. She was a superb secretary."

Bertie wanted no part of such a message. At first he refused, then suggested Preston and he deliver it together. Preston would not go near her. "I'm afraid of her," he confided. "You go. She'll listen to you." Bertie could tell he was serious. Then an attorney should do it, he told Preston. But that seemed too cold . . . too much like what Eleanor had done to him. No, it had to be Bertie, Preston declared. Bianca would trust him.

All right, said Bertie finally, he would go that evening and get the whole ugly business over with. Preston thanked him gingerly and was off to the studio.

When Bertie arrived home that evening, Priscilla was preparing to see a play. Max Reinhardt had a local school for actors. Bertie attended Professor Reinhardt, and he and Priscilla went to the productions whenever possible. "We're going over to see Bianca," Bertie informed her, "and tell her about Preston's settlement."

Priscilla Woolfan, almost timid by nature, had been brought up in a home where voices were never raised. Bianca's frequent outbursts were draining experiences for her. Priscilla was loath to trade an evening of theatre for what promised to be a turbulent exchange with Bianca.

"Well, I don't want to go!" she answered.

"You're going," ordered Bertie, "because I'm not going *alone*." Priscilla relented. "He was afraid of her too," she admitted.

When the Woolfans arrived at Bianca's new apartment, Preston's hunting prints were hung neatly on a wall, his service plates on display in a corner. Bertie parked Priscilla on the sofa, sat Bianca down and began to talk to her. Bianca was strangely subdued, Priscilla observed. She didn't like the feel of this visit; she counted the seconds until they could leave.

Bertie got as far as "Now, Bianca . . ." when the phone rang. It was Max Reinhardt's secretary. The young actress due to star in his premiere performance that evening had fallen ill. He was needed immediately. "Well, that did it," said Priscilla. "That was all he needed. He worshiped Professor Reinhardt. *God* was calling."

Bertie excused himself and flew out the door. Before Priscilla could follow, he was gone. And there she was, left alone, awkwardly, with Bianca. The room fell deathly silent for a moment. Then Bianca's blood began to boil. Red with indignation, she rose and crossed the room to the wall that held Preston's prints. Cursing him fluently in English, French, and Spanish, she carefully removed each print from its nail and smashed it on the floor. Petrified with fear, Priscilla cowered behind a large upholstered chair.

Bianca next selected a service plate and added it to the rubble. And then another. As she worked her way through the corner display her anger dissipated. When Bertie returned, within an hour, the rage had passed completely. Priscilla had emerged from her retreat and was seated limply amid a sea of broken glass and mangled wood. Bianca was wonderfully placid.

The illness had been nothing more than stage fright, but the doctor had received effusive praise for his work. When he floated back into Bianca's apartment, he was flush with adoration and completely oblivious to the mess around him.

Again he sat Bianca down and explained the arrangement. She was not interested in the money, but thanked him all the same, and even offered him coffee. Bertie demurred, turning to the hapless Priscilla. "Let's go," he barked. "I have to get up in the morning!"

The results of Preston Sturges' first two years with Paramount were unfairly mixed. *Hotel Haywire* was altered drastically and deservedly flopped. *Fanny* was postponed and re-edited and underwent several title changes before doing a dismal week at the Capitol in New York as *Port of Seven Seas*. *Easy Living* was filmed intact, but badly in his judgment, and though it started strong it was not very profitable. *Never Say Die* was rewritten for Martha Raye and Bob Hope, which left *If I Were King* (which got oddly mixed notices) as his only unqualified success. And that—for all its embellishments—was considered an adaptation. Sturges returned to work after the first of the new year and began composition of another original—not a comedy this time but an unabashed romance. Again, he hoped they'd let him direct it.

Romantic scenes had always given Sturges trouble. Brooks Atkinson had written that he clearly had no talent for them. Yet he was involved in a great love affair—his courtship and marriage to Louise. And his mind was naturally filled with romantic ideas. So he decided upon a romance—not without humor—and took his title from poetry:

> Beyond these tears, sweet bairn,
> So needful to a better ken

Of light and shade and happiness and pain,
We'll scamper doon a better geen,
Your eyes aspark
Your lips like roses in the rain.
                              —Old Anonymous Scottish Piffle

Sturges wrote *Beyond These Tears* as a classical tearjerker. His plot: a prosecuting attorney takes pity on a woman accused of shoplifting. She'll have to spend Christmas in jail, so he bails her out and offers to take her home for the holidays. Over the course of the next few days, he falls for her. Then the question: Will he let her escape? Will he throw the case? Will she leave him in such a jam? It was a good basis for a picture with two popular stars and Sturges effortlessly sold the idea to both Lewin and LeBaron. Sturges' composing faculty lurched into gear once more. The setup came slowly as he developed his characters in this modern-day *Camille*. But new starts were always rough at first.

"You sweat the fat off your brain for four or five days," he once said, "by writing things that are all hopelessly bad, and then all of a sudden you seem to tune in and good ideas come out of your mouth and you know they are good and admire them as ingenuously as if they were something by Wodehouse."

Beyond These Tears was easily the best romance Sturges ever wrote. Louise sat up with him nearly every night, acclimating herself as best she could to her husband's nocturnal habits. She'd last until four or five in the morning, make sandwiches, then sneak off to bed. But if Preston was still working, his face would appear in the doorway, wanting to know if she was yet asleep and then asking what a "hick" way of saying a particular line would be.

Louise served as an unofficial technical adviser on the script. Her background was similar to that of the characters, and Preston would seek her approval in working them out. If she objected to a line or a phrase, out it came. Preston leaned on her especially for the scenes with the small-town characters and the hero's mother. *Beyond These Tears* was slow and talky and delicate, uncynical; predictable, but not distressingly so. It flowed well and Sturges grew very proud of it. In the space of nine weeks a first draft was completed.

Predictably, when the production people got their hands on it, they had to monkey with it. First they didn't like the title. It was too downbeat, despite its poetic origins. Sturges proposed *The Amazing Marriage*, which was silly, but it seemed to please them. Then Al Lewin unexpectedly broke his contract and, as Sturges had dreaded, the picture was assigned to Mitchell Leisen. And he began to suggest little things—changes in dialogue . . . changes in action. Cuts here and there. Sturges was polite but ignored most of his suggestions. Leisen was no longer encumbered by Lewin or Arthur Hornblow, Jr. He was now his own producer. There would be no one to temper his excesses, save LeBaron himself.

Sturges worked on *The Amazing Marriage* until the middle of June. Leisen was by now not inclined toward rewrites—for which he needed the writer—but rather toward making cuts, which he could do without anyone's advice. The cuts were pointless, Sturges complained, and they fouled his careful pacing. But LeBaron trusted Leisen more than Sturges did. There was little to be said.

Piqued, Sturges began to talk openly of leaving Paramount. There was interest elsewhere, and he truly had to find someplace where he could exert more control before people like Leisen drove him crazy. To placate him, LeBaron let him go ahead with *Triumph over Pain*, the anesthesia picture he wanted to write. Still, Preston was unhappy. He complained about changing the title of *The Amazing Marriage* to *Remember the Night* and grew more argumentative by the day.

LeBaron now had to decide just how important it was to keep Sturges. Was he worth risking a picture on? Was his track record really that outstanding? There were a million considerations in making a writer a director. It just wasn't done; it was tantamount to giving someone a creative stranglehold on a production. It was contrary to the established system.

LeBaron figured he was asking for trouble. He could jeopardize his position with the company, use Sturges only on pictures of his own design. Soon there would be other writers after such a chance. All the really good ones would want to try. To many he would have to say no. And then angered, they would go elsewhere to direct, to try and alter the way things were done.

LeBaron's anxieties remained, even after the deal for *McGinty* was made. For all the risks, though, yes, he concluded, Sturges was worth it. He finally convinced himself there was nothing to lose. He would give Preston Sturges his best shot at directing a picture . . . and suffer the consequences if it didn't work out.

16.

In a seedy dive somewhere in South America, two men converse drunkenly. The bartender, John O'Hara, fills his time between stupors by slipping change from the cash register. His customer, in a state of depression, talks of taking his own life. He's a good man, he says, but he's gone wrong, taken some money.

He gulps his drink and speaks up proudly. "I was the cashier of a bank," he says.

O'Hara chuckles to himself. "*I* was the governor of a state."

This was the beginning of *The Vagrant* as Preston Sturges wrote it in the summer of 1933. As a follow-up to *The Power and the Glory*, it was a scathingly cynical look at a man caught in machine politics. O'Hara bounces from soup line to repeat voter to collector to alderman to mayor and then governor. He is a "reform" candidate, backed by the machine and its controlling force, a mysterious, squat little man known only as "The Boss." When asked what he has to do with the reform party, The Boss pounds his chest. "I *am* the reform party," he says. For the locale, Sturges set his play in the "mythical city of Chicago in the imaginary state of Illinois."

Like *The Power and the Glory*, *The Vagrant* was strong stuff. But unlike a lot of the reform-type pictures churned out by studios like Warner Bros., there was no hopeful resolution, no guarantee of a better tomorrow. O'Hara's change of heart, his desire to work for the public, not the political good, is the thing that brings him down. It was a thesis based upon fact: Sturges had seen and heard too much in Chicago to believe otherwise. Still, *The Vagrant* was not about politics as much as futility and predestination. Sturges was never interested in politics for the sake of politics. "He was very conservative," said Gilletti, "but I never knew him to vote. I guess you could say he was apolitical."

In *The Vagrant*, Sturges set out to show what happened to a man, born dishonest, when he tried to deny his basic nature. "Meat is not good for cows, whiskey is terrible for goldfish," wrote

Sturges in a foreword, "and I propose to show that honesty is as disastrous for a crook as is knavery for the cashier of a bank.

"A man is what he is. So was he made. So will he be."

But regardless of design, *The Vagrant* was certainly perceived as a political story, part of a genre for which there was never much of an audience. Aside from *The Phantom President*, a musical comedy with George M. Cohan, the political melodramas of the sound era could be numbered on one hand. Walter Wanger made two: both *Gabriel over the White House* (1933) and *The President Vanishes* (1934) were pro-Roosevelt fantasies that failed commercially. Frank Capra achieved a sprinkling of political satire in his films for Columbia, culminating in 1939 with *Mr. Smith Goes to Washington*. But when Sturges got his go-ahead in August of that year, *Mr. Smith* was not yet in release, its fate at the box office still a matter of conjecture. Consequently, it was tough to sell a script like *The Vagrant*. "All of the studios have said it is a fine and beautifully written story," Sturges wrote his father in 1933, "but they find the setting too sordid and believe the story is too much concerned with politics to appeal to women." *The Vagrant* became a trunk item; everyone knew about it, but no one wanted to produce it.

Sturges attempted to downplay the political angle, converting the screenplay to a treatment. He changed the title first to *The Story of a Man* and then *Biography of a Bum*. Still no takers. Late in 1935, he tried unsuccessfully to sell it to Universal, and in 1938 he sent it to *The Saturday Evening Post* for serialization. The *Post* gracefully declined, after which Sturges retitled it *Down Went McGinty* and submitted it to Paramount.

When Bill LeBaron finally decided to let Sturges not only write but direct *McGinty*, his first task was to assign him a producer who would complement his talents and keep him on course. For this he picked Paul Jones, a specialist in Bob Hope pictures who had signed both *Hotel Haywire* and *Never Say Die*. Jones was an outgoing little man with a fine sense of humor. Sturges huddled with him while the agreements were drawn up and signed, learning much about scheduling and budgets and working with the casting office. He also went over *The Vagrant* script line by line—to smooth out a narrative now six years old and to change the name of the character from O'Hara to McGinty.

An assistant director was assigned the task of breaking down the script and handling mundane chores with which the director could not be bothered. In this instance, it was important to engage someone who would not be intimidated by either Sturges' haughty manner or his vocabulary.

"I had known Preston around the studio, but just to say hello," recalled George "Dink" Templeton. "The production office called me down and said, 'Look, Preston Sturges, who's a kook and very difficult in many ways and doesn't know his ass from a hot rock, is making a picture.' And they put me with him and said, 'You have to stay with him all the time.'"

Templeton, a handsome ex-football player and actor, was unintimidated by Sturges, yet awed by his talent. Having finished an intensive rewrite, Sturges proceeded to dictate the final shooting script in two days and two nights. "This thing came out," marveled Templeton, "and he didn't change a word in it. God-damn, he was a genius!"

For Preston, the hardest part of his new job was to maintain the integrity of his story and not accede to the suggestions of the producer and assistant director simply to be agreeable. "The hardest part of directing," Willie Wyler once told him, "is resisting the impulse to be a good fellow." Paul Jones sensed instinctively where *McGinty* went too far for popular taste and knew how to get Preston to concur. "Paul Jones was a buffoon," said Dink Temple-ton, "but a smart one. Paul was a joker—he had a great sense of humor. He was a funny little guy but he always had an answer for everything . . . Jones was smart enough to realize Preston knew what he was doing. But Paul would get over certain creative things. He was a creative producer—anything but a paper pusher. It was very important the way he handled Preston."

McGinty would have to star Paramount contract players; with a budget of $325,000, there was clearly no money for free-lancers or loan-outs. First, Sturges and Jones settled on popular heavy Brian Donlevy to play McGinty, and then Akim Tamiroff for the role of "The Boss." Tamiroff was Russian, which Sturges appreci-ated because he could accent his lines. Tamiroff added a new dimension to the character; a subtle, unspoken implication that the person in control was not necessarily an American.

Preston was now, more than ever, concerned that everything should go just right. Every line in the script had to be perfect. He read the script over and over, running the entire picture through in his mind, envisioning the character faces he wanted, the droopy old women running the polling places, the customers in the opening scene in the bar. He worried about the minutest details in the script: Could he handle them? Would his inexperience show? Could he command the respect of the crew and some of the people who clearly hoped for his failure? It was a tall order, not just to make an acceptable picture, but a great picture—on a "B" budget. Bill LeBaron had gone out on a limb for him, wanting to see Sturges succeed brilliantly, and this too increased the pressure. He had waited six long years for this chance. There might not be another.

Sturges worried and paced—bent slightly forward, hands clasped behind him. Whether he was good enough or not, he would have to believe he was and act accordingly. He looked to his "staff"—to Gilletti; to Steve Brooks, his PR man; to Ernst Laemmle, late of Universal, his newly appointed "story editor." If this lasted only eight weeks, Sturges would go out in a blaze of glory. If it lasted longer, he would build a cadre to rival that of DeMille. Most of all, he looked to Louise for support and encouragement. As plans for *McGinty* were formalized. Preston pulled her closer, to share the excitement of his triumph. In the greatest of detail he tried to interest her in planning sessions and casting decisions. The process was undeniably intriguing but Louise could take only so much of it. She was happy for her husband, but she did have obligations beyond Paramount that demanded her attention. As her interest waned, Preston grew more insistent. He also required the Woolfans' attention, as Bertie was fascinated by the movie business and Priscilla had been in it enough to talk knowledgeably.

The casting office suggested hundreds of actors for the various parts in *McGinty*. Aside from McGinty and The Boss, there was Catherine McGinty, the candidate's wife; the unnamed "Politician" who educates McGinty in the ways of big-time politics; the suicidal Thompson, for whose benefit the whole story is told; and "George," Mrs. McGinty's longtime lover. For Catherine, Sturges selected the first name on the list: Muriel Angelus, a British stage and screen actress recently in Paramount's *The Light That Failed*. Thompson was written for Louis Jean Heydt—the original Henry Greene of *Strictly Dishonorable*. Allyn Joslyn made a perfect George. And then Sturges cast the bit parts for faces as much as acting ability.

Willie Wyler suggested Sturges get himself actors with whom he would be comfortable and could use again—a sort of stock company, like John Ford's. Sturges cast faces he could use like set decorations, distinctive and memorable. Some were veterans from the silent days—like meek Arthur Hoyt and blustery Thurston Hall. Others, such as ruffled Jimmy Conlin and burly Dewey Robinson, came from the stage in the early thirties. For The Boss' chauffeur, Sturges cast hulking Frank Moran, a gravelly voiced boxer-turned-actor whom Preston first saw in Deauville in 1914 and who, a year later, fought Jack Johnson for the heavyweight championship.

For The Politician, casting offered twenty-six choices, among them Grant Mitchell, Eugene Pallette, and Sidney Toler. None quite matched Sturges' vision. One day, he heard a dirty story—a type of humor he always professed to hate—from an agent named George Chasin. Sturges laughed uproariously. "Where did you get that?" he asked. Said Chasin, "Bill Demarest told me." Sturges had seen Demarest in a score of recent pictures, including *Diamond Jim* and *Easy Living*. "That's the man I want!" he declared. The cast was then complete.

It looked as if *McGinty* was actually going to be made. A cameraman was assigned, sets were built, and there were conferences about the costumes and the musical score. The starting date was set for December 11, 1939. Sturges prepared himself for a grueling ordeal—emotionally and physically. "I went into training," he said. "This was the big opportunity of my life. I gave up drinking and smoking. I had a masseur waiting for me every night and when he got through with me I had my dinner in bed."

Dink Templeton, after breaking the script down into scenes according to sets and casting needs, projected a thirty-six-day schedule. Late in November, Sturges had copies of the script sent to all the cast members, expecting them to have it committed to memory by the morning of the eleventh. Templeton and Sturges got along very well, although Dink's colorful language was always a point of contention. Sturges professed to disapprove of four-letter words, though he peppered his language with an occasional "goddamn" or "son of a bitch" when out of earshot of women. Usually, he set himself apart from the casual swearing of the crew members and felt an overuse of such language was the sign of a meager vocabulary. Templeton, on the other hand, rarely uttered a complete sentence undotted with expletives, and Sturges protested.

"You understood what I said, didn't you?" demanded Templeton. Yes, conceded Preston, he did indeed. "Well, that's all I care about!" End of discussion.

At first Sturges was uneasy with Brian Donlevy. He had picked the actor specifically because he was no adolescent and could bring a feeling of wisdom and experience to the part. At one point he called to mind what George Jean Nathan had said about Mae West's phenomenal success; that audiences, bored by young ingenues, found it a novelty to look at a woman for a change. Donlevy, forty, had extensive experience on the New York stage, dividing his time after 1929 between Broadway and Hollywood. He had worked for Howard Hawks, Henry King, William Wellman, and Cecil B. DeMille and wasn't afraid to question a line or a situation. During one meeting, the actor objected to the way Sturges read a line. Sturges tensed, fearing the actor intended to walk all over him. He worried for days about the way to carry himself, how to get what he needed from his cast and crew without making enemies. Should he raise his voice? Should lines be changed to placate these people? Should he let Donlevy evolve his own performance and concentrate instead on the supporting cast? Sturges ate carefully and conserved his strength, preparing himself for a fight he hoped would never take place.

The first morning's shooting occurred in a barbershop on Paramount's Stage 6. Dink Templeton remembered actor Donlevy: "You know he had very small shoulders and he was built funny and he was short. He would come in and the first thing he would do was put in his false teeth. Then he would put on a girdle—the goddamnedest tightest girdle. He'd squeeze this thing up. He'd put on his pants and shirt and then he'd put on his platform shoes. He came in looking like he was on his knees, then he looked like he was standing up. Then he'd put on the rug—his hairpiece—and the coat with the padded shoulders and that's what gave him that funny walk."

Donlevy sported a Clark Gable moustache in his early meetings with Sturges, and the director naturally assumed the actor would shave it for the film. But on that first day, the actor appeared on the set in his tramp costume—moustache clearly intact. So this was it, thought Sturges. He was going to fight about a moustache. Sturges called a break, wandering off to pace the circumference of the Paramount lot. He finally decided if conflict was what Donlevy was after, he should just swallow hard and get on with it. He returned to Stage 6, approached the actor's dressing room, and broached the subject:

"I was wondering about that moustache," Sturges began.

"Don't you like it?" the actor asked.

"I certainly do not."

"Then off it comes!" he said, and the crisis was past.

Sturges proceeded as if he had been doing this all of his life. Cameraman William Mellor had lined up the first shot of the morning, but Sturges wasn't sure it was exactly what he wanted. He asked Mellor to hand him the viewfinder, the boxlike instrument that approximates what the camera will see from a given position. Viewfinder in hand, Sturges then roamed the set, afraid to complain that he could see nothing through it. There were several awkward moments until Dink Templeton pointed out that he was looking through the wrong end. Good-naturedly, Sturges joined in the laughter. "That just gives you an idea of what to expect from now on," he told the crew.

"A big problem with him," said Templeton, "was that when he didn't know something, he'd try to bluff his way through. He made a point of dressing unlike everybody else. He had a funny hat and a cane he didn't need. If I remember correctly, he was burlesquing what DeMille had been doing." In the lunchroom, Sturges established a table across from DeMille's. At noontime each day, the producer-director would lunch with his staff and cast, and soon Sturges was doing the same.

Mellor moved his camera and, presently, everything was in place for the first shot of the morning. The scene was relatively simple: McGinty enters the polling place and signals that he's a repeat voter with the code words "Hello, Bill." At that point, "Bill" responds with a phony name, which McGinty must then sign onto the register. Clumsily, McGinty struggles with the name as he writes it out under the suspicious nose of a female election official. Sturges closed in and lingered on the two as their noses practically met. It was a beautiful shot, wordless yet explicit. Everyone realized then that despite his lack of experience, Preston Sturges knew what he wanted and was capable of getting it. Brian Donlevy slapped him on the shoulder and said, "Boy, you're going to be tops!" Relieved, Sturges took the entire cast to lunch.

As filming progressed, the director settled into an efficient pattern of working. With a given scene, he'd first rehearse for a straight-through "master" shot of all the performers. "I didn't think he knew how to direct," recalled Bill Demarest. "He always rehearsed people too much. He'd lose the spontaneity of it." What Sturges looked and listened for was a close facsimile of what he had seen in his mind. The same cadence to the words, the same pitch to the voices. "I always said he was a 'find' director," said Demarest. "He'd give you no direction and then see things he'd want in a scene. He'd pick things out."

"There were always swirls of movement," wrote Idwal Jones, a reporter for the New York *Times*. "He poked the camera at the heart of it, as if the camera were the chief spectator, entitled to the best seat in the house. The players were sufficiently adroit to act as if they were being natural. There were few nursings of a scene, still fewer close-ups. His probable handling of glamour stars would no doubt draw forth a ton of anguished fan mail."

Aside from the funny clothes and the inexperience, Sturges' principal quirk was his insistence that Louise be on the set with him. "And she was always in the wrong goddamn place," said Dink Templeton. "She was in the projection room with him every time we looked at the rushes. He just wanted her around." The rushes looked good. "He was getting great performances and good coverage." Louise found herself most impressed with her husband's ability to direct his actors. "He was a very creative actor himself," she said, "and he had the same insecurities that actors have."

Eagerly, Sturges worked long hours. "He liked to work at night," said Dink, "and I had a hell of a time. We'd start work at nine in the morning. I said, 'Now look, Preston, now we're going into all kinds of overtime so you have to regulate yourself from nine until six. That's the deal. If we're on a scene or on a set we'll go overtime to finish that particular scene. But that's it.' " Sturges responded well to such discipline. "I had to run the guy more or less," Dink said. "You have a schedule and a budget and you have to stay with it."

Sturges settled on nothing less than the best he could get from a scene. He worked hard on perfect master shots and allowed—at Dink's urging—for sufficient coverage, close-ups and the like. Worried, tense, after a week of such action he caught a chill. This he ignored until it developed into a deep, croupy cough. On the fourteenth day of filming, production ground to a halt. Said Preston, "I saved my strength, I treated myself like an egg and as a result of this totally regular and totally unaccustomed manner of living, on the fourteenth day of shooting I was rewarded with pneumonia."

That was it. "The big chance was shot. I knew the picture couldn't wait with all those people on salary. I knew that some cheesy old director with a hundred flops to his debit would be called in to take over and that if the film eventually came out all right, human nature being what it is, people would say, 'Well, you know who did it. After all, Sturges had never directed before and old Hash-face was really due for a hit. Really overdue as a matter of fact.'"

And his fever shot higher. Preston hadn't felt so sick since his appendicitis in 1927. What was especially galling was the fact that he had specifically prepared against such an occurrence. Miserably, he lay in his hospital bed and sweated, his mind clouded with disastrous thoughts. His delirium grew. Hazily, he saw a man standing at the foot of his bed. The man had been sent, he told Sturges, by Mr. LeBaron to tell him that the studio was "enchanted" with what it had seen of his picture. If he were ill for a week, two weeks, or *three* weeks, the picture would be waiting. After that, the cutter, Hugh Bennett, would take over until his return. "My fever slid down like a monkey down a flagpole," said Sturges, "and I was back on the set in ten days." Quickly, he returned to Ivar Avenue, where he conferred with Dink Templeton from his bed. As always, next to Preston sat Louise, bored to tears.

Thanks to the Christmas holiday, *McGinty* lost only four days of actual shooting. Sturges picked up where they had left off and work resumed smoothly. Preston came to feel, though, he was being bullied by the cameraman. With Dink Templeton insisting upon coverage, William Mellor took his director's inexperience to mean he could call the shots as he pleased. He had an especial fondness for over-the-shoulder shots, which Sturges lamely protested. "I don't like this," he complained. "The man I'm interested in is so small and the man I'm not interested in is so large in the foreground." Mellor used a 40mm lens. "That's the only way it can be done," he insisted. Sturges accepted this wisdom sourly; if he directed a second picture, he would not use Mellor again.

As with Bill Demarest, Sturges treated each of his minor players well. During Donlevy's shakedown of Dewey Robinson for protection money, Sturges kept the camera on Jimmy Conlin, the little hophead, as he reacted nervously to the noisy beating.

The rushes were loud, brassy, and well paced. Sturges gained confidence each day and, as he did, his speed increased. When the last shot was in the can, Sturges had finished not only $1000 under budget, but three days early. The studio was very, very pleased.

A rough cut was assembled and previewed. The audiences laughed at the fights between McGinty and The Boss and Bill Demarest was applauded when he showed up with the keys to their jail cells. The film worked beautifully, packed into a running time of eighty-one minutes. The advance word was reminiscent of *The Power and the Glory.* If handled right, the executives thought, it could turn out to be one of the year's "sleepers." Carefully, a campaign was planned. The salespeople thought they could do more with the title *The Great McGinty* and Sturges agreed. Advance one-sheets with the old title had the new one pasted over them. Brian Donlevy toured the country, screening the picture for members of the press. *McGinty*, Sturges was told, would be a terrific success. But he had also heard that about *The Power and the Glory* and remembered only too well what had happened to that. Nervously, he awaited the release, and the first trade showings.

The headline in *The Hollywood Reporter* read: "McGINTY" A SOCKO: STURGES' WRITING, DIRECTION TOPS. The review itself sounded like hype from a studio pressbook:

"Well, boys and girls, here's your answer to great screen entertainment; here's the reply for better pictures; better written, better directed and better acted. Here's the answer to any exhibitor's prayer for a picture that will send an audience out talking, and here's the reason why the motion picture is the greatest institution for entertainment on the earth. Paramount's *The Great McGinty* is all that and a lot of other things. It is, in the first place, a very reasonable cost picture; it's one of the best written jobs we've seen in many a moon; its direction is tops and that on the occasion of a first directorial effort, and it has one of the best acting casts that could be put together.

"If Paramount had a Clark Gable to tie into the picture and maybe the name of a big feminine star to work in his support, the picture would grab about all the coin that's waiting to be spent at the box office."

The premiere followed. *The Great McGinty* opened at the Paramount Theatre in Times Square on August 14, 1940.

"For nigh onto two months," wrote Archer Winsten in the New

York *Post*, "word has been copiously leaking out of Hollywood that *The Great McGinty*, written by Preston Sturges and his first directorial job, was something very special. Now on view at the Paramount Theatre, it lives up to and beyond the advance billing. As a brawling, sharp-witted drama of American political corruption it mixes humor, action, camera, sentiment, and satire in sequences of genuine originality." A night letter from Paramount New York reported the opening-day figures at $5226 with the expectation of another $5000 on day two. "Reviews are unanimously excellent with most of them raves," the letter went on to report. "Paramount Theatre, N.Y., is changing entire theatre front to play up reviews and expects on basis these reviews and word of mouth picture will build rapidly. Audience comment on picture very good."

McGinty did an extremely fine $45,000 in its first seven days and was held over a second week. *Newsweek* hailed the film as a one-man show, "and the man is a screenwriter named Preston Sturges."

The Great McGinty made most all of the "Ten Best" lists for 1940, and although it was not among the twenty top moneymakers, it performed well. The landslide continued through February of 1941, when, on Oscar night at the Biltmore Bowl, Preston Sturges won the first Academy Award ever bestowed in the category of Best Original Screenplay, beating out Ben Hecht, John Huston, Charles Bennett, and Charles Chaplin. In a rented tuxedo he accepted his award before an assemblage of 1300.

"There was a suspicion that I might get this thing only at the last moment," Sturges recalled years later, "and I became desperate because I knew I had to make a speech . . . and since I was supposed to be a humorist (I'm not actually funny at all) I tried to think of something funny. And presently, I thought of something funny. And presently, also, they announced my name. So I marched up and delivered my joke, which was the following:

"I said, 'Mr. Sturges was so overcome by the mere possibility of winning an Oscar that he was unable to come here tonight, and asked me to accept it in his stead.' Forgetting that nobody knew what I looked like and that they thought that I actually was somebody else, so all the applause ceased and I walked dismally back to my table, missing one of the greatest moments of my life."

Sturges could, however, take comfort in the knowledge that he would soon be one of the world's most recognizable motion picture directors. A major two-part biography in *The Saturday Evening Post* would be published in less than two weeks, picturing him at work on the set of his third picture. Before *The Great McGinty* was even in release, he was already at work directing his second.

17.

With the making of *The Great McGinty*, Preston Sturges' life assumed the air of a three-ring circus. "It *was* a three-ring circus," said Priscilla Woolfan, "and there was always someone hanging by their teeth in the center ring." To Sturges, more than half his life was gone and, yet, there was still so much he dreamed of doing. Now, with money and position, he rushed to experience all that life had to offer. Sturges described this philosophy as "living in contemplation of death." Should the whole thing come crashing down tomorrow, he would have no regrets.

When Snyder's closed amid formidable losses and hard feelings in December of 1938, Sturges attempted to sell the fixtures and kitchen utensils. The restaurant had been an irregular pain in his side, never taking off as it was supposed to, never run the way he felt it should be. After months of cash infusions but no results, Sturges sent the Snyder family on its "own sweet way," deciding the life of a restauranteur was not for him. But when he found he could sell his holdings for no more than seven cents on the dollar, he stored the equipment and began looking for a better location.

A pack rat, Sturges saved absolutely everything he owned. Nothing was ever sold or thrown away, although often things were loaned. He saved broken chairs, scraps of notepaper, clothing, and old cars. His sport jackets were famous for their general age and seedy condition. He had shoes in his closet fifteen years old. He would keep the restaurant fixtures and open a new place of his own. But this time, it would be exactly what he wanted . . . no concessions to economy or space. The new eatery would be precisely what Los Angeles needed. He would invent the right restaurant as he would a flying machine . . . or a screenplay.

Sturges kept the engineering company, always teetering on the brink of success though never quite making it. "We are, as usual, on the verge of selling or not selling the first Diesel engine," read a typical communiqué to Solomon Sturges. "In celebration of this, we are building five more." Preston proudly reported that the newly fitted *Recapture* did 14 knots at 850 rpm. This was enough to keep him a happy investor, although he only occasionally visited the facility, and usually as a side trip to a day of sailing.

Between scripts, Sturges amused himself with more designs, for such things as chairs, exercise apparatus, a band saw, a hearing aid, even canned laughter for radio shows. Any of these he could whip up before going to bed at night, but he rarely dated the drawings and they were generally filed and forgotten. The lion's share of his creative thoughts was directed to his writing and to the environment in which he lived. Aside from the restaurant, for which he made countless drawings and design sketches, Preston concerned himself with his home on Ivar and the family he had gathered. In 1939, with Bianca gone, Preston convinced his father to come West. Solomon Sturges was, by this time, in his seventies, ill from syphilis and slowly dying. Still, he was an independent old man. He married his nurse in Chicago and declined living in a second house on the Ivar property. Instead, Preston bought him a cottage near the beach in Santa Monica and placed all the resources of his little empire at his disposal. "He was a very dignified old man," recalled Priscilla Woolfan. "Preston accorded him the greatest respect." On a previous trip westward, Solomon had expressed quiet disapproval of Preston's living arrangement with Mrs. Gilchrist. Bianca was moved to another house the following week.

In Sturges' mind, The Green Hat (as he intended calling his restaurant) would be the definitive Southern California establishment. The way to maximize patronage, he decided, was to appeal to the broadest possible spectrum of consumers. With a fixed overhead, he designed a three-in-one operation similar to the multiplex theatre experiment of the mid-thirties. For what were essentially the costs of running one dining room, Preston Sturges could run several.

When he got the assignment to do *The Great McGinty*, Sturges saw no value in delaying further. If successful, he would be impatient to have a place of his own. In time, he settled on a sizable parcel of land at the westerly intersection of Sunset Boulevard, Havenhurst Drive, and Marmont Lane. Above Sunset, at an altitude approximating Snyder's down the street, was a home that had belonged to the father of actor Chester Morris. That home, now a wedding chapel, for some indefinable reason formed the basis for what Sturges ultimately designed. He pictured three stories, three separate operations. On the street level, a drive-in with counter service. On the second level, an informal restaurant for sit-down dining. The top—the house itself—would be strictly formal, a coat and tie required at all times. This was where Sturges would duplicate the establishments he missed in New York. It was the New York connection that convinced him to name his creation

The Players, after that staid old actors' club in Gramercy Park.

Construction began almost concurrently with the filming of *The Great McGinty*. Sturges decided to leave the old Morris house where it was and, instead of building on top of it, directed that the hill be dug from underneath and that The Players be built from the top down. It was costlier that way—more expensive than demolishing the old house and building from scratch—but Sturges couldn't be budged. "It was just the way Preston wanted to do it," said producer David Lewis. "He didn't need a reason." Even as *McGinty* filmed six days a week, he kept a close watch on every aspect of the work. "They couldn't drive a nail without Preston's OK," said Dominick Maggie, who later became head bartender. "I really think he was having fun with it."

Despite the complicated work on The Players, Sturges considered a full production slate critical to his success as a director. In early January of 1940, with *McGinty* still filming, Bill LeBaron said he had seen enough to merit a second picture and asked Preston what he wanted to do next. Sturges, in turn, had several unfilmed projects—each one, in effect, an unsettled score. There was *Triumph over Pain*, that distasteful biography of W. T. G. Morton that most everyone hated. There was *Two Bad Hats*, a script he had written for Al Lewin that got shelved when Lewin left Paramount. *Song of Joy*, for which there was only a treatment. And, of course, *A Cup of Coffee*, his little three-act play from 1931. It was clearly the failure of *Coffee*, having brought Sturges to Hollywood and having come so close to being made by Universal, that rankled the most. Considering he had written a complete screenplay in 1935, it seemed the logical selection for a quick second picture; a minimum of preparation would allow him to begin shooting it by summer. This would provide a bit of a cushion should *McGinty* fail at the box office—a second chance, if one should be necessary.

There was just one problem with *A Cup of Coffee:* Universal still owned it. Preston didn't know whether LeBaron would be willing to negotiate with them, whether he would consider it worth the trouble. And what if they decided to ask an outrageous price for it? Still, *A Cup of Coffee* was an ideal choice: funny and modest, it could be made for about the same price as *McGinty*. It needed a little work, to be "opened up" as people in Hollywood were fond of saying about plays. Preston took an oversized copy from his files. The title page read:

A
CUP
OF
COFFEE
An
Alleged

Comedy
in
Three
Acts

As with *The Vagrant,* he stapled over this another sheet. This time it read simply:

A CUP OF COFFEE
By
Preston Sturges

He dated it January 23, 1940, and gave it to Paul Jones.

A Cup of Coffee was another essay on the American success syndrome, a microcosm of youthful exuberance indulged by fate. The hero was young Jimmy MacDonald, lowly office worker for the conservative old Baxter Coffee Company. Jimmy thinks the company suffers from a hardening of the corporate arteries and pontificates at length about turning the place around. But Jimmy has his head in the clouds. He is a compulsive contest enterer —slogans, jingles, drawings. He daydreams of winning a fabulous amount of money and marrying Betty Casey—the boss's secretary.

One day Jimmy is fired—with little cause—and is cleaning out his desk when word comes he has won the rival Maxwell House slogan contest with "If you don't sleep at night, it isn't the coffee, it's the bunk!" With this gem of promotional zeal, Jimmy wins $25,000 and a two-year job in the Maxwell House Sales Promotion Department. Jimmy is ready to thumb his nose at Baxter's Best, but the company decides it can't afford to lose a mountain of free publicity and sets about to woo him back.

"These things do a terrible amount of harm," grouses J. Bloodgood Baxter. "They ferment thinking in minds that are not capable of thought. Sixty million husbands will sit down tonight and start work on sixty million plays, novels, political essays, inventions for flying straight up and down while sixty million wives contemplate the sudden wealth of our Mr. James MacDonald and become dissatisfied with their lot. We are a nation of nitwits!"

Jimmy's newfound popularity is intoxicating. He is offered a title, a raise, and a private office with his name on the door. He eagerly proposes to scrap the company's ancient non-slogan ("You'll Like It") and comes up with a replacement—"Baxter's Best—The Blueblood Coffee—It's Bred in the Bean." It's sheer genius, the executives cackle; It's Bred in the Bean, they chant, It's Bred in the Bean. They draw up a contract, but like most other Sturges success stories, Jimmy's rise occasions a fall. The contest official appears to concede a mistake . . . that Jimmy hasn't won after all . . . and, all of a sudden, his contract unsigned, Jimmy is

139

once again plain, unremarkable Jimmy MacDonald—unemployed until finally rehired; given the chance to prove himself as he never was before.

A Cup of Coffee was well developed and cleverly dialogued. Both Jones and LeBaron liked it enough to consult with Universal, and the agreed-upon price was little more than what the Laemmles had put into it—$6000.

The day Sturges finished shooting *McGinty*, he went to work on *Coffee*. Tossing off a screenplay for it, with so much practice, was hardly a chore . . . except for those around him. He still worked late at night, and besides Gilletti, he had Louise sitting up to listen as he spoke.

"He had to have the facial expressions of someone around him," Louise said. "He watched Gilletti's face, but Gilletti finally became not too satisfactory because he learned to control his expressions, whereas I didn't. . . . I think he did eventually think that I should be concerned about every facet of a film."

Sturges streamlined *A Cup of Coffee*, tailoring the Jimmy MacDonald part for Dick Powell as the first picture under Powell's new Paramount pact. Ellen Drew, from *If I Were King*, would play Betty and a starting date was set for the last of May. Sturges worked through March and April, editing *McGinty*, building The Players, and preparing to film *A Cup of Coffee*. As with *McGinty*, preparations went smoothly, helped along by the vast wealth of experience acquired on the previous picture. Sturges stuck with such people as Dink Templeton and the members of his "stock company," but happily rid himself of cameraman William Mellor. Instead he drew Victor Milner, a veteran of silent days and such films as *One Hour with You*, *The General Died at Dawn*, *Union Pacific*, and *The Great Victor Herbert*. Milner was fast, even-tempered, and could wiggle his ears. Most important, he was able to give Sturges exactly what he wanted.

Again, Sturges wrote specific parts for his character people. He retained Bill Demarest, Harry Rosenthal, Byron Foulger, Arthur Hoyt, Jimmy Conlin, Dewey Robinson, Harry Hayden, Pat West, Charles Moore, Robert Warwick, and Frank Moran. He added Franklin Pangborn (from *Easy Living*), Georgia Caine (from *Remember the Night*), Torben Meyer (*The Good Fairy*), Al Bridge (*The Good Fairy, Diamond Jim*), and Jan Buckingham, Fred "Snowflake" Toones, Julius Tannen, Arthur Stuart Hull, and Esther Michelson. He wrote a bit for his friend Georges Renavent and a fairly substantial part for Alexander Carr. The only problems were over the title (L.A. didn't like *The New Yorkers* and New York didn't like *A Cup of Coffee* or *Christmas in July*) and the casting of Carr. These two issues kept the night letters flying but once Carr's casting was approved he still had to be found and agree to the rate.

In early May Sturges wrote the New York office, "Please find Alexander Carr and see if he still looks all right to play part of department store owner in picture starting June 3. Believe he can be located on sidewalk in front of Lindy's." A week later, Carr, who had been working irregularly, demanded $1000 a week with a three-week guarantee. Paramount countered with $750 a week for an eight-day part and Preston wrote to Jack Gilchrist asking him to find Carr and tell him to swallow his pride and accept, that he'd had enough of a time selling the studio on Carr as it was. Carr accepted and came westward the following week for what was to be his final appearance on film.

A Cup of Coffee, retitled *The New Yorkers*, began filming on June 3, 1940. Sturges, now confidently in command, moved the film with obvious expertise. At his side again was Louise. Preston kept her around to provide a certain stability and objectivity. Her opinions were always well formulated.

"I think he believed I would tell him what I thought rather than what I thought he'd like to hear from somebody else," she said. "Because at all times during our relationship he had a great many satellites who would never consider telling him anything but what he would consider to be the acceptable opinion. Yes-men. He had to have it. I don't know whether he really liked it or not; I think he probably really didn't like it but he had to have it."

Sturges was less self-conscious on the *New Yorkers* set, an asset in posing for the publicity department's innumerable production stills. With *McGinty* quickly developing a reputation, Paramount began to sense ready copy in their unusual new director. Sturges posed with a straw hat and cane, directing Powell and Drew, clowning with Dink Templeton, riding a pogo stick around the studio's New York street. He even did a cameo on the first day of shooting. Visiting journalists were encouraged to talk to him; he happily granted them audience in his office in the Director's Building. "Sturges has a weakness for comfort," wrote one reporter, "a trait that endears him to visitors. He has a roomier davenport and more electric fans than the chairman of the company, a prodigious thirst, and a soft-drink cooler of the type favored by proprietors of hot-dog stands." He especially encouraged the photographing of his new restaurant, rapidly nearing completion.

To run The Players, Sturges imported the proprietor of his old 45th Street hangout, Pirolle's. Monsieur Pillet had spent years propping up a business that had run its course. When he wrote to Preston for help in the fall of 1939, Sturges urged him not to "throw good money after bad," but to come West and pilot The Players. The fact that Pillet was not an especially good businessman failed to bother Sturges. Pillet had helped him when he was down, so many years ago, and now Preston was only too proud that he could in some way return the favor.

The great experiment began quietly in the summer of 1940. No ballyhoo, no festivities; one day the doors opened. As with any creation, Sturges allowed for adjustments and expected them. He watched, listened, and made notes to himself. He figured The Players would be an ongoing job of construction and refinement, just as Walt Disney later considered Disneyland. The fact that he was busy stabilizing his movie career kept Sturges off the premises more than he would have preferred, but the first season was a test run; in some ways The Players was a toy to be played with when work was done.

The New Yorkers was completed in twenty-seven days, again on schedule and again on budget. The studio regulars who had feared (or hoped) that *McGinty* was a fluke were reassured: *The New Yorkers* looked to be every bit as good.

Editing continued through July while everyone prepared themselves for the release of *McGinty* in August. Breaths were held as for *Strictly Dishonorable* some eleven years earlier. When it was certain that *The Great McGinty* was an unqualified hit, the title of the new film was set as *Christmas in July* and the first previews held in September. A night letter from New York dated September 16, 1940, reported:

"Christmas in July was received with great enthusiasm by Home Office executives as well as regular theatre audience at preview held Paramount Theatre, N.Y. this afternoon."

The ad campaign, coming hot on the heels of *McGinty*, played up its success and the write-ups on Sturges that were beginning to appear. Ads for the Rivoli, where the picture opened on November 5, pictured Sturges alongside Alfred Hitchcock and John Ford. Teaser ads made liberal use of stills shot at home and on the set: Sturges on his exercycle ("He's riding high!"), Sturges at his pool table ("Your cue for a laugh!"), Sturges in his kitchen ("He's cooking up a hit!"), Sturges on his pogo stick ("He's got the jump!"). A cartoon Santa Claus paraded through each hoisting a sign that read: GENIUS AT WORK. Sturges loved it.

At seventy minutes, *Christmas in July* was a tight little film with much to recommend it. Jimmy's restlessness is apparent in the very first scene. On the roof of their apartment building, Betty is making a case for getting married. But Jimmy isn't buying it; his eyes glow only when he tells her about the Maxford House slogan contest and his entry.

Three office workers concoct a phony telegram, telling Jimmy he has won the Maxford House contest, while the real contest jury, comprised of the stock company and headed by Bill Demarest, is deadlocked. Confused, thinking the contest is actually over, Dr. Maxford writes Jimmy a check. Off Jimmy goes on an elaborate shopping spree for his neighborhood, culminating on the New York street with a fleet of taxicabs loaded with gifts, noisy children, and congratulatory neighbors. Shrewdly, Sturges built the situation with the audience knowing, unlike in the play, that the telegram was phony and that Jimmy's day of glory is quickly going to end. When it does, with the arrival of the irate store owners to repossess the goods, a riot erupts in classical slapstick, with the only distinction being that fish are thrown instead of pies.

The notices for *Christmas in July* were uniformly outstanding. *The Hollywood Reporter* called it ". . . a ten-strike for Sturges as a writer-director." Rival *Variety* labeled it ". . . bright, crisp, refreshing entertainment . . ."

Said *Time* magazine, "As director, Sturges converted this unpretentious plot into a happy, slightly noisy comedy with a Chaplinesque background of pathos. He ably remodeled Powell from the vacuous crooner of Warner Brothers musicals into a convincing prototype of a drudge with a dream of sudden wealth with which he can buy his mother a convertible settee and his girl a fancy wedding. Pale-faced, canyon-mouthed Ellen Drew, a one-time Hollywood soda clerk, was coached into a realistic likeness of a sugary, $18-a-week stenographer. A good dramatist, Sturges kept his characters credible by the simple but neglected technique of letting them act like people."

"How does he do it?" asked Bosley Crowther rhetorically. "Well, through the creation of solid comic characters, for one. His hero—and inevitable heroine—are just nice, honest youngsters, that's all. They want a break so they can get married. But against them are arrayed such a scatter-brained lot of practical jokers, business tycoons, and slightly off-center store clerks that the attainment of the break becomes a gantlet. Then Mr. Sturges contrives some wholly bewitching surprises. Details are worked out with elaborate ingenuity. Things pop out when you least expect them. He keeps you laughing with, not at, his youngsters."

Business for *Christmas in July* was brisk. It was held over in New York and, for such a brief and inexpensive picture, performed admirably. But Sturges' tenure in "B" pictures was drawing to an end. He had proven himself twice now. With the release of *The Great McGinty* in August, Sturges began work on his third script as a director—and his first "A" picture.

18.

Even before their marriage in 1938, Louise and Preston Sturges had discussed having a family. Louise wanted five children; Preston eleven. But 1939 brought them no closer to parenthood and, in 1940, Louise consulted three specialists and underwent two corrective surgeries. Preston wanted a boy—to name after his father—but fully expected their first child to be a girl. A girl, he told Louise, would make a good "toy" for her, would keep her happy and amused and at home. But Louise had plenty to keep her amused already: by 1940, she was devoting a good portion of each week to social obligations, the most prominent of which was a long series of informal parties known as the Sunday Night Suppers.

"We started at first by having a few people over for badminton in the afternoon," Louise recalled. "And then I started—like a damned fool—making preparations so that we would not have to go out that evening. And it snowballed. So eventually it turned out that for about three and a half to four years I would cook for sixteen to thirty-odd people a week."

The Sunday parties became justifiably famous. "You never knew who you were going to meet at a Sunday party," said Priscilla Woolfan. "They were fantastic. They were for Preston. He wanted people he enjoyed being with; terribly interesting people. And there were out-of-town visitors. I'll never forget the nights Alexander King was there. And José Iturbi used to sit and play 'Swanee River' on the piano." Regulars included King, Iturbi and his sister Amparo, the Woolfans, Fran and Dink Templeton, and Lucille and Bill Demarest (who was always careful to let Sturges win at Ping-Pong). Louise enjoyed these gatherings up to a point. "I enjoy cooking," she said, "but not if I have to every blasted weekend." Due to the nature of the weekly guest list, it was imperative to maintain a consistent level of quality. "Because if you get yourself a reputation, you have to keep it up. It's a big bother."

The Sunday obligation took four days a week. "I'd start telephoning on Thursday to get an approximation on how many were coming," Louise remembered. "And then I would go to Farmers Market. And then I would cook Friday and Saturday. And Sunday." In addition, Louise was expected to attend the fights at the American Legion on Friday nights, where Preston held ringside seats. And she joined him at The Players at least one night a week. "I must say I enjoyed that," she admitted. "It was about the only time of the week I saw Preston in a conclave of his peers and less of the satellites. There were some of the best wits of the time gathered around an Algonquin-like round table." The analogy was appropriate: The Players, located at 8225 Sunset Boulevard, was almost directly across from the Garden of Allah, where many veterans of the Algonquin Rose Room stayed when working in town.

The screenplay Sturges completed while in Reno with Louise was called *Two Bad Hats*, from an original story by Monckton *(The Faithful Heart)* Hoffe about a pair of card sharks aboard a luxury liner. In his rush to do yet a third picture in the year 1940, Sturges latched on to it and was ready to go after a quick polish and rewrite. As was his habit with source material, he paid scant attention to the Hoffe story, keeping only the ship and the idea of the father/daughter gambling cheats. What emerged instead was one of the undisputed comedy classics of the 1940s: *The Lady Eve*.

Under producer Al Lewin in late 1938, Sturges originally wrote the film for Claudette Colbert. When it was reactivated in August of 1940, Madeleine Carroll was suggested, first with Joel McCrea, later Fred MacMurray. But Sturges resisted using contract players and, with *McGinty* in release and *Christmas in July* in the can, was in a position to cast as creatively as he pleased. Instead of Carroll, whom he knew would be good in the part but not great, he pumped for Barbara Stanwyck; Sturges thought her superb under Leisen and knew her reputation as a hard-working, devoted professional. At the time of *Remember the Night*, he had told the actress, "I'm going to write a great comedy for you."

"I told him that I never get great comedies," Barbara Stanwyck recalled, "and he said, 'Well, you're going to get one,' and, of course, he followed through." The idea of an "A" picture with an "A" picture cast was naturally intimidating, but Stanwyck was warm and helpful and not inclined to throw her weight around. Preston knew he could work comfortably with her and that counted for almost as much as her talent.

For the male lead, Sturges liked Henry Fonda, who was under contract to 20th Century-Fox. There might be a problem in getting Fonda, he was told, and casting suggested Brian Aherne. But Sturges stood firm and, reluctantly, Y. Frank Freeman began negotiating with Darryl Zanuck. Their final deal called for not only a premium sum of money but a trade: Zanuck, in return for Fonda, wanted Sturges. It was almost an even swap with Paramount, a good indication of just how influential *The Great McGinty* had been. Freeman acceded and the contracts were signed.

With two stars in tandem costing almost as much as *McGinty* in its entirety, Sturges indulged himself to the extent of having Charles Coburn as Stanwyck's father and Eugene Pallette as Fonda's. He then completed the cast with his own stock company: Bill Demarest, Luis Alberni, Frank Moran, Arthur Stuart Hull, Harry Rosenthal, Arthur Hoyt, Jimmy Conlin, Al Bridge, Vic Potel, Esther Michelson, and Robert Warwick.

The Lady Eve began filming on October 12 amid considerable attention. *McGinty*'s reception and the advance word on *Christmas* made it easy for Paramount to plant items in the columns and arrange for interviews. *The Saturday Evening Post* sent profilist Alva Johnston to witness a few days of shooting and extract from Sturges the details of his life for a two-part biography to appear concurrently with *Eve*'s release. Again Sturges performed for the still camera, attired this time in polo shirt, knit muffler, and felt beret. This getup, he explained, made him easier to pick out amid the chaos of his set. Sturges never closed his stages. He welcomed visitors, anyone interested in watching him work. Between shots, he kept Harry Rosenthal off to one side playing the piano. The noisier and more confused the environment, the better he seemed to like it. "He had remarkable concentration," said Charley Abramson. "He could dictate, work on a picture—write it—with the radio going full blast and people in the room talking."

With *Eve* Sturges returned to the kind of freewheeling slapstick comedy he had written in *Easy Living*. As if to underscore the "genius" label the publicity boys saddled him with, he told Hedda Hopper, "I have no success formula. If I have attained any, it's an act of God. What I learned I picked up on sets. I just kept my eyes opened and learned, as my Filipino chauffeur learned to drive an auto. For five years he rode on seats near the bus driver and watched the driver. Then he went out and started driving."

Sturges, however, had formulated a sophisticated understanding of filmed drama that belied his casual comments to people like Johnston and Hopper. And none of his pictures showed this awareness to better effect than *The Lady Eve*. Working again with cameraman Vic Milner, he took an already glib and resourceful script ("A-45 CLOSE SHOT—AN ANNIHILATING PAIR OF FEET AND ANKLES WITH SOME LEG THROWN IN") and played the show out in his mind, seeing two-shots and inserts and noting their duration and values. He knew the speed at which the lines had to be delivered and the volume as well. And he allowed the Stanwyck character to dictate the piece. As she moved, so moved the rest of the story. And since she was fast and clever and resourceful, the film acquired the same attributes.

Sturges told friends that directing Barbara Stanwyck was a rare privilege, that she anticipated his every comment with a perfect grasp of the role. "I think there was a great compatible feeling between Sturges and myself," Stanwyck commented. "I loved the script." And the pace came easily. "First of all . . . the writing was there. The affection and respect I had for him was there—and I had an enormous plus by the name of Henry Fonda."

Fonda made a perfect foil for Stanwyck—the catalyst through whom the whole film worked. It was a magic instance wherein all the elements came together to form an incomparable whole. And Sturges' script was the seed. "The performer can't work miracles," said Barbara Stanwyck. "What's on paper is on the screen. If it isn't there, it isn't on the screen."

For his part, Sturges saw his job as anticipating the interest of the audience and directing accordingly, what Brander Matthews called ". . . the inevitable dependence of the dramatist upon the spectators whose sympathy he must capture and whose interest he must awaken." Sturges once explained the approach to Paramount's director of foreign publicity, Albert Deane:

"Quite a few years ago, 1928 to be exact, when I was new in the theatre and delighted with my job as assistant stage manager, during the representation I used to watch the audience through a peekhole in the cormentor. The thing that astonished me was that all the spectators in the theatre seemed to have their heads attached together so that they all moved in unison. And when I say all, I mean *all*. Nine people did not turn to the right while one turned to the left. *Everybody* turned to the right or everybody turned to the left or everybody looked down. (You can see the same thing at a tennis match.) I was astonished to see six nights a week and two matinees that one thousand people agreed absolutely exactly as to what was the point of principal interest at any one given moment. . . . Granted then that there is one point at which an entire audience looks, the next question is what else do they see while they are looking at this point? And the answer is that they don't see anything. I experimented by looking at objects in a room and noting what my eyes were doing. I found I was making myself an individual shot of the thing I was looking at. I use the term 'individual shot' rather than close-up because, quite obviously, an object does not come closer to you by staring at it. What happens is that your eyes *focus* on that one object and that everything else is out of focus and consequently invisible to the mind. Since the mind sees only the object in focus it becomes larger in *interest* and actually a close-up has been achieved. . . .

"To proceed: when I got into the movies and began taking an interest in films I noticed that in some films I was conscious of the cutting and in some films I was not. Then I began to understand that there is a law of natural interest and that this is what an audience in a legitimate theatre does for itself. The more nearly the film cutter approaches this law of natural interest, the more invisible will be his cutting. If the camera moves from one person to another at the exact moment that you in the legitimate theatre would have turned your head you will not be conscious of a cut. If the camera misses by a quarter of a second, you will get a jolt. (One other requirement is necessary here: the two shots must be approximately the same tone value. If you cut from white to black it is jarring.)

"To sum it up, then, the camera must point at the exact spot the audience wishes to look at at any given moment. To find that spot is absurdly easy: you have only to remember where you were looking at the time the scene was made. My friend Mamoulian told me he could make the audience be interested in whatever *he* showed them, and I told him he was mistaken. It is true that he can bend my head down and force me to look at a doorknob when my reflex wants to see the fade of the girl saying goodbye, but it is also true that it stops my comprehension of the scene, destroys my interest, and gives me a pain in the neck."

The handling of *The Lady Eve* was deft and knowing. Production moved well and finished in forty-one days—almost on budget and only two days over schedule. By now certain patterns had emerged in the Sturges *modus operandi*. He liked his people on the set, even when they weren't working, insisting that everyone view the rushes each day. "We always had to look at them," said Bill Demarest, "every goddamn night. Then he'd start to put the picture together and you'd have to watch that too." Demarest, however, noticed a special deference Sturges paid his two lead actors. During filming one day, Sturges wanted a different reading than he was getting from Stanwyck and Fonda. Softly, charmingly, he used every word, every phrase at his disposal to try and communicate the scene he envisioned. Frustrated, he finally marched away, passed Bill Demarest, who wasn't even in the shot, and yelled, "And don't speak so goddamned slow!"

Said Demarest, "With the big stars, he was careful about what he said, but with the stock company, he didn't give a shit."

Sturges also took to reading the *Christmas in July* notices to all who would listen. His attitudes toward reviewers were contradictory. On one hand, he echoed what Brander Matthews had said when he told Hedda Hopper, "I try only to please the public, not the intelligentsia. I've no patience with those who find solace in 'artistic success.' " On the other hand, he collected every single notice he could lay his hands on, and frequently left yellowing duplicates lying about his office and home.

"It so happens," he once wrote, "that the good opinions of critics, either stage or film, have always meant as much to me as the air I breathe. I live for good reviews and am drunk with pleasure when I get them. They affect me like catnip does a cat and any rumors to the effect that I am a deep drinking man or jolly tosspot were probably started by someone who had seen me rolling around on the floor after I had read a good review. I know, of course, that you can't have the good without the bad, that what goes up must come down, that if you believe them one day you must believe them another, and other depressing philosophies. Nevertheless, I love the critics."

In the case of *The Lady Eve*, Sturges allowed that the film had no moral, taught no great lesson, posed no burning questions. It was simply an amusing story. Still, he pessimistically expected a rough time with reviewers for *Eve*, after the unqualified raves for both *McGinty* and *Christmas in July* and the Academy Award just days prior to its release. He worried needlessly; not only did *The Lady Eve* receive unanimous praise, it outgrossed both his previous films and made the list of the top money-making productions of 1941. Some of the more prominent reviewers were incredulous at such an average. Bosley Crowther banged the gong for his entire fraternity when he wrote, "Now there's no question about it: Preston Sturges is definitely and distinctly the most refreshing new force to hit the American motion pictures in the last five years. A more charming or distinguished gem of nonsense has not occurred since *It Happened One Night*."

There was a general feeling of elation over *The Lady Eve*. The press began referring to Sturges as Paramount's "fair haired boy," "wonder boy," etc.; all the clichés that were annually applied to anyone new and different, regardless of age.

Sturges turned to his third unfilmed pet, *Song of Joy*, and had a copy of the treatment sent to Darryl Zanuck at Fox. Zanuck read it with polite disinterest: he knew it was a trunk item and was unwilling to let Sturges off the hook for anything less than a completely new story. The fact that *McGinty*, *Christmas*, and *Eve* were all trunk items evidently escaped him. *Song of Joy* was doubly awkward in that it required the services of an operatic star, preferably of foreign extraction. Marta Eggerth was still very much around (in *Higher and Higher* on Broadway), but there was not much interest in her and no one else seemed right. *Song of Joy* was a star vehicle without a star, no more feasible at Fox than at Paramount. The opera plot, though, was only a framework, an excuse for a sharp and funny look at Hollywood itself. If there was no selling the plot of *Song of Joy* then the plot could be scrapped.

Sturges decided to replace it with another even less apologetic satire on Hollywood. He could now make just about anything he wished for Paramount; the chance was rare and not to be missed.

In their frustration to have a child, Louise and Preston Sturges avoided their friend Bertie Woolfan. Priscilla Woolfan explained, "Preston never tried to get her to go to Bert—professionally —because that would be against his ethics, you see. Preston had certain very strong morals and he lived by them." In Louise's case, the various specialists she consulted proved ineffectual. When she finally saw Bert—in the late fall of 1940—it was in desperation and without Preston's knowledge. Woolfan performed a tubal insufflation—a relatively simple office procedure—and it was apparently a success. Discounting all the previous consultations, Preston considered Bertie the man who made his son's conception possible. Preston proclaimed his impending fatherhood vigorously when Louise's pregnancy was diagnosed in early February of 1941, and made grandiose plans for the baby's birth. An upstairs room was done over for the nursery and Louise was cared for as the most fragile and precious of patients.

Nineteen forty-one became a year of great productivity and change. By now, Sturges had moved beyond the mere goodwill of the Paramount administration in making his films. He had established an extraordinary reputation and other studios were interested in him. It was therefore not disastrous that Bill LeBaron left Paramount for Fox in February of 1941 or that he was promptly replaced by songwriter-producer B. G. "Buddy" DeSylva. Sturges was now a valuable commodity for Paramount, perhaps not as valuable as DeMille, but certainly important enough to merit the new production chief's respect and accommodation.

DeSylva's reputation stemmed from the songs he wrote for Ziegfeld's *Follies* and the George White *Scandals* and, later, *Good News* and *Hold Everything*. He formed a publishing house (DeSylva, Brown and Henderson) and moved into film work for Fox with *Sunny Side Up* and the futuristic *Just Imagine*. As a writer and producer he alternated in the thirties between Hollywood *(Bottoms Up, Captain January)* and Broadway *(Louisiana Purchase, Panama Hattie)*. DeSylva was a small, abrasive Italian with a production sense limited primarily to musicals. Observers marveled at his being placed in charge at Paramount, reportedly at the behest of general manager Henry Ginsberg. Ginsberg, soft-spoken and inclined to remain aloof from most things creative, was not a strong production man. With Y. Frank Freeman completing the triumvirate, it was clear that DeSylva would enjoy a minimum of interference in shaping the Paramount output. He was a man with considerable power; just what he was there for (Paramount profits were second only to M-G-M's) was uncertain. Paramount's top box-office star was Bing Crosby, with Bob Hope not far behind. Perhaps it was up to DeSylva to cement the studio's dominance in the field of musical comedy. In any event, DeSylva made a special effort to get along with C. B. DeMille, Mitchell Leisen, Sturges, Charles Brackett and Billy Wilder, Mark Sandrich, and Arthur Hornblow, Jr., at least until he could better evaluate each one's potential contribution to the Paramount he envisioned.

Sturges, although suspicious of DeSylva, treated him with respect, hoping he might continue as he pleased. DeSylva praised *The Lady Eve* highly. Almost immediately he asked Sturges to help troubleshoot a flat little comedy called *New York Town* which had been made under Bill LeBaron by producer Anthony Veiller and director Charles Vidor. It was the first Paramount picture DeSylva screened as executive producer and he frankly thought it lousy. What it needed was a better ending, he decided, and he asked Sturges to write and direct one. Sturges said yes, provided no publicity be given the work, and spent several days on the job in early March of 1941. *New York Town* was a "favor" to DeSylva, newly installed and already under the gun. There was obviously little Sturges could do, other than to rethink a limp and inconclusive ending and to add a little noise and slapstick. He turned the last five minutes of the picture into a boisterous scrap between Robert Preston and Fred MacMurray over the hand of wide-eyed Mary Martin. Sturges kept the noise high and the expressions broad and brought the film briefly to life. DeSylva praised his contribution; still there was nothing to salvage the film and it was released quietly that following November.

With his career zooming skyward, Sturges was also pleased with the early popularity of his restaurant, but not with a first-season loss of over $250,000. Charley Abramson had warned him from the start that the multilevel idea was a bad one "because nobody wants to be second-class, especially in a place like Hollywood." Sturges was nonetheless convinced that with adjustments, he could proceed with an official grand opening. The one thing that kept The Players from being a truly all-purpose night spot, he decided, was the lack of live music and a place to dance. So he planned to enlarge the top floor for dancing and create a new room he would call The Playroom. He designed a revolving bandstand, and set Harry Rosenthal to work assembling a group of house musicians. When renovations were about to begin, Sturges closed The Players, announcing its reopening sometime in the fall—after an extensive program of rethinking and remodeling. He then set to work on *Sullivan's Travels*, his fourth consecutive film as writer-director.

"*Sullivan's Travels*," said Sturges, "is the result of an urge, an urge to tell some of my fellow filmwrights that they were getting a little too deep-dish and to leave the preaching to the preachers. Somewhere in a book, I think by Brander Matthews, I read that it was the playwright's job to show conditions but to let the audience draw conclusions. *Sullivan's Travels* could really have been a little pamphlet sent around privately. Maybe it should have been."

Sullivan's Travels is a difficult film to categorize. It is a comedy, yet darkly dramatic in its third act. It is a satire about Hollywood thinking and, at the same time, an apologia for same. Primarily, it is a message picture whose message is that we don't need any more message pictures. It was the first script by Sturges, the writer, for Sturges, the director. As such, it was a very clean job: there was not much revision between the first draft and what finally appeared on screen. And it was never known by any title other than the one it carries. With *Sullivan's Travels*, Sturges created a character, posed a problem, and then allowed that character to carry the situation to its logical extreme. The character, an earnest young film director named John L. Sullivan, has made a fortune spinning confections like *The Big Broadcast of 1938* and *College Swing*. But these aren't enough for him. He is troubled by the fact that he is a maker of comedies—mere entertainment pictures. He aspires to loftier planes, pointing to socially significant productions like *Wild Boys of the Road* and *Grapes of Wrath* for his inspiration. He wants to make a film called *O Brother, Where Art Thou?* and the studio bosses do all they can to talk him out of it. But all they succeed in doing is inspiring him further: he knows nothing of the misery he proposes to film, so he decides to hit the road—in a tramp's costume with ten cents in his pocket—to learn about the world firsthand.

Sturges wrote *Sullivan's Travels* with a specific actor in mind: Joel McCrea. It was a story that demanded the kind of low-key sincerity in which McCrea specialized. Sturges liked the actor's blank, no-nonsense quality that made him a favorite with top directors like DeMille, Wyler, Frank Lloyd, Gregory La Cava, King Vidor, and Alfred Hitchcock. "He knew he could mold me," McCrea said. "Most of the other male stars bring a certain thing; Cagney, for instance, would always be Cagney. But this guy was John L. Sullivan—he couldn't be a movie star. He could be Sturges, he could be me."

McCrea and Sturges had known each other casually for nearly a decade. "I first met Preston out at Fox," he recalled, "where he had just written a script called *The Power and the Glory*. . . . I went over there to see Spence Tracy on the set and I was just sitting there and the script was on the side of the chair so I picked it up and looked at it. It was so good and the dialogue was so good I remarked about it and Preston was there. He was kind of standing in the back and he bowed graciously—I can just see him doing it—and said, 'I'm delighted you think that's a good script.' I said, 'Well, the dialogue is really outstanding.' It was kind of a nice meeting because I was complimenting him without knowing who he was."

The two met again on the set of *If I Were King*, where McCrea's wife, Frances Dee, was playing Katherine de Vaucelles. "He said he wanted to direct," McCrea continued. "He said, 'They never put it on the screen just the way I write it, the way I would like to see it. I guess the only way I'm ever going to see it that way is to do it myself.'"

Three years later, after lunching with Cecil B. DeMille in the Paramount commissary, McCrea passed Sturges' table. "I'd like to talk to you," Sturges told him. "I've written a script for you."

The actor was unconvinced. "No one writes a script for me," he replied. "They write a script for Gary Cooper and if they can't get him they use me."

Sturges laughed. "He got a kick out of that," said McCrea. "He said, 'No, no. This wasn't written for anyone else. It's called *Sullivan's Travels* and it's all original with me, it's not taken from anything. It's all mine.' So I said, 'Well, that's very interesting.' So I went over to his office and he gave me a script and we had a nice visit. I liked him right away. He was a very intelligent fellow and I really was interested in it."

Sturges also had a specific leading lady in mind. His admiration for Veronica Lake began when he saw her in the troubled *I Wanted Wings*, which Mitchell Leisen had taken over after a disastrous start in the hands of another director. It was Lake's first major picture, almost a debut, from which she had already acquired a reputation for being difficult. The publicity people had made quite a thing of her distinctive peekaboo hairdo. Sturges found a fascinating quality in the way she handled her lines, dominating virtually every scene. He approached her one day in the commissary and said, "I saw some of your rushes this morning and I want you to know I think you're going places." Buddy DeSylva thought she was all wrong for *Sullivan's Travels*, that she was best suited for the husky vamp parts she later became known for. They suggested Ida Lupino, Lucille Ball, Claire Trevor, Frances Farmer, Betty Field, and Ruby Keeler. Sturges stood firm. He got Veronica Lake.

And then, of course, Bill Demarest and Torben Meyer, Al Bridge, Jimmy Conlin, Franklin Pangborn, Robert Warwick, Frank Moran, Vic Potel, Harry Rosenthal, Harry Hayden, Arthur Hoyt, Dewey Robinson, Julius Tannen, and Esther Michelson. The budget was set at a little over $600,000 and the schedule at forty-five camera days, more than *The Lady Eve*. Sturges exuded confidence.

"He was what you could call 'intelligently conceited,'" said Joel McCrea. "He knew he was great. He knew what he was doing was good. He didn't question that what he was doing was going to get great reviews from the very first day he started shooting."

Sullivan's Travels commenced production on Wednesday, May 7, 1941, with Sullivan embarking on his journey with a gigantic Sturges-equipped land cruiser dogging his steps. Inside are PR people, a short-wave radio, a kitchen, and a complete support staff required by the studio. Sullivan tries to shake them by hitching a ride on a go-cart, but driver Frank Moran gives chase in a loud, violent ride that ends with the land cruiser lodged in what is left of a farmer's hay wagon.

Filming moved smoothly until they returned to the studio on the twelfth and began work with Veronica Lake. For all of Sturges' faith and support, she proved to be true to her reputation. "She wouldn't know her lines," said McCrea. "This great dialogue and we would go through about fifteen takes while she was learning her lines. Then by the time she got it great, I was just going through the lines, kind of pooped out and tired. She was very unprofessional." As if this weren't enough, Lake then announced that she was six months pregnant. There had been a rumor to that effect, and Preston had broached the subject earlier. "This is going to be a tough film, Ronni," he told her. "I'd never want to see a pregnant gal try to do it." She denied her condition and he accepted her word. But *Sullivan's Travels* was a very spirited film. There was a lot of running, a lot of location work, and a fair amount of slapstick.

"Keeping my pregnancy from Preston hung over my head like a cumbrous weight," wrote the actress in her autobiography. "I certainly didn't want to upset him and the fever with which he approached the film. And yet I was scared to death my condition would cause a problem later on and make completion of the film an impossibility. I knew I had to do something and do it quickly. But I couldn't get up the guts to simply tell him. So I told his wife, Louise."

As usual, Louise was on the set, also six months pregnant. Lake approached her one day and whispered, "Don't tell Preston, but I'm pregnant too."

Louise smiled. "I certainly will not tell him, but I'll give you a two-minute running start to tell him yourself."

This she did. "Sturges was hardly overjoyed. In fact, it took visible restraint to keep from boiling over at me." The studio got a doctor's statement okaying Lake's work on the rest of the picture. The only problem then was how to keep her condition from showing on film. Part of the answer was the floppy bum's outfit she wore during many of her scenes. Otherwise, Edith Head designed her gowns optically so that, if she was shot from carefully positioned angles, her pregnancy was not obvious.

With the problems Lake brought to the film, *Sullivan's Travels* went quickly over schedule. Preston's average of four pages of script a day slipped to almost half. Regardless, the company averaged thirteen setups a day, as compared to *The Lady Eve*'s nine and one half, or *McGinty's* eleven and a quarter. In lieu of Vic Milner, who was on another picture, Sturges drew the legendary John F. Seitz as cameraman, one of the very best in the business. Sturges especially admired Seitz because he was an inventor, a holder of a number of patents for photographic devices. Seitz, in turn, admired Sturges' talent and the somewhat unconventional way he approached his work.

The setup for *Sullivan's Travels* took place in an executive office–screening room where the two studio heads, Mr. LeBrand (played by Robert Warwick) and Mr. Hadrian (Porter Hall and a cigar), try to talk their star director out of *O Brother, Where Art Thou?* Sturges planned to open the film with a film—a brief parody of "social significance" in the form of a climactic fight atop a speeding train (he liked the idea of beginning a picture with "The End"). The lights would then come up and Sullivan would rant about symbolism and moral lessons.

The scene encompassed ten pages of dialogue, four and a half minutes of screen time, approximately four hundred feet of film. It was scheduled for two complete days of shooting, June 5 and June 6. Sturges appeared early on the morning of the fifth and began scanning the set with his viewfinder. "What are you doing?" Seitz wanted to know.

"I'm trying to see where we should cut," answered Sturges.

"I dare you to take it all in one."

Sturges paused. "Well," he replied, "I've never refused a dare in my life." Immediately, he went to Joel McCrea:

"I said, 'Preston, I've never done that—that's two days' work in one day.' He said, 'Well, if we do, it will be through. It'll be lovely, it'll be fine. I will establish a record.' And you had the feeling if you didn't do it it would be OK. He said, 'I can cut it, but I don't want to if I can help it—at least until you get into the office.' "

McCrea was game. "The man was a brilliant writer. He wrote dialogue I could just look at once and do." Bill Demarest agreed. "His dialogue you could learn faster than anybody's," he said. "It flowed. It was always perfectly natural for the situation." Still, doing the scene for an actor without stage training was a monumental task. "But he instilled a lot of confidence in yourself," said McCrea. "And we went ahead and did it."

Seitz laid tracks for the camera and rehearsed the moves with his crew. McCrea, Warwick, and Hall practiced their banter and by ten o'clock they were ready. The scene itself was a nimble give-and-take with Sullivan coming off as a pompously idealistic ass. "You see?" he shouts. "You see the symbolism of it? Capital and labor destroy each other! It teaches a lesson, a moral lesson. It has social significance!"

"Who wants to see that kind of stuff?" asks Hadrian. "It gives me the creeps!"

"The first take was fine," McCrea recalled, "but the camera wobbled a little and Johnny Seitz said something. Preston said, 'Let's just do one more for luck.' We did no more than two or three takes and that was it. Two full days' work."

They were finished by eleven o'clock. Sturges dismissed the company and made a beeline for Frank Freeman's office, where he proudly announced that he had just shot ten pages in the space of an hour. "Everybody at Paramount was talking about what we had done," McCrea continued. "DeMille looked at me and he said, 'Well, you work with these geniuses, these talented men, but my pictures make much more money than theirs do.' I said, 'But C.B., you don't give me a percentage of them. I don't get any more working for you than I do for working with those geniuses.'"

McCrea preferred Sturges. "It was fun working with him. I have to say the money I got paid for it was unnecessary. I don't know any other director (and I worked for some I loved dearly, like Frank Lloyd and Greg La Cava—I loved those men—and George Stevens, too), I never worked with one where I had so much fun. I really felt like I'd do it for nothing."

And Sturges loved and respected McCrea. "The first time I came on the set, Preston was sitting there having his coffee and right away he called to his property man, 'Oscar! Mr. McCrea's coffee!' It was like I was a bigger star than Gable. I never had the feeling I was working with a new director that didn't know. I had just as much confidence as with DeMille."

Filming progressed slowly but productively. Sullivan hits the road, loses the land cruiser, hitches a ride on a truck, and ends up—back in Hollywood. Hungry, he stops at an owl wagon for coffee and a doughnut and meets Vernoica Lake, a would-be actress on her way home. Sturges posed for stills with her, wearing a pajama top. She was chronically late and unprepared but very good. "He got a good performance out of her," said Joel McCrea. "I will say she's good in the picture, but he worked like the devil for it."

The girl latches on to Sullivan and follows him back out into the field. Daringly, Sturges shot a panoramic seven-and-a-half-minute montage of their experiences on skid row—silent, accompanied only by the excellent music of Leo Shuken and Charles

Bradshaw. Deftly the film moves from rowdy comedy to stark drama as the images of despair and loneliness and futility pass across the screen. Sullivan finally decides he's had enough and returns to his hotel room for a hot shower and a wad of five-dollar bills to pass around that evening. But that night Sullivan is robbed by an old bum (Georges Renavent in a small but showy part) and is left for dead. Through a complex series of plot turns, Sullivan winds up on a prison farm with a six-year sentence for assault. Here, in the darkest segment of the film, he is brutalized, cut off from all but the swampland that surrounds him, his contacts in Hollywood believing him dead. Here Sturges set the stage for one of his most memorable scenes, where the chain gang is led—by their brutally magnanimous keeper (Al Bridge)—to an old church for blacks to see a few minutes of comedy on a motion picture screen.

A Mickey Mouse cartoon flashes on the screen and every miserable, stinking man in line breaks into laughter. Sullivan stubbornly surveys the scene, refusing to believe what he is seeing. "Hey, am I laughing?" he demands of Jimmy Conlin. But, finally, Sullivan too is caught up in the merriment. The camera pans the church as the viewers are lifted out of their lives and into the world on the screen. And Sullivan realizes how precious is the gift of laughter.

Said Sturges, "When I started writing it I had no idea what Sullivan was going to discover. Bit by bit I took everything away from him—health, fortune, name, pride, and liberty. When I got down to there I found he still had one thing left: the ability to laugh. The less he had of other things the more important became laughter. So, as a purveyor of laughs, he regained the dignity of his profession and returned to Hollywood to make laughter."

But Sturges didn't necessarily accept the narrowness of such an interpretation. "That was Sullivan's conclusion," he said, "not mine. I don't believe that now is the time for comedies or tragedies or spy pictures or pictures without spies or historical dramas or musicals or pictures without music. I believe that now is the time for all forms of art and that now is always with us. Art, Tolstoy said, is a medium for the transmission of emotions. Without them we exist. The theatre helps to make up for the emotional deficiency in most people's lives and as such is vastly useful."

Sullivan's Travels was finished in early July of 1941—nine days over schedule—at a final cost of $676,687. The Paramount executives reacted favorably, but it was an odd, unusual sort of film, difficult to sell on the basis of content. Instead, a massive ad campaign was planned with Veronica Lake's image dominating. The fact that she was hidden half the time in her tramp's outfit and was not allowed even one passionate embrace with her handsome co-star went unmentioned. They hoped that Lake alone would pull them into the theatre. After that, they counted on the undeniable quality of the film to keep them there.

Toward the end of filming, Preston was on location some fifty miles outside of Los Angeles. Louise's condition was naturally thought fragile and although the baby wasn't due for another seven weeks, the Paramount production manager installed a special telephone hookup just in case. On the night of June 24, word came: the bag containing the baby had broken. Louise was being rushed to the hospital, where an emergency caesarean would be performed. Preston leaped into his car and he and the chauffeur raced toward L.A. at ninety miles an hour, hoping against hope they would get there in time. Preston remembered an elderly floor nurse's comment after viewing X rays of Louise's uterus. Although upside down, the baby looked like a wrestler sitting in his corner with his arms resting on the ropes. "He'll live," the nurse had said. "Look at the way he's sitting there— rarin' to go! You see some of them crouched into their corner as if they were afraid of their own shadow."

They arrived just after sunrise on the morning of the twenty-fifth. The baby had been born at five. There was nothing much to be done, so Sturges gave the elevator man a seventy-five-cent cigar and shook him warmly by the hand.

"My God, you were ugly!" Preston wrote his son years later. "You looked like a hundred-year-old Chinaman who's had his head shrunk by those Central American Indians. I think you weighed two pounds. About a week after you came, you started to turn blue and die. They had to give you a transfusion, but you were so little they couldn't find a vein in your wrist, so they gave it to you through a vein in your temple, while your old English nurse, Mrs. Morrow, held you on a pillow in her arms. During the transfusion you changed seventeen shades and came out of it pink and healthy."

Two months later, when the baby weighed eight pounds and was released from the hospital, Sturges gave the greatest cocktail party of his life. Nineteen seventeen Ivar was crammed with stars and executives. The affair was catered and guests were serenaded by a full orchestra. The event built to a dramatic peak as Preston's old Lincoln pulled into the driveway, Preston standing at the gate to greet his wife and son. The orchestra played "Louise." All gathered around the car as Mrs. Morrow emerged, carrying little Solomon on a pillow and advancing to the strains of Brahms' "Lullaby." The assemblage collectively burst into tears. Preston, embracing his wife and baby, reached into the crowd and brought Bertie Woolfan forward.

"This is the man responsible for giving me a son," he proclaimed. "That is, all but the most *primitive* procedure."

19.

Sturges lost no time in preparing a film to follow *Sullivan's Travels*; on a remarkable winning streak, he dared not break the momentum. In August of 1941 he began writing a new comedy with the provocative title *Is Marriage Necessary?* But the Breen office objected to making light of the institution and the story that Paramount purchased in November of that year—for the customary $10,000—was retitled *Is That Bad?*

Again, Sturges planned to use Joel McCrea in the lead. The story was an articulate screwball comedy along the lines of *The Lady Eve*. Although proud of *Sullivan's Travels*, Sturges expected it to be a less popular film—commercially—than *The Lady Eve*. This, of course, concerned him only to the extent that it concerned Paramount, but an artistic reputation could carry him only so far without receipts to back it up. Sturges had several less than surefire projects up his sleeve (like the unpopular *Triumph over Pain*) and he suspected it would be wise for him to offset each of his more eccentric productions with a good mass-appeal comedy.

Is That Bad? developed from the simple premise that there was no limit to how far a woman could go on her beauty alone. The idea was to concoct a situation where the girl, Claudette Colbert, would be compelled to travel and make her way with virtually nothing. A sort of female John L. Sullivan. Of course, she would be forced to survive on the goodwill of the various males encountered along the way. It was, in a sense, a dissertation on what Sturges called the "Aristocracy of Beauty."

Gerry and Tom Jeffers rent an expensive apartment they can no longer afford. Tom is an inventor, and his invention is a netlike span over a model city that serves as a kind of suspended airport. Tom figures he needs $99,000 to build a prototype, but that money is nowhere to be had. Gerry is frustrated by her inability to contribute to her husband's success: she can't sew, she can't cook, she has little going for her except her looks. She sees herself as nothing but a burden to poor Tom and decides—after an argument over the rent money—to leave him for his own good. She heads for Palm Beach to obtain a divorce and Tom gives chase. It is up to Gerry to keep one step ahead of him.

As with *Eve*, Sturges allowed the woman to propel the story, tossing in a new character wherever necessary. It was, in fact, his casual attitude toward plot development that brought Sturges one of his greatest casting coups.

Charley Abramson was in Los Angeles on business in August of 1941 when, one night after dinner, Preston suggested they take in Ronald Colman's new picture at the Pantages. Not bothering to check the schedule, Charley and Preston walked the few blocks to the theatre, only to find themselves with almost an hour's wait. They went in anyway, and subjected themselves to what remained of the second feature, a musical comedy with Ann Miller and the Three Stooges called *Time Out for Rhythm*. Sturges enjoyed himself, but it was one of its performers, not the film, that fascinated him: radio crooner Rudy Vallée. The New York *Times* described Vallée's dry performance as "petulant." But Sturges noted that whenever Vallée, who had a relatively straight part with little to do, opened his mouth, the audience roared with laughter. Sturges turned to Abramson. "This guy's funny and he doesn't realize it."

Sturges sat through the Colman picture, *My Life with Caroline*, but paid scant attention. He was deep in thought. When they returned to Ivar, Sturges summoned Gilletti. "He started to dictate," Abramson remembered, "and suddenly there was a new character."

When he finished, Charley asked, "What was that?"

"That's the new part for Rudy," Preston replied.

Word that Sturges was interested in him reached Vallée the next day. "When I heard that the possibility was there," he recalled, "I wrote Sturges and said whether or not I get this role in this picture, I want to tell you how much I enjoyed *The Lady Eve*. I said from the beginning with the serpent poking his head through the letters of the title to the end of the picture it was one of the finest things I'd ever seen."

Sturges responded by asking Vallée to lunch at the Paramount commissary. Charley Abramson watched with amusement as Frank Freeman and Buddy DeSylva passed the table and Preston stopped them to say, "I want you to meet Rudy Vallée. He's going to be in my new picture."

The two executives turned a pale shade of green, mumbling only cursory greetings before making a hasty exit. Moments later, word came to Abramson that Mr. DeSylva and Mr. Freeman wished to see him in DeSylva's office. Abramson finished his meal, excused himself, and then made his way to the administration building.

"Listen, you've got to get your friend off this Rudy Vallée kick," DeSylva urged. "He'll ruin the picture. Is he crazy?"

Abramson was unconcerned. "Pardon me," he said, "but I think you gentlemen had better leave him alone. He's done four pictures now and they've all been good." DeSylva and Freeman didn't care, but Abramson persisted. "I'll make a bet with you, in fact. Once this picture's released, you're going to *sign* Rudy Vallée."

"Now cut the kidding," DeSylva said. "This is serious business."

When the film was released in December of 1942, Rudy Vallée's portrayal of Hackensacker, the diffident millionaire, was a sensation. Paramount signed him for $2500 a week.

Sturges completed his screenplay in early November of 1941, solving the problem of the traditional romantic triangle in a new and imaginative manner. Sturges had McCrea pursuing Colbert, Vallée pursuing Colbert, Mary Astor (Vallée's sister, the Princess Centimillia) pursuing McCrea, and set the whole thing to rest by giving both McCrea and Colbert identical twins. This required a quick setup at the opening (during the credits) into which Sturges crammed the makings of an entirely separate film. The last shot then became a trick shot of McCrea marrying both Astor and Colbert, and Colbert marrying both McCrea and Vallée.

Is That Bad? was retitled *The Palm Beach Story* and scheduled to commence filming in late November of 1941. It was budgeted at close to a million dollars (Colbert alone cost $150,000) and expected to take forty-two days to make. Filming stretched on, though, as Sturges spent much time and effort getting the right performance from Mary Astor. "It was not my thing," the actress later wrote. "I couldn't talk in a high, fluty voice and run my words together as he thought high-society women did, or at least *mad* high-society women who've had six husbands and six million dollars."

Somehow, Sturges didn't seem as driven to keep on schedule as he once had. He was more comfortable on the set now, more secure in his position with the studio. Bill Demarest compared working for Sturges with working for Frank Capra:

"If anyone blew a line, Capra never stopped the camera. He'd say, 'All right, take it from that line,' and keep rolling. But with Sturges, when somebody blew a line, they'd stop and the electricians would come in and adjust things and the make-up man and all the others and it'd be twenty minutes before they were ready to shoot again."

Part of the problem was Sturges' insistence upon a perfect master shot before any close-ups could be taken. His words he considered sacrosanct, and he wouldn't stand for even the slightest of adjustments. "He had a great memory," said Demarest. "If you changed anything he'd say, 'Wait a minute,' and, goddamn, he was right."

Sturges nevertheless inspired great loyalty on the part of his cast and crew. "I liked to work with him as a director," said Joel McCrea. "He was a very sympathetic director. Actors that are stood up in front of maybe seventy-five people in a crew, with electricians and everything, do well when they're handled well. And Preston handled his people well."

Sturges seemed to know when he had what he needed in an actor and when extra work would be necessary. "He left me pretty much to myself," recalled Rudy Vallée, "and I did it just about the way I wanted to. I don't think he ever gave me much direction. He never had to with Colbert and the rest of us because we knew what we were supposed to do; our parts were tailored for us." Sturges accented the Vallée character with a yachting cap and pince-nez. "It was his idea," said Vallée, "to cut the pince-nez to the droop of my eyes."

Joel McCrea found *The Palm Beach Story* less demanding than *Sullivan's Travels*, though he was called upon to take a violent tumble down a flight of stairs. Sturges was fond of punctuating his dialogue with slapstick, and did so, in the opinion of some critics, to excess. But he had no trouble selling a star like McCrea on performing such a stunt. "He would have set you up because he was so enthused," said McCrea, "and—really—he would have done it for you first to show you it wouldn't hurt you."

The Palm Beach Story rolled into 1942, finishing in late January, seven and a half days behind, with a final cost just under $950,000. Paramount released *Sullivan's Travels* the following week.

As planned, the ad campaign for *Sullivan's Travels* highlighted Veronica Lake's image and nothing of what the film was about. Since it was his first release in almost a year—since *The Lady Eve*—it was appropriate that some of the attention was directed to Sturges. The advertising people conceived a special introductory scene for the trailer of *Sullivan's Travels* in which Sturges, the director, quarrels with Sturges, the writer, as Joel McCrea and Veronica Lake look on. They also shot trick stills of Sturges seated across from himself, script in hand, blowing a raspberry at his twin, threatening violence, etc.

The publicity people did just about all they could do with *Sullivan's Travels*. The notices were mixed, however, and business didn't hold. Sturges theorized that audiences were expecting another *Lady Eve*. "One local reviewer wanted to know what the hell the tragic passages were doing in this comedy," Sturges reported, "and another wanted to know what the hell the comic passages were doing in this drama. They are both right, of course. Bob Benchley said once that if you want to do a sincere tragedy of a New England rock farm, you'd better start torturing the horses in the first act. He was right also, because if you shape your mouth for ice cream, the best fish tastes like poison."

Bosley Crowther, who liked *Sullivan's Travels* and accorded it a rave, invited Sturges to write a piece for the New York *Times* on its creation and intent. Sturges responded with an article headlined "An Author in Spite of Himself," which appeared in the Sunday edition, February 1. A third of this essay was given over to recollections of the *Park Field Airgnat* and another third to an imaginary dialogue about torching orphan asylums. Finally he got to the point. "Was I Sullivan?" asked Sturges rhetorically. "I am not Sullivan. He is a younger man than I, and a better one— a composite of some of my friends who tried preaching from the screen. I thought they were getting a little deep-dish and wasting their excellent talents in comstockery, demagogy, and plain dull preachment."

Sullivan's Travels managed one month as a *Motion Picture Herald* "Box Office Champion" and then disappeared. Sturges, expecting as much, was glad to have *The Palm Beach Story* waiting in the wings. It was about this time that Sturges conceived his eleven rules for box-office appeal:

1. A pretty girl is better than an ugly one.
2. A leg is better than an arm.
3. A bedroom is better than a living room.
4. An arrival is better than a departure.
5. A birth is better than a death.
6. A chase is better than a chat.
7. A dog is better than a landscape.
8. A kitten is better than a dog.
9. A baby is better than a kitten.
10. A kiss is better than a baby.
11. A pratfall is better than anything.

Due to the quiet reopening of The Players, devoid of the usual bombast of such occasions, it took a while for people to rediscover the place and for the word to spread. Construction on The Playroom was not finished by Christmas of 1941 but plans were under way for its gala opening just after the first of the year. Regardless, the clientele built steadily and it wasn't long before The Players became one of the most popular night spots on the West Coast.

"It was the *top* place," said Dominick Maggie, Sturges' head bartender. "There was nothing like it in the West—nothing like it in the world, for that matter. Anybody of consequence at that time frequented The Players. There were movie moguls; superstars, like Bogart and Barbara Stanwyck, Charlie Chaplin . . . all the stars of that era; writers of all sorts; Orson Welles, Mark Hellinger. Then, when the war broke out, people connected with the services, generals and whatnot. Even potentates came in there."

Though exceedingly busy with moviemaking, Preston was there many nights—to greet guests, table-hop, to enjoy having the most powerful figures in the industry under his roof. Sturges considered the restaurant his own private domain, expecting the same deference accorded a visit to one's home. "It was some place," wrote screenwriter Earl Felton of The Players, "absolutely a marvel, matchless food, service, decor, etc., but with the serious drawback of Preston usually present, turning baleful eyes on any patron he did not know personally."

Sturges often retired to The Players after a day of shooting, arriving between nine and ten o'clock, just as the dinner crowd was thinning and the atmosphere became more relaxed. "Whenever we'd work too late to get home to dinner," recalled Joel McCrea, "he would invite us to dinner at The Players. You could never pick up a check with Preston, either at the commissary or at his restaurant. He always managed to get the check and you couldn't even tell what it was." To Preston, allowing his guests to pay the check at his restaurant would have been tantamount to presenting them with a bill for a meal at his house.

The Playroom opened with appropriate fanfare on January 14, 1942. Printed invitations and newspaper ads augmented the usual word of mouth. Sturges' expansion of the top level of the building eliminated a portion of the upper parking lot. What the floor became was two separate rooms: The Blue Room, occupying the south side of the building, next to Sunset, and The Playroom, which occupied the north. The Blue Room was strictly formal; ties were loaned to customers who came without. The Playroom was built for Harry Rosenthal, who first met Sturges in New York in 1929. "It all started when our photographs appeared side by side in a copy of *Vanity Fair*," Rosenthal told a columnist. He had scored a hit as the piano player in Kaufman and Lardner's *June Moon* at the same time Sturges was the toast of Broadway with *Strictly Dishonorable*. The two were introduced one night in Shubert Alley and became fast friends. Later Rosenthal came West to work in films. Sturges cast him as Louie, the bodyguard, in *McGinty* and made him a charter member of the new stock company.

Sturges had his private table—his round table—at the southeast corner of the mahogany-paneled mezzanine level. From there he could see out toward the Pacific Ocean and still inspect all who entered by way of the staircase across the room. Often he would sit there—in the company of Priscilla and Bert Woolfan—enjoying a leisurely dinner and carefully pointing out the famous and near-famous who had come to dine with him. There were times, however, when Sturges was at a loss to identify an entrant, and he watched such people closely. One night he was in The Playroom observing a couple on the dance floor he found particularly distasteful. "This girl was a little younger than this old buck," recalled Dominick. "Somehow or other, Preston didn't like the way they danced." Sturges summoned Monsieur Pillet.

"You tell that guy to stop his dancing," he ordered, "and not to come back here anymore."

Pillet was incredulous. "I can't do that!" he said. But Sturges was adamant. The man's presence displeased him; that was all that mattered. Moments later, the offending guest was escorted off the premises shouting, "What'd I do?"

Regarding the day-to-day responsibilities of running a famous restaurant, Sturges' inclination was to leave Pillet alone. Pillet was his personal selection, and Sturges felt it only reasonable to trust him. Even at that, there were a lot of things that seemed to demand Sturges' personal attention. These tended to drive the staff crazy, as he had little real business sense and appeared to go overboard in trying to picture The Players as customers did. Dominick, the bartender, dubbed him "The Sultan." Sturges would hold court at his table across the room, occasionally calling to Dominick for refills. This he would do by simply making a broad circular gesture, at which point Dominick was expected to recall the drink of each guest and furnish a fresh one.

Sturges himself drank Black Label Scotch, which sold in 1942 for sixty-five cents. He was in the habit of paying for his drinks with cash. One night, Sturges found himself low on change and had to borrow the money from bandleader Harry Rosenthal.

"You know, you're getting too much for those drinks," he told Dominick. "At the Brown Derby they get less than that."

Dominick explained that the Brown Derby didn't offer entertainment and that The Players made precious little at sixty-five cents. It took Pillet the better part of an hour to convince Sturges this was indeed reasonable. The Players was a cheaper place to eat than any comparable restaurant. "We were serving enormous ham sandwiches downstairs for twenty-five cents," said Dominick. "You couldn't buy that much ham in a market that cheap!"

In its first full year of operation, The Players grossed over $700,000. Yet it is doubtful Sturges ever made a dime from it. He kept it going, providing whatever capital was necessary. It was his second home, an indispensable part of his Hollywood life.

With the press attention that followed *The Lady Eve*, interest grew in writers who felt they could also direct what they wrote.

The studios took note of all the copy generated by Preston Sturges and his "one-man band" and began to think less harshly of writers who wished to follow in his footsteps.

"I knew Preston Sturges as a writer long before I came to America," said Billy Wilder. "We had all seen *The Power and the Glory* and *The Good Fairy*. He was certainly the most important writer who jumped into directing. The fact that he had succeeded helped me in getting from writing into directing."

Wilder, himself with Paramount, prepared a comedy called *The Major and the Minor* which he proposed to direct with his collaborator, Charles Brackett, producing. Sturges enjoyed the idea that he had paved the way for other writers to become directors, and was proud that his success had such far-reaching effects. "He would come on the set," Wilder recalled. "We would have lunch together. We were extremely friendly. I looked up to him—he was older—as the shining light to be imitated, if possible."

All of a sudden, Hollywood was teeming with writer-directors and writer-producers. Besides Brackett and Wilder there were John Huston, Joseph L. Mankiewicz, Delmer Daves, Robert Rossen, George Seaton, Nunnally Johnson, and, of course, Orson Welles, whose *Citizen Kane* bore more than a casual resemblance to *The Power and the Glory*.*

Sturges was especially helpful when the French writer-director René Clair came to the United States after the outbreak of war in Europe. Although Clair was the same age as Sturges, he had been writing and directing films in Europe since the mid-twenties. Now he had come to Hollywood, where he was respected but not necessarily employable. At Universal he made a pleasant Marlene Dietrich picture called *Flame of New Orleans* but the studio wouldn't go for another, and at Paramount, Buddy DeSylva agreed to take Clair on only if Sturges acted as his producer. This Sturges was happy to do, although he had his own projects and would be of minimal help; DeSylva evidently reasoned if Clair made a botch of things, Sturges could always step in and take over.

Clair's film was *The Passionate Witch*, from a novel by the late Thorne Smith, a beguiling fantasy along the same lines as *Topper*. Work on the screenplay began concurrently with *The Palm Beach Story*, allowing Sturges only the slightest influence on the final script. Three writers worked on it, including Dalton Trumbo and

---

*The story is told of a dinner party attended by both Sturges and Welles in Europe in the 1950s. When a guest brought up *The Power and the Glory*, Welles jokingly remarked that he considered it in "extremely poor taste" to mention the film in his presence. Welles liked Sturges but has said, "If his work had any influence on me, I am unconscious of the fact. . . ."

Marc Connelly. Joel McCrea, first cast in the lead, balked at making another picture with Veronica Lake, whom Sturges had sold Clair on over tremendous resistance. Filming got under way in April of 1942 with Lake and actor Fredric March. Sturges admired the finished product but disclaimed any credit for its script or direction. Following its first previews in July under the title *I Married a Witch*, Sturges told Hedda Hopper, ". . . the only person who deserves credit . . . is René Clair. It's going out as a René Clair production. And he's done one of the swellest jobs I've ever seen. After all, he was producing and directing pictures when I was taking nickels from my dad to see them."

Sturges helped write a short for Darryl Zanuck and the Research Council of the Academy of Motion Picture Arts and Sciences called *Safeguarding Military Information* and appeared as himself in an all-star musical called *Star Spangled Rhythm*. For union scale and billing just under C. B. DeMille, Sturges acted in two brief scenes and took a minor pratfall.

It was symbolic of the artistic pratfall Sturges would take with his next film, *Triumph over Pain*. But in *Star Spangled Rhythm*, he merely dislocated a finger. *Triumph over Pain* cost him his position at Paramount . . . and ultimately his career.

20.

The book *Triumph over Pain* engendered a storm of controversy when it was first published. It was the contention of the author, René Fülöp-Miller, that the sole and undisputed discoverer of ether as an anesthetic was a Massachusetts dentist by the name of William T. G. Morton. For this revelation, Morton was vilified—his business ruined, his patents disallowed. His life was one of careful study, modest success, and then great discovery—followed by a brief burst of glory and twenty years of defamation and bitterness.

The dispute concerning *Triumph over Pain* did not surround the events of Morton's "discovery," but whether he was actually the first one to make it. Fülöp-Miller contended that Dr. Horace Wells, a pioneer in the use of nitrous oxide ("laughing gas"), was a buffoon, and that Dr. Crawford Long, who administered ether prior to Morton in the early 1840s, failed to persevere. Admirers of both men were incensed. Indeed, when it became widely known that Paramount had purchased the book—for director Henry Hathaway and actor Gary Cooper—the studio was flooded with letters from dentists and dental groups, protesting the book's findings and urging cooperation with other experts in the field.

Paramount was never enthusiastic about the property, more suited to the Paul Muni/Spencer Tracy school of biography popular at Warners' and Metro. Then both Cooper and Hathaway left the studio and Preston Sturges picked up on the story, dismissing its alleged inaccuracies, embracing instead its marvelous lesson of ingratitude and despair. It was the same kind of dark, everything-right-gone-all-wrong story that Sturges had concocted with *The Power and the Glory;* the success and achievement scenario followed by trial and without a happy ending. It offered something decidedly different in the genre of biography . . . and, in 1942, a chance to direct a film with a theme and structure similar to his most prestigious film of the 1930s.

Sturges wrote the initial drafts of his screenplay in the latter half of 1939, working up to the start of *The Great McGinty*. He then did little more than a polish in early 1942—after finishing *The*

Palm Beach Story—and considered himself ready to start shooting in March.

Triumph over Pain was structured very much like *The Power and the Glory*. Sturges opened his script just after the death of Dr. Morton, with the story told in random flashbacks by Morton's widow and his assistant, Eben Frost (the first patient on whom he used ether). First, Sturges tells of Morton's great triumph; a rousing parade after a surgery performed painlessly, for which Morton has acceded to the demands of the Massachusetts Medical Society to reveal his miracle substance, Letheon, as nothing more than sulfuric ether . . . highly rectified. His dental practice collapses as other dentists rush to open their own "painless" parlors. Then a manufacturer copies the design of his inhaler and, in a matter of weeks, Morton's life is in ruins.

Flash forward seven years: Congress has voted Morton an award of $100,000—long overdue—and Morton borrows on his modest farm in order to make the trip to claim it. But a challenge arises. If Morton is indeed the discoverer of ether as an anesthetic, why has he not gone to court to protect his patents? The President stops just short of signing the bill, advising Morton, with full sympathy, to bring suit against an Army surgeon. The court would, of course, rule in his favor, and the patent would be affirmed. But then the questions arise: Is Morton a phony? Did he steal his idea from Wells? Or his old teacher, Professor Jackson? The press assails Morton's apparent profiteering against the practitioners of painless surgery in the military and, in the end, his patent is disallowed. Bitter, discouraged, Morton returns to the farm without his award, to begin the final decade of his life in obscurity and shadow.

Returning to Frost and Mrs. Morton, Sturges then presents the rest of the tale in chronological order: Morton's pursuance of his sweetheart Elizabeth at an "ether party" in 1840 and then the events leading up to Morton's historic revelation—to save a young girl from a painful operation—in 1848. This is Morton's great triumph, giving Letheon to the world, and the film ends on this note with all the fanfare appropriate to the finest hour in a man's life—not necessarily his last.

Sturges set forth his theme by way of a foreword, spoken as the camera zeros in on the hero's long-forgotten grave:

"One of the most charming characteristics of Homo sapiens, the wise guy on your right, is the consistency with which he has stoned, crucified, burned at the stake, and otherwise rid himself of those who consecrated their lives to his further comfort and well-being so that all his strength and cunning might be preserved for the erection of ever larger monuments, memorial shafts, triumphal arches, pyramids, and obelisks to the eternal glory of generals on horseback, tyrants, usurpers, dictators, politicians, and other heroes who led him, usually from the rear, to dismemberment and death.

"We bring you the story of the Boston dentist who gave you ether. Before whom in all time surgery was agony. Since whom Science has control of pain. It is almost needless to tell you that this man, whose contribution to human welfare is unparalleled in the history of the world, was himself ridiculed, burned in effigy, ruined, and eventually driven to despair and death by the beneficiaries of his revelation."

Under the titles came scenes of a modern operation with which to contrast the barbarism of earlier medicine. Appropriately enough, the first objections to Sturges' approach to *Triumph over Pain* centered on this foreword and its reference to "generals on horseback" during the early days of World War II. Buddy DeSylva did not merely find *Triumph over Pain* distasteful, as had his predecessor, but actually thought it repulsive, about as suitable a subject for general audiences as a VD short. In fact, he contended, the word *Pain* ensured its immediate rejection at the box office. Sturges changed the title to *Great Without Glory* to defuse that argument. DeSylva groused every step of the way—from Sturges' decision to make the film to his intention to cast Joel McCrea in the lead. By now Sturges was his own producer, exerting complete control over his films and blessed—he presumed—with freedom from the interference of the front office. But Sturges' reputation at Paramount was based primarily on a single hit: *The Lady Eve*. His other films had received a lot of attention, but were not exceptional money-makers. DeSylva considered Sturges anything but a sure bet in 1942 and watched him with both suspicion and distrust. When filming started, on April 9, the production chief was barely able to contain his animosity.

Filming also that Thursday morning were *Road to Morocco*, destined to be one of the monster hits of 1942; and *The Major and the Minor*, Billy Wilder's American debut as a director. *Great Without Glory* was perceived as a radical departure for Sturges, but excessive coverage in the press was discouraged; the last thing the company wished to do was to build anticipation for what seemed at the moment to be a surefire disaster. Quietly, Sturges assembled his cast: McCrea, Betty Field, Bill Demarest as Eben Frost, Louis Jean Heydt as Dr. Horace Wells, and Porter Hall as President Franklin Pierce. The stock company filled in the other parts—in period costume—and then Sturges engaged Harry Carey, the popular star of countless silent Westerns, for the role of Professor Warren, the noted surgeon who performs the first painless amputation.

The part of Eben Frost gave Bill Demarest one of his weightiest roles, carrying the entire movie on his formidable shoulders. Demarest was also the principal buffoon of the piece, the man who tells the story and, yet, serves primarily as Morton's guinea pig and the butt of much of the slapstick. His ready testimonial to Morton's expertise ("It was the night of September 30. I was in excruciating pain . . .") is the running gag of the picture. Here Sturges took a great deal of criticism for writing this bleak and unhappy tale with a liberal dosage of comedy and bombast. He had heard this all before with *Sullivan's Travels*. Sturges said, "Unfortunately for me, many people believe in the hand-in-bosom-prematurely-turned-to-marble form of biography and these people are outraged at the idea of anything funny being shown in the foreground of a picture which has a serious background." Sturges saw humor in Morton's first experiments and in the laughing gas Morton's friend, Dr. Wells, administers. He filmed an especially imaginative courtship scene that occurred at the aforementioned "ether party" in 1840. Morton confesses to Elizabeth that he hasn't the money to continue his medical studies and that he intends —instead—to become . . . a dentist. This promptly sours whatever relationship they have, dentists being held at that time in approximately the same esteem as barbers and medicine men. Yet they love each other, a condition made readily apparent when both are encouraged to sniff a little ether and perform for the guests.

The two embrace and the scene dissolves . . . to a similar embrace a few years later between Dr. and Mrs. Morton in his new office, happy as clams and ready for business. Morton begins to search in earnest for an answer to painful dentistry. His patients' screams scare others off, and it is in desperation that he consults with old Professor Jackson and learns once again of the properties of ether.

Sturges pictured Morton as a little dull-witted, a little naïve, something of a dunderhead. Sturges' Morton seemingly backed into his great discovery, more by accident than design. He is forgetful, not especially well versed in medicine, and somewhat sloppy in his methodology. Joel McCrea was surprisingly good in the role, with a distant look in his eyes that lent subtle testimony to the idea that Morton wasn't all that bright.

Yet it was Bill Demarest as the booming Eben Frost who gave the film its juicier moments. The first time Frost appears at Morton's office, Morton unwittingly gives him a lower-grade ether and the patient goes berserk rather than to sleep, crashing through a window and rolling down an awning to the street below. This was the first elaborate stunt Bill Demarest was called upon to perform in a Sturges picture. "Anytime you could get hurt," he recalled, "they had a double on the set. It was usually Jimmie Dundee and he was in your costume and make-up. But with

Sturges, there was always a dare to do it yourself. I made sure the double was there (so he'd get paid), but then I said, 'I'll do it myself,' and I did.''

In one take Demarest went crashing through the candy window, rolled down the awning, landed in the street, got to his feet, and yelled, "The Hessians are coming! Sound the tocsin! Follow me, boys!" and then ran over to the policeman and said, "So there you are, General! I've been looking for you all over the battlefield!"

"I don't know to this day how I got those lines out," he said, "because I had the wind knocked out of me. I couldn't breathe for two minutes!"

Sturges, with a uniformly fine cast, was able to bring *Great Without Glory* in on budget and a day under schedule. It was edited, the prologue filmed (minus the offensive references to the military), and shown to Buddy DeSylva in July. DeSylva criticized the film's construction, saying the story confused him, and would therefore be confusing to the public. Such comments as these began to accumulate and Sturges was at a loss to explain such reactions since *Great Without Glory* was decidedly more chronological than *The Power and the Glory*. Undaunted, he defended his approach to Morton's life, maintaining he really had no choice.

"Unfortunately," said Sturges, "I was not around in 1846 to direct Dr. Morton's life. I had to take it as I found it or construct an entirely fictitious story far removed from fact, as Pasteur was presented with a piece of Semmelweis' work in the Warner Bros. picture. I do not believe in presenting fiction as biography. I believe a biographer has two obligations: he must be true to his subject and he must not bore his public. Since he cannot change the chronology of events, he can only change the order of their presentation. Dr. Morton's life, as lived, was a very bad piece of dramatic construction. He had a few months of excitement ending in triumph and twenty years of disillusionment, boredom, and increasing bitterness.

"My job was not to show the meanness, lack of gratitude, suspicion, and general stupidity of Homo sapiens, which are well known, but rather to show a play about Dr. Morton's life. To have a play you must have a climax and it is better not to have the climax right at the beginning."

When cinematographer John Seitz returned to Paramount after shooting Al Lewin's *The Moon and Sixpence*, Sturges anxiously collared him. "I've been waiting for you for two weeks," Sturges told him. "I want you to see this picture."

Proudly, he ran *Great Without Glory*, certain that Seitz would commend his good judgment. Seitz watched the film in total silence and when the lights came up, Sturges studied his face carefully. "Well, what do you think?"

"Why did you end the picture on the second act?" Seitz wanted to know.

Glumly, Sturges sank back into his chair. "That's exactly what Buddy said."

Slowly, the whole arrangement with Paramount soured. No longer was Sturges the golden boy of 1941, no longer the man who could do no wrong. DeSylva made it clear he intended to assert full authority as executive producer, even though he had indulged Sturges to the point of allowing the film to be made. Now *Great Without Glory* was finished, and although he respected Sturges' talents, DeSylva intended for Sturges to learn a little humility; to recognize his misjudgment and correct the film's obvious deficiencies.

Sturges was not easily swayed. He considered DeSylva's judgment limited at best, but was concerned with what DeSylva could do. His gut feeling told him he had written a fine and serviceable script and had made a wholly admirable film. And he trusted that feeling, just as he had chosen to do with *Recapture* more than a decade before. Dramatically, he *knew* he had made the right decision with the Morton story. DeSylva was full of beans. But he was badly shaken by the respected opinions of others—like Johnny Seitz—whose comments were not so easily dismissed.

Could he have miscalculated his audience so completely? He continually pointed to the example of *The Power and the Glory* and the structure it had, but those who remembered pointed out that that film had flopped and that critics didn't buy tickets. But it was the darkness, the futility of the film that killed it, he countered. The timing wasn't right; it wasn't the construction. But then again, wasn't *Great Without Glory* another cynical lesson in futility? And was that something audiences really needed with the war in Europe quickly gathering momentum? Had Sturges forgotten the message of *Sullivan's Travels*? Or had he considered himself beyond the simple moral it drew?

Great Without Glory was previewed in Glendale as Sturges had intended. Bill Demarest was there, and remembered Buddy DeSylva in the lobby afterward, thumbing through the preview cards. The results were not encouraging. "There's always one guy who'll write 'It stinks,'" said Demarest, "whether it's good or not. The first card said 'It stinks.' Then DeSylva read the next one. It said, 'I was just passing by and I didn't see the picture. I just like to write postcards.' Then he read some more and finally just set the whole stack down. And he said, 'I'll see you at Lucey's* for the next six days!'"

Sturges was unmoved by this initial mixed sampling, but his

*A popular restaurant/bar near the Paramount studios in Hollywood.

colleagues were used to raves at Sturges previews and this reaction was something new and quite different. DeSylva pointed to the indifferent and negative cards and said something definitely was going to have to be done. But just as fervently Sturges embraced the favorable cards—there were a few—pointing to one in particular:

> *Whose performance did you consider best?*
> They were all good.
> *Did the story hold your interest?*
> One of the most informative I've ever seen.
> *What part of the picture should be cut?*
> If you cut anything out of it, you ought to have your heads examined.
> *General Comment*
> Give the studio to Preston Sturges.

DeSylva, unimpressed, put this card in the same pile with the one that said "It stinks."

Sturges' home life suffered as his reputation grew. There was not much time left to play father and husband; only occasionally could he work the family in. His work with the studio, the restaurant, the engine company couldn't wait. His attentions to such items were tendered with urgency. His wealth and position afforded him these things and they would likely not last forever.

Sturges found the life of a famous movie director hard to resist. Not only the money and the press attention, but the fact that he suddenly found himself pursued by all manner of females, those who would crawl into his car and wait for him at night and more prominent ones who would covet his next script and a chance to make a film with him.

"He was a voluptuary," Priscilla Woolfan observed, "but I'm sure he never forced himself on a woman. He was very handsome and very famous; women went after him."

Not that Sturges was away from home all the time; rather he tended to compartmentalize its place in his life. He simply expected it to be there when he wished it. He played with his son at midnight and spent an occasional afternoon in the pool with him. He shot a full case of 16mm color film of the boy—cavorting nude with his nurse, splashing brightly in the water. Occasionally Preston would turn the camera over to Gilletti while he himself stepped into the shot, proudly holding young Mon and flashing his fatherly smile. But he was seldom there and days went by when the baby had no contact with his father. Preston was gone, and Louise was alone . . . the infatuation considerably dimmed as she was relegated to the role of Madame Sturges for photographers and society columns. Preston eventually took up with a shapely young parking attendant whom he chose to make his secretary. Gilletti resigned after *Great Without Glory* to enter the Army. Preston replaced him with this girl, actually a fine secretary. But her place in his life was specific, as was Louise's. "She was his girl," said Priscilla Woolfan of the secretary, "but that was all. She was never included in social functions. I don't recall her ever coming to the house." And Preston kept her until he tired of her.

For her part, Louise tolerated the situation admirably. The vague infidelities, the gradual disaffection, she handled with silence and dignity. But as Preston became more blatant in his philandering, their friends started to divide: one group Preston's, as understanding as possible, the other group Louise's, resentful and disapproving. Louise herself coped as best she could with a young son and an absentee husband. It was something at first that could be handled but then something quite ugly. "Before I was absolutely sure there was anything to it," Louise said, "I sensed it. One night after a preview, an expression of pure venom crossed [the secretary's] face. She looked at me." But, grudgingly, it was something Louise could understand. "He had a great attraction for women," she said. "He was a personable fellow with a great deal of power. And power is a powerful aphrodisiac for women."

As for being a father, Louise commented, "He just wasn't interested. He thought that was something that would come when he was able to converse with him or sit and eat with him. That would come with his post-adolescence." Sturges referred with detachment to his son as "the little boy."

And so it went. He spent his time at the studio and at The Players. With the war on, The Players did well; Sturges seized the opportunity to get the machine shop in on the effort. The diesel engines had never sold, despite Sturges' pouring over $60,000 into the venture. In a genuine effort to turn things around, he converted to a war plant in 1942 and went after government contracts for machine work. "They tried to get some work," said Gilletti, "but none of us really knew how to go about it." Small jobs came in, but hardly enough to show a profit. (Years later, after the shop's demise, he would learn with horror that he had produced—through subcontract—a small fitting that was part of the casing of the atomic bomb dropped on Hiroshima.)

As John L. Sullivan would say, these were troublous times. But Preston Sturges was still safely in Hollywood, and—*Great Without Glory* notwithstanding—still making comedies. *The Palm Beach Story* previewed in mid-October of 1942, and—reassuringly—he had done it again.

"*Palm Beach Story* got very good reception at preview showing today at Paramount theatre, N.Y.," reported a night letter, "both regular audience and Home Office people present. Picture got laughs throughout and applause at end. Sales Department feels in this picture Sturges is back in *Lady Eve* money groove. Please advise Mr. Freeman."

The advertising people prepared posters bearing Sturges' likeness for *The Palm Beach Story*, and it looked as though DeSylva might eventually relent—and allow *Great Without Glory* to go out unhindered. But Sturges' philosophy remained the same: it was essential to keep moving, to keep filming, to keep rolling as long as he could. There was yet much to be done.

Sturges began work on another script—for a rousing and daringly censorable comedy. But the rewards would come too late to help in the conflict ahead. He would make two more films for Paramount, one the biggest hit of his career. Both would be nominated for Academy Awards, but both would be held from release until 1944, after Sturges had left Paramount . . . in a disastrous bid for complete autonomy.

21.

When Preston Sturges began writing *The Miracle of Morgan's Creek, Great Without Glory* had just been assembled and *The Palm Beach Story* was awaiting previews. The conflict between Sturges and Buddy DeSylva had erupted and the chasm appeared to be widening.

The situation was an uncomfortably familiar one. In the days following *Strictly Dishonorable,* New York City crawled with well-meaning advisers like Brock Pemberton, who knew Sturges needed to write another comedy—not a queer tragedy like *Recapture.* These people only served to strengthen the author's resolve to see his play produced, as did the predictors of doom for *The Well of Romance.* Sturges reacted more to questions of his own taste and judgment than the quality of the piece at issue, and usually with disastrous results. In his darkest days, it was this innate faith in himself and his abilities that carried him through—with *The Guinea Pig, The Power and the Glory,* even *The Vagrant.* Now he had assumed the position he had long strived for—and seemingly with more power than at any previous time in his career. He smiled at the irony of *The Power and the Glory* and the ease with which it reached the screen at a time when he had virtually no power or reputation. Now, with an Academy Award and five pictures under his belt, plus a weekly salary of $3250, he had a fine picture languishing in a kind of administrative limbo while Paramount—his willing employer for going on six years—solemnly questioned his excellent judgment and prepared to take the film away from him and cut it to the specifications of an ignoramus like Buddy DeSylva.

It was the kind of situation that naturally played hell with whatever conservative bent Sturges possessed. Again, through pure stubbornness, if nothing else, he would stick to his guns and show the offending parties how needlessly impudent they were. For a more timid soul, it would be time to fall back to safer, more proven territory; to "run for cover," as Alfred Hitchcock later put it. But the forces inside Preston Sturges wouldn't permit such a tactic, and rather than retreat to an easier and safer subject for his next picture, he chose to write a story that no reasonable man could expect to film unhindered. There was, after all, a war going on and censorship was tight. A story about a girl seduced and abandoned by a serviceman was bad enough—but to propose to make a comedy of it was worse. Sturges was clearly asking for trouble, but, amazingly, he encountered little resistance from Buddy DeSylva. DeSylva possibly hoped Sturges would simply hang himself if fed enough rope. Whatever the reasoning, Sturges separated the controversy over the Morton picture from his other affairs with the studio and began writing one of the slickest negotiations of the Production Code ever filmed: *The Miracle of Morgan's Creek*.

The idea dated from 1937, when Sturges was dreaming up stories for the likes of Arthur Hornblow and Al Lewin. At that time he imagined a modern Nativity story with the Virgin Mary in the person of a young, unwed mother-to-be who is saved from suicide by the old town hermit, a part conceived for Harry Carey. But in the wake of *Easy Living*, Sturges' inclinations toward dramatic writing became stalled and *Miracle* spent the next five years fermenting in the dark recesses of his mind where rough ideas—like rough diamonds—were slowly refined. Perhaps in 1937 the idea seemed too close to *Fanny* to be taken seriously. But *Fanny* wasn't a comedy, and when the war broke out the question of promiscuity and illegitimate births took on new prominence.

At Paramount, actress Betty Hutton had adopted Sturges like a groupie, literally begging him to write a part for her. Hutton had been voted a 1941–42 "Star of Tomorrow" for her work with Eddie Bracken in Victor Schertzinger's *The Fleet's In*. A passable singer and dancer, her boisterous personality made her well suited for the kind of military musical popular during the war. And Buddy DeSylva was bullish on Betty Hutton: it was he who had brought her to Hollywood from his own *Panama Hattie* on Broadway. When Sturges began serious dictation of the saga of Trudy Kockenlocker, he imagined Betty Hutton in the lead.

Legend has it that the making of *The Miracle of Morgan's Creek* was prompted by the company's plans to raze a beautiful small-town set that stood unused on the Paramount Ranch. Sturges discovered this and told Buddy DeSylva not to tear it down—that instead he would write a picture for it. And the little town became Morgan's Creek, and its population included Trudy Kockenlocker, Trudy's mouthy little sister Emmy, and the girls' harried father, Constable Kockenlocker.

For the part of Emmy, Sturges settled for young Diana Lynn, who had played a not dissimilar role in Billy Wilder's *The Major and the Minor.* For Constable Kockenlocker, Sturges envisioned no one more perfect than Bill Demarest.

The setup was a classical conflict between father and daughter: Trudy likes a good time, likes to dance and stay out late. Papa, however, is distrusting of any male who looks at his daughter and has about as much faith in her commitment to remaining virtuous as he had in himself at that age. But Trudy gets herself pregnant very near the beginning and the film is not so much about how the problem came to be as what in the world to do about it. Into this mess steps the fourth major character, Norval Jones. Jones is a schnook, the namesake of someone Louise Sturges actually knew in her youth. He is mousy, 4F (sees spots before his eyes), and loves Trudy to the point that he would do absolutely anything for her. Trudy uses poor Norval as a cover to escape from her house on the night of the fateful dance. She leaves him at the movies, borrows his car, and when she reappears the next morning, the car is wrecked, Trudy is pregnant, and—worst of all—she can't even remember the name of the father. Sturges wanted Andy Devine to play Norval, but DeSylva opted for Eddie Bracken and Sturges, who had seen Bracken work with Hutton, had no objections.

"But I didn't want to work with Betty Hutton again," Eddie Bracken recalled. "Not because of Betty—because I loved Betty, I loved working with her—it was just that all the pictures I did with her were my pictures but they were using me to build up Betty Hutton. There was nothing wrong with that except that when I would go to see the movies, I would find about five Betty Hutton numbers in there that I didn't know were in the picture. All of a sudden she was killing all the people with her singing and I became almost a supporting player for Betty. I didn't want to do it again unless I knew the number of songs and had the same amount so that it would at least even itself out. I felt deceived. And what was worse, I felt I couldn't trust anybody.

"So when *Miracle of Morgan's Creek* came up, I didn't want to do it, knowing full well that there'd be five Betty Hutton numbers in it."

Bracken cautiously agreed to meet with Sturges and accepted his word of honor that there would be no Betty Hutton numbers in the picture. Then Bracken read the script and found the whole film was about Betty Hutton—or so he thought.

"Preston said, 'Don't worry. This is the part that'll steal the picture.' So I said, 'OK, let's go.'"

As Sturges was finishing the script and making plans to shoot, Paramount submitted the first 116 pages to the Breen office to see how much trouble they might be in for. Predictably, the one or two cautionary pages a new script normally generated were supplanted by a full seven pages of single-spaced objections. With a starting date rapidly approaching, Paramount's own in-house censor Luigi Luraschi requested a face-to-face meeting with Sturges and Joseph I. Breen to help iron out differences and, in fact, to determine whether the film could ever enjoy MPPDA approval. The conclusion of this lengthy meeting was that it *could*, but that the required changes would be numerous and could possibly undermine the entire film. Said Breen, in his supplemental memo of the next day, ". . . much of this material in the present script . . . appears to us to be unacceptable, not only from the standpoint of the Production Code, but, likewise, from the viewpoint of political censorship." Breen was referring especially to the implying of sexual promiscuity on the part of the armed forces and that as a result illegitimate pregnancies were on the rise. "We should like, again, to repeat the observation we made yesterday, with reference to the imperative necessity of our being extremely careful in handling a subject of this kind because of the delicate nature of the high point of the story. It seems to us to be necessary merely to establish the several points important to the telling of the story, and then 'get away from them.'"

Breen proceeded to note each one of the objections discussed at the meeting, to most all of which Sturges acceded:

"Page 6: We suggest that you change the name of the clergyman from Upperman to something else. This because the name has a comedy flavor which is not good when used in connection with a clergyman.

"Page 8: Scene B-8: This scene, it seems to us, should be carefully rewritten to get away from its present unacceptability. To this end we suggest the substitution of the word 'held' for the word 'committed' in the father's line. We also suggest the elimination from Trudy's speech of the following: '. . . and then kinda . . . out to a roadhouse somewhere and then you know . . . like that . . .'

"Page 15: We again call your attention to the line 'It starts in the church basement,' and suggest, again, that it be amended. We also call your attention, again, to the stuttering of Norval, and we suggest that this be eliminated entirely. [Sturges balked at this.]

"Page 33: Here we have the first broad reference to the fact that Trudy is pregnant. In accordance with the suggestions we made yesterday, we would respectfully suggest that all the material set forth on pages 33, 34, 35, 36, and 37, having to do with the pregnancy of the girl, be drastically cut down and the matter entirely rewritten."

Breen allowed that Trudy's pregnancy was both "agreeable—and necessary for plot purposes," but said it was unacceptable to hit the point several times, as Sturges had. This was the meat of the problem as far as Breen's comments were concerned, although he was also strongly against any reference to Trudy's being drunk at the time of her indiscretion.

Primarily, the code picked at single words and isolated lines, urging caution in dealing with the matters of pregnancy and drunkenness. Sturges was ready for the major objections, promptly marrying Trudy off before her affair occurred and establishing that she was dazed by an accidental conk on the head rather than strong drink. These solutions eased much of the concern over broad sections of the story. Through it all, it was apparent that Breen liked the basic screenplay Sturges had written and his comments were offered with sympathy. There was still much rethinking and rewriting to be done, at the direction not only of Joseph I. Breen and the MPPDA, but of the War Department Pictorial Board, which carefully passed on the portrayal of American servicemen in the picture (the "political censorship" Breen referred to), and of Luigi Luraschi and Paramount itself. These comments are indicative of the responsibility the studio felt in not encouraging undesirable behavior on the part of the citizenry. From Luraschi's office:

"Page B-10: I wonder if you could use possibly a funny toot on the horn to be the signal that Norval has arrived, rather than the sound of brakes and tires, which, of course, are contrary to the rubber conservation program."

With all these reviews occurring and his starting date set for the twenty-first, Sturges did something he had never done before: he began production on *The Miracle of Morgan's Creek* without a completed script, shooting an eight-hour day and then writing most of the night.

Filming began on schedule with Hutton, Lynn, Bracken, Demarest, and the usual collection of Sturges character actors. But there was an urgency to *Miracle* that hadn't previously pervaded a Sturges picture, an uncertainty as to where the film was going when it began, and a competition between two young and ambitious performers.

"Because of the way I was deceived," said Eddie Bracken, "I decided I was going to work every magical trick I ever learned in my life, including upstaging, downstaging, moving with actors, everything I could think of to maneuver myself into position. I came up with the stuttering, and the spots before my eyes, and the nervous twitch, and all the other things that came out. When Betty Hutton was upstage, I'd walk in front of her downstage; I'd be in focus and she'd be out of focus. It was a professional fight on stage, but it wasn't a fight with Betty, it was a fight with the studio."

The picture acquired a kind of kinetic energy, aided by Bracken's determination to hold his ground and Sturges' uncertainty over an incomplete screenplay. Any of the three leading actors—Hutton, Bracken, or Demarest—could well have dominated a less carefully balanced picture. But Sturges tended toward ensemble pieces and even the lesser cast members had showy dialogues, like nasal Al Bridge, who played the lawyer Trudy consults. "The responsibility for recording a marriage has always been up to the woman," he drawls. "Wasn't for her, marriage would have disappeared long since. No man is going to jeopardize his present or poison his future with a lot of little brats hollerin' around the house, 'less he's forced to. It's up to the woman to knock him down, hogtie him, and drag him in front of two witnesses immediately, if not sooner. Anytime after that is too late."

Slight and jittery, far from handsome, Eddie Bracken played Norval Jones to perfection. Betty Hutton was expertly brassy and rambunctious as Trudy, and Bill Demarest gave a performance of Academy Award caliber. Sturges set up long dialogues between Demarest and the daughters. Then, to save time, he specifically picked John F. Seitz, with whom he had shot the long opening to *Sullivan's Travels* and with whom he could shoot these and other wordy scenes without question and without stopping.

Demarest, a tough and crabby old crumb, allows himself to be bullied by both his daughters, especially his youngest. Emmy is vastly superior to his suspiciousness and bluster and when he tells Trudy she can't go to the dance, Emmy informs him he has "a mind like a swamp," then disappears out of frame as he rears back to kick her and falls flat on his rear. Demarest was the butt of a lot of slapstick, which seemed appropriate to the picture's volume and pace.

"Every goddamn thing was falling," he later complained. "They finally called me Pratfall Demarest." After several flat falls winding up to boot young Emmy, he fell two stories helping Norval escape from jail.

Sturges shot two largely expository scenes between Hutton and Bracken in long tracking shots that literally covered blocks. "At four o'clock in the afternoon, the studio heads would come down and have big arguments with Sturges because he didn't have anything shot for the day," Eddie Bracken recalled. "But between four and six in the afternoon, he may have eleven pages." Sturges would spend the day rehearsing the camera and his actors and then—based on the average of three and a half pages a day—suddenly accomplish three days' work in a single take.

With the pressures of simultaneously filming and writing, arguing over *Great Without Glory*, seeing to the release of *The Palm Beach Story*, and the running of his restaurant, Sturges' temper was uncommonly pronounced. He brooked nothing short of perfection on this set and was inclined to explode at even minor infractions. The tension was evident.

"Preston was a Dr. Jekyll and Mr. Hyde," said Bracken. "He was Christ and he was Satan. He would hire Mack Sennett comedy people—people that weren't working—and put them to work, love them, talk to them, and then verbally beat them when they got onto the set. Verbally ridicule them. Brought them down. But as far as they were concerned he was just almost like God. Even though he was beating them verbally. I felt sorry for them many, many times.

"But he would bring everybody down. Betty Hutton and Diana Lynn cried at least ten times on the set from a verbal onslaught of Preston's."

Yet Bracken didn't feel it was simply fatigue that limited Sturges' patience. "He did it to get a performance out of them; to put them off guard and get something good out of them. That was the reason. Not for showing that he was the boss."

And he did indeed get a good performance out of Betty Hutton. "I am not a great singer," she later told *Life* magazine, "and I am not a great dancer, but I am a great actress and nobody ever let me act except Preston Sturges. He believed in me."

Pressure increased as costs mounted and it became evident that *Miracle* would go way over schedule and budget. Y. Frank Freeman dourly expressed his dismay at Sturges' average of only 2.7 pages a day, pointing to one especially costly day when Sturges shot a half-page scene 104 times and then used the second take. With less time to think out a scene, Sturges found it increasingly difficult to direct his actors. "Look at Betty Hutton and Julius Tannen," said Bill Demarest. "He shot their little scene twenty times!"

"Sturges was a perfectionist with a capital *P*," said actor Emory Parnell, who played Eddie Bracken's boss, Mr. Tuerck. "Every word, every inflection had to be letter-perfect."

But Sturges qualified this perfectionism as something more than desperation on the part of a writer who had seen his stuff altered once too often in the hands of other directors. "If anyone should know how a scene should be played," he said, "it is the fellow who wrote it in the first place. Or so I once thought. I agreed with very few directors when I was merely writing. They argued tremendously, and sometimes they lost out. I look upon them now as brave fellows who went down with their colors flying. I don't, as a director, film a scene exactly as the writer—who was myself— wrote it."

Sturges pressed on, still writing, still refining, and finally, when the plot was hopelessly tangled and there seemed to be absolutely no way of unraveling it, he had Trudy give birth to sextuplets—and then filmed a wraparound with Brian Donlevy and Akim Tamiroff as McGinty and The Boss that proceeded to tell the whole story in flashback. With the governor's magical powers, all McGinty needs to do is wave his hand and the terrible tragedy becomes a marvelous spotlight for the glorious state in which they live. Norval and Trudy are married and Sturges' parting words for Norval the schnook are from Shakespeare: "Some are born great, some achieve greatness, and some have greatness thrust upon them."

Filming on *The Miracle of Morgan's Creek* ran into Christmas of 1942 and finished on December 28. A rough cut was assembled in early February and shown to DeSylva, who was, by this time, poring over every line of dialogue, trying to anticipate further offenses to either the MPPDA or the regional censor boards that dotted the country. The Catholic Legion of Decency requested several changes beyond those of the Breen office in order to shift their rating from a "C" (Condemned) to a "B" (Morally Objectionable in Part for All). DeSylva acceded to their changes, and, in late February, Sturges reopened production for a day's revisions. DeSylva then acknowledged there was little chance of their obtaining an "A-2" (Adults) without emasculating the picture, and allowed it to stand as of March 1943.

The Palm Beach Story had done well that last December but not spectacularly, and the reviews were oddly mixed. Bosley Crowther complained it was "generally slow and garrulous." It was the New York *Times*'s first pan of a Sturges picture, and with *Great Without Glory* in disarray, there was fear that Sturges was losing his "touch." And because it was so atypical of Sturges' work, DeSylva doubted that *The Miracle of Morgan's Creek* had much potential as a hit. Certainly the cast was no advantage and it was only the cost of the film and Sturges' name that kept it from looking like a standard "B"; it seemed anything but surefire. Still, the preview audiences roared at it.

Paramount at this time had a tremendous backlog of finished films, so many in fact that they had arranged to sell a total of eleven, including three major features and eight Harry Sherman Westerns, to United Artists in mid-1942. The deal effectively rid Paramount of the Westerns (six were Hopalong Cassidys) and the bait was Sturges and Clair's *I Married a Witch*, which went to U.A. with the others at cost. DeSylva could therefore afford to re-edit *Great Without Glory* (which he did) and hold *Miracle* while other, more "commercial" films took precedence. This annoyed Sturges, who began work on his next screenplay with two pictures in the can and no release dates on the schedule.

Hail the Conquering Hero, Sturges' eighth film for Paramount, began life as a story for Eddie Bracken called *The Little Marine*. Sturges was thrilled with the actor's work in *Miracle* and the two became close friends. "He was a father, big brother, and buddy to me," said Bracken. Intrigued with the premise of the schnook as Great Man, Sturges wrote *The Little Marine* around a variation of the Norval Jones character Bracken had played so beautifully in *Miracle*. This time, however, there would be no Betty Hutton with whom he would have to share the screen. Although the film was Bracken's, Sturges would come to embrace it as his own finest work.

One of the qualities that made *Hail the Conquering Hero* memorable was the utter simplicity of its plot. The initial idea was to write a story about a man who steals a military uniform. And why would someone steal a uniform? To pose as a serviceman. Applied to a Norval Jones-type character, Sturges reasoned that he was 4F and unable to return home. He had a mother and, of course, a girl. And so a deception begins: he writes two letters home about shipping out and arriving in Europe. Then silence. And all the while, he works out the war in a shipyard in San Francisco. One night in a bar he encounters a group of six Marines from Guadalcanal. Sullenly, Bracken buys them beer and sandwiches and tells them his story. He finds the Sergeant who heads the group had served with his father in the First World War ("He was my sergeant. . . . I saw him fall"). With the connection thus established, the Marines decide to help the kid out by taking him home on the train and delivering him into the arms of his mother . . . quietly, in the guise of a wounded hero. The phone call is made before Bracken knows what's happening. And the deception compounds itself for the rest of the film.

Hail the Conquering Hero was a modest picture, designed to be shot on the Morgan's Creek sets with a minimum of fuss. Sturges larded his script with long tracking shots and frenzied crowd scenes peppered with cheering bumpkins and the character people he so loved. The writing took ten weeks and an inordinate amount of revision as the War Department Pictorial Board again examined Sturges' portrayal of servicemen and required adjustments. But the premise was solid and the story compelling.

Sturges finished casting the film in early June. Aside from Eddie Bracken as Woodrow and Bill Demarest as the Sergeant, he selected a young Universal starlet, Ella Raines, for the part of Bracken's sweetheart, Libby. This choice especially annoyed Buddy DeSylva, as Raines was a complete unknown and her first Universal picture, *Corvette K-225*, was not yet in release. But casting had brought her to Sturges' attention and something about her appealed to him. She was appropriately small-town, not a voluptuous beauty; someone whom audiences could readily buy in the part. Sturges had her read for him and gave her the part. Now DeSylva had a picture with even less star power than *Miracle:* Eddie Bracken, William Demarest, and Ella Raines. About the only selling point the studio could find for the film would be the fact that Sturges had made it. And with both *Miracle* and *Great Without Glory* on hold, that might not mean much by the time it got released.

DeSylva didn't like Ella Raines, didn't like her acting, her name, or the fact that they had to borrow her from Universal. He petitioned Sturges to drop her and use one of their own people. But Sturges was in no mood to be conciliatory. His contract was up in December and he was planning to look around; he was certainly not going to tie himself to a man like Buddy DeSylva for the next seven years. He frankly didn't care if DeSylva liked Ella Raines or not. He owed them a picture both written and directed by him. The saving grace of *Hail the Conquering Hero* was that it wouldn't cost much to make. No $150,000 off the top for a star like Claudette Colbert. No expensive exteriors to be built. There was little DeSylva could do other than allow Sturges to go ahead and film. Whatever displeased him would have to wait until filming was over—when DeSylva could again do what he wished.

Shooting began on July 14 and progressed through early September. As the first rushes became available, DeSylva again harped about Ella Raines. Raines, it seemed, was a problem. "Ella Raines couldn't remember her own name," complained one cast member. Sturges himself told the story of the time Raines complained about the color her dressing room had been painted. "I asked her to imagine herself on her deathbed," he related. "She was eighty years old. She was drawing her last breath. Now, at that moment, she recalled herself at twenty, on the threshold of her career, possessed of youth, health, beauty, fame, wealth, and everything else she wanted. I asked her whether she would want to remember, at that last moment, that she had allowed a whole day, or even one of those golden minutes, to be spoiled just because a painter had made the walls the wrong color."

But while DeSylva found Raines an irritant, Eddie Bracken's work was undeniably excellent. "I was courting my wife at the time," recalled Rudy Vallée, "so I took her over to the Paramount lot to watch a scene with Eddie Bracken. And Eddie did that long three- or four-minute scene about the Marines and his dad and reciting all the battles to these boys at the bar in *one take.* Of course, we all applauded and Sturges was so proud of the fact that he had written it and that Eddie could do it in one take."

When Woodrow and the Marines arrive in Oakridge, instead of slipping into town quietly as they had planned, the train is greeted by the entire populace. Sturges surveys the various small-town caricatures. Woodrow's mother (Georgia Caine) stands proudly off to one side. (There was a lot of "momism" built into this picture, not only with Eddie Bracken's Boy Scout devotion but with boxer Freddie Steele's character of Bugsy—a simpleminded fighting man who never had a mother of his own and whose line throughout the story is, "You shouldn't do that to your mother." Sturges wrote a song for the film he called "Home to the Arms of Mother.")

Libby, unknown to Woodrow, has become engaged to Forrest Noble, a handsome young civilian. Noble is in civvies, the dialogue reveals, because he too is afflicted with chronic hay fever. Libby reminds him pointedly that hay fever didn't stop Woodrow.

Forrest's father is the bombastic mayor, played with relish by Raymond Walburn. Mrs. Noble is Esther Howard, the Progressive Band Leader is Vic Potel, and Jimmy Conlin is Judge Dennis. Faced with all this, Woodrow panics. The six Marines stuff him, sneezing and screaming, "Let me outta here!" into a uniform and push him out into the midst of the reception. Woodrow is now trapped in this charade, unable to bring himself to disappoint the townspeople and, especially, Libby and his mother. Worse, all this hero worship refuses to melt away. The mania builds to the point where he is drafted to run for mayor. And frustration builds as the noose tightens and Woodrow is finally brought to his denouncement in as Capraesque a moment as Sturges ever permitted himself.

Hail the Conquering Hero was completed in mid-September and ready for previews by the middle of November. There were two sneaks, the second on December 9, 1943, and the audience comments were carefully tabulated.

"Get rid of some of the sentimentality," ordered one card. "I love my mother, too."

Another said, "Don't wave the flag so much. It's a good yarn, don't spoil it by getting patriotic—it's a comedy, not a drama— also fix that grade C beginning—it crawls."

"Aside from excessive noise which could be toned down, the picture in wartime will be OK. I would not predict a box-office attraction for this film."

"It has a good plot except overdone in parts. It isn't Eddie Bracken's type of picture but he did very well."

"I think *Hail the Conquering Hero* is the best picture I have seen and no other picture could be better."

But the preview of the ninth would result in no further refinements, at least not by Preston Sturges. The cards were mixed, and DeSylva was threatening more cuts and retakes. Sturges' contract expired the following day and he left Paramount to strike out on his own. He had been happy there in the sense that he knew the support people—editors, grips, make-up people, and the waitresses in the commissary—but he was increasingly frustrated by the arbitrary way in which DeSylva meddled in his work. DeSylva recut *Great Without Glory*, putting the sequences in chronological order and cutting for comedy rather than drama, removing every hint of Morton's "great moment" (his sacrifice) until the very last reel. Worse still, he was now making noises about similar action against *Hail the Conquering Hero*. Sturges' agreement with Paramount brought him $3250 a week, a $30,000 director's bonus per film, and absolutely no leverage against such interference. So when negotiations for a new contract began, Sturges demanded a switch on the traditional seven-year contract with options.

"In other words," said Sturges later, "I didn't want to be exposed to a long and humiliating series of experiences such as the one I had just been through with Buddy. No man of value could stand it very long. If he could stand it, he would no longer be a man of value."

Sturges recalled his last meeting with DeSylva and Henry Ginsberg clearly.

"I was very happy here without any contract at all . . ." he told them, "twenty-five hundred a week and thirty days' notice either way. My loyalty and affection to you was my contract and the privilege of giving thirty days' notice was a protection for both sides. I am very anxious to stay here and continue to work for you. I realize quite well that I cannot make the final cutting decisions on a picture because that would make it my property instead of yours, but you must realize also that I work very hard to make a picture, spend many months with it before it is shot, and am certainly closer to it than anyone else.

"Your production head is undoubtedly a better production head than I am, but I am very probably a better director than he is and certainly much more familiar with my immediate problem. Therefore, I ask that at the conclusion of each picture, for a period of two weeks, I have the right to abrogate my contract—not for the purpose of holding a club over your head, because I love Paramount and do not want to leave, but merely to cause your production head, whoever he may be, to treat me with the courtesy due a grown man of known integrity and not like an irresponsible child."

Sturges knew his value on the open market and what people like Zanuck and Goldwyn would pay for his services. It was the closest he could come to "final cut" in the days when such an agreement was unheard of. They refused to go for it. DeSylva wouldn't agree to such an arrangement and Ginsberg supported him. And so Sturges was, as he put it, "forced out" of Paramount

. . . with three pictures unreleased and two in grave danger of alteration.

Sturges spent a restless Christmas, exploring offers and independent production possibilities and monitoring the progress of his Paramount films. *The Miracle of Morgan's Creek* was being readied for release, its success critical to Sturges' future. If it hit big, Sturges would be in a position to dictate terms at another studio. And it would help in his fight to keep *Great Without Glory* and *Hail the Conquering Hero* intact. Sturges refrained from commenting about the break with Paramount publicly; it was in fact several weeks before Louise Sturges discovered it had occurred. But when he spoke of it privately, it was with a real and lasting bitterness toward Buddy DeSylva—the man who forced an end to Sturges' Paramount cycle, the most successful period of his life.

The Miracle of Morgan's Creek opened in New York on January 19, 1944, and Sturges could not have written a better reception. Business was strong from the opening day and the reviews were as fine as for *Strictly Dishonorable, The Great McGinty,* and *The Lady Eve.* Wrote Bosley Crowther, "The watchmen for the usually prim Hays office certainly permitted themselves a Jovian nod when confronted with the irrepressible impudence of Preston Sturges' *The Miracle of Morgan's Creek.* For a more audacious picture—a more delightfully irreverent one—than this new lot of nonsense at the Paramount has never come slithering madly down the path. Mr. Sturges, who is noted for his railleries of the sentimental, the pompous and the smug in his classics, *The Great McGinty, Sullivan's Travels,* and *The Lady Eve,* has hauled off this time and tossed a satire which is more cheeky than all the rest."

Business was startlingly heavy. Extra showings were scheduled on Broadway and the lines were still hours long. *The Miracle of Morgan's Creek* became the number-one topic of conversation— by those who were outraged and those who saw it as the beginning of a new era of freedom for the screen. Critic James Agee, in *The Nation,* wrote that "the Hays office has been either hypnotized into a liberality for which it should be thanked, or has been raped in its sleep."

Within a week, the trade papers had *Miracle* pegged as the undisputed hit of the new year. In theatres throughout the country, *Miracle* played to capacity houses. The national magazines picked up on the film and, once again, Sturges found himself pictured in their pages. Agee, in *Time,* said *Miracle* was "a little like talking to a nun on a roller coaster." Again there appeared thumbnail biographies of the writer-director, just as there had for *The Lady Eve* some three years earlier. *Time* printed an old picture of Sturges on his pogo stick over the caption, "I didn't want to be an artist. . . ."

Best of all, *The Miracle of Morgan's Creek*, being controversial, generated a lot of word of mouth. Audiences who loved the film laughed hysterically. The ones who didn't complained loudly and wrote indignant letters. Sturges answered one, tongue slightly in cheek, with the following:

"In making *The Miracle of Morgan's Creek* I succeeded in pleasing most of the motion picture critics in this country and in England. I was judged by a jury of men and women whose minds, education, and knowledge of playwriting I respect totally. They liked my work and on that I rest my case. It so happens that I intended *The Miracle of Morgan's Creek* as anything *but* evil, meretricious, and destructive of moral standards. I wanted to show what happens to young girls who disregard their parents' advice and who confuse patriotism with promiscuity. As I do not work in a church, I tried to adorn my sermon with laughter, so that people would see it instead of staying away from it. I obviously failed in this since you found it anything *but* funny. For failing to make you laugh then, I apologize, but I refuse to plead guilty to 'contributing to the deliquency of minors.' "

Miracle drew a tremendous amount of repeat business, as its defenders and champions brought their friends to see it. And in a matter of two months it had surpassed the figures amassed by *The Lady Eve*. *The Miracle of Morgan's Creek* became the biggest hit of 1944. In one year it would rake in a total of almost $9 million.

Sturges gloated as every major studio tendered generous offers—including a newly repentant Paramount. DeSylva had made good on his threat to cut the talkier passages from *Hail the Conquering Hero*, but after a disastrous preview of the film in New York in February, Sturges offered to return, free of charge, to adjust *Hail* and *Great Without Glory* to everyone's satisfaction. With *Miracle* taking in millions at the box office, Sturges' judgment began to look not quite so defective and DeSylva was persuaded to relent. Sturges wrote a new ending for *Hail the Conquering Hero* and did four days of retakes in early April with DeSylva's approval. He then spent the rest of that month restoring the film to his original vision. It previewed again with better results, and although Sturges felt comfortable with it, it wasn't a crowd-pleaser like *Miracle*. DeSylva let the film stand, and an ad campaign was designed to lean heavily on the fact it was "from Preston Sturges, who gave you *The Miracle of Morgan's Creek*."

Sturges cynically predicted that *Hail* wouldn't do well alongside *Miracle* and that the critics would react negatively to all the recent praise. And DeSylva, though thinly appreciative of his work with *Hail*, held on to *Great Without Glory*, stoutly refusing to let Sturges touch it. Angrily, Sturges withdrew again, knowing he could never return to Paramount as long as DeSylva remained and figuring the situation would be similar wherever he went. Executives were executives, with the tastes of maggots. There had to be a better way.

Hail the Conquering Hero was released in August of 1944 and the critics, at least, accorded it the same reception as *Miracle*. The notices were uniformly excellent and still more space was given over to Sturges himself. In any year, either picture would qualify as a masterwork; for them both to appear within eight months of one another was incredible. The headline in *Life* magazine read, "A sympathetic satirist of sacred conventions directs his second conspicuous film hit of the year." *Look*'s said, "The 'Toscanini of the pratfall' makes his ninth [*sic*] and last movie for Paramount."

The New York *Times:*

"Don't let anyone tell you that Preston Sturges is just a maker of madcap films, of gloriously impudent satires which are basically frivolous withal. Mr. Sturges is just about the sharpest and most rational Hollywood Magi on the job—a fellow with a searching way of looking at the follies of us rather silly folks. And now that his *Hail the Conquering Hero* has come to the Paramount, you can see this beyond any question that might persist from his former excellent films. For this riotously funny motion picture, this superlative small-town comedy, is also one of the wisest ever to burst from a big-time studio."

Wrote Sturges to Charley Abramson, "I am quite astonished at the reception given this modest little picture. It proves that a good story can lick its weight in stars and pomposity any day. That is a very wholesome and gratifying realization."

Of *Great Without Glory*, scheduled for release in November as *The Great Moment*, Sturges said, "My next picture is coming out in its present form over my dead body. The decision to cut this picture for comedy and leave out the bitter side was the beginning of my rupture with Paramount. They did the same thing to *Hail the Conquering Hero*, but through a last-minute maneuver I was able to get the picture back into shape. I was unable to do so in the case of *The Great Moment*. The dignity, the mood, the important parts of the picture are in the ash can. It will probably get one star and a half in the *News* and I will be advised to stick, hereafter, to what I know."

Business for *The Great Moment* was slack from the start, in spite of a dignified Paramount ad campaign that heralded FROM THE MAN WHO GAVE YOU "THE MIRACLE OF MORGAN'S CREEK"

AND "HAIL THE CONQUERING HERO." Dissuaded by a lackluster response, the ads for the Picture's British release sold it as an outright comedy: HILARIOUS AS A WHIFF OF LAUGHING GAS.

Paramount could not help but sell *The Great Moment* on the strength of *Miracle* and *Hail*, but both critics and audiences were plainly bewildered by DeSylva's butcherblock editing. Even the kind notices were tempered with reserve. The picture, to this day, has failed to find an audience as anything more than an oddity. Sturges, of course, was bitterly disappointed; *The Great Moment* became his first bona fide flop as a director. But what made it worse was that the reviewers knew nothing of Sturges' differences with DeSylva and assumed *The Great Moment* to be in the exact form he had intended. So there was vague confusion over a man who could so expertly produce both *Miracle* and *Hail* and then turn around and make a film like *The Great Moment*. The inevitable comparisons were uneasy and artificial.

"The change of mood is not completely successful," hedged the Chicago *Sun*, "the picture is by no means another *Miracle of Morgan's Creek* or *Sullivan's Travels*."

The New York *World Telegram* said, "*The Great Moment* is one current item that defies any classification. Its theme is serious, the development of anesthesia. But the picture was made by the deft virtuoso of farce and laughter, Preston Sturges, and he couldn't resist slipping in a lot of his own maniacally inspired funny stuff. The result alternates between being diverting and bewildering."

Generally, the film was not slammed as badly as Sturges had predicted. The critical community seemed reluctant to offer a man with his track record anything other than encouragement.

"As a veteran admirer of Sturges pictures," consoled Bosley Crowther, "this writer is fain to agree that a most propitious blend of mood and manner has not been accomplished in this film. Frankly, we feel that Mr. Sturges would rather have kidded his man, that his native bent toward satire inevitably got in his way. But that is not altogether damaging—for our taste, anyhow. We know Dr. Morton much better than we would if he had been sanctified. And the style of presenting this film is one which we'd like to see attempted more frequently by Hollywood. There are ever so many whited sepulchres in the dictionaries of biographies that could do with a little tactful mauling. And Mr. Sturges is the man who could do it, all right."

In spite of *The Great Moment*, 1944 was a red-letter year. Sturges received not one, but two nominations for Academy Awards for his scripts for *The Miracle of Morgan's Creek* and *Hail the Conquering Hero*. And every studio in California was clamoring for his services. But Sturges was no longer interested in working for somebody else; he was interested in making films of his own, under his complete and absolute control. And so he formed a partnership—with one of the most erratic and colorful business-men of the twentieth century.

When told of this, John F. Seitz simply shook his head. "I hope it's successful," he said, "but nobody's ever gotten the best of Howard Hughes."

22.

Preston Sturges left Paramount a different man than the screen-writer who began his tenure there in 1936. Doubtless it was the fact that Sturges wrote and directed eight major films in a four-year period that contributed chiefly to his metamorphosis, augmented as it was by the publicity machine of Paramount Pictures and the attendant media. But all this was coupled with Sturges' own peculiar genius for self-promotion and his playing the role of flamboyant movie director with such obvious relish.

Sturges grew quickly to appreciate the childhood his mother had allowed him, if not for the experience then for the ripping good copy it made for interviewers and critics who wished to probe deeply into his psyche and speculate as to what was responsible for the things he wrote. This, he learned, naturally prompted such people to devote more space to his films, and consequently, to him. And after a while, it was not so much what they said that mattered but simply that they had said *something*.

"I thought he was too eager for publicity no matter where it came from and what was said about him," said Louise Sturges. "His attitude was 'Spell my name right.' In fact, just *say* it."

Sturges caught on to the game of attracting attention in an industry where attention literally meant survival and the competition for it was fierce. That he began writing and directing his films at a time when virtually no one else (save, of course, Chaplin) did was enough to begin with. The childhood anecdotes he could tell by the hour lent further credence to the studio label of "genius," and he easily converted his own individualistic habits of living and working into genuine eccentricities, those charming quirks of personality expected of most all exceptional people. In this respect, he seemed to model himself after Cecil B. DeMille—the undisput-ed king of the Paramount lot whose position Sturges openly coveted and whose flashy attire and regal manner he adopted to a point approaching parody. But Sturges, after all, was a humorist and, admittedly, as big a ham as DeMille. Sturges' table in the Paramount commissary was patterned after DeMille's and, in fact, positioned directly opposite it. Sturges, like DeMille, was always conscious of an audience and played to it whether it was simply Priscilla and Bert Woolfan or a nationally syndicated columnist like Hedda Hopper. "Sturges was always on stage," said Eddie Bracken. "Always."

His office, which began as a modest cubicle in the writers' building in 1936, became a showplace for both friends and journalists. Among the innovations were an antique auto horn with which he summoned his secretary and an elaborate three-sided desk that boxed in said secretary. When dictating, Sturges could pace freely and reverse the time-honored arrangement of the desk-enshrined boss and the free-roaming office help. Sturges was pictured in the pages of *Life* magazine with this creation, which was twenty-five feet in length and supported by a bookcase, file cabinets, and an aquarium on one side. In contrast to this innovational environment was a liberal helping of disarray which, people presumed, was calculated to further distinguish its occupant from his colleagues. "It bears about as much resemblance to a Hollywood office as did the apartment of the late Alexander Woollcott," wrote Alexander King in *Vogue*. "The staff, by now completely demoralized by his distaste for protocol, is constantly serving casual visitors with the best food and drink that can be mustered by the owner of a fine restaurant." No article on Preston Sturges failed to comment on some aspect of his office or his pose as an artist. "We had an hour with him after he had just finished *Palm Beach Story*," reported Idwal Jones in the New York *Times*. "He was disposed half in his swivel chair, half on his desk, in the attitude of a man overcome by sunstroke. Eyes half shut, he was playing with the window cord, and within reach of his head was a telephone on easy-tongs. By his side was one of those red soft-drink tanks, bottles and chunks of ice and labels awash in water. The general aspect of the office was that of a freight caboose after a rough journey overland! Papers, books, and letters were strewn everywhere."

Sturges proudly pointed to the long hours he worked and made much of the fact he slept a maximum of only four hours a night. The trick, he said, was simply in attitude and the brief little catnaps he took whenever things got slow. A book he bought by the case was called *How Never to Be Tired or Two Lifetimes in One* by Marie Beynon Ray. He passed out copies to friends and associates. "But he gave those out as a joke," said Charley Abramson.

At The Players, Sturges installed such amenities as a revolving bandstand, which, he said, allowed him to switch bands without missing a note; and a perambulating wall that enlarged the dining room at the touch of a button. Booths were equipped with tables that swung out for easy seating. On the mezzanine level, he outfitted a barbershop and gave it to his barber (who eventually made enough money to return to Italy and retire). Sturges always had his own hair cut at the house. "When a man reaches the station in life I have," he said, "he has the barber come to him."

Sturges' home was no less a showcase than The Players or the studio, and Louise, whom Alexander King said "looks like a *Vogue* model and talks like Rebecca West," was one of the fixtures. She dutifully posed for pictures and kept up the tradition of the Sunday parties, but it had become only too clear by 1944 that Preston was more interested in appearances than an actual home life and she grew understandably restless. Preston proudly showed her off as he did little Mon, his model trains, his dressing room with the self-designed shoe shelves, his swimming pool, his massive library, his collection of ship models, and his barbecue ovens (of which he had eight). The headline on the *Vogue* article appropriately read, "The Toscanini of the pratfall, writer and director of the new movie 'Hail the Conquering Hero,' he lives his own legend as though it were one of his swaggering, charming, gutsy movies, filled with character bits."

James Agee picked up on this image in *The Nation*, attempting to explain why Sturges functioned as he did. He wrote, " 'Hollywood' is no explanation, surely; 'Hollywood' was made for Sturges and he in turn is its apotheosis; but why? It seems to me that Sturges had reason, through his mother, to develop, as they caromed around high-Bohemian Europe during his childhood, from opera to opera and gallery to gallery, not only his singular mecurialism and resourcefulness, which come especially natural to some miserably unhappy children, but also a wretching, permanently incurable loathing for everything that stank of 'culture,' of 'art.' I gather further that through his stepfather, a stable and charming Chicago sportsman and businessman, he developed an all but desperate respect and hunger for success, enhanced by a sickening string of failures as a businessman and inventor up to the age of about thirty; and that this again assumed the dimensions of a complex. I believe that in his curious career as a never-quite-artist of not-quite-genius he has managed to release and guide the energies of these influences in the only way open to him."

Sturges was able to achieve identity for his Paramount pictures as a body of work comparable to those of Hitchcock, Ford, Chaplin, or Lubitsch. That critics wrote of the Sturges "genius" was enough to establish his own school of Hollywood satire, although Sturges chose to refer to himself more generically as "a modern American humorist, working in film." The fact that he was a colorful dresser with an interesting office and a popular restaurant merely served to strengthen the association between Preston Sturges and the films of Preston Sturges, much as the late Alfred Hitchcock capitalized on the exposure he gained from his weekly television series.

Wrote Bosley Crowther, "In a spotlighted business community which honors and rewards personal flash, Mr. Sturges has quite a reputation for elegant eccentricity. And his worldly and picturesque deportment has all the evident earmarks of an act. As a matter of fact, it is likely that the Jovian humor which distinguishes his films is also applied in studied measure to his conduct in Hollywood. It takes a particular genius to outshine the other 'geniuses.' "

When Sturges announced his departure from Paramount, Billy Wilder was quoted in *The Hollywood Reporter* as saying, "That's fine. Now there'll be only one genius on the lot—me!"

Interestingly, the one quality of Sturges' work that most often dominated criticism was the apparent recklessness with which it progressed. The Sturges pictures seemed to reflect, in their construction and pacing, their creator's own particular impatience with the constrictions imposed upon the filmmaking process and, for that matter, on life itself.

"They are wonderful as comedies," James Agee said, "and they are wonderfully complex and ingenious; they seem to me also wonderfully, uncontrollably, almost proudly corrupt, vengeful, fearful of intactness and self-commitment; most essentially, they are paradoxical marvels of self-perpetuation and self-destruction; their mastering object, aside from success, seems to be to sail as steep into the wind as possible without an instant incurring the disaster of becoming seriously, wholly acceptable as art. They seem to me, indeed, in much of their twisting, the elaborately counterpointed image of a neurosis. It is an exceptionally interesting neurosis, not only because Sturges is a man of such talent, and not only because it expresses itself in such fecund and in themselves suggestive images, but also because, in relation to art, it seems the definitive expression of this country at present—the stranglehold wedlock of the American female tradition of 'culture,' the male tradition of 'success.' "

Said René Clair, a little more to the point, "Preston is like a man from the Italian Renaissance: he wants to do everything at once. If he could slow down, he would be great; he has an enormous gift and he should be one of our leading creators. I wish he would be a little more selfish and worry about his reputation."

The Howard Hughes affair came to fruition not long after Sturges had left Paramount and while the trade papers and gossip columns were still speculating as to what studio would next be home for the maker of *The Miracle of Morgan's Creek*. At one point, Frank Orsatti was very close to a five-year deal with M-G-M, where Sturges would write and direct a screen adaptation of the Philip Barry play *Without Love* for Spencer Tracy and Katharine Hepburn. At the same time, there was much written about an independent production of the Broadway sensation *Harvey* with Sturges adapting and directing. But Sturges was understandably hesitant to align himself with another major studio after what he had just been through with Buddy DeSylva. Instead he chose to throw in with Howard Hughes on a deal that would, in effect, give him his own studio.

Sturges knew Hughes as a regular patron of The Players. The billionaire would come late at night, eat alone in the darkened Blue Room or dine with some obscure starlet, holding the band over till four in the morning. Sturges himself would occasionally dine with Hughes, the nephew of his friend novelist Rupert Hughes, who always referred to himself as the "poor uncle of a rich nephew." The two developed an almost brotherly rapport as they found common interests in aviation and engineering as well as movies, and Sturges and Hughes hit upon the idea of a moviemaking partnership almost concurrently. Hughes was quite deaf and could hear only every third word that Preston spoke. Sturges once recalled a typical exchange, explaining first that Hughes, sensitive about his hearing, resented people raising their voices in his presence. It was therefore rather difficult to get a conversation going, and Hughes spent most of his time devouring salads, which Sturges loathed:

"... Mr. Hughes swallowed the last mouthful of his third salad, looked over greedily at mine, naturally untouched, and spoke for the first time in forty-five minutes.

" 'Aren't you going to eat your salad?' he said, his eyes riveted on the bowl on my side of the table.

" 'I should say not,' I growled, looking away from it in distaste.

" 'I said: aren't you going to eat your salad?' said Mr. Hughes, watching me anxiously.

" 'No,' I said, shaking my head violently. 'Would you care to have it?'

" 'Would you mind if *I* ate it?' said Mr. Hughes hopefully.

" 'Go ahead,' I said and pushed it over to him.

" 'That certainly is very kind of you,' he said with his mouth full of the new salad.

" 'It is really no sacrifice,' I said.

" 'Very kind of you indeed,' said Mr. Hughes, wolfing down another pitchfork full. 'Nothing like a good salad.'

" 'I can't digest them,' I said, being careful not to raise my voice.

" 'So can I,' said Mr. Hughes. 'Very easily.' "

Hughes first suggested a moviemaking partnership. He had been involved in production in one way or another since 1926. Movies were a wonderful hobby, he had decided, and an excellent way to meet girls. He liked *The Miracle of Morgan's Creek*, and took careful note of the money it was making. The two men discussed preliminaries through the latter half of 1943 and into February of 1944.

"They were trying to negotiate a contract," said Louise Sturges, "and they could not get together. They could agree perfectly on their ideas of engineering but not on anything that constituted a good contract."

When The Players proved not private enough for extended dickering, the talks shifted to 1917 Ivar. "Hughes would come in around twelve o'clock," Louise remembered, "and Preston was seeing another woman at that time and he didn't come in till around twelve either. So I would usually let Mr. Hughes in. He was quite deaf. I do not have a voice that carries too well and it's absolute agony for me to have anything to do with the hard-of-hearing. So I would put something in his hand to read, or just say goodnight and walk upstairs and leave him with a huge plate of cookies and milk."

The discussions between the men seemed simple, but their respective lawyers proved them wrong. At each turn, a new clause would cause delays. Hughes' erratic business habits didn't help matters. On the afternoon of February 12, Hughes phoned Sturges to discuss the latter's insistence upon freedom to make outside pictures. Sturges explained that the move was necessary to ensure the viability of his career in case of problems that might prevent production of two Sturges pictures a year. After all, he reasoned, wasn't he the company's number-one asset? Wasn't his professional health synonymous with that of their partnership?

Hughes relented. "We have a deal," he told Sturges.

News of their plans soon reached the outside world. "Last fortnight," *Time* magazine reported on March 6, "two of the most combustible personalities in Cinema, airminded Howard *(The Outlaw)* Hughes and gadget-brained Preston *(The Miracle of Morgan's Creek)* Sturges, announced their cinemanschluss. A new studio was born. Hollywood braced itself for the sort of thing that happens when hydrogen and a match flame meet."

Said Hughes: "I cannot devote any time whatsoever to the motion picture business until the war is over. . . . I did not know of anyone whom I was willing to trust to carry on this business without any attention on my part. Then the opportunity presented itself to make an association with Preston Sturges, whose work I have admired for many years, but who has always been unavailable because of his contract with Paramount. Here is one man in whom I have complete confidence. I am happy to turn over to him full control and direction of all my motion picture activities."

Said Sturges: "I am merely going to keep on making movies just the way I've always done."

Sturges-Hughes, Inc. was off to a shaky start. Almost immediately the new enterprise leased five sound stages and a suite of offices at Harry (Hopalong Cassidy) Sherman's California Studios on Clinton Street, across from Paramount. Sturges was delighted to be in close proximity to the House of DeSylva, and welcomed visits from Paramount friends and co-workers. He busied himself with a proposed slate of twenty productions, the first of which was yet to be determined.

Two months later the lawyers were still at odds. Hughes' initial intention was to hire Preston Sturges as a salaried employee, a proposition Sturges flatly rejected. His aim was to move permanently beyond such status, and he was therefore quite careful to protect his autonomy. As a concession to his interest in the company, Sturges agreed to draw a salary of only $2500 a week, less than the $3250 Paramount had been paying him, and considerably less than the $6000 Frank Orsatti figured he was worth.

"In working for such a sum," Sturges told Hughes, "which is about thirty-five hundred less than what I can command on the open market, I am then investing thirty-five hundred dollars a week in the venture, which I hope to have returned to me through percentage."

The agreement that was hacked out over a six-month period provided that the company be known as California Pictures Corporation, and that the Hughes Tool Company own approximately 37% of it. The stock was divided into three classes totaling 1875 shares. Four hundred forty-six shares of "Class A" stock and 429 shares of "Class B" stock went directly to Preston Sturges, allowing him to nominate and elect a total of five directors. As the company's president, Sturges himself became the sixth. The remaining 1000 shares of "Class C" (non-voting) stock were divided between Sturges' friend and former producer Henry Henigson (292 shares) and the Hughes Tool Company (708 shares). The board of directors divided evenly between the two factions: Sturges, Henigson (secretary), and Frank Orsatti on one side; writer Jules Furthman (vice-president), CPA Harry Kudell (treasurer), and realty operator Joseph A. DeBell on the other.

In exchange for providing most of the operating capital California Pictures (or "Cal-Pix") would require, Hughes insisted upon a ten-year option on Sturges' 446 shares of "Class A," to be exercised at his discretion. To this, Sturges blithely agreed. The contracts were finally signed on August 24, 1944.

Sturges explained the agreement this way: "Howard doesn't have to put up money if he doesn't want to, and I don't have to work for Cal-Pix if I don't want to."

Sturges began discussing production plans in more concrete— but hardly less idealistic—terms. His interests lay principally in six stories: *La Banque Nemo*, a French play by Louis Verneuil about a bank clerk who rises to the presidency (intended for Spencer Tracy); *The Human Strong Box*, a modern variation on an old German play about a man who swallows a valuable jewel; Joseph Hergesheimer's *Three Black Pennies*; *Nine Pine Street*, a play based upon the Lizzie Borden ax murders (to star Lillian Gish and to be directed by D. W. Griffith); *Colomba*, from the Prosper Mérimée novel; and a *Morgan's Creek*ish original about a young girl's adventures in Hollywood, *The Sin of Hilda Diddlebock*.

In December of 1944, California Pictures entered into an agreement with United Artists for the release of the Cal-Pix product. Guaranteed to UA were Hughes' controversial Western *The Outlaw* and two untitled Sturges pictures. Sturges proposed a company logo (the California state flag) and a company motto, "Non Redolemus Pisce," which was as close as he could come in Latin to "We Do Not Smell from Herring."

The writing of the first Cal-Pix production was under way when the UA deal was signed, but it was a rather contrived piece of work that did not flow easily. Sturges had a burning desire to make every Cal-Pix film a unique and admirable production that would distinguish itself not only artistically, but also to the extent that it would not likely have been made by tubular-thinking executives at any of the major studios. By the same token, he realized it was necessary for their first picture not only to be good, but successful.

The commercial aspect of the film was the fact that it was a Preston Sturges comedy; the not quite so commercial aspect was that Sturges wished to star one of his silent screen favorites, a man who had not made a film in seven years and was certainly not considered any threat to Gable or Bogart at the box office—Harold Lloyd. The comedian's silent classics—especially the features of the early twenties—Sturges recalled with especial fondness. He saw them all in New York in those early years of the Jazz Age when he was on his own running the Desti cosmetics shop and courting his first wife. They influenced him, as did the early films of Chaplin and Keaton and Langdon, as well as lesser lights like Raymond Griffith and Reginald Denny and the later comedies of Stan Laurel and Oliver Hardy. Every time someone took a pratfall in a Sturges picture, they paid homage to the creators of the slapstick of the twenties, to which Sturges himself had humbly added a voice. And over the years he had grown to call Charlie Chaplin a friend, and to meet both Langdon and Keaton and to know Langdon's finest director, Frank Capra. And now something inside him urged him to make a picture with one of these great men; to apply the innovation of the talking screen to the character and physical comedy of a man like Harold Lloyd. Not that Lloyd had made no talkies: indeed, he had made six. But Sturges had an idea that built upon the story of one of Lloyd's most famous films, *The Freshman*, and carried it forward twenty years. Langdon was dead and Chaplin worked only for himself. But Harold Lloyd was alive and well and just might do it. Sturges was skittish about approaching him, but convinced he had to have Lloyd to bring it off. There were a lot of reasons for Lloyd to refuse. He was now in his early fifties, wealthy beyond imagination (his Beverly Hills estate sported its own private golf course), and the experience of his last film at Paramount *(Professor Beware)* had not been especially rewarding. He had very little to gain by making another picture at this late date. And he could risk damaging the golden image of the young Harold in the bargain. Lloyd had taken to performing on radio, where his gentle, boyish voice belied his true age, and to producing at RKO. Knowing this, Sturges concocted a phony project, the aforementioned *Sin of Hilda Diddlebock*, and went to Lloyd with the proposal that he join Cal-Pix as a producer-director and add his own special touch to this promising comedy that Sturges could not find time to direct himself.

Flattered, Lloyd encouraged such talk and it became evident to Sturges that Lloyd was a pleasantly bored man who would welcome a chance to become involved in production once more and—Sturges perceived—performing, if the opportunity was right. And so slowly, carefully, Sturges maneuvered Lloyd from directing to performing and transformed *The Sin of Hilda Diddlebock* into *The Sin of Harold Diddlebock;* Lloyd finally said a conditional yes.

Lloyd's agreement was contingent upon Cal-Pix's willingness to meet his fee of $100,000 against 7½% of the gross, a problem because Sturges needed Howard Hughes' approval to enter into such an agreement. Hughes, once the initial Cal-Pix contracts were signed, switched his attentions to such other concerns as TWA, the F-11, and the HK-1—"Hercules," his famous wooden flying boat. He was soon only sporadically available for conference, and almost impossible to reach by telephone. Sturges complained about this lack of communication, at one point threatening to start a column in *The Hollywood Reporter* called "Dear Howard . . . Wherever You Are."

When finally reached, Hughes balked, not so much over the flat fee as the percentage, which he was loath to award any actor (Hughes had never been known for using big stars in his films). Lloyd, he argued, was something approaching a has-been. He hadn't worked in seven years and producers weren't pounding down his door trying to hire him. It was simply because Lloyd could see Preston wanted him so much that he was asking what he was and Hughes felt he would certainly take less if it became apparent the squeeze wouldn't work. Sturges, however, knew Lloyd didn't need the money and wanted merely to reaffirm his value as a star in taking on such an assignment. Sturges pressed the point that the company was still part his, and that if he wanted Harold Lloyd, damn it, it was up to Hughes to trust him. Sturges assured Hughes there would be no other high-priced actors in *Diddlebock*, that they would all be stock company types like Bill Demarest and Jimmy Conlin. He also pointed out that Lloyd was not being unreasonable in his demands when he stopped to consider that Claudette Colbert got $150,000 for *The Palm Beach Story* and that she was supported in that film by three other relatively big names. Hughes finally said okay and the contracts were drawn up.

Harold Lloyd thought Sturges' idea for the film "lovely." Sturges proposed to open with the climactic football game from *The Freshman* in which Harold the water boy is drafted into the game in its closing minutes and becomes—in spite of himself—the hero of the day. As thousands cheer, he is carried to the locker room and offered a job by the president of an advertising firm who has just witnessed his magnificent performance. Harold graduates, brimming with ambition, and proceeds to call upon this man to claim his career. Harold is a stereotypical self-starter, spouting stale platitudes ("Every man is the architect of his own fortune") and substituting zeal for any real intelligence or ability. He is given a chance to start at the bottom—as an assistant clerk in the accounting department. He plasters his wall with a score of homilies of the Elbert Hubbard school and eagerly sets to work. We then see the passage of the decades in the faces of the presidents on the wall calendar. The camera pans back and there, still, is Harold . . . a middle-aged mole of a man, no further along than when he started. Word comes to him that the boss wants to see him.

Harold, it seems, has failed to live up to the high expectations of the company. "You have not only ceased to go forward," the old man tells him, "you have gone backward. You not only stopped progressing, you have stopped thinking. You not only make the same mistakes year after year, you don't even change your apologies. *You* have become a bottleneck!"

Diddlebock pleads innocence, but it does no good. He is paid off, given his savings ($2946.12), and let go—to start all over again at the bottom. Sturges' premise was to take Lloyd's same basic character, place him in middle age with a bankroll in his pocket, nothing to do with his life, and then see what would happen.

"Diddlebock's real sin was his refusal to think," said Harold Lloyd, "to rise from his inertia. The story shows what happens when a man is jolted out of a routine and finds, to his surprise, that he isn't half so afraid of life as he thought. That's why the picture means so much more to me than doing another farce—another gag show. It says that extra something that goes beyond laughs."

Sturges went through five drafts of the Diddlebock script before he was satisfied, then put together a cast and crew exactly as he pleased. This included hiring his Paramount editor (Stuart Gilmore), a blacklisted actor (Lionel Stander), and a respected European cinematographer (Curt Courant) who—due to union restrictions—was unable to work for any of the major studios. He then designed himself a leisurely production schedule of sixty-four days and a budget of over $1 million, making *The Sin of Harold Diddlebock* the most expensive Sturges film ever.

Sturges wrote parts for most all the members of his stock company. "All my actors wear tailor-made parts, down to the woman who sells flowers on the street," he said. "What you see on the screen is the work of one man; what you hear is his voice."

Sturges had come to consider actors like Jimmy Conlin and Frank Moran good-luck charms and he made sure they were in every picture he made. Bill Demarest was no exception. "In fact," said Demarest, "he'd delay the start of a film if I was on another picture." Sturges once autographed a photo for the actor, "To that pillar of strength and cornerstone of comedy known as Bill Demarest." He naturally wanted Demarest in *The Sin of Harold Diddlebock*, especially considering how important the film was to the success of California Pictures. But soon after the release of *The Miracle of Morgan's Creek*, Paramount signed Demarest to a long-term contract, which meant that Sturges had to go to Buddy DeSylva to get him. Sturges called Bill Meiklejohn, head of talent and casting, and said, "I have to have Demarest. I've got a part that runs three weeks." Meiklejohn demurred, saying he would have to clear it through Buddy DeSylva. DeSylva was in no mood to be helpful.

"If he wants him for three weeks, tell him it's $50,000."

Meiklejohn relayed the message. Sturges cringed (Demarest was getting $850 a week in the days of *Sullivan's Travels*) but said "okay." It was, after all, Howard's money and Bill was an investment, even at $50,000.

But DeSylva still wasn't satisfied. "Send the script over," he said. "I want to read it." Sturges sent what he had of the first draft.

DeSylva didn't even bother to read it. "I don't like the part," he said. "You can't have him."

Sturges was furious. DeSylva knew what Demarest meant to him and was simply being vindictive. There was little Demarest could do though, other than break his contract. Then Sturges hit on a plan. In the film, Diddlebock buys a circus and there was a scene with Al Bridge in which a lion sits in the background. Sturges sent his publicity man to propose to Demarest that he sit in this scene in a lion's skin. DeSylva would never know and Sturges would have Demarest in his film. Bill didn't know; he'd have to think about it. "So what happens?" asked Bill Demarest. "Two days later it appears in the trade papers that Bill Demarest wants to be in Preston Sturges' new picture so much that he's going to do it in a lion's skin! That was Sturges. He couldn't have it known that *he* wanted me. I had to want *him*. So naturally DeSylva finds out. And he calls me in and says, 'What's this business?' and I said, 'Where?' He said, 'For Sturges. It's in the paper.' And I said, 'I don't know a thing about it.'"

Sturges took Demarest's refusal to wear the lion's skin as a personal breach of loyalty. Soon after, he took out full-page ads in *Variety* and *The Hollywood Reporter* publicly thanking the actors in *The Miracle of Morgan's Creek* and carefully listing each one with a little comment about the excellence of their performance. The ad was bordered with a dotted line with the inscription "cut along this line." Sturges wrote, "The following talented Ladies and Gentlemen, listed in the order of their appearance in *The Miracle of Morgan's Creek*, are making a fortune for Paramount. They might do the same for you." Next to Bill Demarest's name, Sturges wrote, "... magnificent as Constable Kockenlocker, but now has to be borrowed like a big star ... the Hell with him."

"Imagine that!" said Demarest. "After eight films—'the Hell with him.'" He thought a moment. "You know, in all the time I knew Sturges, I never once felt it was a warm friendship. He never put his arm around me. He never left you with anything. He was like a separate thing walking around by himself. I don't think he had any love for anybody."

When *Hail the Conquering Hero* opened in August, another ad appeared. Again the dotted lines, and again Bill was listed. "Once again magnificent," wrote Sturges, "this time as Sergeant Heffelfinger. Now under contract to Paramount. So long, Bill."

The two men never spoke again.

Making the arrangements to produce *The Sin of Harold Diddlebock* was a monumental task, not because the film was very lavish (it wasn't), but because the filmmakers were literally starting from scratch. The support departments of a major studio—the costumers, the make-up men, the musicians, the special effects technicians—were things Sturges had pretty much taken for granted when he was working for Paramount. But now that he was on his own, each contribution to the final look of a film took on a new significance. Not only did he need the services of a make-up man or a set designer, he had to hire one and then set up an entirely new department. Sturges found that time he would normally devote to the film itself—for writing and casting and such—was increasingly being eaten away by administrative duties for which he had little taste or talent. So, when a deal to purchase the Sherman studios fell through and the stages were engaged by others, Sturges decided to move to the Samuel Goldwyn studios on Santa Monica Boulevard, where there were wardrobe, sound, and camera departments and facilities were not quite so spare.

Sturges obviously enjoyed the attention he received as the head of Cal-Pix. He gleefully promoted the new enterprise whenever the opportunity arose, as much to thumb his nose at Buddy DeSylva as anything. In May of 1945, he put in two weeks as the host of the "Lux Radio Theatre," although he declined Cecil B. DeMille's old job on a permanent basis on the grounds that he found selling soap beneath his dignity. He did, however, endorse Scripto pencils in the pages of the nation's most popular magazines, with a plug for the forthcoming *Diddlebock* prominently displayed. The copy read, "On the set in Hollywood, when production calls for quick changes in a script, Preston Sturges relies on a Scripto Mechanical Pencil."

The Sin of Harold Diddlebock was cast easily, using Jimmy Conlin, Robert Greig, Raymond Walburn, Franklin Pangborn, and the other character actors Sturges had become so comfortable with and could write for so easily. Sturges maintained his administrative offices at the California studios, set up a production office at Goldwyn, and arranged to shoot a few exteriors and the final window ledge sequence at Paramount. *Diddlebock* was budgeted at $1,082,928 and set to begin on September 12, 1945.

Diddlebock began filming under the most bizarre of circumstances. In contrast to past occasions, when Sturges was spending Paramount's money and using Paramount's facilities, he now considered himself entirely on his own turf and no longer worried about discipline and fussy little memos about too low a page average. There was no Buddy DeSylva to hover over him, no studio routine or company policy to restrict his spirit. Sturges began his day with a number from Harry Rosenthal, manning the studio piano, and then settled into a comfortable day's filming. No pressure, no worry. He knew what he wanted from a scene, but he would huddle with Harold Lloyd as a courtesy, to explore fine nuances of character and plot. Sturges not only wished Lloyd to feel comfortable on the set, but he wanted to give Lloyd incentive for the kind of improvisation that frequently resulted in the silent days in some of the funniest routines ever filmed. Lloyd, the soft-spoken Shriner from Nebraska, must have felt somewhat intimidated by Sturges, this articulate foreigner with the vocabulary of Noah Webster who churned out dialogue by the ream and saw physical comedy—as much as he respected it—as subordinate to the spoken word. The differences were evident from the start, Sturges awkwardly insisting that his dialogue remain intact, Lloyd perceiving that Sturges was needlessly substituting talk for action and trying to break the film's static and studio-bound look. What Sturges planned, in effect, was to film as did his friend Charlie Chaplin, who owned his own studio and financed his films entirely with his own money. Chaplin, Sturges knew, thought nothing of shooting only one day a week, writing and thinking the other five while keeping a cast and crew on full salary. This, it occurred to Sturges, was a wonderful way to make pictures . . . without pressures or financial worries and without sacrificing quality to the demands of a shooting schedule. And so he filmed half days, full days, taking his sweet time and welcoming visitors to his set as if he were home, or at The Players. When asked about this manner of working, he would simply say, "It's my money," and end the discussion. Lloyd, used to the routine of making sound pictures and the deadlines they imposed, was clearly bewildered by this attitude but kept to himself, choosing instead to fret over little pieces of physical business that would help the plot along but that Preston might not go for. The two men spoke warmly of each other to members of the press. "Basically, Preston and I think alike, even when our approach is different," said Lloyd. "I like to go on the set with a scene mapped out and work from my head; Preston comes on with a blueprint he's sweated over beforehand to the last detail. He can do his cutting a reel at a time and stay with it indefinitely; it's an effort for me to sit in a projection room with an uncut story. After I've seen three good ideas go through the chopper, I have to come up for air."

As *The Sin of Harold Diddlebock* progressed, it began to take on the look of an expensive Monogram picture, with little action but some of the finest writing Sturges had ever done. The muse by which Diddlebock becomes inspired is alcohol. Approached by a little tout called "Wormy," Harold at first refuses a loan of four dollars, and then, in disgust, peels off a twenty and hands it over. Wormy thanks him profusely and then, perceiving Harold's troubles, suggests a drink to help assuage his misery.

"Did you ever hear of a Texas Tornado?" Wormy asks.

"Not until this moment," replies Diddlebock.

"Oh, ho-ho," pipes Wormy, "you'll be surprised and amazed!" And with that he drags his new friend down the steps to a little cafe owned and operated by bartender Edgar Kennedy.

"Brother Diddlebock is in some kind of trouble," Wormy explains, "And he's about to have his first drink."

"First drink?" says Kennedy, his eyes aglow. "Well, drown my kittens, this is quite a moment." He lowers his voice and leans in. "You mean his first this morning or really his first ever and ever since he was weaned?"

Diddlebock speaks up. "I have never partaken. Now that I've had time—"

Kennedy's mind shifts into high gear at the prospect. "Yes sir . . . You arouse the artist in me." Immediately he sets to work concocting a wonderful new beverage customized to his subject's own particular tastes and needs. "Something you would *remember*," he says.

"I was thinking of a Texas Tornado," Wormy suggests, but Kennedy disapproves.

"Oh, not for an occasion like this, Wormy. A Tornado is a perfectly reliable 'commercial' drink for conventions and hangovers and things like that, but *this* . . . this is almost, uh, is the word *vestal*? I mean it oughta have organ music. I mean opportunities like this come along all too rarely for a man with his heart in his work."

Kennedy sets to work. "Ah, tell me, Mr. Diddleback—"

"—*bock*—"

"—where were you born?"

"What? Nebraska."

Kennedy's eyes light up. "Corn! And in what year please?"

"Nineteen hundred and one."

"Fine, fine. They distilled some very palatable stuff in 1901." He starts rummaging through bottles. "Let me see . . ." He produces a special one. "I wouldn't do this for just anybody."

"I wouldn't want you to for—"

"Oh, you leave it to me."

"You just leave it to him," Wormy agrees.

"Nineteen hundred and one," Kennedy chants, adding a profusion of unidentified ingredients. "Nineteen hundred and one . . . a sort of meeting of old friends . . . brothers under the stars . . . it ought to help your personalities get together . . . or don't you believe in astrology?"

"I've never thought that much about it. If you're making that for me—"

"Do you believe in personalities?"

"I suppose so."

"How about posterity?"

"What?"

"Posterity is just around the corner," injects Wormy.

"Now," says Kennedy, rubbing his hands together, "just a couple of technical questions: would you like it frappé or flambeau?"

"How?"

"Do you like ice skating or Turkish baths?"

"Well, I used to skate a little."

"Frappé!" says Kennedy, icing the glasses. "Now, would you like it sweet or sharp?"

"I don't really—"

"How do you take your coffee?"

"I take milk."

"You've answered my question." He adds some more liquids to the mixture. "Do you prefer showers or sitz baths?"

"Well, we have a shower over the tub, but there's always the danger of stepping on the soap."

"Vodka!" erupts Kennedy. "With vodka you don't care what you step on."

"You can step on snakes!" offers Wormy.

"Now wait a minute," says Diddlebock.

"Just relax," the bartender soothes. "One final question: do you prefer the taste of rosemary or wormwood?"

"Who or who?"

"Do you like Benedictine or absinthe?"

"What?"

"What kind of toothpaste do you use?"

"Sozodone."

"Gotcha!" And Kennedy adds the few chemicals remaining to complete his masterpiece.

"If that's for me—" starts Diddlebock nervously.

"You just leave it to him," comforts Wormy. "What a scientist. Ain't that pretty? They call him 'The Professor.' You just leave it to him."

"Gentlemen!" announces Kennedy. "The Diddlebock!"

The shaker is raised high and three servings are poured. Wormy and Kennedy toast to Mr. Diddlebock's very good health. Diddlebock sniffs it once or twice and then meekly samples it. "Very mild," he says approvingly.

"Nothing to it," Wormy agrees.

"I wouldn't say that," Kennedy cautions, "but it has always seemed to me that the cocktail should approach us on tiptoe, like a young girl whose first appeal . . . is innocence."

Kennedy's caution is well taken; the drink has a Jekyll-and-Hyde effect on the unsuspecting Diddlebock as he alternately howls like a banshee and wonders where the noise is coming from.

Suddenly a new man, he sets out to prove it. He buys a loud suit, makes a bet on a horse that pays twenty to one, and then applies his sizable bankroll to a wild night on the town and the purchase of a small circus. But when stuck with the show's bills and the enormous responsibility for food for the lions and elephants, he is at a loss over what to do or how to do it. It is only when primed with another flask of "Diddlebocks" that he again becomes resourceful enough to hatch the scheme that results in the film's cliff-hanging climax.

Getting there, though, was not as simple or as action-packed as might be imagined. Sturges' easy routine and inherent laziness pushed the schedule far beyond what he had first imagined, as also did the complex special effects sequence photographed by Paramount's John P. Fulton. When *The Sin of Harold Diddlebock* finally wrapped, at the end of January 1946, it was fifty-two days over schedule . . . and more than $600,000 over budget.

23.

"I had been a fashion model in New York," Frances Ramsden recalled, "and I had come out to California to visit friends. One of them introduced me to a screenwriter named Jacques Thery, who had written *Joan of Paris* and one of Ernst Lubitsch's pictures, and he took me to lunch at Paramount studios. As we came through the door there was an enormous round table on the side where Preston Sturges was lunching with a big circle of friends around him. He boomed out, 'Hello, Jacques! How are you?' and Jacques stopped at his table and introduced me. Preston said, 'Why don't you join our table?' So we did.

"I didn't know who Sturges was other than I remember hearing of him because he had married a Hutton. He looked at me and studied me and then said, 'You have a very interesting face, young lady. Have you ever thought of being an actress?' and I said, 'No, I never have.' And he said, 'Well, I think you've got a very interesting face, not like all the other faces they have around here, and I would very much like to give you a screen test. And I *personally* will direct it.'

"I didn't realize that was something unheard of, and I thought to myself, 'Ha-ha. Now when I go back to New York I'll be able to say I was offered a screen test.' "

Ramsden said, "That's very flattering, Mr. Sturges."

And Preston said, "No, I mean it." And he told her to show up the following Tuesday at a specific time.

"I thanked him very much," Ramsden continued, "and I didn't pay any attention to that. Of course I never showed up. Then, three years later, I was in Hollywood and again I was with the same Jacques. We were dining at The Players and I was in the middle of having my dinner when Preston's voice boomed out, 'There's the young lady who never shows up for screen tests!'

"Well, I laughed, and, anyway, I began to join him and his friends at the fights with Max Ophuls—who had a contract with Sturges and his new company—and René Clair and people like that. Then he started taking me out and then, one day, he asked me if I wanted to be in the movie."

The movie was *The Sin of Harold Diddlebock* and Sturges had written a part for a comely young woman who would play the object of Harold Lloyd's affections, thus becoming the first contract starlet of the California Pictures Corporation. As yet he hadn't selected one, but whether she could act or not was not a prime consideration; Sturges had confidence in his ability as a director to get a good performance out of anyone. And he thought there might even be some publicity in the search for a new Sturges ingenue.

Frances Ramsden seemed an excellent choice. Tall, with reddish-blond hair and expressive eyes, she had appeared in the pages of virtually all the well-known fashion journals. Preston liked her not only for her modeling background but for the sophistication in her resonant voice and her quickness in conversation. Not only could he make an actress of her, but she was already presold as a photographic subject and it was almost unbearably easy to get magazine space for such women; Howard Hawks had accomplished it recently with a New York model named Betty Bacall whom he offered a contract and whose name he changed to Lauren.

"But I don't know how to act," Ramsden protested. Waving her objections aside, Sturges arranged for a screen test in which she read the lines of Miss Otis with Preston's friend Richard Hale taking the part of Harold Diddlebock. Sturges worked with her, keeping her face, especially her eyes, animated during the course of the exchange, and when it was cut and shown to Howard Hughes, Preston pronounced himself satisfied. With Howard's approval, she was offered a contract. Soon, Preston Sturges was seen most everywhere with Frances Ramsden on his arm.

Harold Lloyd was a bit overwhelmed by her. When the two first met, Lloyd said, "You know, Preston, she can eat beans off the top of my head."

"Don't worry," replied Sturges. "We'll dig a trench."

Sturges actually wanted very little of Frances Ramsden in *Diddlebock*; he allowed her only three scenes. "You are not yet experienced enough to play anything else but a star role," he told her. He wanted the public to "discover" her for themselves and not to resent the fact that she was in every scene.

"I was scared to death at that time," Ramsden confided. "I'm not an actress and I told him, 'You know, Preston, it's a pity, isn't it, that I'm getting this fantastic opportunity when all these people in Hollywood would give their eyeteeth for this.'

"We'd go to The Players for dinner and then he'd say, 'Come on, Frances, we're going back to the set.' It'd be about eleven o'clock at night he'd go in and tell them to put a work light on. Then he'd say, 'Now we're going to walk it through.' And he'd say, 'You're not going to be frightened,' and he'd take me gently by the hand. He was as gentle as if he were a father talking to a child. And removed all fear. He'd feed me the lines of Harold or someone else—and he'd walk me through to my chalk mark until I had it down cold and I wasn't afraid any longer."

Preston had violins playing on the set during the climactic love scene, in which Miss Otis had to make Diddlebock aware that he had actually married her on the Wednesday he couldn't remember. Lloyd nervously kissed her while watching Preston out of the corner of one eye. Sturges, he had noticed, was extremely possessive of her. He faked the kiss, telling her later, "First time I've been camera-shy in my life."

When the company adjourned to Paramount to film the skyscraper routine, Ramsden watched from the sidelines. The process was slow and painstaking and Lloyd, who insisted upon doing most all his own stunts, was clearly not enjoying himself. One of the problems was the lion, Jackie, from whose chain he dangled a good part of the time. Something in the quality of the actor's voice made the lion nervous. During an earlier scene with Al Bridge, when Lloyd spoke his lines, the lion's ear twitched noticeably. Lloyd extended his right hand for a brief moment and the lion snapped at it. Lloyd gamely finished the scene, then froze as the animal was removed. (The hand had already been partially blown away by a "fake" bomb in the late teens. Lloyd wore a flesh-covered glove to cover the injury.)

"From now on," he said, "I'll not rehearse with this animal and I'll do no close-ups." The rest of the picture was shot with the lion at a prudent distance, or with a stuffed head on a broomstick.

But while Lloyd found the film less than a total pleasure to make, it was obvious to Ramsden that Sturges was delighted. "He was having so much fun, he didn't want to stop the picture. He'd do take after take after take and then we'd wander off to The Players for lunch. One day, he got onto his motorcycle—he had one of those enormous Harley-Davidsons—and then turned to me and said, 'You drive it.' I'd just had a lesson from Freddy Lau, the prop man, and I said, 'All right.' I was as crazy as he was, I guess. You could just see the general manager, Henry Henigson, turn white. Here was writer-producer-director and co-owner of the studio riding pillion with this slight girl, who had just had her first lesson, zooming down Santa Monica Boulevard at forty miles an hour!"

Ramsden's visibility did little to help Preston's ailing marriage, as Louise, who before could choose to ignore such infidelities with secretaries and the like, found herself unable to do so when the woman in question was also the co-star of Preston's new picture and a favorite of the fan magazines. Preston, unconcerned, continued doing exactly as he pleased. "The only thing you'll regret in life," he once said, "are your economies." He not only needed his family, he needed his freedom too. Said Ramsden, "I think the trouble with Preston was he felt that's what he needed—his wife and family—but he really didn't *want* it."

Louise agreed. "He was very happy with the arrangement he had at that time, and he would have continued being married indefinitely." But finally Louise had had enough. His disrespect for her, his contempt, had become too intense and too public. "He didn't like women as people," Louise decided. "I think he trusted me, but he didn't as a rule trust or really like women. He had a great fondness and respect for Priscilla, for instance. But he believed women had tiny, cute little brains that were not capable of great thought. He was a male chauvinist; a charter member of that group." Sturges accorded the same importance to women as he did to money. They were there for only the basest of reasons. When once asked what women were to Sturges, Eddie Bracken replied, "Slaves."

Louise filed suit for divorce in May of 1946 and at once the press descended upon her. "I tried not to pay much attention to that; I left the house around five in the morning and hid so that I would not be caught by one of the columnists. It was a terrible time. Very trying. And eventually Hedda did catch me, doggone her. I don't remember how she did it; it must have been in the middle of the night. I told her as little as I could get away with, but it came out eventually anyway."

The May 13 number of *Life* hit the stands with a photo spread of Frances Ramsden showing off a baggy pair of clamdiggers Sturges designed called "Francie Pants." In light of the divorce proceedings, *Life* headlined the piece, "Frances Ramsden gets some slacks; Preston Sturges a suit for divorce," and went on to describe Sturges' previous marriages. "Last week," the report continued, "his third wife, the former Louise Sargent, sued for divorce on the grounds of 'mental cruelty.' But Hollywood believes the real cause of the divorce is that Preston Sturges was being seen too much with Francie, who herself was divorced only six weeks ago." A tidal wave of similar stories appeared nationwide.

Preston charged publicly that Louise "inhibited" him and that his work required "more stimulating" company. Louise, in turn, accused him of an "ungovernable temper and revengeful disposition." Bertie Woolfan argued with Preston, trying to effect a reconciliation. "Bertie, she *bores* me!" Preston would plead. Finally, he gave up.

"He wanted to experience *all* sensations," Louise remembered. "He had said it before. In fact, he said it to my attorney in the

deposition." She laughed. "I was advised to take this very dignified attorney who had absolutely no experience with divorce cases.
He had never had one. And he in turn gave me to a younger
associate. The day before he was supposed to take Preston's
deposition, I was in his office when a girl popped her head in the
door and said, 'I thought I saw Mr. So-and-so come in here.' My
guy said, no, he isn't came in yet.' " Remembering Preston's fetish
for proper grammar, Louise thought, "Dear God, this is the man
who's going to take Preston's deposition!"

"I left his office in a state of terrible agitation, got in my car,
and apparently I drove right through a safety zone. I was immediately stopped, thank goodness, and the policeman said, 'Have you
been drinking?' and I said, 'No, I've just had something much
worse!'

"That's when I changed attorneys."

Louise's new attorney, Meyer Willner, assembled a property
settlement that included 50% of Preston's interest in California
Pictures and a hefty sum of cash. Preston might have agreed to
such a settlement without contest, except that Louise also wanted
the house. That was where he drew the line: he had spent years
working on that house, remodeling it to his own specifications.
Chances of his finding another as suitable were slim, reduced
further by the amount of work required on even the best of
candidates. Preston's attorney arranged a postponement and
began to negotiate. At that it stalled.

During the course of the divorce battle, Sturges' career stalled
almost as completely. Trouble brewed not so much over *The Sin
of Harold Diddlebock* but, rather, Cal-Pix's second production,
Colomba.

Sturges was enthused about doing the Prosper Mérimée story,
a classical French romance he had read untranslated. The story
was a grim and violent tale of revenge in Corsica in the early 1800s
and Sturges saw it as a fitting contrast to *Diddlebock*, an opportunity to produce a film of great style and beauty. Whether it would go
over commercially was not a prime consideration, as *Diddlebock*
was calculated to make millions. There was, however, enough
blood and romance to please most any audience. Sturges planned
both *Diddlebock* and *Colomba* to film simultaneously, and so
obviously could direct only one.

Max Ophuls, a German expatriate, had made a reputation for
himself as a writer-director working primarily in France in the
1930s. He came to the United States in 1941 after an abortive
attempt to make a film in Switzerland and spent the next four
years trying to get a picture made in Hollywood. When Sturges got
Cal-Pix going, he matched Ophuls to *Colomba* and wrote the
screenplay, as a favor to Hughes, for actress Faith Domergue.

Domergue was the latest in a long string of Hughes contract starlets, a dark New Orleans girl whom Hughes met in 1941 and whose contract he bought from Warner Bros. He promptly boxed her away, putting her first through a year of exercises to lose a lisp, and then two years of diction lessons. She took a year off to get married (to director Hugo Fregonese) and then reportedly tried to break her contract on the grounds that Hughes had failed to use her in anything. That was when Cal-Pix was launched, and Hughes pressed Sturges to find something for her.

Colomba was perfect. It was a story of the struggle between the ancient Corsican tradition of vendetta and the modern concept of law and judgment. Colomba della Rabbia blames the murder of her father on the Barracinis and a long-standing hatred between the two families. And she demands that her brother, Orso, carry out the traditional vendetta against the eldest Barracini son. Orso, however, abroad at the time of the shooting, prefers to stand with the court's ruling in favor of the Barracinis. Colomba despairs that Orso's sense of Corsican heritage has faded and works almost maniacally to rekindle the flame.

Sturges restructured the story so that it was primarily about Orso, keeping Colomba in the shadows as an almost supernatural presence, the voice of barbarism in an enlightened and progressive mind. He gave the character of Lydia Nevil a little boy, contrasting the brutality of the vendetta with the innocence of the coming generation.

When Sturges finished the script for *Colomba* in July of 1945, just prior to the filming of *Diddlebock*, he pronounced it the finest he had ever written. Ophuls was delighted with it, using it in soliciting the services of such stars as James Mason and Madeleine Carroll. But the problem of casting was compounded by Hughes' tightfistedness in refusing to pay major star salaries and in insisting that there not be performers in the film that would likely overshadow the debut of Miss Domergue. Filming was postponed until after the completion of *Diddlebock*, at which time the cast was composed primarily of unknowns. Then Hughes wanted a more commercial title and Ophuls suggested *Vendetta*.

Sturges did a final polish on *Vendetta* in June of 1946 and sold the script to Cal-Pix for $10. Hughes was supposedly happy with the cast (Domergue, George Dolenz, Nigel Bruce, Hillary Brooke), the budget, and the director. He busied himself with his military contracts, in particular the experimental reconnaissance plane, the F-11. The plane had given Hughes problems from the start. Delivery dates were pushed back and then, with the war winding down, the government's order was cut by 80%. Hughes personally chose to conduct a test flight of the craft on the afternoon of July 7,

1946. The plane seemed to perform beautifully, achieving speeds in excess of four hundred miles an hour. But then, without warning, Hughes lost control. Preston and Francie were on their way to San Pedro for a Sunday cruise when a bulletin interrupted the music on the car radio: Howard Hughes had slammed his plane into a house on Whittier Drive in Beverly Hills while attempting to crash-land on a nearby golf course. He was still alive. Without comment, Sturges turned the car and headed for Good Samaritan Hospital.

Hughes proved to be a remarkably resilient fellow; his recovery was astounding. Sturges allowed production on *Vendetta* to begin on schedule: August 13, 1946.

Max Ophuls worked slowly. The original schedule of fifty days proved inadequate for him and on the fifty-ninth day he was still shooting with only about half of the film finished. One day Sturges brought Ophuls to the hospital to meet Hughes, who suddenly became incensed that a thickly accented German was directing his picture. When Hughes returned to his Beverly Hills home to convalesce, Sturges arranged to have the dailies sent up to amuse him. It did more than that: not only did Hughes not like Ophuls' handling of Faith Domergue, he began asking for figures on cost and overtime and when it became apparent that Sturges had permitted Ophuls to fall more than thirty days behind schedule, he called a meeting. He told Sturges to get rid of Ophuls and to finish the picture himself. Quickly.

Ophuls was released the following day although, happily, he was able to get another picture at Universal and there were no hard feelings. Sturges was less than enthusiastic about taking over the film of another director with a style so different from his own. He picked up where Ophuls had left off, but without conviction. The partnership was beginning to sour, like a bad marriage, and Preston could sense it. From a relatively uninvolved financier, Hughes had become a mindlessly meddlesome creature who attempted to tightly rein the entire Cal-Pix operation from his sickbed.

"One must remember that Howard too had been a director," Frances Ramsden later wrote, "and still considered himself one. So as the day's rushes arrived, and as he had a great deal of time on his hands, he began to study the results of each day's shooting in earnest. He was probably comparing how he would handle some scenes or insert this or that piece of business.

"The first intimation of the more than passing interest he was taking was in the phone calls that he began to place to Preston each day. He would suggest a change here or a close-up there. Preston, not yet aware of what was happening, jovially shot down all his arguments. Time passed. A note of impatience began to creep into their voices when they spoke to each other on the phone."

Joel McCrea visited the set one day and was disturbed by the resignation in Sturges' voice. "We had tea," the actor recalled. " 'Well,' Preston said, 'it doesn't really matter. We go on week after week; the money keeps rolling in.' He said Mr. Hughes' money meant nothing to him. I listened to that for quite a while. Finally I said, 'Preston, you've got too much talent to waste on anything like this. I know Howard Hughes slightly—well enough to know that he doesn't mind how much money he spends. You're absolutely right. But neither does he care if the picture's ever released, or if it ever does anything. And if he doesn't like it when he sees it, he'll put it on a shelf. Your talent is too great for that.'

"Of course, he was very gracious and charming and thought I was lovely to say that, but it didn't move him too much."

Sturges' work on *Vendetta* continued to be sluggish and uninspired. He felt himself trapped in a film he no longer cared for, directing a script Hughes had decided he no longer liked. Hughes disliked the little boy (Gregory Marshall) Sturges had added to the story and began suggesting ways to pare his performance. This annoyed Sturges further as his were some of the best scenes in the film. "This picture has one director," Sturges told Ramsden testily, "and that director is *me*."

The matter finally came to a head the day before Halloween. About seven o'clock that Wednesday morning, the phone rang at Ramsden's apartment above the Sunset Strip. The voice was unmistakably Howard's.

"Frances? This is Howard. Is Preston there?"

Sturges took the phone and listened. "Well, okay, Howard . . . If that's the way you feel . . . I'll be at The Players in an hour."

Preston hung up the phone and looked at Francie. "That's it," he said. "Howard's taking over the company."

The pair drove to The Players and had breakfast on the veranda. Precisely at 10:00 A.M., a lawyer from Hughes Tool appeared with a letter on Hughes Productions stationery:

"We hereby elect to exercise our option to purchase 446 shares of the Class A common stock of California Pictures Corporation, as contained in the agreement dated August 24th, 1944."

Tendering a check for $446, the lawyer then asked Sturges to sign the following statement:

"I hereby resign as an officer of California Pictures Corporation, this resignation to become effective immediately."

It was dated October 30, 1946. Sturges signed it with a flourish and then turned to his companion.

"That's that. Come on, darling, let's go sailing." And they did.

The *Vendetta* cast and crew were left assembled on a stage at the Goldwyn studios. No one bothered to tell them what had happened.

Sturges was understandably bitter about the entire affair. Privately, he said, "The whole *Vendetta* episode was regrettable from beginning to end and should teach me never to do favors, since the whole thing was a favor to Mr. Hughes."

Publicly, however, he was more diplomatic. "Interruptions have been frequent in Mr. Hughes' productions," he told the New York *Times*, "but he has never made a failure. Both he and I are doers, and neither of us is content to sit by and watch someone else work. I became an independent producer to get away from supervision. When Mr. Hughes made suggestions with which I disagreed, as he had a perfect right to do, I rejected them. When I rejected the last one, he remembered he had an option to take control of the company and he took over. So I left."

Hughes lost little time in replacing Sturges with director Stuart Heisler *(The Glass Key)*, whose task it was to finish filming the Sturges script to Hughes' specifications. He would then study it and have the script rewritten if it didn't please him. "Since I still own 49% of California Pictures," Sturges said. "I hope that Mr. Hughes will devise as profitable a way to sell *Vendetta* as he did to sell *The Outlaw*."

In spite of their estrangement, Sturges continued to work away on *The Sin of Harold Diddlebock*. A preview had been scheduled for Westwood in early November. Hughes attended that preview himself, appearing only after the lights had been dimmed and plugging himself into a special listening device situated next to Sturges and Ramsden in the back row. He laughed not once during the entire experience and took note of the few walkouts that occurred late in the screening. When the lights came up, both Francie and Preston turned at once to Hughes. His seat was empty.

Sturges decided some tightening was necessary and spent the next thirty-three hours in a cutting room with Francie and editor Stuart Gilmore. He shaved the running time to ninety-one minutes and at that he was satisfied.

The Sin of Harold Diddlebock lacked the polish and drive of Sturges' Paramount pictures. Its pacing faltered—in spite of his careful editing—and it had the overall look of a film that had cost about one sixth the amount it actually had. Dialogue subbed for action in spots, which tended to slow the film even more. Regardless, *Diddlebock* contained a winning performance by Harold Lloyd and some genuinely brilliant sequences. At its trade showings in early 1947, the critics blinded themselves to the film's faults and awarded it notices as fine as any Sturges had yet received.

"A rare, wonderful comedy treat," reported the *Motion Picture Daily*, *"The Sin of Harold Diddlebock* returns Harold Lloyd to the screen in a picture destined to have any theatre rocking with the guffaws of the audience. It is really hilariously funny, sparklingly original, and, from the cashier's viewpoint, a product that just cannot miss in bringing in large grosses."

"This will send all types of audiences into screaming, roaring, howling, and sometimes hysterical laughter," echoed the *Showmen's Trade Review*. "It's undoubtedly one of the funniest comedies ever made and ranks very favorably with Harold Lloyd's previous efforts. Surpasses anything Preston Sturges has done before."

Said *Variety*, "Without setting out to prove anything in particular, *The Sin of Harold Diddlebock* demonstrates conclusively that neither Harold Lloyd nor the comedy technique of silent films has lost any of its entertainment value in the passage of the decades. The picture is surefire box-office wherever the customers are looking for belly laughs."

The film had its world premier at the Lincoln Theatre in Miami on February 18, 1947. In attendance were the Ritz Brothers, Carmen Miranda, Una Merkel, and, representing Cal-Pix, Arline Judge and Harold Lloyd. The audience was responsive, the reviews enthusiastic, and the ensuing business brisk. In subsequent engagements—in Portland, San Francisco, and Fort Wayne, Indiana—the film performed admirably. Sturges was noticeably fortified, but Hughes wasn't. He thought the film slow and over-long and in May of 1947, before the film had a chance at a Los Angeles or New York booking, he pulled it from release. Word got to Sturges that Stuart Gilmore was back on the film, trimming the ending and removing Rudy Vallée, whom Hughes detested. There was no word on when the film might be re-released.

Hughes' cut was undeniably tighter, but Sturges protested the fact that Hughes had dared touch his picture at all, especially with the quality of the reviews it had been getting. Of Hughes' version, Sturges wrote to Bosley Crowther, "I begged him, for Christ's sake, to have a showing of both versions in New York and to ask you and possibly Archer Winsten to give a verdict as to which is better, but he sneered haughtily at this and said he didn't make pictures for critics, he made pictures for the exhibitors and the public."

Hughes shaved nineteen minutes from the running time and, for reasons mysterious to everybody, added a talking horse to the ending. At least he had a better title: *Mad Wednesday*. The film was scheduled for nationwide release in late 1947 and then withdrawn in anticipation of Hughes's purchase of RKO in 1948.

In the meantime, *Vendetta* was almost entirely scrapped, and Hughes commissioned a completely new screenplay. Predictably, he dropped the little boy and once again switched directors. Said

Sturges, "I think it came out the best of anything I have tackled, and it will of course never see the screen as Mr. Hughes had it scrapped, rewritten, and reshot."

Sturges was now at a point where he must have wondered whether Buddy DeSylva was that bad a fellow after all. *"The Sin of Harold Diddlebock* has been renamed *Mad Wednesday* or *Shrove Tuesday* or something equally appropriate," Sturges reported to a friend that summer. "In any case, I am weary of it and have no more interest in it than in news about an old ex-wife.

"I seem to have wasted the last three years horsing around with independent ventures and stock companies and various other efforts all to the accompaniment of gentle laughter from the Collector of Internal Revenue, but as I also wasted the first thirty years of my life, I don't suppose this matters very much."

24.

Preston Sturges resumed major studio moviemaking in early 1947 only slightly humbler than before. Certainly no one was surprised by the disintegration of the Sturges-Hughes partnership, save, of course, the partners themselves. If there was any surprise, it was in the fact that it had lasted as long as it had. Sturges covered his disappointment and humiliation with flip comments about artistic temperaments and Mr. Hughes' genius clashing with his own. Privately, the irritation was much more apparent. "The son of a bitch fired me at seven o'clock in the morning," he reportedly told one friend. "I could have forgiven him if he had waited until noon."

Sturges was once more available to Hollywood. And again the offers came. Most all the majors tendered offers. One independent, Sam Goldwyn, proposed to build Sturges his own office building on the Goldwyn lot. Sturges thought carefully about this one, no doubt feeling the best face-saving tactic was to make the most lucrative deal possible, with whoever chose to offer it. Yet he could not convince himself that life would be any easier under Goldwyn than it had been under DeSylva or Hughes. Goldwyn financed his pictures as Hughes and Chaplin did: completely, and he owned them outright. Goldwyn was no production executive and his risks were not borne by a collection of faceless stockholders. One was dealing strictly with *his* property, and this was an arrangement no better, Sturges decided, than working with an executive producer for one of the majors.

Sturges declined the Goldwyn offer, as he did the offers from Paramount and M-G-M, and went instead to 20th Century-Fox, where he would report directly to Darryl F. Zanuck.

Sturges already had offices at Fox, at the old Western Avenue studios off Sunset. He had moved there with Cal-Pix after Goldwyn had evicted the independents crowding his lot in early 1946. *Vendetta* was filmed at Goldwyn, but Sturges settled on Western Avenue for his offices with the idea that these older studios, seldom used anymore, might be available for purchase by Cal-Pix. He liked the thought of his coming to own the Fox studios that were so significant to his early career. Later, when the California partnership fell through, Sturges bought the Hughes office furniture used at Fox and remained there, very comfortably. More than a dozen rooms on the second floor of the old administration building were given over to the Sturges staff. Sturges himself claimed the former office of William Fox, which sported French windows, green drapes, and a V-shaped skylight.

Zanuck had wanted Sturges since *The Great McGinty* and had made Sturges' loan-out to Fox a condition of Henry Fonda's participation in *The Lady Eve*. But Paramount had never made good on the promise and now Zanuck's offer would, in effect, make him the highest-priced producer-director in the world. The deal appealed not only from the money angle, but because Zanuck truly admired Sturges' films and would respect his talent. Sturges could keep his offices on Western Avenue and even shoot there if he wished. And Sturges pointed out to the press that he did indeed owe Zanuck a picture—morally, if not legally.

The agreement was predicated on the sale of the story *Matrix*, which Sturges had first written for Elissa Landi in 1933 and which had cost him his position at Columbia Pictures. *Matrix* was the ugly duckling of the Sturges trunk, a favorite of its creator but without a champion elsewhere. There can be little doubt that Fox acquired it in December of 1946 to demonstrate goodwill and the seriousness of their advances. The story itself was a distasteful diatribe on the mysteries of love and devotion. The heroine was a beautiful woman who spurns the love of a rich and powerful executive in favor of a weak and inconsequential mate who, by Sturges' reasoning, has aroused her maternal instincts. Sturges' idea was more interesting than his thesis. He wrote in an introduction, "We have all often heard it said: 'She is so lovely! What can she possibly see in that jerk?' This is an attempt at an explanation."

The sale of *Matrix* for $50,000 occurred on December 13, 1946. Three days later, the New York *Times* reported that the basic terms of a deal had been finalized and that Sturges planned to film *Matrix* at Fox with actress Gene Tierney. As with Cal-Pix, Sturges insisted upon outside pictures; his arrangement with Zanuck allowed him one for each picture he made for Fox. His initial thirty-week contract took effect on March 10, 1947. His weekly rate was set at $7825.

Mogul Zanuck treated his new property with deference. He flattered with memos and indulged Preston's illusion of autonomy. Sturges responded just as pleasantly, happily appraising the distance of nine miles between Western Avenue and the main studio at Fox Hills. He had his own little lot, an impressive office, and a sponsor who seemed friendly and tasteful. He decided he was better off here than he could ever have been at Cal-Pix, as he now had all he could ask for as an independent producer with none of the administrative headaches.

Sturges settled down to work, picking at *Matrix* while he lunched with Zanuck and swapped memos and compliments. But Zanuck courted Sturges to request a favor. Gene Tierney was a popular star at Fox, and Sturges might well use her to advantage. She was not, however, the box-office attraction Betty Grable was and Zanuck's plan was for Betty Grable. Grable herself maintained no delusions concerning her potential. "People like to hear me sing, see me dance, and watch my legs," she once told an interviewer. "My legs made me."

Zanuck thought differently. Grable's likability was second to none; he was convinced her public would follow her into more prestigious entertainments, but would gradually become bored if she continued grinding out the same Technicolor musicals indefinitely. In 1946 she was the fourth most popular actress in films. *The Dolly Sisters*, released in November of 1945, was her most profitable film yet. But the war was over and the men who had made her the quintessential pinup girl were returning home to comprise the largest domestic audience the industry would ever know. They would look for Betty Grable, Zanuck reasoned, but not as they once had. She was, in a way, symbolic of an era that had now come to an end. And she would be expected to change and to grow. Grable was Fox's most valuable asset in an increasingly competitive marketplace. It was important to use her wisely.

Betty Grable had been off the screen for more than a year when *The Shocking Miss Pilgrim* was released in February of 1947. It was a period piece about a Boston businesswoman with a Gershwin score and a writer-director named George Seaton. It hadn't turned out well, but it was atypical and more adventuresome than *Coney Island* or *Pin-Up Girl*. Zanuck forged gamely ahead with *Mother Wore Tights*, a nostalgic Lamar Trotti script with Grable and Dan Dailey as a pair of touring vaudevillians with two young daughters. Again, the results were not outstanding, but Zanuck loved it and actually saw it as the turning point in Grable's career. *Mother Wore Tights* placed her forever beyond the simple Technicolor amusements of World War II, he declared. It was time for her to be placed at the disposal of genius. Zanuck told Sturges, "She cannot go backward."

Zanuck wanted Sturges to write a picture for her; a *Miracle of Morgan's Creek*, for instance. Something with a little meat in it, something both the critics and the public would like. If he could do it for Veronica Lake and Betty Hutton, he certainly could do it for Betty Grable. The genius of Sturges and the popularity of Grable—

an unbeatable combination. Sturges hesitated, worried about doing another picture for what he considered a "favor." But Zanuck was too accommodating for him to refuse. Sturges hoped for a long and fruitful association with 20th Century-Fox and this man. He was finally, literally, flattered into doing it. Grable was not untalented and surely he could do *something* with her. And, the ultimate justification, it would open the door to more prestigious, less commercial films.

Once Sturges had consented to do a picture with Grable, Zanuck went to work selling him on a treatment called *The Lady from Laredo*. As long as he had agreed to write and direct a vehicle for Betty Grable, why not try making a Western? It was a genre as foreign to him as the horror film at the time of *The Invisible Man*. But there were indeed some familiar elements: the townspeople would be little more than modifications of the residents of Morgan's Creek. And the setting would be perfectly natural for a man like Al Bridge, who made his living apart from Sturges in "B" Westerns for Republic and lesser companies. Sturges would take a traditional Western setting, the story's plot of a gunslinging saloon singer forced to pose as the new schoolteacher, and the basic characters of any good Western and invest the package with the kind of sophisticated dialogue and slapstick audiences had come to expect of his modern-day comedies.

Sturges began dictating Freddie, the Grable character, as a little girl of six, obediently blowing a row of whisky bottles to smithereens at the patient direction of her old grandpa ("There you go pullin' the trigger again! When all you got to do is close your hand gently like you was squeezin' a sockful of dead mice . . ."). From there the story went to big Freddie in jail, explaining indignantly why she had to shoot her two-timing boyfriend Blackie, and how she happened to shoot the town judge instead. Zanuck was tickled with the first pages and said as much. The scene with the little girl was charming and the setup for Freddie's escape from the law and her subsequent posing as the schoolmarm was skillful and funny.

Sturges pressed on, working slowly but diligently, addressing himself always to the image of Betty Grable and not her character. He added a part for Rudy Vallée and a Mexican sidekick named Conchita. He approached the task of making the picture as if it were a laboratory problem. He examined some twenty-three Grable pictures, starting with the early black and whites for Paramount and RKO. He was reminded that she had appeared in *Child of Manhattan* at Columbia in 1933. He focused on the Fox pictures made since 1940, especially *Down Argentine Way*, in which she had replaced an ailing Alice Faye on a moment's notice. The film was in the bright, sometimes garish Technicolor of the day, and became such a hit that Fox, after 1942, dared not tamper with the formula. There came a long string of such films—*Springtime in the Rockies, Sweet Rosie O'Grady, Billy Rose's Diamond Horseshoe.* Grable inched her way into the top ten in 1942 and remained there for the rest of the decade.

Sturges reasoned that Grable's popularity was based not only on her own pleasing personality and the quality of her singing and dancing, but also on the fact that her pictures were attractive displays of costuming and color, and that there were few enough pictures being made in color that the customers went out of their way to see them. Grable's name was practically synonymous with Technicolor by 1947 and Sturges saw no way out of making *The Lady from Laredo* in Technicolor.

He completed a first draft, titled *The Beautiful Blonde from Bashful Bend,* in mid-August of 1947. Again, Zanuck commended the quality of his work, urging that production commence as soon as possible. Grable had been kept inactive in anticipation of the Sturges script, to which over $200,000 had been charged. Sturges, however, stalled on the question of color. Filming in color was quite expensive at the time, requiring a special camera, three times as much raw stock, brighter lighting, a color consultant, and special processing. Only certain kinds of pictures were made in color: primarily costume dramas and musicals, where the color would clearly add to the pageantry of a given story and contribute measurably to the box office. Generally speaking, big stars didn't need color; Clark Gable, Bing Crosby, Abbott and Costello rarely, if ever, appeared in it. But Betty Grable, it seemed, always had.

The problem was cost, and Zanuck saw a major obstacle to Fox profiting from *The Beautiful Blonde* if it were made in color. The British Labour government had instituted a 75% tax on American movie receipts. In the case of a film that not only charged to budget the salaries of Betty Grable and Preston Sturges but the Technicolor process as well, it was absolutely imperative that the foreign receipts be as high and unencumbered as possible. Forty percent of world gross generally came from foreign markets, and 85% of that 40% from England. The tax could well make the difference between *The Beautiful Blonde from Bashful Bend* turning a profit and ending up in the red. Sturges was adamant. He memoed:

"Miss Grable is the natural child of color. Presenting her without it is like presenting an opera without music. *The Beautiful Blonde from Bashful Bend* is not really a screen play at all, but only a vehicle disguised as a screen play fashioned for the sole purpose of presenting the luscious Betty Grable to her customers in the full color to which they are accustomed. Granted that I have thrown in as many jokes as I can and that I have some facility along this line, and granted that I will throw in some more jokes and tie it all up in the end in a very workman-like way, the picture will still be a very minor effort in both your life and mine. For this waste of our lives, the only excuse can be that the picture was charmingly done and made a great deal of money which we subsequently spent on better ventures."

Zanuck was loath to concur with this line of reasoning, but he was also loath to tell Preston Sturges he couldn't make the film in Technicolor if he truly wished to. Zanuck and his experts considered the English tax temporary, but if they postponed *The Beautiful Blonde* they would be in the awkward position of having spent $234,750 on a presently unproduceable screenplay. *Matrix*, in the meantime, had gone through the usual channels of evaluation and come up a zero. Zanuck inquired if it would be possible to substitute another story for the $50,000 he had paid for *Matrix* and Sturges pleasantly agreed. In the place of *Matrix* he substituted an even older story that dated back to the writing of *The Power and the Glory*. He called it *The Symphony Story*, and said he could write it in the space of eight weeks. This would give Zanuck a picture before the current season was out. "I spritz dialogue like seltzer water," Sturges wrote him. "My trouble has never been in inventing it, but rather in throwing three-quarters of it away."

Reluctantly, Zanuck agreed to the postponement of *The Beautiful Blonde from Bashful Bend*. Grable was given to Fox's other resident genius, Ernst Lubitsch, who didn't seem to mind shooting her in black and white. Preparations went forward on *This Is the Moment** with Grable and Douglas Fairbanks, Jr., and production got under way in late November.

Sturges' thirty-week contract with Fox expired on November 8, 1947. *The Symphony Story* was ready for the cameras on December 2. Sturges described it: "An English conductor, Sir Alfred de Carter, whose family made its money in pills, discovers just before his concert that he is a cuckold. As he starts leading the orchestra, we go into his mind and see his plans for dealing with the situation *as modified by the music he is playing*. There are pieces that soothe the savage breast and pieces that set fire to the seat of your pants; also pieces that make you feel very Christ-like. Having seen all of Sir Alfred's hypotheses we arrive at the end of the concert and see how he behaves in real life as opposed to the projections of himself to music."

The idea had first occurred to him in December of 1932, while he was writing *The Power and the Glory* in an office at Universal. "I had a scene all written and had only to put it down on paper," he

---

*Released as *That Lady in Ermine* (1948). Lubitsch died of a heart attack after only a few days' work and the film was completed by Otto Preminger. The tax threat passed quickly: the film was made in color.

recalled. "To my surprise, it came out quite unlike what I had planned. I sat back wondering what the hell had happened, then noticed that someone had left the radio on in the next room and realized that I had been listening to a symphony broadcast from New York and that this, added to my thoughts, had changed the total."

Sturges wrote his story under the title *The Concert*, then offered it unsuccessfully to both Paramount and Fox in late 1933 as *Unfinished Symphony*. When Darryl Zanuck finally gave it a green light in 1947, he insisted upon a more commercial title than *The Symphony Story* ("We must keep 'symphony' out of the title," he said). Sturges suggested *Improper Relations*, under which the project was known for several weeks, and then *Lover-in-Law*, before ultimately settling upon *Unfaithfully Yours*, the title of the unproduced bedroom farce Sturges had written in 1932.

Unfaithfully Yours was unique in that nothing actually happens to its central character. The imagined affair has not occurred and a good portion of the action takes place only in Sir Alfred's mind.

"That play was autobiographical," said Frances Ramsden. "It is Preston's relationship to me . . . He said, 'One of the reasons I'm frightened to have you is because every man who ever looks at you wants you.'" Approaching fifty, Sturges could be relentlessly possessive, to the point where no actor wishing a part dared speak to Francie in his presence.

His obsession with age was constant, and, at times, all-consuming. *Unfaithfully Yours* was littered with references to youth and the difference in ages. Francie was twenty-four years Sturges' junior. "He trusted me," said Ramsden, "because he never had any reason not to trust me. I never flirted with another man; we never had a lovers' quarrel over another person. But he fantasized. He said, 'You're young, you'll be a great star, you're staying with me because you say you love me,' but he always felt there'd be so much out there for me if I left him."

So much did Frances Ramsden influence the film that Sturges wrote the part of Daphne for her to play. At Cal-Pix there had been requests from other studios for her. Zanuck himself had tried to borrow her, without success, for a picture opposite Tyrone Power. So when Preston suggested using her in *Unfaithfully Yours*, he was amenable. James Mason had been Sturges' first choice for Sir Alfred, but had become unavailable due to some contractual problems. Rex Harrison was an inspired second choice, perfectly suited for delivering the elegant dialogue Sturges wrote with such ease. There was, however, a major hitch in using Francie: she had a bad back which had plagued her since the age of five.

Wrote Sturges to Bosley Crowther on November 1, "Just for your very private ear there is a heluva race starting here on Tuesday. Zanuck has told me I can pencil Francie in opposite Rex Harrison in the new picture. She is just out of the hospital again after another attack of spinal disc trouble which they now find will heal only with a major operation. Without the operation I could not in fairness put her in the picture as her back might give way at any moment. The operation requires two months convalescence. She will be operated upon in the Hollywood Presbyterian Hospital Tuesday, November 4th. The picture starts January 5th."

Sturges proceeded to polish the script and finished casting with Barbara Lawrence, Kurt Kreuger, Lionel Stander, Rudy Vallée, Edgar Kennedy, and the usual complement of character actors. The scheduled starting date came and went. Francie's recovery was rapid (thirteen days after surgery, she bumped into her doctor at a party while dancing the rumba), but Zanuck stalled. He studied the script, presumed to edit it a bit, then decided the cast was too weak to carry a picture as expensive as *Unfaithfully Yours*. Although happy with the script and cast as set, he worried about Harrison being popular enough to carry the film on his own. Zanuck decided he wanted Gene Tierney (who had done *The Ghost and Mrs. Muir* with Harrison) instead of Frances Ramsden. Preston understood and agreed to the change. Then, in deference to Ramsden, Tierney withdrew and Linda Darnell replaced her. Filming began on Stage 5 at Fox Hills on February 18, 1948. The budget was set at just under $2 million and the schedule at a comfortable fifty-six days. The set was jammed with visitors; the press covered the event in force.

At questions about the hefty budget for the picture and trends for economy, Sturges balked. "Anybody can make money in good times, even with lousy pictures," he told the reporters. "Now is the time to put good money into *good* pictures."

Unfaithfully Yours was filmed in much the same atmosphere that *The Sin of Harold Diddlebock* was, but with the necessary discipline Darryl Zanuck was able to exert. He wrote daily memos (as many as half a dozen), but allowed Sturges his head. Sturges, in turn, directed the film as a show as much for the crew and visitors as for the public. He wore a bright red fez throughout the production ("So the director is always easy to find"), and bragged that he generally worked twenty hours a day and slept only four (not quite true, but close).

The Los Angeles *Times'* Philip K. Scheuer witnessed the filming of a small fire in Sir Alfred's dressing room one morning and reported the following: "While flames encouraged by liquid gas turned the room into an inferno and real firemen stood by, chewing their nails, Harrison and Sturges took turns at playing the hose on everyone they could reach—in and out of camera range."

Unfaithfully Yours contained some of the slickest dialogue Preston Sturges had ever written, owed in no small sense to the fact that Rex Harrison's part was, in effect, that of Sturges himself. The mannerisms, the endearments, the phrases, the attitudes, the rages—they all were his.

August (Rudy Vallée) informs Sir Alfred that he has had his wife tailed by detectives. Sir Alfred is outraged: "You dare to inform me that you have had vulgar footpads in snap brim fedoras sluicing after my beautiful wife??"

With the seed of infidelity planted in Sir Alfred's head, Sturges set the stage for the varying pieces of music: Rossini's *Semiramide* Overture (murder), Wagner's *Tannhäuser* Overture and Venusberg Music (forgiveness), and Tchaikovsky's *Francesca da Rimini* (Russian roulette). The payoff comes when he returns home after the performance and tries to implement, with violent incompetence, each of these plans.

The completed film displayed a tightness of expression and, yet, an equal joy of exhibition. An extended sequence of Sir Alfred rehearsing the orchestra in the *Semiramide* Overture established no more than wonder for musicians coming together to create music. Sturges' camera lovingly surveyed the spectacle from above and behind, slowly drawing closer to the conductor and noting every nuance of movement and its corresponding effect.

Unfaithfully Yours was unflinchingly flamboyant, from its nimble use of sound (not only musical, but with effects as minor as wallet zippers, wheezing sandwich bread, and melodious clock chimes) to its transitions from Sir Alfred's podium into his mind—shot in single continuous takes that begin with medium shots of Harrison leading the orchestra and move quickly into the black of the eyeball, retaining perfect focus at all times. The effect, after decades of technical advancement, is still breathtaking.

It was, of course, absolutely crucial that Harrison appear to be the eminent conductor he supposedly was. The task of teaching the actor—who couldn't read music—to conduct credibly for the camera fell upon actor-conductor Robin Sanders-Clark. Harrison and Sanders-Clark worked for seven weeks perfecting a system of counting beats. "I went out there every night," the conductor recalled. "Sometimes we'd work until two or three in the morning. I first of all had to teach him how to conduct four-in-a-bar, three-in-a-bar, two-in-a-bar, so on, which I did. And then he had to learn the pieces like he learned lines. He couldn't read the music. So I'd take, for instance, the *Semiramide* Overture and say, 'It starts at four bars with a timpani. The fifth bar, the violas and cellos enter, and, on the ninth bar, the horns enter. So he absolutely learned it like that. I showed him where all the sections of the orchestra would be and he had to count mentally. Also, I had an off-camera mike and I would prompt him, always a bar or two bars ahead."

The scheme worked beautifully. Harrison gave a fine account of himself and carried the whole film on the basis of his performance.

Sturges brought *Unfaithfully Yours* in on schedule and $4000 under budget. Though Zanuck thought it a "wonderful, wonderful comedy," he felt that the picture had been scheduled for a week more than was necessary and that it would have to be a tremendous box-office hit (on the scale of *The Miracle of Morgan's Creek*) to make any money. Sturges, confident this would be the case, took a good long time editing the footage. Zanuck estimated that Sturges was allowed 300% more time to edit than any other director in Fox history. By the time of the first preview, in Riverside on June 3, the film ran 126 minutes and clocked ninety-four walkouts. Zanuck insisted the film be cut to no more than one hour and forty-five minutes and, on June 11, took charge of the additional cutting himself. Most preview cards indicated what the producer had feared: viewers either loved it or detested it. It would be a very long shot to break even under such conditions.

Unfaithfully Yours was virtually complete by the July 4 holiday, and then—as if it didn't have a rough enough chance for acceptance on its own merits—it made the nation's newspapers by virtue of one of Hollywood's greatest scandals: the Carole Landis suicide.

Married to actress Lilli Palmer, Rex Harrison had been romantically involved with the blond actress, and when news of her death—from an overdose of Seconal barbiturates—reached the public, the attention of the entire nation fell upon him. Reporters staked themselves out at his house, and dogged him through a brightly lit coroner's inquiry and public funeral at Forest Lawn. *Unfaithfully Yours* and Joseph L. Mankiewicz's *Escape* were Harrison's two films in reserve. His questionable pull at the box office dwindled to nil.

"The studio could have given me some support," the actor wrote years later, "but as far as I know, no statement was made. The atmosphere in the front office was strained when I went there very much later, and visiting one of the sets I heard someone say, 'After all, it happened to Fatty Arbuckle.' "

Sturges, numbed by the tragic event, could not speculate on what effect the adverse publicity might have on his film's success. It was shown to the New York office, where it was well received, and the decision was made to hold it for a November release.

Discounting *Diddlebock*, it would be the first Sturges picture in general release in four years—since *The Great Moment* in 1944. They allowed it a big and appropriate advertising campaign. Sturges nervously awaited the verdicts of the East Coast critics. A full-page ad in *The Motion Picture Herald* read:

TIMED TO BRING YOU YOUR HAPPIEST HOLIDAY SEASON . . .
MADE FOR HOLIDAY GROSSES ANY TIME!

Unfaithfully Yours opened at the 6200-seat Roxy Theatre on November 6, 1948. The notices were remarkably mixed, paralleling the trade press comments of a week earlier.

The Hollywood Reporter: "*Unfaithfully Yours* is typically Preston Sturges—a fanciful film dealing with an idea instead of a plot. The characters are original and amusing in the usual Sturges style, and the tone of the picture is a blending of high comedy and slapstick. This traditional formula accounts for some moments of rare good humor, but aside from these, *Unfaithfully Yours* appears slight, repetitious, and forced."

Film Daily: "An adroit fun fest from Preston Sturges. It is slick farce and will probably delight every audience segment."

Bosley Crowther, in the New York *Times*, stated, "It is too bad that Preston Sturges is not compelled by law to turn out at least one movie—maybe two—a year."

The Roxy's first-day receipts were among the lowest in its history; certainly the lowest Fox had had in years. It was hoped an enthusiastic review by critic Alton Cook in the *World-Telegram* would spark a growth of interest. Said Darryl Zanuck, "If it doesn't, we are certainly in for one of the biggest beatings in history."

Business improved that weekend, but still remained slack. In desperation, the studio tried opening the film in five theatres in Los Angeles with the ad campaign of a murder mystery, not even hinting at its comedic elements. Shrouded in cobwebs, Harrison resembled the villain in a Sherlock Holmes film. On all accounts, *Unfaithfully Yours* died a horrible death, generally dismissed as "class entertainment" with no mass appeal. And the failure dealt a heavy blow to the Sturges career. He could not afford another.

25.

In spite of his record income from 20th Century-Fox, the drain on Sturges' cash reserves was fierce. Never one to consider saving a virtue, he found whatever funds he had been able to accrue after wartime taxation eaten up by that bottomless pit of fiscal whimsy, The Players.

Business dropped off appreciably as the restaurant entered the latter half of the 1940s, with postwar inflation and a tradition of employee theft making matters worse. "There was a lot of leakage," Dominick Maggie confirmed. "Preston was a very trusting guy." Cries of "86!" would go up whenever he entered the building. Said one employee, "The entire texture of the place changed when Preston was there."

The pillage was not merely confined to ashtrays and matchbooks: whole sides of beef disappeared. Vegetables went out under jackets and overcoats; even cases of liquor. And Preston's ears were impervious to talk of such things. It was beyond his comprehension that his employees would do that to him. "Don't spoil my day," he would say. End of discussion.

It is doubtful that Sturges ever made a profit on The Players, even in the best of times. He staunchly refused to take steps to shelter his income, preferring to plow whatever earnings there were back into the building with mechanical improvements and additions like the barbershop. At one time he had wanted to build a helicopter pad in the upper parking lot for the purpose of flying in fresh fish. The neighbors objected, however, and Sturges finally dropped the idea.

The decline in business was probably due to changing tastes and the metamorphosis the Sunset Strip underwent in the late forties and early fifties. The Players was devoid of the kind of intimacy regulars found at places like Chasen's and the Brown Derby. Always more of a novelty than a tradition, it was the "in" place to go only for a while. As Sturges began his apparent four-year hiatus from filmmaking, The Players began to fall from favor. The famous faces were replaced by faces not so famous and—increasingly—by tourists.

Sturges saw a more sinister reason for the drop in patronage and maintained it to the day of his death. It stemmed from a nasty incident that occurred toward the end of the war, involving —ironically—his old adversary Ben Schulberg.

As Sturges explained it in 1959, ". . . Schulberg, incensed at my refusal to fire an old manager of a restaurant of mine . . . who had unfortunately drawn his ire, started a rumor that I was anti-Semitic. Now the Jews, on subjects like this, are no more intelligent than any other group of people, so without bothering to ascertain the truth of the allegation, they immediately boycotted my restaurant and ruined it."

Schulberg, it seems, had engaged in a shouting match at the restaurant with a former writer of his who, during the course of the exchange, made some rather intolerant remarks about the Jews and Schulberg in particular. Indignantly, Schulberg demanded that Monsieur Pillet eject this man, which Pillet declined to do. Schulberg then petitioned Sturges, by letter and telegram, to dismiss Pillet, and, of course, Sturges refused. Instead, he responded with a letter that included the following passage:

"If instead of blaming me and my hard working manager . . . you and other prominent Jews would do something to stem the deplorable wave of anti-Semitism which seems to have started in the armed forces, you would be spending your time to better purpose. This is very much more serious than the animosity of a former writer for his former producer. The slogan: 'to clean up the Nips and come back and clean up the Jews . . .' seems, unfortunately, to be widespread in use among men in uniform."

This comment evidently served only to make Schulberg angrier. The very idea of a Jewish boycott was ludicrous to anyone who knew Sturges well. His Jewish friends included Charley Abramson, Oscar Serlin, Willie Wyler, the Laemmles, Al Lewin, Charlie Chaplin, David Lewis, Ernst Lubitsch, and scores of others. When someone asked Harry Rosenthal how come he was working for an anti-Semite, he snarled back, "Auntie *What?* I wisht I'd a had the concession to smuggle Gentiles into his last Christmas party!"

By 1946 The Players was clearly in trouble. In the past, Sturges had thought nothing of spending $2000 a week on improvements and whims and in making up deficits and payroll. Now his response was to redecorate—to change the entire look of the place. The cost was not excessive: $100 to $150 a week for supplies and a painter, and another hundred or so for a carpenter named Joe Santana. He estimated three weeks, maybe four, to repaint the mezzanine and the top level and rid the building of the predominant pink of which he had grown so tired. He hired a very creative artist by the name of Maxine Merlino, who made sketches of whole walls with painted curtains, padding, windows, and Roman columns. Sturges approved some, reworked others, and changed his mind after they had been painted. Walls were painted and repainted and The Players began to look like the Palace of Versailles. "I got so good at painting Roman columns," said Maxine Merlino, "that people would go over and touch them."

Sturges had his own peculiar way of doing things. "Half the time," said Merlino, "when you thought you had a solution to a problem that was the sensible, pragmatic one, it wasn't Preston's way. He'd have another way of doing it, so we'd rip it out. Preston's way was not always the practical, functional way, but it was always the way with flair."

Merlino worked an average of sixteen hours a day, Sturges prodding her on. "You're only as tired as you feel," he told her. He once presented her with a copy of *How Never to Be Tired or Two Lifetimes in One*, but she refused to read it. Staggering off to bed at one or two, she would return the next morning to find notes written on the backs of menus:

> Maxine dear—
> It seems to me that maybe the capital over the door should be painted a little more *freely*—maybe that would take away the Forest Lawn machine chiselled look. Call me at Granite 1831 if you wish to discuss the matter—
> PS.

Repainting was only the beginning. By the time Sturges began work at Fox he had decided to go ahead with an idea of Eddie Bracken's to turn The Playroom with the revolving bandstand into a dinner theatre. He then added the notion of making the room not only adaptable to dining and staging, but to dancing and film showings. He envisioned, in fact, an entire evening's entertainment within the same four walls—a room that converted at the touch of a button. Building such a room was, needless to say, a task of sizable proportions. Not only would he have to get a zoning clearance, he would have to enlarge the top level considerably, adding dressing rooms and a scenery dock, and even at that there would be precious little space.

"Part of it is a little tricky," Sturges wrote to a friend in the summer of 1948, "as the stepped pit of the auditorium has to turn into a dance floor, complete with ringside tables, in two minutes. I have also devised a new (I believe) method of shifting scenery by a sort of overhead switchyard composed of garage door tracks. There will also be 16mm rear projection for sound film and 35mm front projection. I will have a permanent stock company and we will give regular three act plays like *Saturday's Children* or *Little*

Accident or *Successful Calamity* or *Children of Darkness* or such, for which we will pay the regular stock royalties. The novelty of all this is that it will not be an experimental theatre or group, groping for some new form of expression or new talent, literary or dramatic, but merely a theatre. That is to say: a room in which people gather in mass to hear the words of playwrights mouthed by actors. The financial problem should be solved by a two dollar cover charge. The room will seat between two hundred and three hundred. The most I can lose is a fortune."

Sturges' cash reserves were further depleted by the fact that his draw at Cal-Pix had been substantially less than what he had been getting at Paramount. And there was also the divorce, which was granted, after fifteen postponements, on November 12, 1947. The settlement called for $57,500 in cash, 50% of Preston's interest in Cal-Pix, 20% of his annual literary income (up to $9000), $45 a week child support, a $20,000 trust fund for Mon, and two automobiles. He accepted the outcome with dignity; at least he got to keep the house.

The engineering company expanded to eleven employees and was kept busy machining stainless steel valves for an oil company and selling bronze gimbal candelabra and other yachting novelties through local newspaper ads. They also built boats Sturges added to his fleet: there were three by the summer of 1948 and two more in the works.

That summer was an especially wearing one for Sturges. He was bothered by the fact that Zanuck had recut *Unfaithfully Yours* (although he had pronounced himself happy with the final cut), and wished he were out of his commitment to direct *The Beautiful Blonde from Bashful Bend*, which he was to start preparing in August. He would escape for the weekends on long cruises—usually to Catalina—with Francie and Maxine and Caroline Wedderburn, his secretary, and a large pot of bouillabaisse. There he would anchor in the Fourth of July cove, where there were few yachts, and lapse into semisomnambulistic trances, reclining toward the stern, hand resting on the tiller, his eyes gazing far off into the distance. "He would sit that way for *hours* on end," said Maxine, "almost as if he were brooding. He would not talk. But if I would walk by, he might say something very sweet to me like, 'Those slacks look nice on you,' or 'I'm going to get you a new sweater. That color isn't right.' He loved to watch me go swimming and would throw quarters for me to dive for."

He was not particularly good company on these trips. "We all got bored," Maxine continued. "I know Francie got terribly bored. And we somehow didn't do things unless he suggested we do them. If we suggested them, he would find wonderful little ways of saying that we couldn't do them. He never wanted us to go ashore, for instance."

It was as if he wanted his privacy and yet could not bear to be alone. One Saturday morning during a record heat wave in July of 1948, Preston called the Woolfans and said, "Let's go down to the boat and get out of this heat."

At San Pedro, they took the *Island Belle*, his thirty-two-foot "grand islander," but didn't go outside the harbor. The three were lazy and they just sat and enjoyed the cool breeze and the food packed from The Players. Darkness fell. Large padded cushions were pulled out onto the deck, and Sturges and the Woolfans remained awake throughout the night. There were stars and a moon and the two men talked as Priscilla lay between them.

"There was no subject they did not explore," said Priscilla. "And eventually, the moon went down and the stars were changing, and they got around to the subject of 'What's up there?' and 'What's beyond?'

"And they both agreed. They felt—no proof—that there was *something*. 'Or else,' Preston asked, 'why is this life such agony at times?' "

On Sunday the heat returned, and eventually they returned to port. The next day was Monday and Bertie had to get some sleep. At Preston's house, the Woolfans got into Priscilla's car.

"Are you leaving me?" Preston wanted to know.

"Preston, I have to sleep," said Bertie. "Tomorrow is Monday. I have to get up early." The next day, at noon, Bertie returned to collect his favorite sweater, which he had left behind.

"How could you go yesterday and leave me alone?" asked Preston. "I can't understand it. I was so depressed, I wrote this poem," which he offered on a sheet of stationery that displayed his profile.

> Cold are the hands of time—
> that creep along relentlessly
> Destroying slowly
> but without pity
> That which yesterday was young.
> Alone our memories
> resist this disintegration—
> And grow more lovely with the passing years.

Bertie said, "Give it to me." Preston did, and wrote "For Bertie" at the bottom.*

---

*Bertie kept this poem till his death, believing Preston had composed it that evening. It was some thirty years after the fact that Priscilla learned it had appeared under Preston's entry in Rouben Mamoulian's autograph book in 1936. Six years later, it came out of the mouth of the "Wienie King" in *The Palm Beach Story*.

Filming began on *The Beautiful Blonde from Bashful Bend* in late September of 1948. In Technicolor, the film was budgeted at $2,192,000, making it the most expensive Betty Grable film to date.

The Beautiful Blonde was cast with stock company types, but, oddly, not Frank Moran, Julius Tannen, nor even Jimmy Conlin. Zanuck cast much of the picture himself, not wishing to give Sturges free reign on a film this costly. Cesar Romero, a Zanuck favorite, was cast as Blackie and Olga San Juan would play Grable's sidekick, Conchita. By the time shooting commenced, Sturges had lost whatever enthusiasm he once held for the project and regretted once more getting involved with a picture that was not wholly his own doing. There was no line, no typically Sturges idea to carry the action along. It was, as he had said earlier, only a vehicle disguised as a screenplay, and he had lost, over the space of a decade, the faculty he once had for writing such things. Not that it was a bad script; it read well. But the rushes lacked the old bounce of his Paramount films. His disinterest was evident to the cast and crew and, eventually, to Zanuck. "I needed the money," he later said with a shrug. "I got four hundred and sixty-four thousand for it."

The strain between Zanuck and his director became pronounced as *Unfaithfully Yours* neared release and anxiety over its box office grew. When his worst fears were confirmed, Zanuck scrutinized Sturges' performance on *The Beautiful Blonde* as if he were the parent of a wayward child requiring constant supervision. He didn't like Sturges' original ending and suggested the judge get shot yet a third time, which Sturges rejected out-of-hand. Zanuck then noted that the rushes were sluggish and that the film had fallen behind schedule. The memos became increasingly hostile.

Sturges later told a friend that he knew it was time to leave when he could no longer open a Zanuck memo without a momentary twinge of fear.

"He tried so very hard to get along with Zanuck," said Priscilla Woolfan. "He was very unhappy." The Woolfans had little indication of the trouble at Fox until one day while visiting the set. Priscilla had once acted in a picture at Goldwyn with an actor named Tom Moore. Moore had been a popular star and Priscilla recalled the experience of working with him fondly. Moore had a minor part in *Unfaithfully Yours* and wanted desperately the part of Betty Grable's grandfather in *The Beautiful Blonde*. He wrote to Sturges personally, and when he noticed Priscilla on the Sturges set, he approached her.

"I understand you and your husband are very close to Mr. Sturges . . ." he said to her. "There's a part in this picture that I'd love to play. . . . I haven't done anything in such a long time. . . . I know I could do this part well. Could you please ask Mr. Sturges to give it to me?"

Priscilla, momentarily stunned, replied graciously.

"I'll try. Tonight we'll be having dinner with him alone. I give you my word I'll try."

Priscilla waited that evening until just the proper moment to broach the subject. It was before dinner, and Preston had had his first drink. He was relaxed and receptive as Priscilla told her story. When it was over, tears welled in his eyes.

"If I could possibly give him the part," he said, "I would give it to him. I know what a fine actor he is, and I know he was a big star . . . but Zanuck won't even let me cast a minor role now. *In my own picture*. Priscilla, I'm having an awful time."

Preston Sturges being denied authority over a minor part in one of his pictures distressed Priscilla greatly. Suddenly, the seriousness of the Fox situation became apparent. "I don't know . . ." Preston said. "I'll get through it some way. . . ." He had an awful gut feeling about this picture, but he honored his commitment without question. Even Betty Grable turned away from him, perhaps sensing his disinterest and impatience.

"My relationship with Betty Grable has always been a mystery to me," he said later. "We were the best of friends and getting along fine until one day [Ray Klune], the head of the Fox production department and also of its News Gathering Service (if I make myself clear) visited my set and was closeted with Miss Grable in a portable dressing room for about one half hour. I have no idea what he said, but immediately thereafter Miss Grable became the reverse of polite and stupefied everyone on the set, the day we finished the picture (generally a happy day), by walking off without saying goodbye to me. I have always had the greatest respect for her acting ability and I had continued to sing her praises although her unflattering remarks about me had been repeated to me many times. I thought (and think) that she was a young Mae West. Maybe she disagreed with me."

Betty Grable told a columnist, "I was so mad I left the set after the last scene of the picture without even saying goodbye to anyone in the crew. That's the first time I've done that since I've been in the business."

Sturges' estrangement from Darryl Zanuck was soon complete, though Sturges regretted his inability to make economical pictures at the studio on Western Avenue, as had been his original intention. Zanuck took *The Beautiful Blonde from Bashful Bend* out of his hands after witnessing a preview in Pomona. "I walked around the block ten times," Zanuck recalled later. "I didn't know what to do."

The film was recut and Zanuck ordered a day's retakes done

under the supervision of an old-time comedy director. It was a foregone conclusion that Sturges' contract would not be renewed at a time when Sturges critically needed money for The Players. He began work on his dinner theatre, then fell behind on his food bills. There was a desperate tone in his final memo to Zanuck: "When I remember that I made *The Lady Eve* for $660,000 and *The Miracle of Morgan's Creek* for $775,000, I am outraged to see the slow, demoralizing, enthusiasm-sapping, absurdly expensive methods of film production that are growing like a cancer in the heart of this industry, making ruinously dangerous, as you said yourself a year ago, all forms of interesting experimentation and removing all the long shots from a business that always has been, and always will be, a gamble. I sincerely believe that only an invention in shooting and production techniques can shake us out of our lethargy and that is why I keep returning, with almost rude insistence, to the idea of making some pictures for you in the old studio on Western Avenue. I am certain that I can shoot a big picture in twenty-four days maximum. I am certain that I can do at least two pictures a year. I have done it before and you have heard of all of them. It means working sixteen hours a day, but I like to work sixteen hours a day and when you are doing what you want to do, sixteen hours pass like sixteen minutes. All of this I am perfectly willing to do on any equitable basis whatsoever. It can be straight salary plus originals, or drawing account against percentage of the gross, or a separate corporation. The more pictures you get out of me for a year's pay, the better I will like it. Give it some thought, my dear Darryl, before you chase me from this excellent company."

There was no reply.

When *The Beautiful Blonde from Bashful Bend* was released in May of 1949, it became justifiably infamous as Betty Grable's first starring flop. It signaled the gradual decline of her worth as a profitable attraction, as well as the relatively rapid fall from grace of Preston Sturges. It wasn't simply that a Sturges picture had been less than excellent; *The Beautiful Blonde* was not essentially Sturges. Even his lesser films—*The Sin of Harold Diddlebock* and *The Great Moment*—were unique by virtue of a concept and execution that were distinct and identifiable. In contrast, *The Beautiful Blonde from Bashful Bend* was merely a tired and undistinguished comedy that could have been written (and directed) by any one of a dozen lesser talents. There wasn't even enough action to make a good "B" Western. Sturges had reached that plateau where his films were no longer gauged against the works of others, but rather against his own greater achievements. As an effort to rank alongside *Sullivan's Travels* and *The Miracle of Morgan's Creek*, *The Beautiful Blonde from Bashful Bend* was miserably inadequate.

Said Archer Winsten in the New York *Post*, "This is a dreadful loss to Hollywood production. It comes at a time when the fresh satire and rowdy humor of Preston Sturges are most grievously missed. It comes without explanation, like darkness at noon, or a blow from behind. For *The Beautiful Blonde from Bashful Bend* is dull, flavorless, and labored. If it didn't say, right up there on the screen, that Preston Sturges wrote, directed, and produced it, I wouldn't ever believe it. Even now I keep thinking the studio must have finished the picture as a labor of sabotage and given him the triple credit as a parting curse."

Even the fan mail was negative: "So Hollywood wonders why the American people are turning more and more to foreign films?" wrote a woman from Chicago. "Imagine paying 98¢ to see that farce! As the saying goes, 'We should have stood in bed,' or at least have demanded a refund."

Seconded a man from Columbus, Ohio, "I was lured in, like a gullible moth by a candle, by a clever title and a lovely leading lady. My command of our language is above average, but I cannot find words which will express my reaction to this film. To say that it 'stinks' would be vulgar, and besides, it would be an over-statement. I can inadequately describe it as pitiful."

A gentleman in New York simply wrote, "I was always an admirer of yours in the past. I saw your picture *The Beautiful Blonde from Bashful Bend*. HOW COULD YOU?"

Sturges' friend Rupert Hughes reported that the common theatre audiences seemed to like it. Preston was cheered, but found the information of little consolation. "I'm glad you told me they laugh at the goddamned thing," he replied glumly. "I have never had the heart to see it."

26.

Sturges' clash with Darryl Zanuck, coupled with publicity surrounding the cost of *The Beautiful Blonde* and his extraordinary salary, did him immeasurable harm. Critics commented on the gap of four years between *The Great Moment* and *Unfaithfully Yours*, a break in training which, as Bosley Crowther noted, could prove fatal to a champion. "Like a boxer who takes too long a lay-off, Mr. Sturges has slowed up a bit. And this is something his public will be the first to note and deplore."

There was still interest in him; almost immediately Sturges jumped from Fox to M-G-M. His price, however, dropped considerably, and with it, his prestige. The deal struck by Dore Schary, vice-president in charge of production, was what is known today as a "step" deal, in which a story is commissioned, then a screenplay, the company having the option of terminating each step of the way. It was an inexpensive, cautionary approach to dealing with a man who was now suspected of being "difficult" and "costly." The money involved was considerably less than he had gotten at Fox: $25,000 upon completion of a script and another $25,000 after any revisions the studio deemed necessary.

The story Sturges had for M-G-M was an entirely new idea concocted especially for Clark Gable. It was about a Henry J. Kaiser type of industrialist who is ordered by his doctor to spend six months "resting" in a small town. Sturges called his story *Mr. Big in Littleville* and, later, *Nothing Doing.*

The part of Charles "Big Kim" Kimble suited the fifty-ish Gable better than the tired romantics he had played of late and anticipated the kind of hard-driving, self-made character he later played in films like *Key to the City* and *Teacher's Pet.* The key to Gable's character was his pace—jetting around the country overseeing a vast business empire. One could easily imagine him owning The Players in Hollywood and passing out copies of *How Never to Be Tired or Two Lifetimes in One.*

Sturges clearly admired this man. Big Kim's awkward compliance with the doctor's orders was written with heartfelt empathy for a man both misunderstood and almost forcibly removed from his natural environment. He is sent to a hamlet called West Bismark ("Elevation 2 Ft."), where he is to have no contact with the outside world.

Big Kim's restlessness soon gets the better of him. He sets to work to revitalize the old carriage works on the outskirts of town and by the time his "rest" is over, he has transformed West Bismark into a center of both industry and tourism.

Nothing Doing was everything *The Beautiful Blonde from Bashful Bend* was not. It was modest, clever, and perfectly suited to the talents of the actor for whom it was written. It was not a vehicle; it was a classical Sturges comedy cut from virtually the same cloth as *Sullivan's Travels* and *Hail the Conquering Hero*. In short, Sturges chose to write the picture he had described to Darryl Zanuck in his final memo at Fox: a big picture he figured he could shoot in the space of twenty-four days maximum. And he would demonstrate just how inexpensive a new Sturges film could be.

Without being planned that way, Sturges' pictures had become progressively more costly. *Diddlebock*, he now acknowledged, cost far more than it should have. If he wished to survive, the only solution was to retreat from his $2 million rut. He told Dore Schary as much, and he meant it. The only excuse for a runaway budget was sloppiness. It was a trend the studios could no longer afford.

Sturges' career was now at its lowest ebb in fifteen years. He was under contract only at arm's length. He preferred not to consider the possibility of *Nothing Doing* not being made, but his anxiety over it was well founded. He had everything riding on this one motion picture; he had gone through most all the major studios: Paramount, Fox, Columbia, Universal, even RKO in the sense that it was now owned by Howard Hughes. M-G-M and Dore Schary offered him a final chance to prove himself in the cold, gray world of profits and losses. The stakes he himself had established made him unacceptable as anything other than a big, big winner. He not only wrote, he directed and produced. And he was still as expensive as the biggest stars. The control he demanded was conceded to only a handful of his colleagues. In the space of two years, Zanuck had lost almost $4 million on him.

As if the situation at Metro were not enough, Sturges pressed forward on the construction of his dinner theatre, shoveling every spare cent into it. The obstacles were formidable: besides the design problems and the shortness of capital, it took some time to get a zoning clearance on the property itself. The city refused a permit to add a theatre to the building, so the plans finally approved were for a large underground "storeroom." It was the first storeroom they had approved with a proscenium arch, an inspector declared, winking as he signed the permit.

By Monday, June 13, 1949, Sturges needed $20,000 to finish the theatre and another $80,000 or so to satisfy the various debts The Players had independently accrued. He owed $64,000 of that to the purveyors. When *Nothing Doing* came through, he asked the Orsatti agency to defer its commission until he could pull some of his liabilities into line. If he could only get the theatre finished and open, he said, it would generate enough income to help compensate for the losses on the rest of the business. But on the aforementioned Monday, as Sturges arranged to meet with his creditors to ask for more time, he found his name included—much to his horror—among the people the IRS reported as having earned the most money during 1947. Sturges, with $370,000, was third in the nation, right behind Charles P. Skouras of National Theatres and Fox-West Coast ($810,000) and the president of American Tobacco ($484,202). "The face on my chicken dealer was really something to see when I continued to tell him I just hadn't the money. He kept waving the newspaper under my nose and saying, 'But . . . but . . . but . . .' "

His alleged financial worth dogged him everywhere. "That bothered him," said a close friend, "because, he said, nobody was worth that kind of money to write. He figured out one day how many dollars per word that was. He said, 'Look at the *real* writers—Molière, Balzac—and what they made. It's outrageous.' " Most of it went for confiscatory taxes, he told all who asked; the bite was 86% on unsheltered income over $200,000. Compounding the problem was the release of *The Beautiful Blonde from Bashful Bend* in May, which only served to confirm the worst of the rumors concerning its quality. Desperate for cash, he met with Dore Schary and producer Larry Weingarten at M-G-M in an effort to interest them in buying *Strictly Dishonorable* for *South Pacific's* Ezio Pinza. Sturges offered a package, independent of *Nothing Doing*, that consisted of *Strictly Dishonorable*, *Matrix* (which, he pointed out, had interested M-G-M producer Voldemar Vetluguin), and the screen rights to Hergesheimer's *Three Black Pennies*, which he had acquired at Cal-Pix. Both men rejected the proposal, saying they weren't interested in package deals. Sturges then counterproposed *Strictly Dishonorable* on the condition that he write, produce, and direct it. This they said they would think about, and Sturges returned to *Nothing Doing*. But they communicated no further and in October the deal was apparently cold. There was talk of taking *Strictly Dishonorable* to Warners' for Humphrey Bogart. Sturges said, "This is idiotic, as they could look for two hundred years and not find anything as good for Pinza."

With Buddy DeSylva on the set of Sullivan's Travels.

Holding court at the Paramount commissary, 1941. Veronica Lake and Joel McCrea are in costume for Sullivan's Travels.

Directing Joel McCrea and Claudette Colbert on the set of The Palm Beach Story *(1942).*

Sturges' most inspired piece of casting: Rudy Vallée as John D. Hackensacker III in The Palm Beach Story.

The famous stock company, plus one, on the set of Palm Beach Story. *Top row: Dewey Robinson, Robert Warwick, Sheldon Jett, Torben Meyer, Jack Norton, Vic Potel, Jimmy Conlin, Bottom row: Robert Greig, Chester Conklin, Sturges, Claudette Colbert, Roscoe Ates, William Demarest.*

Directing a typical exchange between William Demarest and Eddie Bracken for The Miracle of Morgan's Creek.

Harold Lloyd preferred Sturges to Jackie the Lion in this pose on the set of The Sin of Harold Diddlebock, *1946.*

Sturges in the kitchen of The Players, with manager Alexis A. Pillet.

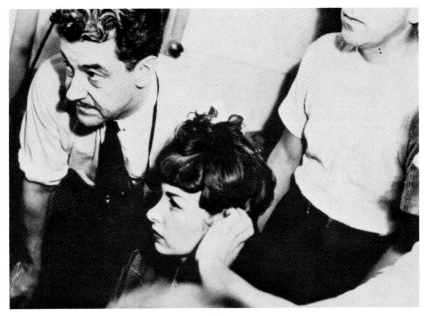

Sturges oversaw every detail of Francis Ramsden's screen debut.

At work in his home at 1917 Ivar.

Opposite: On the set of Vendetta, *over which he briefly assumed command, in 1946; at the Sturges Engineering Company, c. 1947.*

Bertie Woolfan.

Sturges in his office at the Fox Western Avenue Studio. The wraparound desk was his own design.

Directing Linda Darnell in Unfaithfully Yours—Newsweek *cover, May 10, 1948.*

Top: with Henry Henigson and Mon Sturges, Christmas, 1948; bottom: with Nanette Fabray and composer Hugh Martin during preparation for Make a Wish.

Preston and Sandy during rehearsals at The Players.

London, 1954: Sandy, Preston, little Preston.

One last premiere.

Preston and Tom-Tom, Paris, 1957.

With Bob Hope in a scene from Paris Holiday.

Paris, 1958.

Inexplicably, *Nothing Doing* vanished from the schedules in mid-October and, as with Thalberg in 1933, Sturges' relationship with M-G-M soured. "Again I am in a sort of miasma at M-G-M," he reported to Henry Henigson. "I have always worked my damnedest to make a good impression."

Refusing to be deterred, Sturges hammered away at the *Strictly Dishonorable* deal. He dropped the requirement that he adapt it and direct it, pushing instead for an outright sale. Sadly, without Sturges' employment as a condition, they were once again interested. But then came the question of ownership: *Strictly Dishonorable*, Sturges discovered, was no longer his.

"Brock Pemberton gave Preston an agreement to sell his share of *Strictly Dishonorable* for $1000," Charley Abramson recalled. "Then Brock Pemberton died, and I thought, 'This isn't going to get past the M-G-M lawyers. Pemberton was only part owner.'

"There were the backers. They owned a big piece. Sure enough, Preston got a wire from M-G-M New York saying, 'Mr. Sturges, we're sorry, but we'll have to call the deal off. The only way we can do this is if you can get a release from each of the backers.' Preston didn't have any money. A wire came to the lawyer, Walter Rubin, from Preston Sturges, saying, 'Put it in the hands of my pal, Charley Abramson. You can reach him at Famous Artists. He'll take care of you.' This was the call I got from Rubin.

"I began. The first one I went to was the Perry girl. Her mother was dead, and she now owned the interest. I persuaded her to give a release for Preston. No money. Then I got hold of Gilbert Kahn (another backer was his father, Otto Kahn). And I persuaded him.

"Then it came to some other guy whom I didn't know, a millionaire, and he had a firm of Irish lawyers. They were tough; I couldn't even get to see them. Finally I sent them a wire that said, 'I want to see you. I don't understand your attitude. I'm asking for an appointment. I want to talk business.' I called them on the phone and somebody finally answered and gave me an appointment. He said, 'We have no rights,' and I said, 'Well, you can advise your client.' He said, 'The client's dead.' I said, 'They have heirs, don't they? Mr. Sturges made a lot of money for them, and here are the releases from Mr. Kahn and the others. They are grateful to this man, who is in difficulty now. You're not going to get any money out of it.' 'I've got a partner,' the man said, and I said, 'I'd like to meet your partner.' I put in a hell of a pitch.

"It took me three months. Every day I worked at it, and, finally, I got all the releases."

Once the backers had signed releases, there was still the matter of Universal International, which owned the film rights via the 1931 movie the Laemmles had made. The deal M-G-M finally agreed to was a hefty one: $110,000, with $50,000 of it going to Universal. Sturges would neither write the screenplay nor direct it. The finished product bore almost no resemblance to the play.

The setbacks took their toll. The lack of money, the borrowing, the depression translated into bouts of drunkenness. Preston had always been fond of alcohol and had a tremendous capacity for it. That he now let it take control of him was by choice rather than accident. His relationship with Frances Ramsden suffered, although she stuck by him doggedly until it was finally clear that Preston intended to hit bottom. He accepted her sympathy, her comfort, but did nothing to encourage their relationship. He kept a large oil portrait of his mother over his bed, the one in which she had died. Sometimes he remembered her telling him that if he got heartsick and weary to lie down there and she would put her arms around him and everything would be all right.

The press, of course, had been looking for a wedding announcement, as Francie and Preston were together constantly since Preston's highly publicized divorce. "Preston Sturges will be free to remarry on November 12th," Hedda Hopper wrote in October of 1948, "and like a lot of observant people here, I've presumed that on the following day he would marry his long-time companion and leading lady, Frances Ramsden. 'I am not going to marry Preston,' says Francie, 'but I hope to make pictures for him. It's all so embarrassing. He's never asked me to marry him.' "

Francie's frustration was understandable. There were fights about his drinking, his carelessness with money, his depressions. He quarreled with even his closest friends—Bert Woolfan and Charley Abramson—about the quagmire into which he was sinking. It was as if Preston wished to get it all over with and begin again with nothing. "When I've lost it all," he said, "I'll take a pencil and piece of paper and start the whole thing over again." And he truly believed he could.

His restaurant was his ace in the hole, his mistress, his anchor in Hollywood. As long as he could keep his head above water, as long as he could hold on to The Players, all was not lost. If he couldn't make films for the moment, he could return to the theatre. He had come from the stage; he was a child of Broadway, not Hollywood. He didn't own a studio, but he was building a theatre. And with it he could work to repair his reputation. Suddenly, The Players was more than just an amusement—it became his lifeline. He would write and direct in it, and create a showcase for his new plays. And as he did so, he would continually remind those in power of what he had recently been to them and what he could be once more.

Francie finally decided there was nothing more she could do for him. When she announced her intention to leave, Preston was glum but refused to stop her. There had been one too many arguments over money and marriage and his drinking. She hoped that her threat would have an impact when nothing else would. But he had been anticipating her decision and, in fact, encouraged it. There was nothing more he would do or say. Tearfully, reluctantly, Francie stuck to her decision. And Preston refused to budge.

Philosophically, Preston told of a theory he had: "It implies that our memories are bookkeeping systems with a separate account for every single person, animal, or thing we have to do with in our lives. Does our dog forget himself on the carpet? . . . Flip! Flop! The ledger opens to his account on the debit side and there, all too plain, are all the other things he has done since he was a puppy. The carpets he chewed up. The time he ate your passport the night before you were to leave for England. The furniture he has knocked over, the time he stuck his paws in your face and nearly put your eye out . . . all, all is there . . . you are not irritated by a little acid on the carpet but by a long life of crime and you beat him accordingly. That is why parents fall off the handle at a slight whimpering from a child. It isn't one whimper they hear, it is a whimper four years long.

"My theory indicates that it's very dangerous for newly in love couples to permit themselves the slightest discourtesy or anger toward each other. They may say, after wiping away the tears, that they have forgiven and forgotten the incident, but they are wrong. It is written forever in indelible ink on the debit side of their ledger. The trouble with Francie and myself is that our ledgers were overflowing."

And so he let her go. Patiently, he endured Priscilla's continual lectures. "You can't let her go," she implored. "You mustn't let her go. She has so much that is right for you."

Preston remained firm. "These things are very painful," he said. "They must be endured."

"And what will become of her?" she asked.

"She is the most resourceful woman I know," he replied. "No matter what happens to her, she'll always land on her feet."

Priscilla tried every tactic she could think of. "In my opinion," she said, "Preston was deeply in love with Francie." She refused to concede defeat. In frustration she said, "Do you know what you want in a woman? You want a combination of Potiphar's wife, Aspasia beloved of Pericles, and the Blessed Virgin. And no such woman exists!" For one time in their long friendship, Preston had no comeback.

The time came a few days later to take Francie to the depot. Priscilla asked Preston if he would come. "I will come later," he answered and they left without him. At Union Station were Francie, Priscilla, and the secretaries Caroline Wedderburn and

Jill MacDonald. Preston appeared at the very last moment, silvery hair uncombed, his arms filled with long-stemmed roses. The two embraced and wept quietly. Priscilla and the others kept their distance as the train pulled away and Preston's rumpled figure stood alone.

"I think I'll ride back with him," whispered Priscilla to Caroline, who nodded in agreement. She went up to Preston and took his hand. "I left my car at your house," she said. "May I ride home with you?" They made the journey back to Ivar in silence. Before disappearing inside the empty house Preston asked, "Where's Bertie?"

"He's at the office, Preston."

"Will I see you tonight?"

The Woolfans had made other plans. "Yes, of course," Priscilla told him. Preston squeezed her hand and in a moment was gone.

27.

Preston's drinking accelerated after Francie's departure. He withdrew almost completely into The Players, working, eating, and sometimes sleeping there. He borrowed $7000 from Rudy Vallée and a like sum from Howard Hughes, using *The Destiny* as collateral. He staked a great deal on the completion of his theatre.

His moods would fluctuate radically, betraying the emptiness in his life. "There was a period of—oh, maybe a year or so when he was extremely sad and moody and brooding," said Maxine Merlino. "He was feeling empty because there was a vacuum in his life. . . . We spent a lot of time together then. Oftentimes I'd go home with him and we'd have dinner together and he'd talk and talk." Priscilla Woolfan remembered one night around this time when one of the waiters at The Players phoned her husband to report that Preston was alone and very drunk. The Woolfans drove to the restaurant and Bertie was directed to the mezzanine level, where Preston lingered in a stupor. Rallying, an expression of utter helplessness and shame crossed his face. He implored his friend to remain and send Priscilla home in a cab. "Don't let her see me like this," he begged, unconsciously borrowing a line from *The Great McGinty*. Bertie returned to Priscilla and complied; he spent the rest of the night there.

When she arrived on the scene, Sandy Nagle, Preston's fourth wife, was a godsend. "I don't know why," said Maxine Merlino, "my intuition said, 'There's Preston's next girl friend,' She fit the image that I felt he was searching for." She wore her hair in the same style as Frances Ramsden, with giant china-blue eyes that contrasted with Francie's in color and shape. She lived in a house above The Players, up a road that resembled a driveway from the street. She walked that road daily, to and from her work at Blue Cross.

She recalled, "The very first time I met Preston was because there was an electric sign on the side of the building that said 'The Players' and it was shooting sparks. I thought it was going to start a fire, so I ran to the nearest open door to sound the alarm. Workmen were stacking planks and Preston was there, wearing old baggy corduroy pants, moccasins with no socks, and an old Hawaiian shirt. He was carrying lumber. I said, 'Would one of you be kind enough to tell whoever owns this building that he's about to have a fire?' Preston said that it was very kind of me to stop by and he would take care of that . . .

"I thought he was in the construction crew. Every time I came home after that, he would step out and say, 'Perhaps you would like to see what we've done today.' And I thought that was really nice. He was so proud of his work."

Anne Margaret Nagle, nineteen, had moved to California with her first husband, and was separated when she first met Preston Sturges. "One of those childhood marriages," she said. She grew up in Washington, D.C., Virginia, and Boston, and finished her schooling in Connecticut.

"He'd always be hauling lumber, and wearing those wretched clothes. He would point to the hugest mud pit you've ever seen but describe, as if it was there, the fantastic theatre he was going to build—the chandeliers, the cupids, the candles, the carpets, and the elevators that arranged the seating.

"I never got the impression that he was there when I came home on purpose. He just happened to be there—crossing the driveway, or carrying the lumber, or looking up at the building. On the second night he said he should have introduced himself, said his name, and hesitated for that millisecond famous people allow for reaction. Nothing happened, of course. I said mine, and that it was nice to have met him, and I thought to myself that it was too bad that his mother hadn't given him a three-syllable first name so it would have had a better rhythm. I had never heard the name before.

"Three days later, he was out doing something with the lumber and he said, 'Just a moment, I have something I want to show you.' He disappeared and came back with a book under his arm, and he said, 'I don't want you to think I'm a total bum.' He opened it for me and said, 'There's my name.' There was a long listing. It was *Who's Who*."

The chance meetings became a fixed routine. "A couple of times, he asked me if I'd care to come in and have a Coca-Cola. He'd just go over to a phone and push a button and say, 'Bring up a couple of Coca-Colas.' A waiter would bring them up, but I had no idea there was any connection. I thought what a really nice boss he had. There was never a check, never any question."

He asked her one night if she'd care to have dinner there and she asked, "Will they let you?"

"I think so," he told her.

Sturges worked principally with two Spanish waiters who had been with him for years. They performed most of the unskilled labor, functioning chiefly on loyalty and praise; Sturges' enthusiasm was contagious. If Mata had done a particularly marvelous piece of shoveling, Sturges would invite everyone over to watch. "Do it again, Mata," he would urge. "Now have you ever seen anything as fine?"

One night, he told Sandy that he was having trouble writing because he didn't have anyone who could work with him at night. He asked if she would type for him, explaining that he usually dictated to someone with a typewriter.

"Oh, I could never type that fast," she said.

"There's nothing to it," he said. "When I'm thinking, I scarcely speak."

She started to work with him at The Players. After a week he said, "This isn't going to work. All my books are at the house."

"The minute he said, '. . . at the house,' I thought, 'Oh, spit!' Then I didn't know what to do, because I had left Blue Cross to work for him. I felt so stupid."

Yet he had been so courtly, never so much as touching her on the shoulder. They began working at the house on a script called *A Present for Uncle Popo* under a self-imposed deadline. "One night," said Sandy, "we worked all the night. He would dictate, lie down on the sofa, get up, walk around, and then sit. Finally, his secretary of the day, Caroline Wedderburn, arrived about ten o'clock the next morning. I can still remember her face when she came in and saw me there. She had never seen me in her life. I think she thought the whole typing story was a ruse. Until she saw my typing.

"I thought there was a real urgency to *Uncle Popo*, but half the time, you couldn't drag him out of The Players until three. Then he would get to work. Then, he said, the easiest thing to do was for me to live in the house. 'Then, when I'm ready to work, you'll be ready to work.'

"I said. 'Well, I couldn't do that,' and he said, 'Why not?' He assured me of his honorable intentions and said no thought was further from his mind than taking advantage of me."

Sandy moved into a second house on the Ivar property, furnished with, among other things, his Cal-Pix office furniture. Next, Preston declared the second house wasn't close enough, and that she would have to move into the main building. Sturges began talking marriage as a joke: "I don't know whether to marry you or adopt you." Maxine Merlino described a scene where Sturges lovingly watched Sandy and nine-year-old Mon climb a tree. "Isn't she sweet?" he would ask of no one in particular.

The building progressed as the money came in: masons and electricians were hired on a day-to-day basis. The floor was installed in June of 1950, divided into panels measuring seven by twenty-four feet apiece. To support them, Sturges invented a mechanical screw-jack system that would raise and lower them at about a tenth the cost of hydraulics. Four jacks supported each panel, and were driven by a single one-and-a-half-horsepower motor. The system was smooth, quiet, and since one motor propelled each floor section, there was no synchronization problem.

Once the floor was in place, Sturges' spirits rose considerably. "My new theatre is nearly completed," he wrote to his friend John Hertz, Jr., in July of 1950, "and is quite certain to be a big financial hit. I am certain that it will be a forerunner and model for theatres to be built hereafter. One of the problems facing the motion picture exhibitors of the future will be to give the public something that television *cannot* give. I have given considerable thought to this and am reasonably certain that I have discovered the correct line of attack. My six one-act plays will go into rehearsal in August and open early in September. The theatre will provide a complete evening of pleasure and the ads will say: 'Preston Sturges Presents . . . The Players Acting Company . . . in . . . A Perfect Evening In the Theatre . . . 6 One Act Plays 6 . . . *A Minute . . . The Monkey's Paw . . . Barber Shop Blues . . . The Boor . . . Hello Out There . . . The Dear Departed.*' You will be hearing much news of this. Even *Popular Mechanics* is giving the mechanical features of the theatre five pages."

More money came in when the Hollywood Freeway crossed Ivar and Preston, instead of surrendering the main house to the wreckers, had it cut in three pieces and moved up Hollywood Boulevard to a parcel of land on Franklin Avenue. Whatever funds were left over were promptly swallowed by the theatre.

A job came up when the theatre was nearing completion and Sturges was loath to turn anything down. A young man named Harry Rigby, an ardent fan of Sturges', had come to him with an idea to turn *The Good Fairy* into a musical for Nanette Fabray. Rigby had never produced a show before. Although Sturges didn't take him too seriously (and warned him that he was "extremely inexperienced in musical shows") he told him he would be delighted to do it. Much to Sturges' surprise, Rigby was able to get the project on its feet. In mid-August, Sturges went east with Sandy ("my secretary Mrs. Mellon") for a series of conferences with Rigby and composer-lyricist Hugh Martin ("The Trolley Song"). They discussed a story line and a string of song ideas and then Sturges returned to L.A. to oversee the furnishing of his theatre and to write the first draft of *The Good Fairy* at night. Remarkably, it took him only five days to complete. Unsure of his expertise with musical numbers, he qualified most of his suggestions. Nonetheless, the script was solidly plotted and genuinely funny. There then came a give-and-take between coasts as the songs were integrated and modified. "Hugh Martin was doing his work in New York and Preston was doing his here," recalled Sandy, "and Hugh would send songs. And for every song received Preston would respond with a note, 'put it back in the trunk and write a song that goes with this scene.' And poor Hugh would say, 'But Mr. Sturges, it's a beautiful song,' and he'd say 'You're right, it's a beautiful song, but we're writing for this play.' "

Sturges' script was larded with clever little dialogues between the most minor of characters, characters he wrote as if he were writing a movie. The characters spoke pages of dialogue before even a hint of the first song, and then pages more before the second. The girl was an orphan, as in the original, but instead of working in a movie theatre, Sturges placed her in the chorus of the Folies Bergère, where she proceeded to ruin an elaborate production number. Sturges' preliminary description of this number ran over two pages: a lavish, naughty salute to American industry called "Viva the U.S.A." Scantily clad female replicas of Airwick, Coca-Cola, Rinso, and Yuban would invade a starving European seaport by way of the U.S. Marshall Plan. Into this pageant steps Nanette, with shattering incompetence.

The first draft of *The Good Fairy* was too talky and long, the accent on comedy instead of music. Rehearsals began in New York on February 9, 1951, as Sturges tackled a second, more acceptable version titled *Suits Me Fine*. Contritely, he replaced much of the clever dialogue with utilitarian lines that served only to bridge the gaps between numbers and nudge the plot along. The story became a succession of not very good songs and Sturges soon lost his enthusiasm. Under still a third title, *Make a Wish*, the show opened in Philadelphia, in very rough shape, on March 12. The notices were poor. *Variety* praised Nanette Fabray (as did all the critics) and found the show in need of "radical doctoring." Sturges foresaw his further involvement to be of little value. After a difficult week in Philadephia, he gratefully withdrew and returned to California. Abe Burrows *(Guys and Dolls)* was recruited to follow the show into New York. Burrows told the New York *Times'* Sam Zolotow that he was "making a few suggestions and was glad to give any advice out of friendship to the management," but an unidentified company member told another reporter that Burrows "had the cast working around the clock as he turned out new material as though he were a mimeographing machine."

Said Sturges, when he arrived back in Los Angeles to prepare the opening of his dinner theatre, "I stayed with *Make a Wish* in New York and Philadelphia as long as I could within the limit of my somewhat restricted time. There is no rift between the management and myself other than there is normally during the excitement of a production."

By the time *Make a Wish* opened at Broadway's Winter Garden on April 18, the show bore little resemblance to *The Good Fairy* or to Sturges' adaptation of same. The critics singled out for praise Nanette Fabray and choreographer Gower Champion, who staged a showstopping ballet called "The Sale." They panned most of the other elements of the show. Little of the Sturges influence was evident.

Burrows or no Burrows, it was Sturges who received sole credit for the book of *Make a Wish*. It was Fabray's first starring show and reviews were typically headlined 'MAKE A WISH' MADE BY NANETTE FABRAY. The show was what *Life* magazine dubbed a "summer musical" and, in that context, it was a mild success.

Within days of his return, Sturges had the theatre ready for operation. Rehearsals commenced immediately and on April 2 a small 1 x 6 ad appeared in *The Hollywood Reporter*. Headlined SLIGHTLY CONFIDENTIAL, it read:

"Concerning the out-of-town or Oxnard opening of Preston Sturges' new theatre venture, upstairs over The Players restaurant: having looked at the map and discovered where Oxnard is, it has been deemed wiser to hold the out-of-town opening in town. Therefore, beginning tonight, April 2, 1951, at 8:30 p.m., and continuing roughly for a couple of weeks, there will be presented, in the new and enormously complicated electro-elevating Playroom Theatre, a series of catch-as-catch-can, try-it-on-the-dog, squares-kindly-stay-away, let's-keep-it-in-the-family dress rehearsals for the purpose of finding out if anything works.

"This ambitious extravaganza, consisting of five one-act plays, preceded by, followed, and interspersed with the startling music of the one and only Red Nichols and his extraordinary Five Pennies, and temporarily known as the Disasters of 1951, may be viewed for the temporary pot-luck price of $1 for the five plays plus $1 for the succeeding concert and jam session. Also plus tax. The plays, subject to change without notice, are: *Barbershop Blues*, *The Monkey's Paw*, *The Boor*, *Hello Out There*, and *The Dear Departed*. Come at your own risk. First come, first served. The box office opens at noon and telephone reservations will be held until 6 p.m. The purchase of food or drink is not required but basket parties will be frisked at the door. Anyone wishing to crash the gate for free will please ask for Sergeant-at-Arms Frank Moran or one of the gentlemanly members of his squad. Members of the Press are welcome but will kindly keep their traps shut until the Grand Gala Soup & Fish Opening, complete with Searchlights, Stars, Suckers, and Sables. This will be held at a later date and expensively advertised. For further information call The Players, 8225 Sunset Blvd. Hillside 7303."

"For the theatre dining, he offered a choice of three dinners," said Sandy. "He got that idea from Ray's Round-Up, which was an all-you-can-eat-for-one-price restaurant serving only three entrées: roast beef, turkey, and something else. Ray told Preston it was marvelous. You knew exactly what your food costs were going to be; nothing happened to the beef, nothing happened to the turkey. 'Great idea,' said Preston, embracing it at once.

"So the waiters, trained to cater to a la carte customers, and all the French chefs poised to produce wonders were to wear two hats: fast food dispensers in the theatre, French cuisine on the floor below."

In contrast to the rococo theatre he had created, with gold and crystal, mirrors tinted peach color, velvet chairs, and table lamps that got brighter when moved, Sturges engaged Red Nichols and his Five Pennies to surprise and delight the patrons.

The curtain went up at 10:30 P.M., Nichols playing the overture. All tables had to be cleared of plates before the entertainment could begin. Sturges hoped to make his money on the liquor served between and after the plays. Cocktails, dining, theatre, and dancing took place in the same room. As a means of selling drinks it was a failure because, Sturges later figured, people had no wish to remain in the same room for six straight hours. The first-night cast included Cathy O'Donnell, Harold Gordon, Al Bridge, Margaret Brewster, Eddie Firestone, Frank Marlow, and Keith McConnell. Red Nichols and his Five Pennies alone got a union minimum of $1250 a week.

"When he was on," said Sandy, "you couldn't hear yourself swallow."

The gala opening took place on April 24—called "Theatre at Ten." Gone were two of the five one-acts; three hundred customers filled the room. Said Sturges to *Time* magazine, "People seeing theatre in the same building with a restaurant have their mouths shaped for cabaret. But tragedy isn't something you have to go into mourning for. Theatre in which you eat is the oldest form of theatre."

The customers enjoyed the novelty of the surroundings and seemed to love the plays. The critics hated the food and found the casts of decidedly mixed quality. Sturges went further into debt with his policy of one-acts, and then decided to fall back upon the security of a classic farce.

Eddie Bracken agreed to star in a Sturges-directed production of *Room Service*, gratis, to help pull the operation out of its rather sizable hole. The scheme worked: *Room Service* opened on July 25, 1951, and was a whopping success.

"Preston Sturges' presentation of the 1937 hit by John Murray and Allen Boretz is staged at the top of the actors' lungs," reported *Variety*, "and rightly so. Sturges is billing it in his theatre-restaurant as 'Probably the Funniest Bedroom Farce Ever Written.' If it's not that, it's certainly a very funny show."

Sturges cast Teddy Hart in the role of Englund, the stage manager, which the actor had created in the original Broadway production fifteen years earlier. He cast three of his treasured stock members, Al Bridge, Julius Tannen, and Frank Moran, in featured roles, and, for good measure, cast Sandy in the part of Hilda, the girl who falls for Bracken. The show did capacity business for weeks. Said Sturges, "At last the value of the idea is becoming apparent." The engineering company, which he had turned over to three ex-employees in exchange for a share of the profits and a small amount for use of the machinery, was beginning to pay off. He was talking to Paramount about going back to work. He was once again seeing the light at the end of the tunnel.

On the morning of August 15, 1951, after the Tuesday evening presentation of *Room Service*, the paying audience was asked to leave and 250 invited guests witnessed the marriage of Sandy and Preston on the theatre's stage.

28.

Had Sturges not clung stubbornly to the one-acts with which he opened his new theatre, had he not sunk further into debt those first two months, *Room Service*, he figured, would have put him in pretty good shape. He began talking of television, a new horizon for him. He had spoken of it with great seriousness as early as 1949, when it was still fashionable in the movie industry to regard the medium with contempt. To Bosley Crowther he wrote, "I am as of this moment tremendously enthusiastic about television. Not about what I have seen on these sulphurous little screens but what I see in my head, what I know can be done with the technical equipment now available. Unless television gets into the hands of the same real estate men and candy butchers who inherited sound film from the movies, it will discharge the obligation that talking film failed to do and will diffuse to the smallest hamlets in the farthest parts of the world the treasures of literature and of music. I hope this will happen."

Six months later, Sturges found himself in a store that sold TV sets. "I saw two things . . ." he later said, "and saw the light. The first thing I saw was the hair on the back of a man's hand. He was giving a drawing lesson. The second thing was a panning shot across some dress models, winding up on the cloak-and-suiter himself, who didn't know he was in the shot and was scratching his pants. It was the movement of the camera and the quite excellent lighting that impressed me. I hurried out of the shop knowing that I could tell any story on television."

With a great burst of enthusiasm, Sturges called some people he knew at ABC, who gave him a tour of their facilities and hoped that someday there would be enough money in television to tempt him into the fold. One night, KTLA's Klaus Lansberg originated his "City at Night" program from The Players and Sturges was surprised to start receiving offers to emcee quiz shows and write and direct pilots ". . . for practically nothing . . . with promises of great riches to follow." These he declined in favor of a project completely his own. Again, he wanted both control and ownership;

it was not difficult for him to envision his new theatre as a potential TV studio.

Not surprisingly, when Sturges conceived a pilot of his own, he set it at The Players. He noted the medium's voracious appetite for new material, that at the rate it was chewing through cooking shows and old Westerns there would be nothing left to show but sporting events by the 1952 election. He paused to consider the pressures of having to create the equivalent of seventeen new features a year; the fact that he had been a fast writer for the movies meant nothing in television. He had written *Strictly Dishonorable* in six days, but he hadn't written fifty-one other plays that same year. The solution, he decided, lay in the same one-act dramas that had proven so deadly in his dinner format. His mind envisioned a national showcase of fine one-acts both new and old. Some he could write himself. Others might come from new playwrights, and still others could be commissioned from more established artists. Tying the whole package together would be Sturges, who would introduce each week's installment from the stage of his theatre.

The treatment Sturges prepared for a pilot, which he called "The Sturges Stories," began with a shot of The Players and then cut inside where Sturges himself could be seen taking tickets and bantering with members of the audience. Rushing backstage, Sturges prepares to go on:

"CUT TO CAMERA NUMBER 3   This catches Mr. S.'s head sticking through the curtains. Nervously he says, 'All ready?' CAMERA pans to the can-can girls dressing and making up at a wheeled dressing table. One of the girls says, 'We're always ready . . . you know that . . . like the Marine Corps . . . Semper Fidelis." Mr. S., who is visible in the mirror, now says, 'No Latin, please . . . you're supposed to be can-can girls!' 'Can we help it if we're all PhD's?' says another very pretty girl adjusting her stockings. 'Shut up, will you?' says Mr. S. in the mirror. 'You let out stuff like that and our sponsor will divorce us.' 'Who *is* our sponsor, by the way?' says another can-can girl. 'Have we got one?' 'Sufficient unto the day is the evil thereof,' says the reflection of Mr. S. 'Ask me no questions and I'll tell you no lies.'

"CUT TO CAMERA NUMBER 1   Mr. S. from the rear. Across the back of his coat is the sponsor's slogan. Mr. S. turns into CAMERA and says, 'Have we got a sponsor!' Now he looks at his watch, vaults over the desk again, knocking down the props which have once more to be picked up, he arranges himself once more, tries a few more smiles, examines his teeth in a mirror, and answers the phone. 'Of course I'm ready . . . if those musicians will ever stop playing . . . all right, see what you can do.' He hangs up the phone. 'What a life! And what do you get for it? A fortune!' "

Sturges would have found it easy to get "The Sturges Stories" produced locally, but since there would have been no money in it, he held out for a network contract. Even with *Room Service* playing, he had to stall his creditors and seek enough money from jobs to keep The Players running. "Preston," asked Eddie Bracken, "why are you giving up your time, your talent, and your greatness for a dot on a map and forgetting about the whole world?" But with no firm work, Preston—by necessity—had to turn The Players into a profit-making enterprise.

"We played it for eighteen weeks," said Bracken, "and I didn't take any salary at all. Sturges was in trouble and I wanted to help him. For eighteen weeks I worked there for nothing and he was doing six thousand dollars *a night*. Packed. You couldn't get in. And at the end of the eighteenth week, he was further into debt than when we had started. That's when I quit."

The money kept the theatre solvent, but there wasn't enough to retire previous debts or support the remainder of the business. They did other plays there, notably Sherwood's *The Road to Rome*, which did well for its first couple of months. But *Room Service* had prompted a special kind of word of mouth. Perhaps people felt funny about going to a theatre amid the nightclubs on the Sunset Strip. Preston, after *Room Service*, was more convinced than ever that the idea had value. "There was a period of time when no one could get to Preston," said Priscilla Woolfan. "If anyone could, Bertie could. His business manager, Milton Cashy, came to Bertie and said, 'I hear you can out-yell him.' "

Cashy wrung his hands over the crumbling affairs of his client. The Players had posted substantial losses for eight straight years. Wages were in arrears, Social Security, withholding, and real estate taxes were unpaid. Payments on the second, third, and fourth mortgages were ignored, placing the loans in default. Sturges worked away at his TV deal, at staging new plays at the restaurant, and on screenplays at night. He worked again on *A Present for Uncle Popo* and yet another draft of *Matrix*. He wrote to Frank Freeman at Paramount, reiterating how much he had always loved the company and how he so wanted to work there again. He commented on what he called "the absurdly increasing cost of pictures," and proposed a production system which called for the lighting and preparation of sets at night, minimizing the time in which eighty to one hundred people would sit around on full salary waiting for four or five men to light a set. This, he said, would call for the director to work extra hours, but the savings in actual production costs would be substantial. "Twelve to fifteen days should be ample for a big picture of fine quality," he estimated.

Freeman responded pleasantly, and although he didn't close

the door on a new Sturges picture, neither did he provide much encouragement. Frustrated, dispirited, Sturges kept after him. Rudy Vallée saw him one night at The Players; he and his wife attended the show and talked with Sturges for several hours afterward. "Finally he said the most amazing thing to us," Vallée recalled. "With complete desperation written in his face, he said, 'Rudy, they won't even use me as a writer.' "

He drank heavily. "I saw him at times when I could hardly endure it," said Priscilla Woolfan. "And I saw the expression on his face. He was facing facts. I think he did know what had happened to him. And so he drank to oblivion; he drank to despair."

"But when he got in a position where he was pushed against the wall," said Sandy, "and he would fall into one of those black depressions, *zingo*! He would just get something from somewhere and *boom*! He'd get up and he would fight. Some spring would rise up inside of him . . . all of a sudden, he'd get an idea—perhaps this would work—and he would go. But he wouldn't weigh anything. It was just *zing* and then he'd start telephone calls and meetings, whatever it'd take to get that thing going. And once he got on that track, that was it. Bertie could come, Milton Cashy, anybody could say, 'Now, Preston, stop and try to think a moment,' and get nowhere. 'Sell the Players. It's worth a fortune.' No way would he sell that Players. Because it wasn't making money. That was the reason."

Preston said it would be "giving up" and thus "unmanly" to sell The Players. He wouldn't consider selling it and he never considered filing for bankruptcy. In late 1951, the government slapped a blanket lien on his assets, known and unknown. "At one point," recalled Sandy, "he said it was like presiding over the dissolution of an empire. Because he would just shore everything up to save this over here and that over there would start to go. He couldn't catch up."

Less than five years after earning the third highest salary in the nation, Preston didn't have the money to pay a $6.00 gas bill. "The Nietzschean belief in living dangerously is splendid," he decided, "but probably should be modified to: live dangerously, but with a small income."

Work was scarce. Television had the movie industry, already crippled by divestiture, in a state of near panic. Weekly movie attendance dropped from a record high of 90 million in 1945 to 60 million in 1950. The market for "B" pictures was virtually eradicated.

It wasn't until January of 1952 that Paramount called, after a year and a half of notes between Sturges and Freeman. It wasn't so much the studio's desire to put Sturges back to work as the simple realization that no one was better suited to write Betty Hutton's next picture. The property in question was the 1948 Broadway musical *Look, Ma, I'm Dancin'*, which starred Nancy Walker and Harold Lang. Paramount bought it for Betty Hutton and Gene Kelly. They commissioned a screenplay by Jerome Robbins, who conceived the original, and Arthur Laurents. It then went through a succession of hands, notably screenwriter Ian McLellan Hunter and producer Joe Sistrom. When scenarist Laurence Stallings was assigned it in late 1951, he considered the problem of taking a singular and independent work like *Look, Ma, I'm Dancin'* and adapting it into a vehicle for a specific performer. In a memo he evaluated the material (praising Hunter's work, deploring Sistrom's), and ended, philosophically, with a brief critique on the use of Hutton herself. Wrote Stallings, "Because she has an explosive force, a vivid personality, a sort of bragging charm, it seems to me that the picture-makers at Paramount have always relied upon her gifts, rather than their own, in putting her new pictures across the screen . . . there is, of course, the notable exception which Preston Sturges once made of her; when she was actually treated like a human being and given an opportunity to play a few appealing scenes."

The mention of a success long past served to unite Sturges and his old producer, Paul Jones, one last time. The studio agreed to pay $35,000 for a Sturges script and the chances of his directing it looked good. That was enough; a hope, a foothold at the studio where his greatest triumphs had occurred. Sturges dropped whatever else he was doing and moved back onto the lot, into a tiny office barely big enough for Preston to pace and Sandy to type. Gone were the suite of offices, the secretaries, the famous desk, the auto horn, and the Coca-Cola cooler. But Preston was grateful for another chance and determined to put the nightmare of the last two years behind him.

He began by reading the other drafts, the memos, notes, and the original show, and then, his imagination ignited, he discarded them all. He had never written a straight adaptation in his life; he wanted to come as close to an original as he could.

"His first thought," said Sandy, "was not 'what have they done with *Look, Ma, I'm Dancin'*? We'll use that idea and go.' His first thought was to take you over New York City, then zoom in on some really lousy part of town, then to a sign reading 'Dance Studio,' and then into a tiny office where you see Gene Kelly with a huge stack of letters. The camera goes to an ad that he's had posted in the paper—'New York City, Home of Ballet,' etc.—an enormous, glamorous ad offering dance lessons by mail. Kelly is reading the responses from the hinterlands. One of the letters is from Betty Hutton. She's from some tiny little town in Pennsylvania.

"You see her trying the mail order lessons and, of course, we had to learn all about the ballet, and the positions. The first position, the fifth position—all that, and her with nothing more to go on than an illustration in a book. And then finally, after sending her money, she gets a certificate that says she's a dancer. So she goes to New York. She knows she's going to be famous, and she wants to see this man who's given her her whole life.

"That's how *he* conceived *Look, Ma, I'm Dancin'*—not so it would be a Sturges story, but simply to facilitate the telling of it in his mind. Small-town dancer. What's the worst kind of small-town dancer that could arrive on the scene in New York? A mail order school graduate."

Sturges went through several false starts and three complete versions, each one drawing closer to the content of the original play. He wrote parts for the members of his stock company and changed the name of the heroine (Jessica Jones, Edie Stampham-mer, Elvy Johnson) with each rewrite. The basic idea of the original, a touring ballet company on the strawhat circuit, re-mained. Sturges concocted a cross between *Hail the Conquering Hero* and W. C. Fields' *The Old-Fashioned Way*, telling the story of the rise of the Hutton character from awkward country girl to Broadway star. In doing this, he opened in the present day and flashed back, contrasting a show about Hutton's life with the actual events upon which it is based.

The Sturgeses remained six months at Paramount, doing a draft, submitting it for review, receiving comments, then doing it again. Unfortunately, Sturges found himself tied to Betty Hutton at the very end of her career. Inordinately difficult, she had married the dance director on her last picture and suddenly insisted that he be engaged to direct *Look, Ma, I'm Dancin'*. The studio balked, Hutton walked out on her contract, Paramount left it at that. *Look, Ma, I'm Dancin'* died in its tracks; the film was never made.

William Wyler, preparing *Roman Holiday* at Paramount, got word of Preston's predicament and tried to help. Over the space of two years, four writers had worked on *Roman Holiday*, most recently Ben Hecht. "I didn't need anything really," Wyler re-called. "I did it simply in an effort to help him, and put him to work. I didn't think there was much involved, because I had a script already and the script was satisfactory, but I told the studio I needed more. It needed some rewriting.

"So I went to Preston and said, 'Look, here's a job I was hoping would turn out better. Maybe you can think of a couple of new scenes, or some good jokes to liven it up a bit. Basically the story's good.'"

Sturges took the material, read it, and met with Wyler again the next day. "There's one good line in it," he told Wyler. "That's all."

"He was not generous with his praise of other people," Wyler noted. "Especially other writers. He said, 'I'll have to do some rewriting on this.'

"I said, 'Now, Preston, we don't need very much.'

"He said, 'Just let me handle it.'

"I said, 'But you're not getting enough money to do a whole script.'

"He said, 'I'll do it, and it won't cost the studio a penny more.'

"I said, 'Well, go ahead and do what you want to.'"

Sturges took the Hecht script and completely rewrote it. He kept the structure and the form of the scenes but changed every word of dialogue. Where Hecht had written one line, Sturges wrote two. Where Hecht had written two, Sturges wrote three. "We didn't leave that little office except to go to the bathroom," Sandy remembered. "We were there five days and four nights and we never went home. He was *so* anxious to do a good job on it that we didn't even go to The Players. In fact, we really didn't even sleep."

Proudly, Sturges presented Wyler with his new *Roman Holiday*. "*Completely* rewritten," said Wyler. "I read it and said, 'Preston, remember you said there was *one* good line? Where is it?'

"He said, 'I decided not to use it.'"

Wyler couldn't use the script. "It wasn't as good as what we had," he said later, "but he just had to make it *his*. With all of his pictures, he was a true auteur. He had to create the story, direct it, everything. You can't blame a man for that, but maybe if he had been more flexible he might have survived longer."

Hopefully, Preston talked with Frank Freeman about *Matrix* and the possibility of doing *Look, Ma* with another actress. Freeman was pleasant, attentive, but frustratingly noncommittal. The story was out that Sturges was in trouble, that he owed most everyone in town. He withdrew once more into The Players but the money he got for *Look, Ma* and *Roman Holiday* was gone in a matter of weeks, the Internal Revenue Service claiming half right off the top. Slowly, his creditors closed in.

Priscilla Woolfan was at Preston's house one day, visiting with Caroline Wedderburn. Preston entered the room and said, "Caroline, I want to write a letter." He dictated a letter and Caroline left promptly to post it. Wearily, he turned to Priscilla and said, "Somehow, I've gotten myself in the most awful predicament and I don't honestly know how I did it." It had become necessary, he told Priscilla, to let Caroline go, as there was no money left with which to pay her. "When a big man falls, it makes an awful splash," he said glumly. "It is quite possible I may never make another picture."

29.

There was no work into 1953. Preston remained at The Players, sketching ideas for screenplays and TV shows, but writing none of them. Through it all, Sandy's presence made it bearable. "Sandy was so young," said Priscilla Woolfan. "She adored him and Preston needed that."

From Sandy, Preston drew a new purpose for living. "Through Sandy, I live again," he told Eddie Bracken. "It's like a blind man being able to see. I've seen everything, and now I'm seeing it all again through her eyes."

A child was born to the couple in late February, 1953, a five-pound boy named Preston. Sturges first saw the baby in a nurse's arms as he left the delivery room. As she parted the blanket to reveal his face, the baby winked at his father. "I have produced a genius!" Preston exclaimed.

Sturges had the time to dote on little Preston that he'd never had for Mon. "When we had Preston," Sandy explained, "he didn't have tons of monies. He was working at home and when we went to The Players, we threw the baby in the basket and took him with us. And so he knew him as a constant, fascinating presence from the time he was born. He would go into the nursery when Preston was three weeks old and come out and say, 'Well, I've just had a great conversation with my son.' I'd say, 'Oh? What did he say?' and he would of course make up this totally fantastic conversation."

Preston now feared he would lose The Players to creditors and desperately tried to lease it. He went to see Dominick Maggie, his former bartender, who had opened his own restaurant on Beverly Boulevard. "I was interested in *buying* The Players," said Dominick, "and I was going to put Harry Rosenthal back in there and try to make it similar to what it was before. But when Harry died, I just gave up the idea. Rosenthal was the key."

By the time a new job came up, in July of 1953, there was little left to hold Preston in Hollywood. It took him to New York by way of San Francisco. It was the last he would see of California; he would never return.

Carnival in Flanders was based on the classic 1935 French film *La Kermesse Héroïque*, about a Flemish town and its bid to save itself from invasion with the subterfuge of a carnival. The show had begun in New York, lavishly mounted, with music by Johnny Burke and James Van Heusen and a troubled book by at least four writers. The producers planned a long tour—three and a half weeks in Philadelphia and two months on the West Coast—to whip it into shape. The reviews in Philadelphia, where it opened on June 8, were terribly mixed. *Variety* said the show "has a number of undeniable assets, but plenty of deadwood too," and called the book "cumbersome." When it arrived in Los Angeles in July as part of the local Civic Light Opera season, the notices didn't improve. *Variety* estimated the show as being $80,000 over budget and reported its box office in L.A. set a "new low" for the Civic Light Opera. Sturges came in as the trades reported a lawsuit against the producers by the show's former general manager. Bretaigne Windust, the original director, resigned, and the Los Angeles *Times* reported Sturges would rewrite the show and direct it.

Preston left for San Francisco on August 2, 1953, and for New York, with Sandy and the baby, a month later. Lucinda Ballard, who designed the costumes, recalled the show as "an unmitigated disaster." John Raitt, co-starring with Dolores Gray, so hated his costume, a black velvet design with lace collar, that he took to wearing his own pair of tuxedo pants in lieu of the lower half.

Carnival in Flanders was a mess. Sturges viewed the original film, did his own translations, and rewrote most of the existing material. "The play was so *awful*," said Sandy. "Just dreadful. Then, of course, given the writing assignment, he wrote and then the actors couldn't learn all those new lines in time. And re-rehearse. And re-stage. It just could not be done."

Lucinda Ballard said, "He was so harried . . . he almost went insane. Because the producers had run out of money as I recall. There was really a question as to whether it would open or not."

It did open, at the Century Theatre, on September 8, 1953. With little chance other than to climb aboard a sinking ship, Sturges received a black eye for his trouble. The New York reviews were unanimously poor. *Variety* called it a "large, ornate, humorless, tuneless bore." Sturges, the paper commented, had turned the original Gallic satire into "pompous hokum with touches of labored slapstick in place of wit."

This was the first play Sturges had directed outside of The Players and his instinct was to stage the action as he would for film. But without the benefit of cutting and sound and the meticulous timing he had on the set, he was lost and his old tricks were of use to him no longer. Sturges' direction, said *Variety*, was "heavy-handed and occasionally hackneyed." The show opened on a Tuesday and closed the following Saturday. There was a total of six performances.

All of this would have dealt a further blow to Sturges' confidence had he not, in the meantime, lined up a new film. The producer was Lester Cowan, best known for *The Story of G.I. Joe* and a couple of W. C. Fields' pictures, who asked Sturges to write the screenplay and possibly direct an adaptation of George Bernard Shaw's play *The Millionairess* with Katharine Hepburn. Hepburn had recently done it on Broadway and was determined to see it filmed. Cowan told her, "There's only one man who can match Shaw's wit on the screen pictorially. That man is Preston Sturges."

Hepburn admired Sturges' work enormously. She said, "Certainly *Miracle* and *Conquering Hero* were unique. An extraordinary contribution. Like nothing before or since." She agreed with Cowan's judgment and opted to work with Sturges on the screenplay in New York. Cowan and Sturges made the following deal: $1250 a week for eight weeks, beginning October 1, then four weeks at $500, four at $750, four at $1600, and the final two at $1850.

The Millionairess proved to be a tough job. Shaw, in his will, had stipulated that his plays could in no way be altered for the screen. Cowan protested to the estate, which finally allowed a variance of 20%. Such rigid adaptation was new to Sturges, used to changing whatever he wished. He opened the piece up in the most respectful of manners, composing a few minor scenes only hinted at in the play, and visually accelerating the pace with a series of imaginative montages. Hepburn was clearly perfect for the role of Epifania, her rages and tirades well suited to the Sturges bent for slapstick. The opening shots got the film off to a rousing start, with the credits superimposed on a succession of slamming doors and breaking furniture.

Hepburn sat with Sturges as a kind of surrogate producer during the course of the writing, offering support, encouragement, and keeping the project on track. "With me on *The Millionairess* he was full of ideas," she said. "Too many almost. But in a way —there—his spirit seemed doomed or broken almost. I think by then he had had many reversals, but I never talked to him about it. Or about personal matters. I wouldn't hazard a guess as to what or why."

The first draft, disciplined and unerringly faithful, timed out at two hours, roughly thirty minutes longer than Cowan's projections. A considerably tighter version was completed on January 8,

1954, and pronounced brilliant by all concerned. Sturges looked forward with great enthusiasm to directing the film in England. Producer Cowan budgeted a forty-day schedule with plans to shoot the film in CinemaScope and Eastman Color.

"Lester was usually off to England every other weekend," said Sandy, "making deals. He'd come back and make statements like, 'Now we've got Alec Guinness,' 'Now we've got Alastair Sim,' 'Studios are set,' none of which turned out to be true. Then one day Katharine said, 'Well, Lester, if everything's all ready, why are we here?' He said, 'You're quite right. We should be in London by Monday.' I got my passport in four hours."

Cowan and Hepburn flew to London while Sturges and his family booked passage on the *Queen Mary*. Sandy, in a panic, bought several cases of Gerber's baby food for little Preston. "The pediatrician made it sound as though we were going to a desert where people ate dogs in the street," she recalled.

On the eve of their departure, the Sturgeses were sitting in the lobby of the Algonquin Hotel with Sir Cedric Hardwicke and Charles Laughton when two bellboys emerged from an elevator struggling with one of two steamer trunks. "Sandy," asked Laughton, "what have you got in those trunks?"

"Baby food," she replied.

"Well, that's very wise." He nodded. "But, you know, we have babies in England, too."

The crossing took seven days. Cowan cabled news of prospective co-stars for Hepburn that seemed like a Who's Who of British actors—Guinness, Sim, Robert Donat, and Michael Redgrave were all mentioned as strong possibilities.

The ship docked at Southampton and production, Sturges was informed, was only a week or so away. He continued to polish the script, then one day attended a luncheon at the House of Lords and was introduced to Alec Guinness—who, by that time, according to Cowan, had definitely agreed to do the picture.

"Of course, they knew each other by reputation," said Sandy, "and they exchanged the standard compliments. Then Preston mentioned how happy he was that Alec was going to be in his film, and Alec was delighted to hear he was going to be in the film, but wanted to know *what* film.

"Then we realized that Alec Guinness had never even *heard* of the film, much less said that he would do it. And then he wanted to do it, but during the shooting dates that we had, he was scheduled to be at the Abbey Theatre in Dublin."

A deal with J. Arthur Rank turned cold and Sturges' weekly payments halted. Filming dates became less fixed. Cowan talked of plans to film not only *The Millionairess*, but *Johnny's Sister*, *The Three Black Pennies*, and a Sturges original called *The Great Hugo*.

By March, the project looked dead and Sturges decided in April that it would be wise to get out of the country before taxes became due on the money they had brought in. Since arriving, Cowan had paid him only $1000.

Said Sturges, "The picture was to cost two hundred and twenty-five thousand pounds over and above the American money, but the recent experience with Shaw plays turned into pictures was so disastrous that the Rank people did not want to put up more than one hundred and seventy-five thousand pounds. This brought everything to a full stop."

Preston was used to such things by now, but Hepburn was shattered by the project's demise. "Certainly the greatest disappointment of my life," she said later. "I still read the script today; it's just wonderful."

Talk of the project continued through the end of 1956. When *The Millionairess* was finally filmed, it was the year following Preston's death. Cowan's option on the property had long since lapsed. Sir Anthony Asquith made it: with Peter Sellers, Sophia Loren . . . and Alastair Sim.

30.

Lester Cowan kept insisting *The Millionairess* was not dead, that he had formed a partnership with Walter Chrysler, the younger, and that the financing they needed would materialize momentarily. In fact, he encouraged Preston to write *The Great Hugo*, a cynical fable of pacifism and war Alec Guinness was enraptured with, a film he said he would make "anytime, anywhere."

There was really no point in returning to Hollywood. Creditors had forced the sale of The Players in December of 1953 and the engineering company not long afterward. There were no jobs waiting. Only the house on Franklin, its seams unmended, and the debts still owed. As close as they were to France, Preston decided to take Sandy and the baby there—to show Sandy Paris and the places where he had lived as a boy. This would also keep him handy should any of the Lester Cowan projects come to fruition.

"He tried to buy a truck," recalled Sandy, "because in three months we had accumulated a toy store. Every time he left the hotel, he came home with a present for the baby. So we had rocking horses, and bears, and cars, and blocks, plus all those steamer trunks to get out of the country. But he couldn't find a truck, so instead he bought an old 1922 Rolls-Royce that had been converted into what they called a 'shooting brake.' It was like a station wagon.

"So we tooled out of there and that thing was *packed*. We drove down to Dover and picked up a ferry to Belgium. Not only was the inside stuffed, but we had things roped onto the top. When we docked in Belgium, he called Vely Bey, one of his erstwhile stepfathers, who was then married to the widow of a chocolate manufacturer. They invited us to visit, so we stayed at their house two nights."

Upon entering France, the Sturgeses came to a border inspection station, stopping behind a Volkswagen with French license plates. Preston watched apprehensively as the officials almost dismantled the little car before passing it.

Their turn came. "Passport," the officer demanded. The man examined their papers and then haplessly surveyed the crush of things atop and within the Rolls. "Monsieur," he said hopefully, "you have nothing to declare, have you?"

"No," Preston replied.

"Pass!" the officer shouted, obviously relieved.

In Paris they settled at Le Royal Malesherbes, where Preston went to work on *The Great Hugo*. Cowan kept in touch, promising backing, but then Sturges heard rumors that Cowan had made a deal in Hollywood with his *Millionairess* script, and that the film would shoot with Hepburn and her friend George Cukor directing. Sturges conferred with Charley Abramson, who advised him that since Cowan had failed to live up to the terms of their contract, the script was not his. Communication between Cowan and Sturges subsided, and work on *The Great Hugo* lost its urgency.

In Germany, George Templeton had been appointed chief of the motion picture programming office of the U.S. High Command. "He got in touch with me," Dink recalled, "and I asked him to come over and work with us in Germany. They supplied housing, you went to the PX, you went to the commissary; everything was cheap. I had Dwight Taylor there, and Virginia Van Upp, for God's sake. I had Jack Moffitt. I had Ted St. John over there, and he had just won the Academy Award for *The Greatest Show on Earth*. It was a living. But Preston wouldn't come over. There was no way I could convince him."

Sturges' arrival in Paris generated a lot of publicity: his films, slapstick—if not idioms—intact, had become quite popular. Old friends began looking him up: René Clair, Marcel Pagnol. As a favor to Pagnol, he volunteered to write the English subtitles for Pagnol's episodic *Letters from My Windmill*. This became a sizable task: there were twenty-five hundred separate titles. The job finished, Sturges was still unsatisfied. He composed a prologue for American audiences in which he appeared to introduce his colleague and his work, and to engage with Pagnol in a brief dialogue on the desirability of subtitles over dubbing:

STURGES: Do you think the American people will *read* subtitles?

PAGNOL: Why not? Are they so different? In silent films people read subtitles with *pleasure*— if by this method audiences of one country can enjoy the best work from another country without the idiocy of dubbing and hearing a young man from Provence talking to his grandmother in Brooklynese or fractured French—it seems to me the audiences should be willing to learn to read!

The two men directed each other. "I must be a better director than he," said Sturges good-naturedly when he saw the completed film, "because he comes out wonderfully and I come out lousy."

The publicity paid off. Believing Sturges to be British, French producer Alain Poire asked him to direct a film based upon a series of columns in the Paris newspaper *Le Figaro*, the humorous impressions of the French people by a fictional Englishman. The screenplay was to have been written by Pierre Daninos, the author of the supposed writings of Major Marmaduke Thompson, but, according to Sturges, "he was so busy with his success that he never got around to it." So to get the project moving, Sturges found himself writing in French for the first time in some forty years.

He actually wrote three complete screenplays. The first, *Forty Million Frenchmen*, was a charming original "about a French author having invented a fictitious Englishman, and one day the fictitious Englishman appeared in Paris and said, 'I mislaid my notebooks, what have you done with them?' At the end it came out that he was a war hero who had lost his memory fighting for France, and the French author admitted that he had taken his notebooks—which he hadn't, of course—and gave this man who had no identity an authentic identity."

During the course of the writing, however, the columns were collected into a book entitled *The Notebooks of Major Thompson* and became a nationwide best seller. The producers, afraid now to make a film that differed from the content of the Daninos writings, demanded another screenplay and Sturges reluctantly complied. "So I took one chapter called 'The Dear Hereditary Enemy,'" he said, "and, from three pages of this chapter, made a conjugal comedy in seven or eight scenes about the English Major and his French wife, and the dispute as to how their half-English, half-French child will be brought up, whether it will learn the facts of history from the English or French point of view—which are diametrically opposed, of course."

This solution was the best possible under the circumstances and Sturges did all he could to make it work. He developed a dialogue between the Major and his wife, and then interlaced their exchanges with brief Daninos-based essays on various comparisons of the French and English cultures. He also proposed a unique plan for releasing the film in English, as he considered its proper exposure in the United States (especially Los Angeles) critical to his making another American film.

His plan was exceedingly simple: write another script in English, tailored for English-speaking audiences, hire bilingual actors, and shoot each scene twice—once in French and again in English. He figured the added cost of filming to be approximately 30%. "The picture will be amortized on the Continent, then proceeds from the English-language version will be so much gravy."

Sturges prepared to film for the first time in six years. Casting the French parts was easy—Gaumont, the producing company, set actress Martine Carol, who, at the time, was the most popular star in France.

"Can she speak English?" Sturges asked.

"Perfectly," they assured him.

Sturges worried more about casting the part of the Major. He wrote his screenplays for Alec Guinness and wanted—at various times—David Niven, Brian Aherne, Rex Harrison, and James Mason. He finally settled—for a variety of reasons—on British musical comedy star Jack Buchanan, who was enjoying a sort of postwar revival in his native land. Buchanan loved Sturges' script; filming began in late July of 1955 in and around Paris—mostly on location. French moviemaking, Sturges discovered, was the most casual of enterprises. The Paris studio was just that—a Paris studio. Four walls. There was no make-up department, no scenery shop—nothing. Things in France had to be arranged from scratch. "It's a whole different concept," said Sturges, "based on your own ability to get out of tricky situations. In Hollywood, they're used to being babied, having every wish anticipated; here you must do more for yourself."

It turned out that neither of the co-stars had heard of the other. Jack Buchanan, a veritable institution in Great Britain for over thirty years, caused no glimmer of recognition when his name was mentioned to Martine Carol. Likewise was Buchanan's response when alerted to his good fortune in working with the wildly popular French actress . . . the two separated by a mere twenty miles of water.

Sturges worked under a variety of handicaps. Martine Carol spoke an English so heavily accented as to throw the most studious of dialecticians into fits. Much of her dialogue was learned phonetically and it was a chore for her to deliver it at all, let alone well. It was her appearance in the film, however, that made the financing possible—if one had Martine, one had a picture. Like it or not, Sturges was stuck with her. Buchanan's French was in much the same condition as Carol's English. The two found it impossible to pick up their cues in complex exchanges and had to be posed so they could nudge each other when the cues came up. This effectively shot Sturges' famed and colorful pacing all to hell. Nonetheless, he spoke glowingly of the challenge of French filming, and outlined the problems with remarkable good humor.

"I find working in French studios perfectly delightful," he told the BBC's Gordon Gow in a radio interview. "There's an unexpected quality to it. It's very pleasing to me because I began in the theatre that way. I put my first play on Broadway for twenty-five hundred dollars, including an out-of-town tryout, and it worked all right and started me off. The system in France is called *débrouillard*—which means 'now you're in it, get yourself out of it.' Everyone laughs about it, but nothing counts except what you eventually get on the screen. How you get it doesn't matter. I had Jack Buchanan and the French comedian Noël-Noël down at the Austerlitz station one day, and I had a rather difficult boom shot to do. This large, heavy camera had to rise about seven feet into the air, and turn while rising to follow the progress of the two actors—they get into the car on one side and the camera picks them up through the window on the other side. Well, I looked to see what our piece of apparatus was like. It was a highly ridiculous old boom, and we had no lead weights for it. I'm used to working with enormous booms that work perfectly, and these fellows were trying, with a few pieces of iron, to counterbalance the weight of the camera and get it to rise seven feet into the air. I knew that they always succeeded and I wasn't particularly worried. Presently the whole crew disappeared, and they came back a few minutes later while I was talking to an American journalist on the platform. I looked round and saw they had taken all the manhole covers and all the loose pieces of iron from the station, and tied them to the back of this boom with rope—and the shot was perfect. It couldn't have been better if they'd had a boom that cost half a million dollars.

"That's the kind of thing we do constantly. You often pick up an actor in the middle of the street—if you want a cab, for instance, you just stop a passing cab and say, 'Do you think you could act?' to the driver. He generally says, 'Yes, I'd be delighted to,' and he means it. In America, it would be an actor and a specially hired cab, but over here if you need a French taxicab for your scene, you just stop one and say to the driver, 'This is your role, would you go over there and get made up?' And the perfectly amiable old man does quite well.

"Another thing: one day we were making some inserts of Ursula's feet. Ursula is Major Thompson's first wife, and there's a scene in which he says, 'By constantly telling me to wipe my feet when I came in, she finally attracted my attention to hers.' Here I had to show some rather eccentric shoes that Ursula was supposed to have worn, and I needed somebody to pose for the feet. There was no one available, so I looked around the set and there was a make-up lady there. I said, 'Would you mind posing for the feet?'

"She said, 'Well, I haven't got any stockings on.'

" 'Well,' I said, 'that doesn't matter—we'll borrow stockings from the wardrobe.'

"So we borrowed the wardrobe lady's stockings, put them on the make-up lady, borrowed some shoes from my wife, and started making inserts of the feet. The result is exactly as good as if it had cost a thousand pounds."

To keep on schedule and help bury the American stories of his costly ways, Sturges eventually got two crews going simultaneously and finished both the films for a cost of about $540,000. Given the situation though, his work was more that of a skilled craftsman than an artist and his achievement was in getting film done at all, rather than doing it well.

Said assistant director Pierre Kast, "We were all in the Bois de Vincennes to shoot a fox-hunting scene—all actors, horses, and the lot—except for a pack of hounds. Standing to one side, Sturges waited, then decided it was too late to find the dogs and useless to get mad about it. So he rewrote the script, making it read, 'One day, when we had *lost* the pack . . .' and the sequence turned out funnier than before."

Les Carnets du Major Thompson opened in Paris with the festivities usually associated with world premieres. Tuxedo-clad and looking every inch the distinguished Hollywood director, Sturges posed for pictures, smiled and laughed, but a nagging uncertainty told him that he was in for a hard time. "Once the picture started," said Sandy, "he wasn't happy at all. He got very uncomfortable as the thing unfolded."

The film had been made from a source about as filmable as a cookbook. When the pieces were edited together, there was no preview, no tryout, no way to perfect the timing or identify the things that didn't work. The opening night reception was polite, no more. Subsequently, *Major Thompson* placed ninth among first-run pictures in Paris for the year 1956. Respectable, perhaps, but based to what extent on the success of the book? Sturges worried more about the English-language version, where the book would be of no help.

"The problem, as I see it in this case, has always been getting them in," Sturges wrote Walter Reade, the film's U.S. distributor. "Insofar as America is concerned, the book title means nothing. . . . Noël-Noël means nothing. . . . Jack Buchanan as the star is a hindrance. . . . Martine Carol means very little . . . and everybody thinks I'm dead! I'm not kidding! They teach my scripts in the public schools, and some kid who had been studying me nearly fainted when he was introduced to me one day. He thought he was talking to a ghost!"

Sturges' plan for the American release was twofold: it would be necessary to set up the premise of the film and its best-selling parent, and it would be necessary to change the film's title.

"My view is that the English version should commence with a narrative sequence to establish from the very beginning what the picture's about. Not everyone has read the book, or even heard about it, and to start the film with the breakfast scene—much more heavily played in the English version than in the French—is from which there is no recovery afterwards."

The Notebooks of Major Thompson became, at Sturges' suggestion, *The French, They Are a Funny Race*. It was a line from the World War I song "Mademoiselle from Armentières." The entire rhyme was, "The French, they are a funny race—they fight with their feet, and fuck with their face."

"We wish to make it clear," said Sturges, "that ours is an *adult* picture."

Reade's company, Continental Distributing, gave Sturges $2000 to come to New York for the film's opening. He arrived the morning of Sunday, May 5, 1957, and remained for two weeks, giving interviews and appearing on both radio and television, including a session with "Night Beat" host Mike Wallace. *The French, They Are a Funny Race* opened at the Baronet Theatre on May 20, and the reviews of the next day were not encouraging.

Major Thompson was primarily a film for the French. For all its amusing little commentaries, the gentle eccentricities were funny through a recognition and identification that were lost to American audiences. The film was spoken entirely in English, but there was cheating in the sense that dialogues heard in France were, in America, merely paraphrased in the ornate and long-winded voice-overs of the Major himself. Sturges concluded Jack Buchanan's nasal croon was too much for the average American listener, except in extreme moderation. When the film employed the Narratage technique of *The Power and the Glory*, Buchanan's voice began to wear on the most devoted of listeners.

The scenes between Buchanan and Martine Carol were just as wearing, as it was extremely difficult to understand the simplest of lines through the actress' remarkably thick accent. Sturges wrote intricate dialogue for Carol and Buchanan as he had for Rex Harrison in *Unfaithfully Yours* and discovered—too late—that the task of proper delivery was quite beyond them. Typical of Buchanan's monologues are the six single-spaced pages given him in a discussion of French driving habits:

". . . The mere fact of being passed plunges M. Charnelet into a vile mood," a snippet reads. "He recovers his good humor only in passing someone else. Betweentimes his family had better watch itself. Woe unto Madame Charnelet if at the command of her husband, she doesn't lay her hand instantly on the lower half of France. . . ."

Typical of the lines Martine Carol was required to learn phonetically is one she delivers to her husband, the Major. "You know very well I'm teasing you and I never say anything against you except you are escape from a sanatorium of eccentrics . . . but that your family is of high quality and extremely respectable . . . but all joking left aside, it would give you something to do . . . to writing a book . . . and a man like you who has done so much for his whole life . . . is much better he is doing something than spending his time to drink and play bridge. . . ."

Marvelous subtleties never left the printed page. Actors struggled to speak their lines while audiences struggled to understand them.

"To turn this rag, tag, and bobtail of epigram, anecdote, whimsy, and general small beer into a movie was, according to Sturges, 'like trying to make a film of the telephone directory,'" said the blindly favorable *Time* critic. "But, except for a few wrong numbers, Director Sturges has done the trick with a controlled crackpottiness that will take many moviegoers back to *The Great McGinty* and even further back to the bladder farces of silent days."

The reviewers obviously wanted the film to be good; wanted badly to believe that Sturges had done it again. Bosley Crowther was disappointed. "It isn't fair for Mr. Sturges to be so mellow," he wrote. "It isn't fair to us—or to the French."

The film's best moments, as universally noted in the press, were the ones that contained little dialogue and relied instead on the director's physical instincts. When the Major meets his first wife in flashback and the two share a drink aboard their hunting steeds, the picture comes alive. The scene ranks among the best of Sturges' work. But it lasts on the screen only a few precious moments.

"Thank God for the *Time* review," Sturges wrote Continental Distributing's Frank Kassler. "I have no idea whether the picture is going or not, but I am more than ever persuaded that A GOOD CINEMATIC SUBJECT, made inexpensively in Europe with the American market in view, can make a fortune. It's too damned bad that in my over-anxiety to be cooperative I allowed Poire to persuade me to take out the more violent scenes I had shot: The Ventouses—The French and English schoolboys—especially the Chiropractors—so that Bosley could say I had mellowed. Years ago, when I started directing, William Wyler gave me one piece of advice. He said the hardest thing about directing was 'resisting the impulse to be a good fellow.' If you fight for what you believe in, they say you are 'hard to handle' and you don't get any work. If, through a desire to be 'easy to handle,' you give in about things you know are wrong—and there are no previews to find out who is right—the critics say you have 'mellowed' and don't know your business. It's a hard world!"

Variety reported the picture as doing well in the United States, but Continental Distributing maintained that business was bad.

Sturges was inclined to believe them, but despite artistic differences, he continued to embrace the concept of foreign production for the U.S. market. If he could only have free rein on one such picture, he told anyone who would listen, he could virtually guarantee a hit. *Major Thompson* was profitable in Europe, and made its guarantee to Gaumont back for Walter Reade. But it was not a *hit* in America, and Reade cooled to the idea of backing a Sturges picture made in France *in toto*. He left the door open, though, for a possible partnership, and it was upon hopes such as this that the next two years of struggle hinged.

31.

Several pictures came within flinching distance after *Major Thompson*. John Shepridge, Famous Artists' representative in London, worked hard for Sturges, but there seemed to be only talk—no money—in Europe in the late fifties. Said Sturges of Shepridge, "He is an extremely nice man, but every time he starts a deal for me, it seems to have been kissed by death."

One proposal in early 1956 was for Sturges to write and direct a picture with Michael Wilding and Cesar Romero titled *Long Live the King* in Sweden and Germany, filming versions in both German and English. Sturges liked the plot, detailing the adventures of a king who insures his throne so that he collects as long as he is *not* king, but the necessary financing never came through and Sturges' fee—$25,000 for writing plus $25,000 for directing—was never met. That same year, producer-director Chester Erskine expressed an interest in filming Sturges' script for *The Millionairess*, but that again was just talk.

A picture in Rome was proposed for Carlo Ponti with British actress Katie Johnson (*The Ladykillers*), called *The Respectable Widows Fray*. Director Howard Hawks wanted Sturges to write a comedy for him, but the two could not come to terms.

"All I need is *one* chance to make *one* good picture," Sturges wrote John Shepridge. "The rest will take care of itself. So far, the producers have always insisted on a choice of story, which made true success impossible. . . . Poire with his insistence upon shooting a non-cinematic book . . . The one thing I've always done best is the writing of a story . . . but this required a confidence in another man which only very few and great men have. Great companies had it because they *had* to have it."

In Hollywood, Paramount remade *The Lady Eve* with George Gobel, Mitzi Gaynor, and David Niven. Although Sturges, by virtue of the original, received co-screenplay credit with Sidney Sheldon, most of the film was a line-by-line lift. Sturges marveled at the studio's complete lack of faith in him—that they would rather regurgitate one of his old pictures and hire lesser talents like Sheldon and director Norman Taurog than to commission an original for Gobel from Sturges himself. To his friend John Hertz, Jr., he wrote dejectedly, "I am persuaded that the only way that I, at least, will ever get out of hock in this race I am running with the Grim Reaper is by doing my writing and directing over here. . . . I mean someplace in Europe."

Said Sandy, "He said now he was beginning to understand how the mother of Howard Hughes felt, because—apparently —Howard Hughes' father either had nothing or had a lot of money. And she was always scared that he would die here instead of there. And that's what he was trying to do—to die with money instead of without."

He refused to buy life insurance. "If they called it Death Insurance, which is what it really is, they'd never sell a policy."

Sturges' big story of the late fifties was a screenplay called *The Gentleman from Chicago*, which he completed just prior to his visit to America. "It is the story," he said, "of a Chicago gangster of Italian origin, deported by the U.S. government and condemned by the Italian government to live in the small village where he was born. Unwanted at first, his celebrity slowly brings prosperity to the village. His presence also gives it protection, a fact he demonstrates rather charmingly at the end by exterminating legally a gang of twenty-nine men who have come to prey upon the village's new prosperity."

It was *Nothing Doing* with a different twist, and Sturges thought it one of the best things he had ever written. He wrote it in French and translated it into English in March of 1957, at which time he submitted it to both Paramount and United Artists through their Paris offices. Neither expressed interest and Sturges set about beating the bushes for workable deals. He had obtained a firm commitment from actor-singer Eddie Constantine—another American expatriate—to play the title role and hoped to generate sufficient interest on the strength of Constantine's considerable popularity in Europe. During 1957, Sturges negotiated with both John Wayne's Batjac Productions and Sir Michael Balcon's Ealing Films to make *The Gentleman from Chicago*, but neither effort came to anything. In July of that year, for a fee of $1000, Sturges played a one-day part as a French playwright in Bob Hope's *Paris Holiday*. " . . . Bob seemed delighted with my acting talent," he later wrote. "I cannot say the same, but to my astonishment I *did* remember six pages of lines, spoken with a heavy French accent. He predicts a new career for me—which I am far from coveting."

Sturges pushed for the French-language rights to Robert Sherwood's comedy *The Road to Rome*, which he had produced at The Players in early 1953. His task was not made easier by Sherwood's death in late 1955, nor the animosity he felt for

Sturges as the result of a *Variety* review that described The Players presentation as a "cafe production." Sherwood had demanded that the show close and Sturges—who had put every dime he had into it—told him to go to Hell.

And so it went. Sturges had a story for anybody—and with the proper financing, he told them, he could turn it into a hit picture. *The Great Hugo, The Three Black Pennies, The Human Strong Box, Matrix,* and others. Not one deal could he make after *Major Thompson.* "I feel like a ghost trying to make contact," he told Sandy.

In Paris, he felt it important to be seen and would frequent the Café Alexandre on the Avenue George V, across from Fouquet's. "He would be sitting on the terrace every time I came to Paris," Billy Wilder recalled, "drinking brandy and inviting chums to come and join him and—actually—to buy him a brandy."

And there he drank—sometimes until three or four in the morning. Talking of stories, pictures, and past successes, and the need for just one more chance to come to bat.

"But his was the case of the strikeout fear," said Wilder. "You go to bat and you hit singles, doubles, you hit them out of the ball park, and then comes a series of strikeouts. You strike out, and you can't even bunt anymore. There was a loss of self-confidence and a sense that the money men were dealing with a burnt-out but enormous talent. And, of course, bad luck . . . ."

But Sturges was not written out. All he needed was to enjoy again the position, respect, and resources he had once had, and he would surely make more classics for the screen. He was running a race with death, he said, and he approached age sixty with apprehension. His mother had died just short of her sixtieth birthday and Sturges somehow felt that he too would not survive that age.

The birth of a second son to the Sturgeses, Thomas Preston ("Tom-Tom") occurred in June of 1956. It made Preston all the more conscious of his age and position, and what he had yet to do with his life. It took little to send him into uncharacteristic fits of self-pity.

"If you went out of the house when he had a cold," said Sandy, "you were abandoning him in his hour of need. One time he had a cold, and I was going to take the babies to the park for their afternoon outing. It was winter and there were seven thousand pieces of snowsuit on each of them. He said, 'That's how it should be—youth belongs to youth. Your *old* husband will lie here alone, with no one to bring him any soup.' And he meant it. Not as heavily as he would lay it on, but he *really* meant it."

In a fit of anger, Frances Ramsden once told him he would die both broke and alone, with no one to grieve for him. That image became a useful manipulative tool he used shamelessly.

In mid-1957, theatrical producer Max Gordon told Sturges he wanted a play from him for Broadway. That play—Sturges decided— was the half-written *Matrix* in his Hollywood files. The script, stored amid boxes of documents and typescripts dating back thirty years, would be difficult to find. At first he said he would return to Hollywood himself to retrieve it. "Then," said Sandy, "I reminded him that he was the type of person who could be sent into a bedroom containing only a bed with a white spread on it and be asked to bring back a black pocketbook in the middle of the bed, and who would come back and say, 'I can't find it.' He said, 'You're quite right,' and so I went home to get it."

Sandy took the children and left with a one-way ticket for two months. The money for their return, Preston was sure, would take only weeks to materialize.

Sturges had two projects for European production—*The Gentleman from Chicago* and a farce he called *I Belong to Zozo*—thus he resisted returning to California himself. But living apart from his family was both expensive and depressing. If the plays failed to find backers, if the picture found no financing soon, he would have no choice but to return to L.A. He made contingency plans he called "Operation Tentfold." It meant giving up his apartment, selling his French car, taking his Rolls back to England and selling that, and then returning—"pitifully," he said—to California. "It is true that I will find some kind of work in California," he said, "be it TV or house painting, but the move seems a stupid one. At six thousand miles' distance I am not very apt to get either the picture or the play on their feet. I could come back here and live in a hotel, it is true, but you don't do very good work without a base to work from . . . or so I believe."

And so he stayed. Alone, depressed, his drinking accelerated once more. In California, Sandy went to work in Bertie Woolfan's office. Preston sent a small check each month, writing letters as optimistic as possible, but which betrayed his loneliness and insecurity. He found a pair of Tom-Tom's socks behind the radiator in his reading room and fastened them to the wall with a thumbtack.

Sturges aimed *I Belong to Zozo* for Paris production during the fall 1957 season. To Charley Abramson he wrote, "I have finished my first play in French and it is terribly funny. I had [playwright] George Marton read it, however, and he told me on the telephone this morning that it is 'dated.' This is because it is a farce. He may be right. Maybe the only successful plays these days are about homosexuals or depressed young men in love with their grandmothers. I don't know. Personally, I have always enjoyed a truly funny farce and believed that the reason one did not see more of them was that there are never, at any one time, many people who know how to write them. I wrote it with the classical number of doors, which is to say five, and took great pride in the mechanical sequence of entrances and exits. This is not easy to do. I even made up a little verse about it: amateurs who toy with farces . . . often wind up on their arses. I think it is the funniest play I have ever written in my life and should have the audience gasping for breath."

His other major project, Sherwood's *The Road to Rome* (the French rights for which took him three years to obtain), lapsed into coma when it was accepted for production by producer Lars Schmidt, who, in turn, committed it to the schedule of actress Ingrid Bergman, whom Schmidt was soon to marry. Bergman wanted time to perfect her French and ordered a rewrite. In place of Sturges, she wanted Luchino Visconti to direct, and this Sturges refused to allow. Schmidt courteously withdrew and Sturges began to search elsewhere. There was scattered interest, but nothing definite on which to base a future. The Sherwood estate granted Sturges the rights for a period of five years for a fifty-fifty split of the revenues. Sturges proclaimed his reverence for the material to all who would listen, claiming at the same time to have made the play more palatable for French tastes. "I have been told that a number of the passages have a new and quite enchanting sound to the French ear . . . due to my rendition of Mr. Sherwood's English . . . as opposed to the words that would have been used by a run-of-the mill French translator."

Preston pursued another film with even greater fervor. In October of 1957, he prepared a treatment for a film based on a series of *New Yorker* articles about a Wall Street con man called *The Metamorphosis of Philip Musica*. Musica, aka F. Donald Coster, was a former convict and bootlegger who bought the brokerage firm of McKesson and Robbins in the late 1920s and brought it back into full bloom. Sturges spoke of the caricaturing of the leading investment bankers, brokers, and counselors of the nation with relish. ". . . It is the loud puncturing of these pompous and pious personages which will supply the greater part of the fun in this epic of an East Side barber's son," he wrote in a press release. Here, at last, was a subject worthy of him and his films of the forties. Sturges signed the contracts, but the check that was issued him bounced.

Primarily, *The Gentleman from Chicago* was the center of attention during most of 1957 and 1958. A contract was signed with Gray Films, a French production organization that had made Jacques Tati's *Mon Oncle*. Early in November 1958, Sturges, understandably gun-shy, asked if there was any possibility the deal might not go through. "How can it not go through?" was the reply. "It *has* gone through!"

Reassured, Sturges sent most of the money he had left to his family in Hollywood. Within days, the ax fell. As he recalled, "On the very day I was sent for to sign my contract and pick up my first thousand-dollar check, Columbia Pictures announced a film to be made with Cary Grant—based on a story about a deported gangster—written by Art Buchwald. Gray Films dropped my deal like a hot potato. The fact that I had written mine a year before Buchwald meant nothing to them—or the fact that such stories are always in the public domain."

The cancellation of *The Gentleman from Chicago* left its author financially stranded. Sturges wrote to Stanley Donen, producer-director of the Buchwald picture, *A Gift from the Boys*,* slamming the script and urging Donen to acquire Sturges' instead. But a third writer appeared with a deported gangster story and accused both Buchwald and Sturges of plagiarism and threatened a lawsuit. Donen shied from the Sturges script and Sturges was left with an unsalable screenplay.

In desperation, he wrote to Eleanor Hutton—Mrs. Leon Barzini—his second wife. When they parted in the early thirties, Preston had told her that she could pay him the disputed $100,000 "when and if she wanted to." He would never ask her for anything, he said, "unless I were ill or desperate." Now, he described his condition and humbly requested help. At stake were ". . . the immediate necessities of two very small boys, their young mother, another boy of seventeen, and his mother. I said necessities—not Christmas presents. This unfortunate little group has only me to look to at the moment—and as a provider, just now, I am a thundering flop. Completely cashless; I mean really and truly, not figuratively speaking."

But in this, possibly his darkest hour, came luck. Sturges had a strong sense of Irish luck, a luck he reasoned came from the fact that his mother had been born with a caul, part of the amniotic sac which sometimes envelops the head—an identifying mark placed upon the heads of favored infants by the Little People of Ireland. These people led charmed existences, it was said, and the protection of the caul extended sometimes to the succeeding generation. Before Eleanor could respond, before the cars could be sold, there was a cable from New York. A new play was in trouble, this time a comedy. The director had withdrawn. And the co-producer—at the urging of his playwright—believed in the old Sturges magic. Money was cabled, and Preston left just days before Christmas. To return to New York and to Broadway once more.

---

*Released as *Surprise Package* (1960).

32.

Sturges arrived in New York on Christmas Eve, 1958, and installed himself at the Algonquin Hotel on 44th Street. The new play was called *The Golden Fleecing* and the playwright was Lorenzo Semple, Jr. His producers were Elliott Nugent and Courtney Burr (they had done *The Seven Year Itch* together) and Nugent himself had planned to direct it. Nugent cast the play, hired the theatre, announced a tryout in Atlantic City in late January, then suffered a nervous breakdown. With a history of mental illness, no one cared to predict just how long he might be out. And so they had to find a new director. Semple had an inspiration: his play was a comedy and, like Harry Rigby before him, he remembered with great fondness the Sturges films of his youth. He decided that Sturges would be the perfect choice to direct and convinced Courtney Burr.

The honeymoon was brief. At Burr's instigation, Sturges fired most of Nugent's cast. When new actors were hired, he began picking at the play, demanding rewrites and changes. "I've been around a lot longer than you," he told the young playwright, "and I know about comedy, and this isn't funny."

Sturges was irritable, unsure of himself directing something new he hadn't written. Again, as with *Carnival in Flanders*, he directed as he would for film. He tried injecting slapstick, tried reworking the script so he could see it more clearly. The end results were alienation and failure.

"Rehearsals went forward, but there was a hole at the center," wrote actress Chris Chase, whom Sturges cast as the ingenue. "An entire scene wouldn't be working, yet Preston would take an hour to fuss over a single word, and some of the actors began writing him off. Retroactively. 'He never was any good,' I heard one man telling another. 'So-and-so did all the movies Sturges got credit for.' Sure, and a little colored boy wrote Irving Berlin's music."

Nugent returned to see the play on the fifteenth of January: Sturges and his cast were fired the following day. On January 21, *Variety* announced that Nugent had returned. The play would rehearse an additional two weeks, the paper reported, then play its tryouts in both Atlantic City and Washington, D.C. But again, for Nugent, the task was beyond him. When the play finally opened, in October of that year, Burr was in partnership with Gilbert Miller and the director was Abe Burrows.

An agent approached Sturges in mid-January, urging him to write his autobiography. Sturges had had a title for years: *The Events Leading Up to My Death*. He agreed and a contract with Holt was negotiated for an advance of $7500. He began dictating on February 11, 1959, usually working at night. The Algonquin generously provided an office. Preston began slowly, straining his memory, recounting only with great difficulty the events of his early childhood. He asked his editor for copies of his mother's book and *Best Film Plays of 1943–44*, which included the scripts for both *Miracle* and *Hail the Conquering Hero*. He wrote thirty pages the first month, seventy-four the next. He put virtually every memory he could muster down on paper. As a result, he digressed quite a bit, and the manuscript grew long and cumbersome. In the middle of his chapter on the Lycée Janson, for example, he got to writing about gymnasiums and wandered off into boxing. From there it was only a short hop to the career of Frank Moran, and Preston devoted five pages to what he called "the longest count in the history of boxing."

Fittingly, Preston began his book with an epitaph:

> Now I've laid me down to die
> I pray my neighbors not to pry
> Too deeply into sins that I
> Not only cannot here deny
> But much enjoyed as life flew by.

Alternately, Sturges worked on an English translation of *I Belong to Zozo*, in which he said he would cast Blanche Yurka and Edward Everett Horton. He then got a deal going through NBC and David Sarnoff, with whom he had once dined. He wrote to Sarnoff with proposals for two series: "The one series is called *Station F.A.T.E.* (which has been broadcasting on more wave lengths than you knew existed, for much, much longer than you suspect) and the other *It Happened Exactly Here*. The device in this case is a visible tie-up between the present and the past, by showing the local AS IT IS TODAY of some celebrated event of the past. For instance: we want to show the assassination of Abraham Lincoln in Ford's Theatre. A small amount of research will pinpoint not only the location of the theatre but the exact location of the box where The Great Emancipator sat. It may be the shelves of a grocery store today or the bathroom of a colored family's apartment or a place in the air over the roof of the garage.

Wherever it is, it is not difficult to find out and a couple of surveyor's instruments and stretched lines will give authenticity and interest to the moment the narrator says, 'IT HAPPENED . . . EXACTLY . . . HERE!' I can hear the fanfare of trumpets, don't you? As we start to dissolve, and the voice of the narrator begins, 'It was a cold night in February 1865, the 16th to be exact . . .' or a hot night in July, or whenever the hell it was. But I am sure that you get the idea, which covers all of history and can never run out of interesting facts. The gimmick is good as it really does hook the present to the past. The final dissolve naturally brings you back to the opening shot: the surveyors pick up their instruments, and the narrator concludes with, 'AND IT HAPPENED . . . EXACTLY . . . HERE! I thank you.' "

Sarnoff was intrigued enough to schedule a pilot. Sturges authorized Charley Abramson and Famous Artists to negotiate the contract, which called for a fee of $25,000 as producer, director, and writer, and an additional $2500 for appearing on camera as "The Producer." A knowledgeable friend estimated the cost of the series at $150,000 per episode but Sturges said, "That seems high to me."

At work on his book, the NBC deal pending, Sturges again saw a way out of his troubles. Sandy and the family made plans to come east, where young Preston would start school in the fall. In June, a backer was found for *The Gentleman from Chicago*, a Canadian multimillionaire who owned five insurance companies. Sturges was wary at first; he had watched so many deals disintegrate. "Until he shakes hands," said Preston, "your hopes are high."

But this time it was different. Here he was not talking with producers who could *get* the money—he was talking to the money itself. And the deal was quite firm. "He would have had an office," Eddie Bracken remembered. "All he had to do was write. They would have financed him and he wouldn't have to worry about money anymore. He showed the people *The Miracle of Morgan's Creek* and *Hail the Conquering Hero* in one night at the Algonquin Hotel. I was there with the backers to, again, do my friend a favor and help him promote and talk this thing out. He wasn't drinking at the time. It was the *turn* for Sturges."

And in June, a contract was signed. First would come *I Belong to Zozo*, a farce comedy, then a musical, based upon *The Gentleman from Chicago*. Third would be a motion picture made from that musical.

Said Bracken, "I recall the very wonderful and nostalgic feeling I had that night—for a great man, a good friend, a man that did a lot for me. I loved it. His treatment of me, what he said of me always built my ego up to a tremendous high. And the ideas he had—this was the old Sturges talking. It was still there."

Sturges' last weeks were busy and filled with hope. He still dwelled on his errors, but from the healthy perspective of a man on the rise. He resolved that this time things would be different. His inclinations toward excess would be tempered with the responsibility he now felt toward his friends and young family. In June, he wrote to Mon on the occasion of the boy's eighteenth birthday. "I took a complete physical check-up the other day," he said in closing, "and to my horror the doctor told me I was good for another twenty-five years. This gives me time to take up another profession, such as dentistry for instance . . . although I think I will stay in the one I am in now. I may not get around to treating you to a college education until you are forty, and your brothers both six feet also, but sooner or later I'll come through with something for all of you."

It was the sort of sentiment he wrote at the beginning of his book. One night in the Algonquin his thoughts turned to his wives and children and the chicken dealer he had owed so much back in 1949.

He wrote, "Like an actor between engagements, I am probably merely *between* fortunes, but it is a fact that of the vast and depressing sums I earned I managed to save exactly . . . nothing. Or, more accurately, slightly *less* than nothing . . . since I arrived in Hollywood broke but without any debts . . . and departed with quite a few.

"Is this upsetting? To me? Not at all. Men of intelligence need very little, and writers have always worked better hungry, as François Villon, Honoré de Balzac, and Edgar Allan Poe will now sing for us in three part harmony . . . but it is very upsetting to the chicken dealer, and for his sake I regret it bitterly, as I do for the loyal friends who stood by me and for the patient ladies I had the honor of being married to . . . but my principal regret is directed toward those several young males burdened with my name, but not necessarily with my useful knack of increasing the value of a piece of paper by scribbling on it. It is of these I hate to think: heartbreaking in angular unbending suits, painful grammar, and white sidewall haircuts . . . plodding hopelessly in some one-building university . . . sans languages . . . sans voyages abroad . . . sans opportunities to meet first class minds . . . in short, sans any of the remarkable advantages my remarkable mother managed to wring from a reluctant world and shower upon the head of her unappreciative son. When I think of the oceans I crossed and recrossed . . . the countries I've lived in . . . the operas and concerts I furiously attended . . . the museums and catacombs I was shoved into, pushed through, and dragged out of . . . then set against all this the meager opportunities awaiting my mother's grandsons . . . unless . . . yes, I said unless . . .

"You can never tell when an old yegg is going to crack another crib ... and *this* time unless they plug me during the getaway ... the boys will all be dressing at Brooks Brothers ... and their mothers at Balenciaga."

APPENDIX 1
THEATRE CHRONOLOGY

1. Hotbed (1928)

Author: Paul Osborn. Producer: Brock Pemberton. Directors: Brock Pemberton, Antoinette Perry. Theatre: Klaw, New York. Opening: November 9, 1928. Number of Performances: 19

Rev. David Rushbrook	William Ingersoll
Hattie	Josephine Hull
Lila	Alison Bradshaw
John	Richard Spencer
Lawrence Binnings	Preston Sturges
Professor Clark	Carl Anthony
Louis Willard	Richard Stevenson
George Courtenay	Walter Greenough
Dean Slawson	Paul Gilmore
Professor Kimball	Leigh Lovel
Professor Staton	Charles Abbe

2. The Guinea Pig (1929)

Author: Preston Sturges. Producer: Preston Sturges. Director: Walter Greenough. Settings: William Bradley Studio. Theatre: President, New York. Opening: January 7, 1929. Number of Performances: 64

Miss Snitkin	Rhoda Cross
Seth Fellows	Robert Robson
Sam Small	Alexander Carr
Wilton Smith	John Ferguson
Helen Reading	Ruth Thomas
Robert Fleming	John Vosburgh
Catherine Howard	Mary Carroll
Natalie	Audree Corday

3. Frankie and Johnnie (1929)

Author: John M. Kirkland. Producer: A. H. Woods. Director: John D. Williams. Settings: P. Dodd Ackerman. Costumes: Mrs. Sidney Harris. On Tour: Spring 1929.

Danny	Edgar Nelson
Lazy Ike	Charles Henderson
Nellie Bly	Leona Maricle
Lady Lou	Georgie Drew Mendum
Count	Kenneth Burton
Jimmie	Ralph Wordley
Frankie	Grace Kern
A Man	Ray Earles
Lily	Grace Peters
Pansy	Helene Sinnott
Johnnie	Louis Jean Heydt
John Walsh	Preston Sturges
Margy, the Dove	Mary Brett
Margy's Man	John Altieri
Pansy's Visitor	George Colan
Reynolds	Jack Clifford

4. Strictly Dishonorable (1929)

Author: Preston Sturges. Producer: Brock Pemberton. Director: Brock Pemberton, Antoinette Perry. Settings: Raymond Sovey. Costumes: Margaret Pemberton. Theatre: Avon, New York. Opening: September 18, 1929. Number of Performances: 557.

Giovanni	John Altieri
Mario	Marius Rogati
Tomaso Antiovi	William Ricciardi
Judge Dempsey	Carl Anthony
Henry Greene	Louis Jean Heydt
Isabelle Parry	Muriel Kirkland
Count Di Ruvo	Tullio Carminati
Patrolman Mulligan	Edward J. McNamara

5. Recapture (1930)

Author: Preston Sturges. Producer: A. H. Woods. Director: Don Mullally. Settings: P. Dodd Ackerman. Theatre: Eltinge, New York. Opening: January 29, 1930. Number of Performances: 24.

Mrs. Stuart Romney	Cecilia Loftus
Rev. Outerbridge Smole	Hugh Sinclair
Monsieur Remy	Gustave Rolland
Gwendoliere Williams	Glenda Farrell

Monsieur Edelweiss	Joseph Roeder
Auguste	Meyer Berenson
Henry C. Martin	Melvyn Douglas
Patricia Tulliver Browne	Ann Andrews
Capt. Hubert Reynolds, D.S.O.	Stuart Casey
Madame Pistache	Louza Riane

6. The Well of Romance (1930)

Libretto and Lyrics: Preston Sturges. Music: H. Maurice Jacquet. Producer: G. W. McGregor. Director: J. Harry Benrimo. Settings: Gates and Morange. Costumes: Eaves, Schneider & Blythe. Theatre: Craig, New York. Opening: November 7, 1930. Number of Performances: 8. Musical Numbers: "At Lovetime," "The Well of Romance," "Be Oh So Careful, Ann," "Hail the King," "Melancholy Lady," "Dream of Dreams," "I'll Never Complain," "Cow's Divertissement," "Mazourka," "Fare Thee Well," "Intermezzo," "The Moon's Shining Cool," "One Night," "I Want to Be Loved by an Expert," "German Country Dance" (Pantomime), "Rhapsody of Love," "For You and for Me," "Serenade."

Ann Schlitzl	Laine Blaire
Wenzel	Tommy Monroe
Frau Schlitzl	Lina Abarbanell
Gertrude	Elsa Paul
Mildred	Mildred Newman
Louise	Louise Joyce
The Grand Chancellor	Louis Sorin
The Princess	Norma Terris
Poet	Howard March
Lieutenant Schpitzelberger	Louis Rupp
Second Lieutenant	Syuleen Krasnoff
Third Lieutenant	Eugene Racine
General Otto	Max Figman
A Gypsy	Edis Phillips
Joseph	Joseph Roeder
A Waiter	Pat Walters
First Guardsman	Rowan Tudor
Second Guardsman	James Libby
Butterfly (the Cow)	Lo Ivan (Front) Ruth Flynn (Rear)

7. Child of Manhattan (1932)

Author: Preston Sturges. Producer: Peggy Fears. Director: Howard Lindsay. Settings: Jonel Jorgulesco. Theatre: Fulton, New York. Opening: March 1, 1932. Number of Performances: 87.

Miss Sophie Vanderkill	Helen Strickland
Eggleston	Joseph Roeder

Otto Paul Vanderkill	Reginald Owen
Spyrene	Ralph Sanford
Clifford	Charles Cromer
Flo	Judy Abbot
Madeleine McGonegal	Dorothy Hall
Gertie	Mitzi Miller
Buddy McGonegal	Jackson Halliday
Mrs. McGonegal	Maude Odell
Martha	Jacqueline Winston
Lucinda, Limited	Franz Bendtsen
Constance	Joan Hamilton
Myrtle	Eileen Bach
A Girl	Elizabeth Young
Yvette	Louise Sheldon
Lilly	Peggy Fish
Gladys	Mary Orr
Jewel	Geraldine Wall
Aunt Minnie	Jessie Ralph
Lucy McGonegal	Harriet Russell
Nurse	Florence John
Doctor	Alexander Campbell
John Tarantino	John Altieri
Charley	Alexander Campbell
Panama C. Kelly	Douglas Dumbrille
A Waiter	Charles Hubert Brown

8. Make A Wish (1951)

Book: Preston Sturges (Uncredited: Abe Burrows). Based upon the play *The Good Fairy* by Ferenc Molnár. Music and Lyrics: Hugh Martin. Producers: Harry Rigby, Jule Styne, Alexander H. Cohen. Director: John C. Wilson. Dances and Musical Ensembles: Gower Champion. Settings and Costumes: Raoul Pene Du Bois. Theatre: Winter Garden, New York. Opening: April 18, 1951. Number of Performances: 103. Musical Numbers: "The Tour Must Go On," "I Wanna Be Good and Bad," "What I Was Warned About," "Suits Me Fine," "Hello, Hello, Hello," "Tonight You Are in Paree," "Who Gives a Sou?" "Make a Wish," "I'll Never Make a Frenchman of You," "Paris, France," "When Does This Feeling Go Away?" "Over and Over," "The Sale" (Ballet), "That Face," "Take Me Back to Texas with You."

Dr. Didier	Eda Heinemann
Dr. Francel	Phil Leeds
Janette	Nanette Fabray
Ricky	Harold Lang
Poupette	Helen Gallagher
Policeman	Howard Wendell
Marius Frigo	Melville Cooper
Paul Dumont	Stephen Douglass

294

The Madam	Mary Finney
Felix Labiche	Le Roi Operti
Sales Manager	Howard Wendell

9. Carnival in Flanders (1953)

Book: Preston Sturges (Uncredited: George Oppenheimer, Herbert Fields). Based upon the screenplay *La Kermesse Héroïque* by Charles Spaak, Jacques Feyder, Bernard Zimmer. Music: James Van Heusen. Lyrics: Johnny Burke. Producers: Paula Stone, Mike Sloane, Johnny Burke, James Van Heusen. Director: Preston Sturges (Uncredited: Bretaigne Windust). Special Ballet and Musical Numbers: Helen Tamiris (Uncredited: Jack Cole). Settings: Oliver Smith. Costumes: Lucinda Ballard. Theatre: Century, New York. Opening: September 8, 1953. Number of Performances: 6. Musical Numbers: "I'm One of Your Admirers," "Take the Word of a Gentleman," "How Far Can a Lady Go?" "The Plundering of the Town" (Ballet), "The Small Things," "The Delicate Stronger Sex," "The Sudden Thrill," "It's a Fine Old Institution," "Unaccustomed As I Am," "It's a Matter of Military Tactics," "Here's That Rainy Day," "For a Moment of Your Love," "In the Clear Light of Dawn," "The Carnival Ballet," "Ring the Bell," "The Very Necessary You," "It's an Old Spanish Custom," "A 17-Gun Salute," "You're Dead."

Siska	Pat Stanley
Jan Breughel	Kevin Scott
Tailor	Paul Reed
Butcher	Paul Lipson
Barber	Bobby Vail
Innkeeper	Lee Goodman
Mayor	Roy Roberts
Cornelia	Dolores Gray
Martha	Dolores Kempner
Courier	Matt Mattox
Three Mourning Women	Sandra Devlin
	Julie Marlow
	Lorna Del Maestro
1st Officer	Ray Mason
2nd Officer	George Martin
3rd Officer	Jimmy Alex
Duke	John Raitt
1st Citizen	Wesley Swails
2nd Citizen	Norman Weise
Lisa	Jean Bradley
Katherine	Undine Forrest
Orderley	William Noble

10. The Conquering Hero (1961)

Book: Larry Gelbart. Based upon the screenplay *Hail the Conquering Hero* by Preston Sturges. Music: Moose Charlap. Lyrics: Norman Gimbel. Producers: Robert Whitehead, Roger L. Stevens. Director and Choreographer: Bob Fosse. Settings: Jean Rosenthal, William Pitkin. Costumes: Patton Campbell. Theatre: ANTA, New York. Opening: January 16, 1961. Number of Performances: 8. Musical Numbers: "Girls! Girls!" "Five Shots of Whiskey," "Hail, the Conquering Hero," "Must Be Given to You," "Wonderful, Marvelous You," "Truth," "Won't You Marry Me?" "The River Bank," "Only Rainbows," "The Campaign," "One Mother Each," "I'm Beautiful," "Rough Times," "Yours, All Yours."

Doorman	Lee Barry
PFC Doyle	Walter Farrell
PFC O'Dell	Bob Dixon
Cpl. Ganz	Bill McDonald
PFC Pasco	Bernie Meyer
Sgt. Murdock	Lionel Stander
Nightclub Performer	Marilyn Stark
Master of Ceremonies	Bob Kaliban
Waiter	Eric Kristen
Nightclub Manager	William Le Massena
Woodrow Truesmith	Tom Poston
MP	Burt Bier
Bartender	Samye Van
A General	T. J. Halligan
Conductor	Dan Morgan
Mayor Noble	Fred Stewart
Judge Callan	William Le Massena
Forrest Noble	John McMartin
Whiteman	Bob Kaliban
Mrs. Noble	Edith Gresham
Rev. Cox	Geoffrey Bryant
Sue Anne Barnes	Jane Mason
Ronnie	Richard Buckley
Mrs. Truesmith	Elizabeth Kerr
Libby Callan	Kay Brown
Gene	Kenny Kealy
Doc Johnson	T. J. Halligan
The Enemy Captain	John Aristedes
Effie	Brina Dexter

APPENDIX 2
FILM CHRONOLOGY

1. The Big Pond (1929)

Producer: Monta Bell. Director: Hobart Henley. Dialogue Director: Bertram Harrison. Based upon the play by George Middleton, A. E. Thomas. Scenario: Robert Presnell, Garrett Fort. Dialogue: Preston Sturges. Photography: George Folsey. Editor: Emma Hill. Sound: Ernest Zatorsky. Musical Arranger: John W. Green. Song: "Livin' in the Sunlight, Lovin' in the Moonlight" by Al Lewis, Al Sherman. Song: "This Is My Lucky Day" by Lew Brown, B. G. DeSylva, Ray Henderson. Songs: "Mia Cara," "You Brought a New Kind of Love to Me" by Irving Kahal, Pierre Norman, Sammy Fain. Studio: Paramount Long Island Studio. Production and Distribution: Paramount. Release Date: May 1930. Running Time: 72 minutes.

Pierre Mirande	Maurice Chevalier
Barbara Billings	Claudette Colbert
Mr. Billings	George Barbier
Mrs. Billings	Marion Ballou
Toinette	Andree Corday
Ronnie	Frank Lyon
Pat O'Day	Nat Pendleton
Jennie	Elaine Koch

Note: A French-dialogue version, *La Grande Mare*, was filmed simultaneously. It was directed by Henri Bataille and featured Chevalier, Colbert, Corday, Pendleton, Lorraine Jaillet, Maude Allen, Henry Mortimer, and William Williams.

2. Fast and Loose (1930)

Director: Fred Newmeyer. Dialogue Director: Bertram Harrison. Based upon the play *The Best People* by David Gray, Avery Hopwood. Screenplay: Doris Anderson, Jack Kirkland. Dialogue: Preston Sturges. Photography: William Steiner. Sound: C. A. Tuthill. Studio: Paramount Long Island Studio. Production and Distribution: Paramount. Release Date: November 1930. Running Time: 70 minutes.

Bronson Lenox	Frank Morgan
Marion Lenox	Miriam Hopkins
Alice O'Neil	Carole Lombard
Henry Morgan	Charles Starrett
Bertie Lenox	Henry Wadsworth
Carrie Lenox	Winifred Harris
George Grafton	Herbert Yost
Lord Rockingham	David Hutcheson
Millie Montgomery	Ilka Chase
Judge Summers	Herschel Mayall

3. Strictly Dishonorable (1931)

Producer: Carl Laemmle, Jr. Director: John M. Stahl. Assistant Director: Joe Tarrillo. Based upon the play by Preston Struges. Screenplay: Gladys Lehman. Photography: Jackson Rose. Editor: Arthur Travers. Art Director: Herman Rosse. Sound: C. Roy Hunter. Make-up: Jack P. Pierce. Production and Distribution: Universal. Release Date: November 1931. Running Time: 91 minutes.

Gus, Count Di Ruvo	Paul Lukas
Isabelle Parry	Sidney Fox
Judge Dempsey	Lewis Stone
Henry Greene	George Meeker
Tomaso	William Ricciardi
Mulligan	Sidney Toler
Waiter	Carlo Schipa
Waiter	Samuel Bonello

4. Child of Manhattan (1932)

Director: Eddie Buzzell. Assistant Director: Dave Selman. Based upon the play *Child of Manhattan* by Preston Sturges. Screenplay: Gertrude Purcell, Maurine Watkins. Photography: Ted Tetzlaff. Sound: Lodge Cunningham. Production and Distribution: Columbia. Release Date: February 1933. Running Time: 70 minutes.

Madeleine McGonegal	Nancy Carroll
Paul Vanderkill	John Boles
Eggleston	Warburton Gamble
Aunt Sophie	Clara Blandick
Mrs. McGonegal	Jane Darwell
Buddy	Garry Owen
Lucy	Betty Grable
Bustamente	Luis Alberni
Aunt Minnie	Jessie Ralph
Panama Kelly	Charles Jones
Dulcey	Tyler Brooke
Louise	Betty Kendall

5. They Just Had to Get Married (1932)

Director: Edward Ludwig. Assistant Director: Eddie Snyder. Based upon a play by Cyril Harcourt. Screenplay: Gladys Lehman, H. M. Walker (Uncredited: Preston Sturges). Additional Dialogue: Clarence Marks. Photography: Edward Snyder. Editor: Ted Kent. Sound: Gilbert Kurland. Make-up: Jack P. Pierce. Production and Distribution: Universal. Release Date: January 1933. Running Time: 69 minutes.

Sam Sutton	Slim Summerville
Molly	ZaSu Pitts
Hume	Roland Young
Lola Montrose	Verree Teasdale
Marie	Fifi D'Orsay
Hampton	C. Aubrey Smith
Radcliff	Robert Greig
Montrose	David Landau
Lizzie	Elizabeth Patterson
Fairchilds	Wallis Clark
Mrs. Fairchilds	Vivian Oakland
Rosalie Fairchilds	Cora Sue Collins
Wilmont Fairchilds	David Leo Tollotson
Bradford	William Burress
Mrs. Bradford	Louise Mackintosh
Langley	Bertram Marburgh
Clerk	James Donlan
Tony	Henry Armetta
Mrs. Langley	Virginia Howell

6. The Power and the Glory (1933)

Producer: Jesse L. Lasky. Director: William K. Howard. Assistant Director: Horace Haugh. Dialogue Director: Preston Sturges. Photography: James Wong Howe. Editor: Paul Weatherwax. Art Director: Max Parker. Sound: A. W. Protzman. Musical Direction: Louis De Francesco. Musical Score: J. S. Zamencik, Peter Brunelli. Costumes: Rita Kaufman. Production and Distribution: Fox. Release Date: August 1933. Running Time: 76 minutes.

Tom Garner	Spencer Tracy
Sally	Colleen Moore
Henry	Ralph Morgan
Eve	Helen Vinson
Tom Garner, Jr.	Clifford Jones
Mr. Borden	Henry Kolker
Henry's Wife	Sarah Padden
Tom (the Boy)	Billy O'Brien
Henry (the Boy)	Cullen Johnston
Mulligan	J. Farrell MacDonald
Edward	Robert Warwick

7. Imitation of Life (1934)

Producer: Carl Laemmle, Jr. Director: John M. Stahl. Assistant Director: Scotty Beal. Based upon the novel by Fannie Hurst. Adaptation: Preston Sturges. Screenplay: William Hurlbut. Photography: Merritt Gerstad. Editors: Phil Cahn, Maurice Wright. Art Director: Charles D. Hall. Sound: Gilbert Kurland. Make-up: Jack P. Pierce. Production and Distribution: Universal. Release Date: November 1934. Running Time: 106 minutes.

Beatrice Pullman	Claudette Colbert
Stephen Archer	Warren William
Elmer	Ned Sparks
Aunt Delilah	Louise Beavers
Jessie Pullman (Age 3)	Baby Jane
Jessie Pullman (Age 8)	Marilyn Knoylden
Jessie Pullman (Age 18)	Rochelle Hudson
Peola Johnson (Age 4)	Seble Hendricks
Peola Johnson (Age 9)	Dorothy Black
Peola Johnson (Age 19)	Fredi Washington
Martin	Alan Hale
Landlord	Clarence Hummel Wilson
Painter	Henry Armetta
Doctor Preston	Henry Kolker
Butler	Wyndham Standing
French Maid	Alice Ardell
Mr. Carven	Franklin Pangborn
Restaurant Manager	Paul Porcasi
Hugh	Walter Walker
Mrs. Eden	Noel Frances
Tipsy Man	Tyler Brooke

8. Thirty Day Princess (1934)

Producer: B. P. Schulberg. Director: Marion Gering. Assistant Director: Art Jacobson. Based upon the story by Clarence Budington Kelland. Adaptation: Sam Hellman, Edwin Justus Mayer. Screenplay: Preston Sturges, Frank Partos. Photography: Leon Shamroy. Editor: June Loring. Art Director: Hans Dreier. Associate: Bill Inhen. Sound: J. A. Goodrich. Production and Distribution: Paramount. Release Date: May 1934. Running Time: 74 minutes.

Princess Catterina	Sylvia Sidney
Nancy Lane	Sylvia Sidney
Porter Madison III	Cary Grant
Richard Gresham	Edward Arnold
King Anatol	Henry Stephenson
Count	Vince Barnet
Baron	Edgar Norton
Managing Editor	Robert McWade
Spottswood	George Baxter

Mr. Kirk	Ray Walker
Parker	Lucien Littlefield
Lady-in-Waiting	Marguerite Namara
Mrs. Schmidt	Eleanor Wesselhoeft
Doctor at Gresham's	Frederick Sullivan
First Detective	Robert E. Homans
Second Detective	William Augustin
Policeman	Ed Dearing
Spottswood's Friend	Bruce Warren
City Editor	William Arnold
Sergeant of Police	Dick Rush
Radio Man	J. Merrill Holmes
Gresham's Butler	Thomas Monk

9. We Live Again (1934)

Producer: Samuel Goldwyn. Director: Rouben Mamoulian. Assistant Director: Robert Lee. Based upon the novel *Resurrection* by Leo Tolstoy. Adaptation: Maxwell Anderson, Leonard Praskins. Screenplay: Preston Sturges (Uncredited: Thornton Wilder). Photography: Gregg Toland. Editor: Otho Lovering. Art Director: Richard Day. Production Designer: Sergei Sudeikin. Sound: Frank Maher. Musical Director: Alfred Newman. Costumes: Omar Kiam. Studio: United Artists. Production: Samuel Goldwyn. Distribution: United Artists. Release Date: October 1934. Running Time: 85 minutes.

Katusha Maslova	Anna Sten
Prince Dmitri Nekhlyudov	Fredric March
Missy Kortchagin	Jane Baxter
Prince Kortchagin	C. Aubrey Smith
Aunt Marie	Ethel Griffies
Aunt Sophia	Gwendolyn Logan
Matrona Pavlovna	Jessie Ralph
Simonson	Sam Jaffe
Theodosia	Cecil Cunningham
Korablova	Jessie Arnold
The Red Head	Fritzi Ridgeway
The Colonel	Morgan Wallace
Tikhon	Davison Clark
Kartinkin	Leonid Kinskey
Botchkova	Dale Fuller
Judge	Michael Visaroff
Judge	Edgar Norton

10. The Good Fairy (1934)

Associate Producer: Henry Henigson. Director: William Wyler. Assistant Director: Archie Buchanan. Based upon the play by Ferenc Molnár. Screenplay: Preston Sturges. Photography: Norbert Bodine. Editor: Daniel Mandell. Art Director: Charles D. Hall. Sound: Joe Lapin. Gowns: Vera West. Make-up: Jack P. Pierce. Production and Distribution: Universal. Release Date: January 1935. Running Time: 98 minutes.

Luisa Ginglebusher	Margaret Sullavan
Dr. Max Sporum	Herbert Marshall
Konrad	Frank Morgan
Detlaff	Reginald Owen
Schlapkohl	Alan Hale
Dr. Schultz	Beulah Bondi
Dr. Motz	Eric Blore
Telephone Man	Hugh O'Connell
Joe	Cesar Romero
The Barber	Luis Alberni
Head Waiter	Torben Meyer
Doorman	Al Bridge
Moving Man	Frank Moran
Moving Man	Matt McHugh

11. Diamond Jim (1935)

Producer: Edmund Grainger. Director: A. Edward Sutherland. Assistant Director: Joseph McDonough. Based upon the book by Parker Morell. Adaptation: Harry Clork, Doris Malloy. Screenplay: Preston Sturges. Photography: George Robinson. Editor: Daniel Mandell. Art Director: Charles D. Hall. Sound: Gilbert Kurland. Musical Direction: C. Bakaleini-koff. Musical Score: Franz Waxman, Ferdinand Grofé. Gowns: Vera West. Make-up: Jack P. Pierce. Production and Distribution: Universal. Release Date: August 1935. Running Time: 90 minutes.

Diamond Jim Brady	Edward Arnold
Lillian Russell	Binnie Barnes
Jane Matthews/Emma	Jean Arthur
Jerry Richardson	Cesar Romero
Sampson Fox	Eric Blore
Horsley	Hugh O'Connell
Pawnbroker	George Sidney
Harry Hill	William Demarest
A. E. Moore	Robert McWade
John L. Sullivan	Bill Hoolahahn
Bartender	Lew Kelly
Brady (the Child)	Baby Wyman
Brady (the Boy)	George Ernest
Brady's Father	Robert Emmett O'Connor
Brady's Mother	Helen Brown
Brady's Aunt	Mabel Colcord
Secretary	Fred Kelsey
Station Agent	Charles Sellon

Physician	Purnell Pratt
Minister	Tully Marshall
Poker Player	Al Bridge

12. The Gay Deception (1935)

Producer: Jesse L. Lasky. Director: William Wyler. Assistant Director: Al Schaumer. Screenplay: Stephen Avery, Don Hartman. Additional Dialogue: Arthur Richman (Uncredited: Samson Raphaelson). Photography: Joseph Valentine. Art Director: Max Parker. Sound: S. C. Chapman. Musical Direction: Louis de Francesco. Song: "Paris in the Evening" by Preston Sturges, Ted Snyder. Gowns: William Lambert. Studio: Fox. Production: Fox. Distribution: 20th Century-Fox. Release Date: September 1935. Running Time: 75 minutes.

Sandro	Francis Lederer
Mirabel	Frances Dee
Miss Channing	Benita Hume
Lord Clewe	Alan Mowbray
Spellek	Akim Tamiroff
Consul General	Lennox Pawle
Lucille	Adele St. Maur
Mr. Squires	Ferdinand Gottschalk
Mr. Spitzer	Richard Carle
Peg De Forrest	Lenita Lane
Joan Dennison	Barbara Fritchie
Bell Captain	Paul Hurst
Adolph	Robert Greig
Ernest	Luis Alberni
Gettel	Lionel Stander
Jail Attendant	Al Bridge
Bank Teller	Jack Mulhall
Waiter	Torben Meyer

13. Next Time We Love (1935)

Producer: Paul Kohner. Director: Edward H. Griffith. Assistant Director: Ralph Slosser. Based upon the story "Say Goodbye Again" by Ursula Parrott. Screenplay: Melville Baker (Uncredited: Preston Sturges). Photography: Joseph Valentine. Editor: Ted Kent. Art Director: Charles D. Hall. Sound: Gilbert Kurland. Musical Score: Franz Waxman. Gowns: Vera West. Make-up: Jack P. Pierce. Production and Distribution: Universal. Release Date: January 1936. Running Time: 87 minutes.

Cicely Tyler	Margaret Sullavan
Christopher Tyler	James Stewart
Tommy Abbott	Ray Milland
Michael Jennings	Grant Mitchell

Madame Donato	Anna Demetrio
Frank Carteret	Robert McWade
Kit	Ronnie Cosbey
Mrs. Talbor	Florence Roberts
Otto	Christian Rub
Professor Dindet	Charles Fallon
Asst. Stage Manager	Nat Carr
Swiss Porter	Gottlieb Huber
Hanna	Hattie McDaniel
Designer	Leonid Kinskey
Juvenile	John King
Ingenue	Nan Grey

14. Love Before Breakfast (1935)

Producer: Edmund Grainger. Director: Walter Lang. Assistant Director: Phil Karlstein. Based upon the novel *Spinster Dinner* by Faith Baldwin. Screenplay: Herbert Fields (Uncredited: Preston Sturges). Additional Dialogue: Gertrude Purcell. Photography: Ted Tetzlaff. Editor: Maurice Wright. Art Director: Albert D'Agostino. Sound: Charles Carroll. Musical Score: Franz Waxman. Make-up: Jack P. Pierce. Production and Distribution: Universal. Release Date: March 1936. Running Time: 90 minutes.

Kay Colby	Carole Lombard
Scott Miller	Preston Foster
Mrs. Colby	Janet Beecher
Bill Wadsworth	Cesar Romero
Contessa Campanella	Betty Lawford
College Boy	Douglas Blackley
Stuart Farnum	Don Briggs
Fat Man	Bert Roach
Charles	Andre Beranger
Brinkerhoff	Richard Carle
Steward	Forrester Harvey
Southern Girl	Joyce Compton
Friend	John King
Telephone Girl	Nan Grey
Captain	E. E. Clive

15. One Rainy Afternoon (1936)

Producer: Jesse L. Lasky. Director: Rowland V. Lee. Assistant Director: Percy Ikerd. Based upon the screenplay *Monsieur Sans Gene* by Slovenskee Liga Pressburger, Rene Pujol. Screenplay: Stephen Avery. Additional Dialogue: Maurice Hanline. Photography: Peverell Marley, Merritt Gerstad. Editor: Margaret Clancy. Art Director: Richard Day. Sound: Paul Neal. Musical Direction: Alfred Newman. Musical Score: Ralph Irwin.

Song: "Secret Rendezvous" by Preston Sturges, Ralph Irwin. Song: "One Rainy Afternoon" by Harry Tobias, Ralph Irwin. Costumes: Omar Kiam. Studio: United Artists. Production: Pickford-Lasky. Distribution: United Artists. Release Date: May 1936. Running Time: 80 minutes.

Philippe Martin	Francis Lederer
Monique Pelerin	Ida Lupino
Toto	Hugh Herbert
Maillot	Roland Young
Count Alfredo	Erik Rhodes
M. Pelerin	Joseph Cawthorn
Yvonne	Countess Liev de Maigret
Judge	Donald Meek
Cecile	Georgia Caine
Minister of Justice	Richard Carle
Leading Man	Mischa Auer
Hortense	Angie Norton
President of Purity League	Eily Malyon
Prosecutor	Ferdinand Munier
Theatre Manager	Murray Kinnell
M. Pelerin's Secretary	Phyllis Barry
Maillot's Secretary	Lois January

Note: Although there is no evidence that Sturges contributed anything other than the lyrics of "Secret Rendezvous" to this film, he always listed it among his credits.

16. Hotel Haywire (1937)

Producer: Paul Jones (Uncredited: Henry Henigson). Director: George Archainbaud. Assistant Director: Stanley Goldsmith. Screenplay: Preston Sturges (Uncredited: Lillie Hayward). Photography: Henry Sharp. Editor: Arthur Schmidt. Art Director: Hans Dreier. Associate: Robert Odell. Set Decoration: A. E. Freudeman. Musical Direction: Boris Morros. Make-up: Wally Westmore. Production and Distribution: Paramount. Release Date: June 1937. Running Time: 66 minutes.

Dr. Zodiac Z. Zippe	Leo Carrillo
Dr. Parkhouse	Lynne Overman
Phyllis	Mary Carlisle
Bertie Sterns	Benny Baker
Mrs. Parkhouse	Spring Byington
I. Ketts	George Barbier
Judge Newhall	Porter Hall
Genevieve Sterns	Collette Lyons
Frank Ketts	John Patterson
Elmer	Lucien Littlefield
O'Shea	Chester Conklin
Switchboard Operator	Terry Ray
Reception Clerk	Nick Lukats

Mrs. Newhall	Josephine Whittell
Reilly	Guy Usher
O. Levy	Teddy Hart
Fuller Brush Salesman	Franklin Pangborn

17. Easy Living (1937)

Producer: Arthur Hornblow, Jr. Director: Mitchell Leisen. Assistant Director: Edgar Anderson. Based upon a story by Vera Caspary. Screenplay: Preston Sturges. Photography: Ted Tetzlaff. Special Effects Photography: Farciot Edouart. Editor. Doane Harrison. Art Director: Hans Dreier. Associate: Ernst Fegte. Musical Direction: Boris Morros. Costumes: Travis Banton. Make-up: Wally Westmore. Production and Distribution: Paramount. Release Date: July 1937. Running Time: 88 minutes.

Mary Smith	Jean Arthur
J. B. Ball	Edward Arnold
John Ball, Jr.	Ray Milland
Mr. Louis Louis	Luis Alberni
Mrs. Ball	Mary Nash
Van Buren	Franklin Pangborn
Mr. Gurney	Barlowe Borland
Wallace Whistling	William Demarest
E. F. Hulgar	Andrew Tombes
Lillian	Esther Dale
Office Manager	Harlan Briggs
Mr. Hyde	William B. Davidson
Miss Swerf	Nora Cecil
Butler	Robert Greig
1st Partner	Vernon Dent
2nd Partner	Edwin Stanley
3rd Partner	Richard Barbee
Jeweler	Arthur Hoyt
Saleswoman	Gertrude Astor

18. Port of Seven Seas (1937)

Producer: Henry Henigson (Uncredited: Carl Laemmle, Jr.). Director: James Whale. Assistant Director: Joseph McDonough. Based upon the play *Fanny* by Marcel Pagnol. Screenplay: Preston Sturges (Uncredited: Ernest Vajda). Photography: Karl Freund. Montage: Slavko Vorkapich. Editor: Frederick Y. Smith. Art Director: Cedric Gibbons. Associates: Gabriel Scognamillo, Edwin B. Willis. Sound Recording: Douglas Shearer. Musical Score: Franz Waxman. Costumes: Dolly Tree. Make-up: Jack Dawn. Production and Distribution: Metro-Goldwyn-Mayer. Release Date: July 1938. Running Time: 81 minutes.

César	Wallace Berry
Panisse	Frank Morgan
Madelon	Maureen O'Sullivan
Marius	John Beal
Honorine	Jessie Ralph
Claudine	Cora Witherspoon
Brueneau	Etienne Girardot
Captain Escartefigue	E. Allyn Warren
Boy	Robert Spindola
Customer	Doris Lloyd

19. College Swing (1937)

Associate Producer: Lewis Gensler. Director: Raoul Walsh. Assistant Director: Rollie Asher. Dance Director: LeRoy Prinz. Based upon an idea by Ted Lesser. Adaptation: Frederick Hazlitt Brennan. Screenplay: Walter DeLeon, Francis Martin (Uncredited: Preston Sturges). Photography: Victor Milner. Editor: LeRoy Stone. Art Director: Hans Dreier. Associate: Ernst Fegte. Sound: Harold Lewis, Howard Wilson. Musical Direction: Boris Morros. Songs: "I Fall in Love with You Every Day," "What a Rhumba Does to Romance," "The Old School Bell," "You're a Natural" by Frank Loesser, Manning Sherwin. Songs: "Moments Like This," "How'dja Like to Love Me," "What Did Romeo Say to Juliet?" by Frank Loesser, Burton Lane. Song: "College Swing" by Frank Loesser, Hoagy Carmichael. Costumes: Edith Head. Make-up: Wally Westmore. Production and Distribution: Paramount. Release Date: April 1938. Running Time: 86 minutes.

George Jonas	George Burns
Gracie Alden	Gracie Allen
Mable	Martha Raye
Bud Brady	Bob Hope
Hubert Dash	Edward Everett Horton
Ginna Ashburn	Florence George
Ben Volt	Ben Blue
Betty	Betty Grable
Jackie	Jackie Coogan
Martin Bates	John Payne
Dean Sleet	Cecil Cunningham
Radio Announcer	Robert Cummings
Skinnay	Skinnay Ennis
Slate Brothers	Themselves
Prof. Yascha Koloski	Jerry Colonna
Prof. Jasper Chinn	Jerry Bergen
Grandpa Alden	Tully Marshall
Dr. Storm	Edward J. Le Saint

With Bob Mitchell and St. Brandan's Choristers

20. Never Say Die (1938)

Producer: Paul Jones. Director: Elliott Nugent. Assistant Director: Harold Schwartz. Based upon the play by William H. Post. Screenplay: Don Hartman, Frank Butler, Preston Sturges. Photography: Leo Tover. Special Effects Photography: Farciot Edouart. Editor: James Smith. Art Director: Hans Dreier. Associate: Ernst Fegte. Set Decoration: A. E. Freudeman. Sound: William Wisdom, Walter Oberst. Musical Direction: Boris Morros. Song: "The Tra La La and the Oom Pah Pah" by Ralph Rainger, Leo Robin. Costumes: Edith Head. Make-up: Wally Westmore. Production and Distribution: Paramount. Release Date: April 1939. Running Time: 82 minutes.

Mickey Hawkins	Martha Raye
John Kidley	Bob Hope
Jeepers	Ernest Cossart
Jasper Hawkins	Paul Harvey
Henry Munch	Andy Devine
Poppa Ingleborg	Siegfried Rumann
Prince Smirnow	Alan Mowbray
Juno	Gale Sondergaard
Mama Ingleborg	Frances Arms
Kretsky	Ivan Simpson
Dr. Schmidt	Monty Woolley
Kretsky's Bodyguard	Foy Van Dolson
Julius	Donald Haines
Chemist	Gustav von Seyffertitz

21. If I Were King (1938)

Producer: Frank Lloyd. Associate Producer: Lou Smith. Director: Frank Lloyd. Assistant Director: William Tummel. Based upon the play by Justin Huntly McCarthy. Screenplay: Preston Sturges. Photography: Theodore Sparkuhl. Special Effects Photography: Gordon Jennings. Editor: Hugh Bennett. Art Director: Hans Dreier. Associate: John Goodman. Set Decoration: A. E. Freudeman. Sound: Harold C. Lewis, John Cope. Musical Direction: Boris Morros. Musical Score: Richard Hageman. Costumes: Edith Head. Make-up: Wally Westmore. Production and Distribution: Paramount. Release Date: November 1938. Running Time: 100 minutes.

François Villon	Ronald Colman
Louis XI	Basil Rathbone
Katherine de Vaucelles	Frances Dee
Huguette	Ellen Drew
Father Villon	C. V. France
Captain of the Watch	Henry Wilcoxon
The Queen	Heather Thatcher
Rene de Montigny	Stanley Ridges
Noel le Jolys	Bruce Lester
Tristan l'Hermite	Walter Kingsford

Colette	Alma Lloyd
Robin Turgis	Sidney Toler
Jehan le Loup	Colin Tapley
Oliver le Dain	Ralph Forbes
Thibaut d'Aussigny	John Miljan
Guy Tabarie	William Haade
Colin de Cayeuix	Adrian Morris
General Dudon	Montagu Love
General Saliere	Lester Matthews
General Barbezier	William Farnum
Burgundian Herald	Paul Harvey
Watchman	Barry McCollum

22. Remember The Night (1939)

Producer: Mitchell Leisen (Uncredited: Albert Lewin). Director: Mitchell Leisen. Assistant Director: Hal Walker. Screenplay: Preston Sturges. Photography: Ted Tetzlaff. Editor: Doane Harrison. Art Director: Hans Dreier. Associate: Roland Anderson. Set Decoration: A. E. Freudeman. Sound: Earl Hayman, Walter Oberst. Musical Score: Frederick Hollander. Song: "Back Home in Indiana" by James F. Hanley, Ballard MacDonald. Song: "Easy Living" by Ralph Rainger, Leo Robin. Song: "A Perfect Day" by Carrie Jacobs Bond. Costumes: Edith Head. Make-up: Wally Westmore. Production and Distribution: Paramount. Release Date: January 1940. Running Time: 94 minutes.

Lee Leander	Barbara Stanwyck
John Sargent	Fred MacMurray
Mrs. Sargent	Beulah Bondi
Aunt Emma	Elizabeth Patterson
Frances X. O'Leary	Willard Roberston
Willie	Sterling Holloway
Judge (New York)	Charles Waldron
District Attorney	Paul Guilfoyle
Tom	Charley Arnt
Hank	John Wray
Mr. Emory	Thomas W. Ross
Rufus	Snowflake
"Fat" Mike	Tom Kennedy
Lee's Mother	Georgia Caine
Mrs. Emory	Virginia Brissac
Judge (Rummage Sale)	Spencer Charters

23. The Great McGinty (1940)

Associate Producer: Paul Jones. Director: Preston Sturges. Assistant Director: George Templeton. Screenplay: Preston Sturges. Photography: William Mellor. Editor: Hugh Bennett. Art Director: Hans Dreier. Associate: Earl Hedrick. Set Decoration: A. E. Freudeman. Sound: Earl Hayman, Richard Olson. Musical Score: Frederick Hollander. Costumes: Edith Head. Make-up: Wally Westmore. Production and Distribution: Paramount. Release Date: August 1940. Running Time: 81 minutes.

Dan McGinty	Brian Donlevy
Catherine McGinty	Muriel Angelus
The Boss	Akim Tamiroff
George	Allyn Joslyn
The Politician	William Demarest
Thompson	Louis Jean Heydt
Louie	Harry Rosenthal
Mayor Tillinghast	Arthur Hoyt
Bessie	Libby Taylor
Mr. Maxwell	Thurston Hall
The Girl	Steffi Duna
Madame LaJolla	Esther Howard
Chauffeur	Frank Moran
Catherine's Girl	Mary Thomas
Catherine's Boy	Donnie Kerr
The Lookout	Jimmy Conlin
Benny Felgman	Dewey Robinson
Manicurist	Jean Phillips
Cop	Lee Shumway
Pappia	Pat West
Secretary	Byron Foulger
Dr. Jarvis	Richard Carle
McGinty's Valet	Charles Moore
Policeman	Emory Parnell
Cook	Vic Potel
Watcher	Harry Hayden
Opposition Speaker	Robert Warwick

24. Christmas in July (1940)

Associate Producer: Paul Jones. Director: Preston Sturges. Assistant Director: George Templeton. Screenplay: Preston Sturges. Photography: Victor Milner. Editor: Ellsworth Hoagland. Art Director: Hans Dreier. Associate: Earl Hedrick. Sound: Harry Lindgren, Walter Oberst. Musical Direction: Sigmund Krumgold. Make-up: Wally Westmore. Production and Distributuion: Paramount. Release Date: November 1940. Running Time: 70 minutes.

Jimmy MacDonald	Dick Powell
Betty Casey	Ellen Drew
Dr. Maxford	Raymond Walburn
Mr. Baxter	Ernest Truex
Bildocker	William Demarest
Schindel	Alexander Carr

The Announcer	Franklin Pangborn
Tom	Michael Morris
Dick	Rod Cameron
Harry	Harry Rosenthal
Mrs. MacDonald	Georgia Caine
Mr. Schmidt	Torben Meyer
Mr. Hillbeiner	Al Bridge
Mr. Jenkins	Byron Foulger
Mrs. Casey	Lucille Ward
Mr. Zimmerman	Julius Tannen
Mrs. Schwartz	Ferike Boros
Mr. Waterbury	Harry Hayden
Furniture Salesman	Vic Potel
Mild Gentleman	Arthur Hoyt
Large Gentleman	Robert Warwick
Thin, Sour Gentleman	Jimmy Conlin
Large, Rough Gentleman	Dewey Robinson
Cashier	Arthur Stuart Hull
Sophie's Mother	Esther Michelson
Patrolman Murphy	Frank Moran
Sign Painter	Georges Renavent
Porter	Snowflake
Man (Shoeshine Stand)	Preston Sturges
Secretary	Kay Stewart
Man with Telephone	Pat West
Secretary	Jan Buckinham
Porter	Charles Moore

25. The Lady Eve (1940)

Associate Producer: Paul Jones (Uncredited: Albert Lewin). Director: Preston Sturges. Assistant Director: Mel Epstein. Based upon the story "Two Bad Hats" by Monckton Hoffe. Screenplay: Preston Sturges. Photography: Victor Milner. Editor: Stuart Gilmore. Art Director: Hans Dreier. Associate: Ernst Fegte. Sound: Harry Lindgren, Don Johnson. Musical Direction: Sigmund Krumgold. Costumes: Edith Head. Make-up: Wally Westmore. Production and Distribution: Paramount. Release Date: February 1941. Running Time: 97 minutes.

Jean	Barbara Stanwyck
Charles Pike	Henry Fonda
"Colonel" Harrington	Charles Coburn
Mr. Pike	Eugene Pallette
Muggsy (Ambrose Murgatroyd)	William Demarest
Sir Alfred McGlennan-Keith	Eric Blore
Gerald	Melville Cooper
Martha	Martha O'Driscoll
Mrs. Pike	Janet Beecher
Burrows	Robert Greig

Gertrude	Dora Clement
Pike's Chef	Luis Alberni
Bartender	Frank Moran
Guest at Party	Evelyn Beresford
Guest at Party	Arthur Stuart Hull
Piano Tuner	Harry Rosenthal
Lawyer	Julius Tannen
Lawyer at Telephone	Arthur Hoyt
Steward	Jimmy Conlin
Steward	Al Bridge
Steward	Vic Potel
Wife	Esther Michelson
Husband	Robert Dudley
Purser	Torben Meyer
Passenger	Robert Warwick

26. New York Town (1941)

Producer: Anthony Veiller. Director: Charles Vidor (Uncredited: Preston Sturges). Assistant Director: Stanley Goldsmith. Based upon a story by Jo Swerling. Screenplay: Lewis Meltzer (Uncredited: Preston Sturges). Photography: Charles Schoenbaum. Editor: Doane Harrison. Art Director: Hans Dreier. Associate: William Pereira. Sound: Hugo Grenzbach. Musical Direction: Sigmund Krumgold. Musical Score: Leo Shuken. Costumes: Edith Head. Make-up: Wally Westmore. Production and Distribution: Paramount. Release Date: November 1941. Running Time: 94 minutes.

Victor Ballard	Fred MacMurray
Alexandra Curtis	Mary Martin
Paul Bryson, Jr.	Robert Preston
Stefan Janowski	Akim Tamiroff
Sam	Lynne Overman
Vivian	Eric Blore
Shipboard Host	Cecil Kellaway
Gus Nelson	Fuzzy Knight
Bender	Oliver Prickett
Master of Ceremonies	Ken Carpenter
Toots O'Day	Iris Adrian
Brody	Edward J. McNamara
Henry	Sam McDaniel
Peddler	Philip Van Zandt

27. Sullivan's Travels (1941)

Associate Producer: Paul Jones. Director: Preston Sturges. Assistant Director: Holly Morse. Screenplay: Preston Sturges. Photography: John F. Seitz. Special Effects Photography: Farciot Edouart. Editor: Stuart Gilmore. Art

Director: Hans Dreier. Associate: Earl Hedrick. Cartoon Clip: "Playful Pluto" (1934), Walt Disney Productions. Sound: Harry Mills, Walter Oberst. Musical Direction: Sigmund Krumgold. Musical Score: Leo Shuken, Charles Bradshaw. Costumes: Edith Head. Make-up: Wally Westmore. Production and Distribution: Paramount. Release Date: January 1942. Running Time: 90 minutes.

John L. Sullivan	Joel McCrea
The Girl	Veronica Lake
Mr. LeBrand	Robert Warwick
Mr. Jones	William Demarest
Mr. Casalsis	Franklin Pangborn
Mr. Hadrian	Porter Hall
Mr. Valdelle	Bryon Foulger
Secretary	Margaret Hayes
Butler	Robert Greig
Valet	Eric Blore
Doctor	Torben Meyer
The Mister	Al Bridge
Miz Zeffie	Esther Howard
Ursula	Almira Sessions
Chauffeur	Frank Moran
Bum	Georges Renavent
Cameraman	Vic Potel
Radioman	Richard Webb
Chef	Charles Moore
Trustee	Jimmy Conlin
Labor	Jimmie Dundee
Capital	Chick Collins
Mr. Carson	Harry Hayden
Counterman (Owl Wagon)	Roscoe Ates
Preacher	Arthur Hoyt
One-Legged Man	Robert Dudley
Sheriff	Dewey Robinson
Colored Preacher	Jess Lee Brooks
Public Defender	Julius Tannen
Man at Railroad Shack	Emory Parnell
Cop	Edgar Dearing
Woman (Poor Street)	Esther Michelson
Old Bum	Chester Conklin
Railroad Clerk	Howard Mitchell
The Trombenick	Harry Rosenthal
Mrs. Sullivan	Jan Buckingham
Counterman (Roadside)	Pat West
Desk Sergeant	J. Farrell MacDonald
Yard Man	Perc Launders
Dear Joseph	Paul Jones
Director	Preston Sturges

28. Safeguarding Military Information (1941)

Produced by the Research Council of the Academy of Motion Picture Arts and Sciences; Darryl F. Zanuck, Chairman. Screenplay: Preston Sturges. Studio: Paramount. Release Date: August 1942. Running Time: 9 minutes.

29. The Palm Beach Story (1942)

Associate Producer: Paul Jones. Director: Preston Sturges. Assistant Director: Hal Walker. Screenplay: Preston Sturges. Photography: Victor Milner. Editor: Stuart Gilmore. Art Director: Hans Dreier. Associate: Ernst Fegte. Sound: Harry Lindgren, Walter Oberst. Musical Score: Victor Young. Gowns: Irene. Make-up: Wally Westmore. Production and Distribution: Paramount. Release Date: December 1942. Running Time: 88 minutes.

Gerry Jeffers	Claudette Colbert
Tom Jeffers	Joel McCrea
Princess	Mary Astor
John D. Hackensacker III	Rudy Vallée
Toto	Sig Arno
Mr. Hinch	Robert Warwick
Mr. Osmond	Arthur Stuart Hull
Dr. Kluck	Torben Meyer
Mr. Asweld	Jimmy Conlin
Mr. McKeewie	Vic Potel
Wienie King	Robert Dudley
Manager	Franklin Pangborn
Pullman Conductor	Arthur Hoyt
Conductor	Al Bridge
Colored Bartender	Snowflake
Colored Porter	Charles Moore
Brakeman	Frank Moran
Orchestra Leader	Harry Rosenthal
Wife of Wienie King	Esther Howard
Ale & Quail Club	William Demarest, Jack Norton, Robert Greig, Roscoe Ates, Dewey Robinson, Chester Conklin, Sheldon Jett
Prospect	Harry Hayden
Nearsighted Woman	Esther Michelson
Officer in Penn Station	Edward J. McNamara
Waiter in Diner	Mantan Moreland
Proprietor of Store	Julius Tannen
Jewelry Salesman	Byron Foulger
Taxi Driver	Frank Faylen
O'Donnell	J. Farrell MacDonald

30. The Great Moment (1942)

Producer and Director: Preston Sturges. Assistant Director: Edmund Bernoudy. Based upon the book *Triumph over Pain* by René Fülöp-Miller. Screenplay: Preston Sturges. Photography: Victor Milner. Editor: Stuart Gilmore. Art Director: Hans Dreier. Associate: Ernst Fegte. Set Decoration: Stephen Seymour. Sound: Harry Lindgren, Walter Oberst. Musical Score: Victor Young. Make-up: Wally Westmore. Production and Distribution: Paramount. Release Date: November 1944. Running Time: 83 minutes.

W. T. G. Morton	Joel McCrea
Elizabeth Morton	Betty Field
Professor Warren	Harry Carey
Eben Frost	William Demarest
Dr. Horace Wells	Louis Jean Heydt
Dr. Jackson	Julius Tannen
Vice-President of Medical Society	Edwin Maxwell
President Pierce	Porter Hall
Dr. Heywood	Franklin Pangborn
Homer Quinby	Grady Sutton
Betty Morton	Donivee Lee
Judge Shipman	Harry Hayden
Dr. Dahlmeyer	Torben Meyer
Dental Patient	Vic Potel
Senator Borland	Thurston Hall
Priest	J. Farrell MacDonald
Mr. Abbot	Robert Frandsen
Morton's Butler	Robert Greig
Mr. Chamberlain	Harry Rosenthal
Porter	Frank Moran
Cashier	Robert Dudley
Colonel Lawson	Dewey Robinson
Mr. Stone	Al Bridge
Mrs. Whitman	Georgia Caine
Sign Painter	Roscoe Ates
Mr. Gruber	Emory Parnell
Mr. Whitman	Arthur Stuart Hull
Frightened Patient	Chester Conklin
Streetwalker	Esther Howard
Receptionist	Byron Foulger
Patient	Esther Michelson
Mr. Burnett	Jimmy Conlin
Presidential Secretary	Arthur Hoyt
Whackpot	Sig Arno
Little Boy	Donnie Kerr
Morton's Little Boy	Billy Sheffield
Morton's Little Girl	Janet Chapman
Morton's Little Girl (Older)	Tricia Moore

31. I Married a Witch (1942)

Producer: Preston Sturges. Director: René Clair. Assistant Director: Art Black. Based upon the novel *The Passionate Witch* by Thorne Smith, completed by Norman Matson. Screenplay: Robert Pirosh, Marc Connelly (Uncredited: Dalton Trumbo). Photography: Ted Tetzlaff. Special Effects Photography: Gordon Jennings. Editor: Eda Warren. Art Director: Hans Dreier. Associate: Ernst Fegte. Set Decoration: George Sawley. Sound: Harry Mills, Richard Olson. Musical Score: Roy Webb. Costumes: Edith Head. Make-up: Wally Westmore. Studio: Paramount. Production: Paramount. Distribution: United Artists. Release Date: November 1942. Running Time: 76 minutes.

Wallace Wooley	Fredric March
Jennifer	Veronica Lake
Dr. Dudley White	Robert Benchley
Estelle Masterson	Susan Hayward
Daniel	Cecil Kellaway
Margaret	Elizabeth Patterson
J. B. Masterson	Robert Warwick
Tabitha	Eily Malyon
Town Crier	Robert Greig
Vocalist	Helen St. Rayner
Justice of the Peace	Aldrich Bowker
Wife	Emma Dunn
Martha	Viola Moore
Nancy	Mary Field
Harriet	Nora Cecil
Allen	Emory Parnell
Rufus	Charles Moore
Prison Guard	Al Bridge
Guest	Arthur Stuart Hull
Bartender	Chester Conklin
Young Man	Reed Hadley

Note: I Married a Witch headlined a package of Paramount-produced features sold to United Artists in September of 1942. According to the trade press, Paramount didn't need all the completed film it had on hand. United Artists, conversely, needed more product than the independent producers with U.A. distribution contracts could supply. The package included *Witch, The Crystal Ball* (with Ray Milland and Paulette Goddard), *Young and Willing* (with William Holden, Susan Hayward, and Eddie Bracken), two Harry Sherman productions *(American Empire* and *Silver Queen)*, and six Hopalong Cassidys. The three non-Sherman titles were released under the banner of "The Cinema Guild," apparently a euphemism for United Artists Productions, under which the films were copyrighted.

32. Star Spangled Rhythm (1942)

Associate Producer: Joe Sistrom. Director: George Marshall. Assistant Director: Art Black. Screenplay: Harry Tugend (Uncredited: Arthur Phillips). Sketches: George Kaufman, Arthur Ross and Fred Saidy, Melvin Frank and Norman Panama. Photography: Leo Tover, Theodore Sparkuhl. Editor: Paul Weatherwax. Art Director: Hans Dreier. Associate: Ernst Fegte. Musical Direction: Robert Emmet Dolan. Songs: "He Loved Me Till the All-Clear Came," "Old Glory," "A Sweater, a Sarong, and a Peek-a-Boo Bang," "That Old Black Magic," "Let's Hit the Road to Dreamland," "Sharp as a Tack," "I'm Doing It for Defense," "On the Swing Shift" by Johnny Mercer, Harold Arlen. Make-up: Wally Westmore. Production and Distribution: Paramount. Release Date: December 1942. Running Time: 99 minutes.

Pop Webster	Victor Moore
Polly Judson	Betty Hutton
Jimmy Webster	Eddie Bracken
B. G. DeSoto	Walter Abel
Sarah	Anne Revere
Mimi	Cass Daley
Hi-Pockets	Gil Lamb
Mr. Freemont	Edward Fielding
Mac	Edgar Dearing
Duffy	William Haade
Sailor	Maynard Holmes
Sailor	James Millican
Tommy	Eddie Johnson

with Bing Crosby, Bob Hope, Fred MacMurray, Franchot Tone, Ray Milland, Dorothy Lamour, Paulette Goddard, Vera Zorina, Mary Martin, Dick Powell, Veronica Lake, Alan Ladd, Eddie "Rochester" Anderson, William Bendix, Susan Hayward, Jerry Colonna, Macdonald Carey, Marjorie Reynolds, Betty Rhodes, Dona Drake, Lynne Overman, Gary Crosby, Johnnie Johnston, Ernest Truex, Arthur Treacher, Sterling Holloway, Cecil B. DeMille, Preston Sturges, Ralph Murphy, Walter Catlett, Katherine Dunham, Walter Dare Wahl and Company, the Golden Gate Quartette, Slim and Sam.

33. The Miracle of Morgan's Creek (1942)

Producer and Director: Preston Sturges. Assistant Director: Edmund Bernoudy. Screenplay: Preston Sturges. Photography: John F. Seitz. Editor: Stuart Gilmore. Art Director: Hans Dreier. Associate: Ernst Fegte. Set Decoration: Stephen Seymour. Sound: Hugo Grenzbach, Walter Oberst. Musical Score: Leo Shuken, Charles Bradshaw. Song: "The Bell in the Bay" by Preston Sturges. Costumes: Edith Head. Make-up: Wally Westmore. Production and Distribution: Paramount. Release Date: January 1944. Running Time: 99 minutes.

Norval Jones	Eddie Bracken
Trudy Kockenlocker	Betty Hutton

Emmy Kockenlocker	Diana Lynn
Constable Kockenlocker	William Demarest
Justice of the Peace	Porter Hall
Mr. Tuerck	Emory Parnell
Mr. Johnson	Al Bridge
Mr. Rafferty	Julius Tannen
Newspaper Editor	Vic Potel
Governor McGinty	Brian Donlevy
The Boss	Akim Tamiroff
Wife of Justice of the Peace	Almira Sessions
Sally	Esther Howard
Sheriff	J. Farrell MacDonald
First MP	Frank Moran
Cecilia	Connie Tompkins
Mrs. Johnson	Georgia Caine
Doctor	Torben Meyer
U.S. Marshal	George Melford
The Mayor	Jimmy Conlin
Mr. Schwartz	Harry Rosenthal
Pete	Chester Conklin
McGinty's Secretary	Byron Foulger
McGinty's Secretary	Arthur Hoyt
Man	Robert Dudley
Man Opening Champagne	Jack Norton
Hitler	Bobby Watson
Mussolini	Joe Devlin
Nurse	Jan Buckingham
Head Nurse	Nora Cecil
Nurse	Judith Lowry
Soldier	Freddie Steele

34. Hail the Conquering Hero (1943)

Producer and Director: Preston Sturges. Assistant Director: Harvey Foster. Screenplay: Preston Sturges. Photography: John F. Seitz. Editor: Stuart Gilmore. Art Director: Hans Dreier. Associate: Haldane Douglas. Set Decoration: Stephen Seymour. Sound: Wallace Nogle. Musical Direction: Sigmund Krumgold. Musical Score: Werner Heymann. Song: "Home to the Arms of Mother" by Preston Sturges. Make-up: Wally Westmore. Production and Distribution: Paramount. Release Date: August 1944. Running Time: 101 minutes.

Woodrow Truesmith	Eddie Bracken
Libby	Ella Raines
Sergeant	William Demarest
Forrest Nobel	Bill Edwards
Mayor Noble	Raymond Walburn
Corporal	Jimmy Dundee
Mrs. Truesmith	Georgia Caine

Political Boss	Al Bridge
Jonesy	James Damore
Bugsy	Freddie Steele
Bill	Stephen Gregory
Juke	Len Hendry
Mrs. Noble	Esther Howard
Libby's Aunt	Elizabeth Patterson
Judge Dennis	Jimmy Conlin
Reverend Upperman	Arthur Hoyt
Dr. Bissell	Harry Hayden
Chairman of Committee	Franklin Pangborn
Progressive Band Leader	Vic Potel
Mr. Schultz	Torben Meyer
Regular Band Leader	Jack Norton
Western Union Man	Chester Conklin
Officer	Robert Warwick
Conductor	Dewey Robinson
Porter	Charles Moore

With Julie Gibson and the Guardsmen

35. The Sin of Harold Diddlebock (1946)

Producer and Director: Preston Sturges. Assistant Director: Barton Adams. Screenplay: Preston Sturges. Technical Director: Curtis Courant. Photography: Robert Pittack. Special Effects Photography: John P. Fulton. Editor: Thomas Neff. Art Director: Robert Usher. Set Decoration: Victor A. Gangelin. Film Clip: *The Freshman* (1925), Pathé. Sound: Fred Lau. Musical Score: Werner Heymann. Love Theme by Harry Rosenthal. Make-up: Ted Larsen (Uncredited: Wally Westmore). Studio: Samuel Goldwyn. Production: California Pictures. Distribution: United Artists. Release Date: February 1947. Running Time: 91 minutes.

Harold Diddlebock	Harold Lloyd
Miss Otis	Frances Ramsden
Wormy	Jimmy Conlin
E. J. Waggleberry	Raymond Walburn
Bartender	Edgar Kennedy
Manicurist	Arline Judge
Formfit Franklin	Franklin Pangborn
Banker	Rudy Vallée
Max	Lionel Stander
Barber	Torben Meyer
Harold's Sister	Margaret Hamilton
Circus Manager	Al Bridge
Mike	Frank Moran
Coachman	Robert Greig
Professor Potelle	Vic Potel
Bearded Lady	Georgia Caine
Banker	Robert Dudley

James Smoke	Jack Norton
Banker Blackston	Arthur Hoyt
Snake Charmer	Gladys Forrest
Doorman	Max Wagner
With Jackie, the lion	

Note: Howard Hughes had *The Sin of Harold Diddlebock* pulled from release before it could play either New York or Los Angeles. A re-edited version, titled *Mad Wednesday*, was finally released through RKO in January of 1950. The additional cutting was done by Sturges' regular Stuart Gilmore under Hughes' supervision. Added to the shortened climax were two shots of Robert Greig's horse singing to himself. These were animated by Jerry Fairbanks Inc. Hughes cut Rudy Vallée from the film, although Vallée can be glimpsed in the bidding scene toward the end. The running time of *Mad Wednesday* is 72 minutes.

36. Vendetta (1946)

Producer: Howard Hughes (Uncredited: Preston Sturges). Director: Mel Ferrer (Uncredited: Max Ophuls, Preston Sturges, Stuart Heisler, Howard Hughes). Assistant Director: Edward Mull. Based upon the novel *Colomba* by Prosper Mérimée. Adaptation: Peter O'Crotty. Screenplay: W. R. Bernett (Uncredited: Preston Sturges). Photography: Franz Planer, Al Gilks. Editor: Stuart Gilmore. Art Director: Robert Usher. Sound: William Fox, Vinton Vernon. Musical Direction: C. Bakaleinikoff. Musical Score: Roy Webb. Including selections from *Tosca* and *La Bohème* by Puccini, and "Torna a Surriento" by Di Curtis. Aria from *Tosca* sung by Richard Tucker. Make-up: Norbert Miles. Studio: Samuel Goldwyn. Production: California Pictures/Hughes Productions. Distribution: RKO-Radio. Release Date: December 1950. Running Time: 84 minutes.

Colomba Della Rabbia	Faith Domergue
Orso Della Rabbia	George Dolenz
Lydia Nevil	Hillary Brooke
Sir Thomas Nevil	Nigel Bruce
Padrino	Donald Buka
Mayor Barracini	Joseph Calleia
Brando	Hugo Haas
Prefect	Robert Warwick

37. I'll Be Yours (1946)

Producer: Felix Jackson. Associate Producer: Howard Christie. Director: William A. Seiter. Assistant Director: William Holland. Based upon the play *The Good Fairy* by Ferenc Molnár. Adaptation: Preston Sturges. Screenplay: Felix Jackson. Photography: Hal Mohr. Special Effects Photography: David Horsley. Editor: Otto Ludwig. Art Director: John B.

Goodman. Set Decoration: Russel Gausman. Sound: Lawrence Alcholtz, Charles Felstead. Musical Direction: Walter Schumann. Musical Score: Frank Skinner. Orchestrations: David Tamkin. Song: "Granada" by Augustin Lara. Song: "It's Dream Time" by Walter Schumann, Jack Brooks. Song: "Love's Own Sweet Song" by Emmerich Kalmán. Costumes: Travis Banton. Make-up: Jack P. Pierce. Production: Universal. Distribution: Universal-International. Release Date: January 1947. Running Time: 93 minutes.

Louise Ginglebusher	Deanna Durbin
George Prescott	Tom Drake
Wechsberg	William Bendix
J. Conrad Nelson	Adolphe Menjou
Mr. Buckingham	Walter Catlett
Barber	Franklin Pangborn
Captain	William Trenk
Blonde	Joan Fulton
Usherette	Patricia Alphin
Stage Door Johnnie	William Brooks

38. Unfaithfully Yours (1948)

Producer and Director: Preston Sturges. Assistant Director: Gaston Glass. Screenplay: Preston Sturges. Photography: Victor Milner. Special Effects Photography: Fred Sersen. Editor: Robert Fritch. Art Director: Lyle Wheeler. Associate: Joseph C. Wright. Set Decoration: Thomas Little, Paul S. Fox. Sound: Arthur L. Kirbach, Roger Heman. Musical Direction: Alfred Newman. Music: Gioacchino Rossini, Richard Wagner, Peter Ilyitch Tchaikovsky. Costumes: Bonnie Cashin. Make-up: Ben Nye. Production and Distribution: 20th Century-Fox. Release Date: November 1948. Running Time: 105 minutes.

Sir Alfred de Carter	Rex Harrison
Daphne de Carter	Linda Darnell
Barbara	Barbara Lawrence
August	Rudy Vallée
Anthony	Kurt Kreuger
Hugo	Lionel Stander
Sweeney	Edgar Kennedy
House Detective	Al Bridge
Tailor	Julius Tannen
Dr. Schultz	Torben Meyer
Jules	Robert Greig
Dowager	Georgia Caine
Telephone Operator	Isabel Jewell
Telephone Operator	Marion Marshall
Doorman	J. Farrell MacDonald
Fire Chief	Frank Moran

39. The Beautiful Blonde from Bashful Bend (1948)

Producer and Director: Preston Sturges. Assistant Director: William Eckhardt. Based upon a story by Earl Felton. Screenplay: Preston Sturges. Photography: Harry Jackson (Technicolor). Technicolor Consultants: Natalie Kalmus, Leonard Doss. Special Effects Photography: Fred Sersen. Editor: Robert Fritch. Art Director: Lyle Wheeler. Associate: George W. Davis. Set Decoration: Thomas Little, Stuart Reiss. Sound: Eugene Grossman, Harry M. Leonard. Musical Direction: Alfred Newman. Musical Score: Cyril Mockridge. Song: "The Beautiful Blonde from Bashful Bend" by Don George, Lionel Newman. Song: "Every Time I Meet You" by Josef Myrow, Mack Gordon. Song: "In the Gloaming" by Meta Orred, Annie F. Harrison. Costumes: Rene Hubert. Make-up: Ben Nye. Production and Distribution: 20th Century-Fox. Release Date: May 1949. Running Time: 79 minutes.

Freddie	Betty Grable
Blackie	Cesar Romero
Charles Hingleman	Rudy Vallée
Conchita	Olga San Juan
Basserman Boy	Sterling Holloway
Doctor	Hugh Herbert
Mr. Jorgensen	El Brendel
Judge O'Toole	Porter Hall
Roulette	Pati Behrs
Mrs. O'Toole	Margaret Hamilton
Basserman Boy	Danny Jackson
Mr. Hingleman	Emory Parnell
Sheriff	Al Bridge
Joe	Chris-Pin Martin
Sheriff Sweetzer	J. Farrell MacDonald
Mr. Basserman	Richard Hale
Mrs. Hingleman	Georgia Caine
Mrs. Smidlap	Esther Howard
Conductor	Harry Hayden
Messenger Boy	Chester Conklin
Freddie (Age 6)	Mary Monica MacDonald
Dr. Schultz	Torben Meyer
Bartender	Dewey Robinson
Dr. Smidlap	Richard Kean
Grandpa	Russell Simpson
French Floozy	Marie Windsor

40. Strictly Dishonorable (1951)

Producers and Directors: Melvin Frank, Norman Panama. Assistant Director: Joel Freeman. Director of Opera Sequences: Vladimir Rosing. Based upon the play by Preston Sturges. Screenplay: Melvin Frank, Norman Panama. Photography: Ray June. Editor: Irvine Warburton. Art Director:

Cedric Gibbons. Associate: Hans Peters. Set Decoration: Edwin B. Willia, Hugh Hunt. Sound: Douglas Shearer. Musical Direction: Lennie Hayton. Original Operatic Scene: Mario Castelnuovo-Tedesco. Costumes: Helen Rose. Make-up: William Tuttle. Production and Distribution: Metro-Goldwyn-Mayer. Release Date: July 1951. Running Time: 86 minutes.

Agustino Caraffa	Ezio Pinza
Isabelle	Janet Leigh
Bill Dempsey	Millard Mitchell
Marie Donnelly	Gale Robbins
Countess Lili Szadvany	Maria Palmer
Mama Caraffa	Esther Minciotti
Uncle Nito	Silvio Minciotti
Harry Greene	Arthur Franz
Tomaso	Sandro Giglio
Harry Donnelly	Jugh Sanders
Luigi	Mario Siletti

41. Letters from My Windmill (1954)

Producer: Jean Martinelli. Director: Marcel Pagnol. Based upon the stories "The Three Low Masses," "The Elixir of Father Gaucher," and "The Secret of Master Cornille" by Alphonse Daudet. Screenplay: Marcel Pagnol. English Subtitles: Preston Sturges. Photography: Willy Faktorovitch. Editor: Monique Lacombe. Art Director: Robert Giordani. Associate: Jean Mandaroux. Sound: Marcel Royné. Musical Score: Henri Tomasi. Make-up: Paul Ralph. Studio: Marseille Studio. Production: Mediterranean Film Company. Distribution: Tohan Pictures. Release Date: December 1955. Running Time: 120 minutes.

"The Three Low Masses"

Dom Balaguere	Henri Vilbert
Garrigou / The Devil	Daxely
The Old Woman	Yvonne Gamy
The Marquis	Keller
The Chef	René Sarvil

"The Elixir of Father Gaucher"

Father Gaucher	Rellys
The Abbot	Robert Vattier
Father Sylvestre	Christian Lude
M. Charnigue, apothecary	Fernand Sardou

"The Secret of Master Cornille"

Master Cornille	Edouard Delmont
Alphonse Daudet	Roger Crouset
Vivette	Pierrette Bruno

42. Les Carnets du Major Thompson; The French, They Are a Funny Race (1955)

Producers: Alain Poire, Paul Wagner. Director: Preston Sturges. Assistant Directors: Pierre Kast, Francis Caillaud. Based upon the book *The Notebooks of Major Thompson* by Pierre Daninos. Screenplay: Preston Sturges. Photography: Maurice Barry, Christian Matras, Jean Lallier. Editor: Raymond Lanny. Art Director: Serge Pimenoff. Associates: Robert André, Robert Guisgand, Claude Moesching. Sound: Jene Rieul. Musical Score: Georges Van Parys. Costumes: Suzanne Revillard (Pinoteau). Make-up: Jean-Jacques Chanteau, Alexandre S. Ranesky, Maguy Vernadet. Studio: Paris-Studios-Cinéma Billancourt. Production: S. N. E. Gaumont-Paul Wagner. Distribution: Gaumont (France); Continental Distributing (U.S.A.). Release Date: December 1955 (France); May 1957 (U.S.A.). Running Time: 105 minutes (France); 82 minutes (U.S.A.).

Major Thompson	Jack Buchanan
Martine Thompson	Martine Carol
M. Taupin	Noël-Noël
Miss Ffyth	Totti Truman Taylor
Ursula	Catherine Boyl
M. Fusillard	André Luguet
Mlle. Sylvette	Genevieve Brunet

43. The Birds and the Bees (1955)

Producer: Paul Jones. Director: Norman Taurog. Assistant Director: John Coonan. Dance Director: Nick Castle. Based upon the story "Two Bad Hats" by Monckton Hoffe. Screenplay: Sidney Sheldon, Preston Sturges. Photography: Daniel L. Fapp (Technicolor, VistaVision). Technicolor Consultant: Richard Mueller. Editor: Archie Marshek. Art Director: Hal Pereira. Associate: Roland Anderson. Sound: Gene Merritt, Gene Garvin. Musical Score: Walter Scharf. Songs: "Each Time I Dream," "The Birds and the Bees," "La Parisienne" by Mack David, Harry Warren. Song: "Little Miss Tippy-Toes" by Harold Adamson. Costumes: Edith Head. Make-up: Wally Westmore. Studio: Paramount. Production: Gomalco. Distribution: Paramount. Release Date: May 1956. Running Time: 94 minutes.

George Hamilton	George Gobel
Jean Harris	Mitzi Gaynor
Colonel Harris	David Niven
Gerald	Reginald Gardiner
Mr. Hamilton	Fred Clark
Martin Kennedy	Harry Bellaver
Duc Jacques de Montaigne	Hans Conried
Mrs. Hamilton	Margery Maude
Purser	Clinton Sundberg
Assistant Butler	Milton Frome

Butler	Rex Evans
Waiter	King Donovan
Mrs. Burnside	Mary Treen
Jenkins	Charles Lane
Ship Bartender	Steven Geray

44. Paris Holiday (1957)

Producer: Bob Hope. Associate Producer: Cecil Foster Kemp. Director: Gerd Oswald. Assistant Director: Paul Feyder. Based upon a story by Bob Hope. Screenplay: Edmund Beloin, Dean Riesner. Photography: Roger Hubert (Technicolor, Technirama). Editor: Ellsworth Hoagland. Sound: Frances Scheid, Robert Biart. Musical Score: Joseph J. Lilley. Song: "Every Day's a Holiday in Paris" by Jimmy Van Heusen, Sammy Cahn. Costumes: Pierre Balmain. Production: Tolda Productions. Distribution: United Artists. Release Date: May 1958. Running Time: 100 minutes.

Robert Leslie Hunter	Bob Hope
Fernydel	Fernandel
Zara	Anita Ekberg
Ann McCall	Martha Hyer
American Ambassador	Andre Morell
Serge Vitry	Preston Sturges
Judge	Jean Murat
Doctor Bernais	Maurice Teynac
Shipboard Lovely	Irene Tunc
Golfer Patient	Roger Treville
Inspector Dupont	Yves Brainville

45. Rock-a-Bye Baby (1958)

Producer: Jerry Lewis. Associate Producer: Ernest D. Glucksman. Director: Frank Tashlin. Assistant Director: C. C. Coleman, Jr. Dance Director: Nick Castle. Based upon the screenplay The Miracle of Morgan's Creek by Preston Sturges. Screenplay: Frank Tashlin. Photography: Haskell Boggs (Technicolor, VistaVision). Technicolor Consultant: Richard Mueller. Special Effects Photography: John P. Fulton, Farciot Edouart. Editor: Alma Marcrorie. Art Director: Hal Pereira. Associate: Tambi Larsen. Set Decoration: Sam Comer, Robert Benton. Sound: Gene Merritt, Charles Grenzbach. Musical Score: Walter Scharf. Songs: "Dormi, Dormi, Dormi," "Why Can't He Care for Me?" "The Land of La-La-La," "The White Virgin of the Nile," "Love Is a Lonely Thing," "Rock-a-Bye Baby" by Harry Warren, Sammy Cahn. Costumes: Edith Head. Make-up: Wally Westmore. Studio: Paramount. Production: York Productions. Distribution: Paramount. Release Date: July 1958. Running Time: 102 minutes.

Clayton Poole	Jerry Lewis
Carla Naples	Marilyn Maxwell
Henry Herman	Reginald Gardiner
Sandy Naples	Connie Stevens
Papa Naples	Baccaloni
Mr. Wright	Hans Conried
Dr. Simkins	James Gleason
Bessie Polk	Ida Moore
Mrs. Van Cleve	Isobel Elsom
Judge Jenkins	Alex Geary
Clayton (Age 12)	Gary Lewis
Carla (Age 10)	Judy Franklin
M.C.	George Sanders
Choreographer	Nick Castle

INDEX

Coward, Noel, 84, 88
Crosby, Bing, 4, 151, 226
Crowther, Bosley, 143, 149, 163, 184,
    189, 192, 197, 220, 229, 232, 242,
    257, 276
Cukor, George, 74, 270
Cup of Coffee, A (film), *see Christmas
    in July*
Cup of Coffee, A (play), 67–68, 76

Dailey, Dan, 224
Daninos, Pierre, 271
Darnell, Linda, 229
Daves, Delmer, 166
Davis, Owen, 84
Deane, Albert, 147
Dear Departed, The, 252, 254
DeBell, Joseph A., 200
Dee, Frances, 153
Demarest, Lucille, 144
Demarest, William, 129–130, 132,
    134, 140, 142, 144, 145, 148, 153,
    155, 161–162, 170–172, 173,
    179, 182, 183, 185, 186, 203,
    204–205
DeMille, Cecil B., 4, 111, 113, 129,
    130, 131, 150, 151, 152, 153, 156,
    167, 194–195, 206
Dempsey, Mary, *see* Desti, Mary
Denny, Reginald, 201
d'Este, Mary, *see* Desti, Mary
Desti, Mary, 8–13, 14–18, 19–21, 22,
    24–25, 27–28, 30–31, 32, 62,
    63–64, 67, 91
DeSylva, B. G. ("Buddy"), 150–151,
    153, 160–161, 166, 170, 172–174,
    177–179, 184, 185–192, 198, 200,
    204–205, 206, 221, 222
Devine, Andy, 179
Diamond Jim (film), 5, 101–103, 105,
    130, 140
Dietrich, Marlene, 4, 166
Disney, Walt, 142
Dolenz, George, 216
Dolly Sisters, The, 224
Domergue, Faith, 215–216, 217
Donat, Robert, 267
Donen, Stanley, 283
Donlevy, Brian, 128, 130–131, 132,
    134, 184
Douglas, Melvyn, 57
Dove, Billie, 70
Down Argentine Way, 225
*Down Went McGinty, see Great
    McGinty, The*

Drew, Ellen, 140, 141, 143
Dumbrille, Douglas, 70
Duncan, Isadora, 11, 12–13, 15, 16,
    17, 24, 27, 30, 32, 63
Duncan, Temple, 11, 64
Dundee, Jimmy, 171

Easy Living (1937), 5, 6, 109–111,
    113, 123, 130, 140, 146, 178
Eaton, Mary, 70
École des Roches, 16, 19
Edwards, Gus, 70
E. F. Hutton & Company, 61
Eggerth, Marta, 105, 106, 149
Erskine, Chester, 278
Escape, 231
Events Leading Up to My Death, The,
    x, 285

Fabray, Nanette, 252, 253, 254
Fairbanks, Douglas, 74
Fairbanks, Douglas, Jr., 227
Faithful Heart, The, 145
Famous Artists, 278, 286
Fanny (American film version), *see
    Port of Seven Seas*
Fanny (film, 1932), 97
Farmer, Frances, 153
Farnum, William, 114
Farrell, Glenda, 57
Fast and Loose, 74–75
Faye, Alice, 225
F. B. Keech & Company, 33
Felton, Earl, 164
Ferguson, John, 46
Field, Betty, 153, 170
Fields, W. C., 4, 262, 266
Firestone, Eddie, 255
Fish, Hamilton, 25
Flame of New Orleans, 166
Fleet's In, The, 178
Fleischer, Max, 4
Flynn, Errol, 115
Fonda, Henry, 145–146, 147, 148
Ford, John, 93, 129, 142, 196
*Forty Million Frenchmen, see French,
    They Are a Funny Race, The*
Foulger, Byron, 140
Fox Film Corp., 81–82, 85, 86, 87, 92,
    93, 150, 152
Fox, Sidney, 73
Fox, William, 85, 223
Frankenstein (film), 77
Frankie and Johnnie (play), 47, 49, 57

Marshall, Herbert, 99
Martin, Hugh, 252–253
Martin, Mary, 151
Marton, George, 281
Marx Brothers, The, 4
Mason, James, 216, 228, 272
Matrix, 93, 223, 224, 227, 244, 259, 263, 280, 281
Matthews, James Brander, 34, 37, 39, 40, 43, 49, 65, 148, 152
May, Ada, 70
"Maybe You'll Be My Baby," 36
Mayer, Louis B., 108
Meiklejohn, Bill, 204
Mellon, Sandy, *see* Sturges, Anne ("Sandy")
Mellor, William, 131, 133–134, 140
Mencken, H. L., 25–26
Menken, Grace, 70
Menken, Helen, 70
Mérimée, Prosper, 201, 215
Merkel, Una, 220
Merlino, Maxine, 235, 236–237, 249, 251
Metamorphosis of Philip Musica, The, 282
Metro-Goldwyn-Mayer, 3, 5, 85, 93, 107, 108, 111, 116, 151, 168, 222, 242, 243, 244–246
Meyer, Fred S., 105
Meyer, Torben, 140, 153
Michelson, Esther, 140, 146, 153
Milestone, Lewis, 70
Miller, Ann, 160
Miller, Gilbert, 285
Millionairess, The (Sturges screenplay), 266–267, 270, 278
Milner, Victor, 140, 146, 155
Minute, A, 252
Miracle of Morgan's Creek, The, 177–184, 186, 189–190, 191, 192, 198, 199, 204, 205, 224, 231, 240, 266, 285, 286
Miranda, Carmen, 220
Mr. Big in Littleville, see Nothing Doing
Mr. Smith Goes to Washington, 127
Mitchell, Grant, 129
Mocambo, 118
Moffitt, Jack, 270
Molière, Jean Baptiste Poquelin, 12, 39, 71, 244
Molnár, Ferenc, 98
Monet, Claude, 12
Monkey's Paw, The, 252, 254

Monogram Pictures Corporation, 207
Mon Oncle, 282
Moore, Charles, 140
Moore, Colleen, 86–88
Moore, Tom, 238
Moran, Frank, 129, 140, 146, 153, 154, 204, 254, 256, 285
Morehouse, Ralph, 42
Morell, Parker, 101
Morgan, Frank, 113
Morris, Chester, 137, 138
Mossies, Mae, 12
Mother Wore Tights, 224
Motion Picture Producers and Distributors of America (MPPDA), 98, 180, 181, 184
Mounet-Sully, Jean, 12
Mudge, Estelle, *see* Sturges, Estelle
Mullally, Don, 57
Muni, Paul, 168
Murray, John, 256
Mutiny on the Bounty (film, 1935), 115
"My Cradle of Dreams," 36, 58
My Life with Caroline, 160
"My Wife's Gone to the Country, Hurrah, Hurrah," 35

Nagle, Anne Margaret, *see* Sturges, Anne ("Sandy")
Nana (film), 95
Nathan, George Jean, 130
National Broadcasting Company, 285, 286
Negri, Pola, 70
Nesbit, Evelyn, 25
Never Say Die (film), 113–114, 123, 127
Never Say Die (play), 113
New Yorkers, The, see Christmas in July
New York *Times*, 47, 53, 63, 66, 132, 160, 163, 184, 195, 219, 223, 232, 253
New York Town, 151
Next Time We Love, 104
Nichols, Red, 254–255
Nine Officers, 111
Nine Pine Street, 201
Niven, David, 272, 278
Noël-Noël, 273, 274
Notebooks of Major Thompson, The, see French, They Are a Funny Race, The

United Artists, 3, 184, 201, 279
Universal International, 245–246
Universal Pictures, 3, 76, 77, 82, 85,
    93, 96, 97–101, 103, 104,
    105–106, 107, 111, 127, 129, 138,
    140, 166, 185, 186, 217, 227, 243
Untold Story, The, 10

Vagrant, The, see *Great McGinty, The*
Vajda, Ernest, 111
Vallée, Rudy, 160–161, 162, 186, 220,
    225, 230, 360
Vanderlip, Frank A., 46
Van Upp, Virginia, 270
Veiller, Anthony, 151
Vendetta (aka *Colomba*), 215, 216,
    217–219, 220, 222
Verneuil, Louis, 201
Vetluguin, Voldemar, 244
Vidor, Charles, 151
Vidor, King, 152
Villon, François, 6, 114–116, 287
Visconti, Luchino, 282

Wagner, Frau, 11
Walburn, Raymond, 187, 206
Walker, James J., 70
Walker, Nancy, 261
Walker, Stuart, 100
Wallace, Mike, 275
Walska, Ganna, 12, 25
Wanger, Walter, 73, 74, 127
Ward, Fannie, 70
Warner Bros., 3, 85, 86, 92, 93, 115,
    126, 143, 168, 216, 244
Warner, Jack L., 70
Warwick, Robert, 140, 146, 153, 155,
    156
Wayne, John, 279
Webb, Millard, 70
Wedderburn, Caroline, 236, 247–248,
    251, 263
Weingarten, Larry, 244
We Live Again, 95–96, 97
Welles, Orson, 164, 166
Wellman, William, 130

Well of Romance, The (*see also Silver
    Swan*), 65–66, 71, 177
Wells, H. G., 77
West, Mae, 4, 98, 130
West, Pat, 140
West, Rebecca, 196
Whale, James, 77, 98, 111, 113
Wharf Players of Provincetown,
    41–42
Wild Boys of the Road, 152
Wilder, Billy, x, 151, 166, 170, 197,
    280
Wilder, Thornton, 96
Wilding, Michael, 278
Willner, Meyer, 215
Windust, Bretaigne, 256
"Winky," 19
Winsten, Archer, 134, 220, 241
Wiseman, Sir William, 70
Without Love (play), 198
Wodehouse, P. G., 124
Woods, A. H. ("Al"), 57, 70
Woolfan, E. B. ("Bertie"), 89, 90,
    120–123, 129, 144, 150, 158, 164,
    195, 214, 237, 238, 246, 248, 249,
    260, 281
Woolfan, Priscilla Bonner, 90–91,
    119, 120–123, 129, 136, 137, 144,
    150, 164, 174, 175, 195, 214, 237,
    238–239, 247–248, 249, 259, 260,
    263, 264
Woollcott, Alexander, 195
Worst Woman in Paris, The, 94
Wyatt, Jane, 97–98
Wyler, William, 97–100, 103, 111,
    116, 128, 129, 152, 234, 262–263,
    276

Yurka, Blanche, 285

Zanuck, Darryl F., 145, 149, 167, 188,
    222–229, 231, 232, 238–240, 242,
    243
Zolotow, Sam, 253
Zukor, Adolph, 70